THE TEXAS BOOK

FOCUS ON AMERICAN HISTORY SERIES

Center for American History
University of Texas at Austin

Edited by Don Carleton

PROFILES,
HISTORY, AND
REMINISCENCES
OF THE UNIVERSITY

The Texas Book

EDITED BY RICHARD A. HOLLAND

University of Texas Press   *Austin*

Publication of this book was generously supported by the
Jess and Betty Jo Hay endowment at the University of
Texas Press.

"The Week James Michener Died," by James Magnuson,
reprinted with permission from the December 1997 issue
of *Texas Monthly*.

"The Search for William E. Hinds," by Walter Prescott
Webb, copyright © 1961 by *Harper's Magazine.* All rights
reserved. Reproduced from the July issue by special permission.

Selections from *North Toward Home* reprinted with
permission from JoAnne Prichard Morris and David Rae
Morris. *North Toward Home*, Houghton Mifflin Company
(1967); reprinted by Vintage Books (2000) and University
Press of Mississippi (2000).

"Remembering Texas" (1984) by J. M. Coetzee. Copyright ©
by J. M. Coetzee, 1989. All rights reserved.

First paperback printing, 2012

Requests for permission to reproduce material from this
work should be sent to:
    Permissions
    University of Texas Press
    P.O. Box 7819
    Austin, TX 78713-7819
    www.utexas.edu/utpress/about/bpermission.html

♾ The paper used in this book meets the minimum requirements of ANSI/NISO Z39.48-1992 (R1997) (Permanence
of Paper).

LIBRARY OF CONGRESS CATALOGING-IN-PUBLICATION DATA

The Texas book : profiles, history, and reminiscences of the
University / edited by Richard A. Holland.— 1st ed.
    p. cm. — (Focus on American history series)
Includes bibliographical references.
ISBN-13: 978-0-292-74546-9

1. University of Texas — History. 2. University of Texas
at Austin—History. 3. University of Texas—Biography.
4. University of Texas at Austin—Biography. I. Holland,
Richard (Richard A.) II. Series.
LD5333.T49 2006
378.764'31—dc22   2006004520

Contents

THE TEXAS BOOK

RICHARD A.
HOLLAND } # Introduction

The University of Texas is celebrating its 125th birthday, and by most measures of excellence it ranks as a worldwide success in higher education. The competition to enter the University is intense, yet approximately thirty-nine thousand undergraduate students enroll in a given year, with another eleven thousand students enrolling in UT's one hundred seventy graduate programs. The faculty and student body includes winners of the Nobel Prize, the Pulitzer Prize, the MacArthur "genius award," and Rhodes and Marshall scholarships; many have become members of state, national, and foreign learned societies. The athletic programs are thought to be the best overall in the country, and the libraries and archives are lauded in every educated part of the world. Texas alumni have left their marks in law, engineering, geology, business, journalism, and all fields of the sciences, arts, and entertainment.

Yet if one looks back over its history, the institution has frequently not been at this level of prosperity and accomplishment. In fact at some junctures in the past the University's integrity as a center for higher education has been deeply compromised, and more than once its very existence has been seriously threatened.

The University of Texas reflects the state of Texas, and that can be complicated. Texas has always been perceived as a setting for action, not book learning, and a robust frontier spirit of anti-intellectualism has existed since Sam Houston served as president of the republic. On the other hand, no single place in the United States has the richness and diversity of the cultures of the Lone Star State, located as it is as the western-most part of the South, at the bottom of the Midwest, as the gateway to Mexico, and as the place where the West begins. Add to this a certain native competitiveness and ebullience and you have traits that in a university produce excellence not only in sports but also in academic fields as rarefied as classics and biochemistry.

As the University has matured, some of these considerations may seem a bit dated—after all, a century and a quarter after its founding UT receives less than 20 percent of its funding from the legislature, foreign students in Austin number over four thousand and come from a hundred different countries, and Texas high-tech companies are crucial to the U.S. economy. But as one reads through the essays that follow, one theme that emerges is how long it has taken the University to rise to its present position and how hard-earned its status is.

The Texas Book is a selection of essays about the University—some short and personal, some long and historical, and some that together bring to life a handful of notables who have walked the Forty Acres. There are villains, such as Governor Jim (Pa) Ferguson, who tried to destroy the University; heroes, such as UT president Robert Vinson, who fended off Ferguson; and a few visionaries, most notably Harry Ransom. This being the University of Texas we're talking about, on occasion outsized characters loom large. Some are faculty members, including the contrarian English professor J. Frank Dobie, who publicly called the top of the Main Building tower "a Greek outhouse." Some are students, including Willie Morris, who championed freedom of the press during the repressive period when he was editor of the *Daily Texan*. And one is a regent, Frank C. Erwin Jr., who, though a lightning rod to the student protestors of the sixties, may have been equal parts villain, hero, and visionary.

What *The Texas Book* is not is a beginning-to-end narrative history. This book is a selection, combining new pieces written for this anthology with chapters that have been previously published. Its three sections—Profiles, History, and Reminiscences—are each arranged in a chronological sequence. The book ends with the words of Barbara Jordan, a black Texan who was denied admittance to the University during the days of "separate but equal"; she became a prominent member of the U.S. Congress and at the end of her life was a distinguished presence teaching at the LBJ School of Public Affairs.

In the beginning, the founders of the Republic of Texas wanted there to be a University of Texas. The town of Austin was laid out in 1839 to be the capital of the Republic, and in November of that year the Congress of the Republic met there for the first time. One of their decisions at this initial meeting allocated over two hundred thousand acres of land toward the establishment of two state colleges. But it was not until 1876, after decades marked by Texas' entering the United States, seceding from the Union, losing in

the war, and suffering through Reconstruction, that a new state constitution was drafted. It specified that the legislature was to establish, organize, and support a "university of the first class" to be called "The University of Texas" and to be located by popular vote. The state constitution also included a gift of land, a million acres of unsurveyed land in West Texas.

Governor Oran M. Roberts was a strong advocate for the University, and he signed the enabling legislation on March 30, 1881. Austin was chosen as the site for the main campus in September of that year, and Galveston was picked to house a "medical department." The plot of land chosen for the new college, in Austin, was a few blocks north of the new Capitol building, then under construction. It was one-sixteenth of a section—forty acres. This was not a huge allotment when one considers that another important government institution located in Austin, then called the State Lunatic Asylum, had been allotted 380 acres in 1857 prior to its construction in the area of present-day Guadalupe Street between 38th and 45th.

Laying the cornerstone for the first Main Building must have been quite a scene. A procession traveled from the Travis County Courthouse downtown to the uncompleted Capitol, and then up to barren College Hill. A huge crowd of over two thousand made the march; it was a colorful assemblage comprised of University and government officials, Confederate veterans, members of fraternal orders, and several bands.

The principal speaker at the ceremony was thought to be the most learned man in all of Texas—Dr. Ashbel Smith, a medical doctor who held three degrees from Yale University. In earlier decades he had helped fight yellow fever epidemics on the Texas coast and had been Sam Houston's chargé d'affaires to France and England during the era of the Republic of Texas. On this day, November 17, 1882, Dr. Smith was the new president of the University Board of Regents. One sentence in the flowery rhetoric of his speech now sounds prescient, as if he were looking forward forty years: "Smite the rocks with the rod of knowledge, and fountains of unstinted wealth will gush forth."

The West Texas rocks filled with oil were not smitten until the 1920s, but the University made do in its early decades, although the physical plant was a little, shall we say, spotty. Old Main, sitting on the crest of the hill, was not completed until 1899, and everything from classrooms to the library to the president's office was housed there. There were structural problems with the building from the beginning, and its style, a version of American college Gothic, was outdated by the time it was completed. The building that was truly central to the identity of the young university was the men's dormitory, B. Hall, the "B" standing for George Washington Brackenridge, a Texas regent for twenty-five years.

Five of the essays that follow touch on this early period. My essay on "the two George Washingtons," Brackenridge and Littlefield, is political in nature and traces the ups and downs of the University from 1886, the year of G. W. Brackenridge's appointment as regent, to 1920, the year that Brackenridge and his worthy adversary, G. W. Littlefield, both died. David Dettmer's chapter on B. Hall is a deep socioeconomic examination of the class of students who lived in the quarters set aside for the "poor boys." If Texas's evolution from rural to urban is an almost tacit theme in this book, in Dettmer's essay the theme is writ large.

Larry Speck's knowledgeable contribution on the formative period of UT architecture grounds the reader in the modern as well as the original place. We can only imagine what Cass Gilbert, who was designing what would be the tallest building in the world in New York City (the Woolworth Building), must have thought when he first arrived in Austin on the train and laid eyes on College Hill, empty except for some blue-bonnets and a few mismatched buildings. This was in 1910. Gilbert drew the first coherent campus master plan and created the one UT building now generally acknowledged as a masterpiece—then called the University Library, now named Battle Hall.

Meade Griffin's reminiscence of his college days is a rare thing—a modest and articulate presentation of daily life as it was lived close to a hundred years ago. Walter Prescott Webb's "The Search For William E. Hinds" was published in the July 1961 issue of *Harper's*. When Webb wrote the magazine article he was an acclaimed UT historian, known for two landmark books, *The Great Plains* and *The Great Frontier*, but the essay is set in 1904, when Webb was a bookish boy with no prospects, working dawn to dark on a dirt farm outside Ranger, in Eastland County. The story is a mystery that portrays Webb's lifelong search for a generous stranger from Brooklyn who paid his way through the University.

Webb and his friend J. Frank Dobie were both born in 1888, but Dobie made his reputation earlier than Webb, who was awarded a Ph.D. by the University somewhat as a courtesy after he published *The Great Plains* in 1931. Dobie had joined the faculty in 1914 and left to enlist in World War I. He taught folklore and literature proudly without a doctorate and feuded with his colleagues in the English department, who returned his scorn. Don Graham, who now teaches Dobie's "Life and Literature of the Southwest" class, examines Dobie's extensive library, pointing out that Dobie was the state's only real literary figure for decades, this despite his often hiding behind a cowboy exterior, spinning yarns on the radio, and performing rope tricks.

If the poor boys lived in rough-and-ready B. Hall, the domestic style of the faculty and staff was scarcely more elevated. Another prominent campus figure was John Lomax, who went on to fame as a musicologist for his collections of cowboy songs and his discovery of the blues artist Leadbelly; in the first decade of the twentieth century Lomax was University registrar and secretary of the University Alumni Association. Although university salaries were notoriously low, Lomax and his wife Bess built a fine brick house on West 26th Street a few blocks from campus. Yet to help make ends meet, the couple and their three children kept a milk cow and raised chickens for eggs. On the other hand, during the same era, Walter Webb was known to be wise in the ways of investing in Austin real estate, and J. Frank Dobie and his wife Bertha lived in a pleasant two-story house where Dobie could be found entertaining his friends with a bottle of Jack Daniels in a back yard that sloped down to Waller Creek. The folklorist's fame was such that he sometimes received mail simply addressed to "J. Frank Dobie, Austin, Texas."

Funded for the most part by West Texas oil, the building boom that made the campus what it is today occurred in a remarkable flurry of construction that lasted twelve years. In the portico at the top of the Main Building's front steps there is a plaque that comprehensively documents this building boom. Twenty-four buildings are listed as having been completed between 1925 and 1937. The early ones included Garrison Hall in 1926, and Gregory Gym in 1930. During one of the bleakest years of the Depression, 1933, eight buildings were put up. These included the Texas Union, the Architecture Building (now Goldsmith Hall), the gracious Home Economics Building (now Mary E. Gearing Hall), and the beginning of the new Main Building, which took over three years to complete. By 1936, the year of the Texas Centennial, the Forty Acres was just about filled up and had jumped Speedway Street to the east and 24th Street to the north.

Overseeing this remarkable creation was the new supervising architect, Paul Phillipe Cret, who extended Cass Gilbert's vision of a unified campus. Overseeing the never-ceasing noise and flying dust on campus were the chair of the Building Committee, W. J. Battle, and the University president, H. Y. Benedict. Battle was a distinguished professor of classics who briefly had served as president of the University back in the difficult Pa Ferguson days. Benedict was a much loved salt-of-the-earth administrator from Weatherford, Texas, who spoke to everyone he passed on campus. It was a shock the day in 1937 when he fell to the sidewalk in front of the YMCA building on Guadalupe Street and died of a cerebral hemorrhage. One of the projects that Benedict left behind was an unfinished history of the University.

Joe B. Frantz's profile of Richard Fleming presents us with another Edwardian gentleman, born two years after Dobie and Webb. Fleming was by nature a hell-raiser, as demonstrated by his founding the campus's first underground newspaper, *The Blunderbuss*, in 1913, his first year in law school. Frantz presents him over fifty years later, having retired from being a wealthy corporate attorney in New York, working on campus for a dollar a year, tending his collection of writings by university students and faculty. Those who knew Mr. Fleming listened closely to his stories of attending regents meetings in the old meeting room on the second floor of the Main Building. When Frank Erwin would propose something that displeased him (this happened frequently), Fleming would strike his handsome walking stick on the parquet floor and mutter "scandalous."

If the 1930s were a period of growth and optimism on campus, the early 1940s were just the opposite. Homer Price Rainey's tenure as UT president (1939–1944) was marked almost from the start by conflicts with regents appointed by governors W. Lee (Pappy) O'Daniel and Coke Stevenson. If Governor Ferguson's attempts to defund the University back in the second decade of the nineteenth century was the first attack on the University, in effect this was the next one, but this time it came from the inside. *The Handbook of Texas* neatly summarizes the situation:

Several on the board pressured Rainey to fire four full professors of economics who espoused New Deal views. In 1942 the regents fired three untenured economics instructors and a fourth who had only a one-year appointment for having attempted to defend federal labor laws at an antiunion meeting in Dallas. Rainey protested in vain. Regent D. F. Strickland wrote Rainey that the president of the University of Texas had no business suggesting anything to the regents and that if the abolition of tenure would make it more difficult to recruit out-of-state professors, Texas would be better off. (*Handbook of Texas Online*, s.v. "Rainey, Homer Price")

The last straw was the regents' ham-handed attempt to fire an English professor for assigning John Dos Passos's novel *U.S.A.* in a sophomore reading list. After Rainey expressed his grievances to a general faculty meeting in October 1944, the regents quickly fired him, giving no cause. The resulting protests were large and loud and divisive—twenty-five years later the Rainey demonstrations were viewed as precursors to student protests over the Vietnam War. In educative terms, the University had a black mark against it when the American Association of University Professors censured the institution. The term of this academic quarantine was nine years.

Michael Gillette elaborates on this particular group of close-minded regents in his survey of UT's struggles to desegregate itself in the 1940s and 1950s. Gillette quotes Regent Orville Bullington, a UT graduate who practiced law in Wichita Falls: "There is not the slightest danger of any negro attending the University of Texas, regardless of what Franklin D. or Eleanor [Roosevelt] or the Supreme Court says, so long as you have a Board of Regents with as much intestinal fortitude as this one has." This stark pronouncement, made in 1944, is a reminder that not only have the state of Texas and the University traveled a long social distance, but that they also started a long way back. *Sweatt v. Painter* was neither the beginning nor the end of this struggle.

Three other chapters deal with race and the University, each one differently. Bobby Hawthorne's essay on the University Interscholastic League traces the uneasy relationship that the League had with the University, and specifically brings up one example of a failure to integrate a high school basketball game that speaks volumes about the racial politics of

Texas in the early sixties. Julius Whittier was UT's first black football scholarship recipient who lettered—he played the 1970 through 1972 seasons. His reminiscence comes from the other side, i.e., as one of the first African-Americans to be recruited to play sports at the University. Douglas Laycock, while professor of constitutional law at the UT Law School, was deeply involved in the University's legal struggles to create more diversity in the student body. His essay clearly presents the court challenges to UT's entrance requirement formulas over the last two decades, and is a ringing endorsement for a future campus that truly represents the state's population.

Chad Oliver came to the University in 1946 as a bright young man wearing a Crystal City (Texas) High School football letter jacket. Oliver's reminiscence is the first sighting of Harry Ransom in our chapters, and it is an apt introduction. Oliver went on to obtain two degrees from UT and a Ph.D. from UCLA. He returned to Austin, where he eventually chaired the Anthropology Department and became a productive science fiction novelist.

Willie Morris' chapter is taken from his classic memoir *North Toward Home*, published in 1967. His account of coming to Austin from Yazoo City, Mississippi, reminds us that by the early fifties, the University of Texas had a reputation that traveled beyond the confines of state borders. Willie (everyone seemed to call him that) had an illustrious career at Texas, editing the *Daily Texan* during a politically repressive period. His penchant for practical jokes made him a natural to live with the subversive wild men who inhabited the new Brackenridge Dormitory. When he was a senior in 1956, Morris became the University's fifteenth Rhodes Scholar. (Since Morris, there have been twelve more Texas students so honored, five of them since 1990.)

Returning from his studies at Oxford University, Willie returned to Austin to edit the liberal political fortnightly, the *Texas Observer*. Then he moved to New York where he transformed venerable *Harper's* magazine into a platform for the best of the 1960s New Journalism. John Schwartz is another Austin to New York success story. Now reporting for the *New York Times*, Schwartz was the 1980–81 *Daily Texan* editor. His chapter focuses on the symbolic power of the UT Tower, discussing how his generation of students missed seeing the view from the top after its closing in 1974. For Schwartz, the Tower's closely supervised reopening becomes a cause for celebration and optimism.

Willie Morris was not the only student journalist who ran into censorship at the hands of the Texas Student Publications Committee. Leading the way was the smart and funny and dirty-minded staff of the *Texas Ranger* magazine. The impulse to shock appears to be a natural part of college life, but the "Rangeroos" at their best did it with first-class humor and artistry. The chapter that interviews two *Ranger* editors reminds us of the tremendous creative talent on campus during the heyday of the magazine in the fifties and sixties. Two characters who emerge in the interviews went on to become heroes of the counterculture: cartoonist Gilbert Shelton and singer Janis Joplin.

Harry Huntt Ransom first came to Texas as an instructor in 1935 and during the next forty years left an indelible mark on the campus. By the time Willie Morris was fighting for campus freedom of the press, Ransom had risen to be dean of the College of Arts and Sciences. During the next ten years (1956–1965), Ransom became president and soon chancellor of the University, and the fine arts and liberal arts were transformed and began to receive worldwide notice. Ransom's drive to excellence manifested itself in the building of a great library. Some would say there was already a pretty good library in place, but Ransom went world class. Two chapters deal directly with Ransom's most creative period: Harold Billings's atmospheric study of Ransom's office in the Main Building and its second-most important occupant, Frances Hudspeth; and Richard Oram's compelling tale of Ransom's landmark library acquisition, the Hanley Collection, that has its own atmosphere when it brings in the collector's wife, Tullah Hanley, a beautiful exotic dancer.

If you were lucky enough to be on the Texas campus during Ransom's salad days, the cultural opportunities that were available seem almost unbelievable in retrospect. The same year that Texas novelist Katherine Anne Porter appeared on campus for a reading wearing an evening gown and opera-length gloves, poet T. S. Eliot read in Gregory Gym, and appeared delighted when presented with a big Stetson hat. The author of *Brave New World*, novelist Aldous Huxley, lectured in Batts Hall auditorium—the rumor was that he visited campus to get longevity advice from the eminent UT biochemist Roger Williams. The two big venues were the Texas Union ballroom and homely old Gregory Gym, where one might variously see Arturo Toscanini conduct the NBC Symphony and Louis Armstrong play "The Bucket's Got a Hole in It." The most elegant presentation I personally witnessed was a concert by the tuxedoed Modern Jazz Quartet, set up in the round in the middle of the gym's hardwood floor.

Three chapters are by students from this era: William Hauptmann, who went on to the Yale Drama School and to success on the stage in New York when he won a Tony Award for his book for the musical "Big River"; Betty Sue Flowers, who has had a notable publishing and administrative career and is currently director of the LBJ Library and Museum; and South African novelist J. M. Coetzee, who was at UT on a Fulbright Scholarship in the middle sixties. In 2003 he was awarded the Nobel Prize for Literature.

Bill Hauptmann majored in drama and profiles the distinguished Shakespeare director B. Iden Payne. Betty Sue Flowers re-creates a pivotal era during which she transformed herself from a freshman living a sheltered existence in Scottish Rite Dormitory in 1965 to a witness of some of Frank Erwin's strong-arm tactics in the Texas Union Chuck Wagon four years later. John Coetzee's brief reminiscence talks about the unexpectedness of being free to roam the rare literary treasures that Ransom's library provided him, particularly the manuscript notebooks for Samuel Beckett's novel *Watt*. Coetzee links the terror of Charles Whitman's shooting spree from the top of the Tower in August 1966 with his feelings about the Vietnam War.

From the outset, as editor of this collection of essays, I knew I had to deal in some fashion with Board of Regents' chairman Frank C. Erwin Jr. It was a problem because of Chairman Frank's very nature: big, boisterous, larger than life, he was a man as intensely loved by his friends, who were many, as he was intensely disliked by those he pushed around, who were legion. So I drew the short straw and came up with an essay about a man whose life deserves a sizable book. The final result is a kaleidoscopic piece that examines multiple aspects of the Chairman's colorful life. The title is borrowed from Wallace Stevens' poem "Thirteen Ways of Looking at a Blackbird."

The final profiles are of two important campus personages who died in the late 1990s: Américo Paredes and James Michener. Both figures represent the outsider to campus who became an important part of its culture—Paredes as a Mexican-American intellectual, and Michener as a globe-trotting celebrity writer who decided to settle in Austin. English professor José Limón studied under Paredes, who almost singlehandedly created the field of Mexican-American folklore. Jim Magnuson is the director of the James A. Michener Center for Writers (located in Dobie's old house above Waller Creek) and well aware of the importance of Michener's personal contact with the students his generosity attracted.

The last words are delivered in the unmistakable voice of Barbara Jordan, the congresswoman from Houston who became a Richard Nixon nemesis during Watergate. Her 1986 commencement address, delivered in front of architect Paul Cret's tower, is a call for kindness and mercy, but not weak versions of either. Speaking at a briefing on higher education in 1987 in favor of increased funding for UT, she alludes to the University's segregated past by saying that for a long time she "couldn't come here . . . but I can now." She closes with a clarion call to "retain the greatness of this institution."

A good time to walk on campus these days is the weekend following commencement in the spring. The parents in their SUVs have moved the computers, clothes, and DVDs out of Jester and Kinsolving dormitories, the sorority and fraternity houses are on schedule for their summer repairs, the enormous sets of bleachers set up for commencement in front of the Main Building are being dismantled. As likely as not, the Longhorn baseball team is getting fine-tuned for another appearance at the College World Series. There is a brief interim before the Boys State delegates arrive and the summer sports and music camps commence. Even parking is a little relaxed. There is the feeling that a large and important enterprise is pausing to take a breath.

So what do we see on the walk? A handsome, packed, urban landscape, many buildings being buffed for the next round of academic endeavors. Some of the newest buildings on the north periphery of campus have an old look, with overhung roofs made of Mediterranean-style red tile. The buildings that really are old, like beautiful Battle Hall and the oldest structure on the original Forty Acres, the Gebauer Building, give off an undeniable impression of solidity and tradition.

But the pause is only momentary. Construction crews appear to have been waiting until the minute graduation was over to start knocking something down or building something new. The year of this walk (2005), it's the old Student Health Center building on Dean Keeton Street (a.k.a. 26th) that is going down and the new women's dorm going up on Whitis across the street from All Saints Church. Over behind Gregory Gym it's the new outdoor lap pool, lined on two sides with date palms, a hint of a luxurious oasis just off 21st Street. Just when you think every square inch has been filled up, there's one more thing.

Without all the people, the walker starts to notice how many big trees there are, how the statue of Martin Luther King Jr. is placed so that it has a nice view of the LBJ fountain, and how the Ransom Center has transformed itself into an inviting oasis of its own—on a hot day you can walk right through the cool, dimly lit lobby and look at pages of the Gutenberg Bible.

The University estimates that there are about four hundred fifty thousand living alumnae, and by September it feels like all of them are between you and where you're headed. As developed as the physical campus is, it is not really transformed into itself until it is full of people. On a normal Tuesday or Wednesday in October or April there are thought to be something over seventy thousand students, faculty, and staff on the campus. Let's make it seventy-five thousand, to include the many visitors here for meetings, tours, or just to look around.

A good spot to survey this fast-moving scene is up on the portico of the Main Building. From there you can imagine Cass Gilbert and Paul Cret drawing sketches for their master plans, Battle and Benedict overseeing construction, Frank Erwin glowering over his reading glasses at a crowd of hostile students, or Barbara Jordan, preaching a message of love and mercy in front of the slogan carved into stone that so impressed the young Willie Morris: "Ye shall know the truth and the truth shall make you free."

Profiles

DON
GRAHAM

J. Frank Dobie
A Reappraisal

By the time of his death in 1964, J. Frank Dobie had achieved an extraordinary reputation as a regional spokesman for the Southwest, especially for Texas. He was our Frost, our Faulkner, our Sandburg—the local sage who spoke for the region. Carl Sandburg was the one closest in temperament and achievement to Dobie. They were friends, and, staying in Dobie's Austin home once, Sandburg said to his host, upon noticing their similar locks of tousled white hair: "Frank, we look like a couple of authors."[1] Certainly Dobie did, with his shock of white hair and sunny, open face; a smile of apparently legendary charm; and overall, a sort of cowboyish appeal that never left him. Unlike the others, however, Dobie did not build his reputation out of imaginative literature; he wrote neither poems nor novels. He was part folklorist, part historian, though neither of those disciplines would be comfortable with claiming him entirely as one of their own. He rewrote and retold tales drawn from oral and print sources, and so he was not a folklorist per se, a collector of folk tales; nor was he a historian like his friend Walter P. Webb. He was a finder and a popularizer of regional historical and folkloric materials whose preferred form was the anecdotal essay rather than the sustained narrative.

Dobie was born in 1888, the same year as T. S. Eliot and Raymond Chandler. This is strange company when one thinks about it. Eliot went on to create some of the greatest of modern poetry, and Chandler became the best hard-boiled detective writer in the U.S. Dobie became a pioneer literary regionalist; he became Mr. Texas. This honorific title bestowed upon him by his biographer Lon Tinkle doubles back on itself as soon as Dobie is measured by any yardstick other than regional.[2] Both Eliot and Chandler were supremely well educated; Chandler in English schools, Eliot at

Don Graham is J. Frank Dobie Regents Professor in American and English Literature at the University of Texas. His books include Cowboys and Cadillacs: How Hollywood Looks at Texas, Giant Country: Essays on Texas, Lone Star Literature: From the Red River to the Rio Grande *(ed.), and* Kings of Texas: The 150-Year Saga of an American Ranching Empire. *This essay was first published in the January 1988* Southwestern Historical Quarterly.

J. Frank Dobie, photographed by Russell Lee. *From the Russell Lee Photograph Collection, Center for American History, the University of Texas at Austin. (DI 02381)*

Harvard. Dobie came out of a patrician but decidedly provincial culture in South Texas. His family valued learning, sending all the children to college at a time when, early in the twentieth century, most Texas families had neither the means nor the imagination to conceive of such an enterprise.

Dobie was perforce a provincial with a taste for a wider world. He made several forays into that world, to New York for an M.A. at Columbia, to western Europe during a tour of duty in Europe in World War I, and to England for a celebrated year at Cambridge during the Second World War. But most of Dobie's life, and nearly all of his imaginative energy, was devoted to his native region, the Southwest. In that capacity it can be said that he invented southwestern literature, finding a historical precedent in the English romantics who seized upon border ballads and the speech of the common man to inform literature with a new spirit. He also tried to create literature, and it is this phase of his long and influential career that I wish to address upon the occasion of his centennial. Not forgetting his role as liberal spokesman, defender of civil liberties, influential teacher, fierce advocate of the

unfettered mind, pioneer in the study of southwestern literature and folklore, I want instead to consider him as a writer because in the long run, his writing is what will increasingly have to bear the test and scrutiny of time.

To begin, I want to examine Dobie's response to the imaginative writing of the postwar Southwest. For it is there, in his reaction to the new, that the essential Dobie aesthetic may be located. He was an avid reader, and he had the library to prove it. Among Dobie's many books, easily the most influential was his *Guide to Life and Literature of the Southwest*, first published in 1943 and "enlarged in both knowledge and wisdom" in 1952.[3] It is a characteristic Dobie work because it is, in the purest sense, bookish. Dobie was a bookman. Gertrude Stein saw through Ernest Hemingway's manly prose and said that he smelled of the museum; well, Dobie, too, smelled of libraries. His *Guide* generated dozens of courses in southwestern literature and, though unavoidably dated, remains a lively, engaging introduction to the literature of the region. The book grew out of Dobie's own pioneering course offered for the first time in 1930, in the Department of English at the University of Texas. According to legend, when Dobie proposed such a course, it met with opposition from the English faculty, who declared that there wasn't any literature of the Southwest. So Dobie said, all right, I'll teach life; there's plenty of that.[4] In respect to belles lettres, the English department was right (and here it must be remembered that at this time courses in American literature were only beginning to find a place in the curricula of many institutions). A significant body of imaginative writing did not yet exist when Dobie began to offer the course. The creation of such work was already underway, however, by such writers as Harvey Fergusson, Katherine Anne Porter, Oliver La Farge, Paul Horgan, and others. By 1943, when the *Guide* appeared, there was enough fiction in the region to warrant a separate section, but the majority of the book was devoted to other kinds of writing—journals, histories, autobiographies, and folklore. The fiction section contained sixteen authors. When Dobie revised the book in 1952, he added only four new writers to the fiction section.

Since Dobie did not revise his bibliography a third time, there is no public record of his opinion of fiction published after 1952. But fortunately there is another record of Dobie's response to contemporary writers of southwestern fiction. His extensive personal library, consisting of 12,177 volumes (8,905 titles), contained many works of fiction, and from the prefatory remarks and marginalia in these volumes it is possible to view Dobie's reaction to the writing that appeared in the years from 1952 to 1964.[5] He was the embodiment of Ralph Waldo Emerson's "creative reader"; he seems never to have picked up a book without a pencil at hand. Unvarnished opinions sprinkle the pages of books that engaged his attention; the prefatory remarks often sparkle with delight or dislike. Two further things should be noted about the collection. Dobie appears not to have read everything that he owned. By the late 1930s and certainly by the 1950s his fame was so great that few authors could resist sending him copies of their work—both vanity-press authors and those with reputable houses. Dobie received a great many more "authentic reminiscences of life on the frontier" by grandmothers, garrulous uncles, and antiquarians than even the most dedicated of regionalists would have time for or could tolerate. He received, in short, a great deal of bluebonnet or cow-chip literature. Many of these volumes he dismissed with an unread harumph. But he also dismissed some notable fiction with the same peremptory gesture.

In addition to making pertinent remarks of approval, disapproval, or queries in the margins, Dobie nearly always made a summary judgment, usually placed among the front matter and running from a brief sentence or so to statements two pages long. Most of these entries are dated, and most are signed variously: Frank Dobie, J. Frank Dobie, J.F.D. His practice of recording his impressions goes back to his early acquisitions, in the 1920s and 1930s, and continued unabated through the books he read during the last years of his life. In the late 1950s some of the judgments begin to sound like self-conscious pronouncements, retrospective annotations on books read long ago. How else to explain an entry dated 1960 on the flyleaf of Upton Sinclair's *The Jungle*, published in 1906? Of course it's possible that Dobie didn't read the book until 1960. In any case, the practice of recording his impressions conveys the sense of a literary figure whose word, he was certain, would be valued by whoever chanced to peruse those remarks in the future.

The myriad annotations also suggest that fiction was not Dobie's favorite genre. Fiction was a distant fourth behind poetry, essays, and history. Though he read novels and directed M.A. theses on southwest-

J. Frank Dobie and Walter Prescott Webb on campus. *From the Prints and Photographs Collection–J. Frank Dobie, Center for American History, the University of Texas at Austin. (DI 02382)*

ern fiction, like his famous friends Roy Bedichek and Walter Prescott Webb he seems always to have been slightly suspicious of the claims of fiction. Dobie adhered to the criterion of authenticity and truth, whether local or universal, and he revered Nature with a capital *N*. Fiction was often capricious in its treatment of each of these standards. With fiction, Dobie did not always know the right things to look for; he was essentially an academic critic, though he would have been repelled by such a label. Educated in the Genteel Tradition, he never escaped from its pieties.

As we look at the novels that Dobie owned and read, we can begin to assess the nature of his response to the burgeoning output of fiction in the 1950s and 1960s. Fiction, of course, had been written in Texas, in the Southwest, since the 1820s, but all of it in the nineteenth century, from dime novels to fat pre-Michenerized Alamo novels, was popular trash. All the best writing about the Southwest through the formative years of Dobie's reading was nonfiction, or presumed to be, the chief case in point being Andy Adams's disguised novel, *The Log of a Cowboy*, which Dobie insisted was the "best book that has ever been written of cowboy life, and . . . the best book that ever can be written of cowboy life."[6] But in the post–World War II era fiction was the new arena of excellence, and Dobie, temperamentally at least, wasn't well equipped to be its best arbiter. Nobody in Texas of his generation was.

Not surprisingly, considering his years of devotion to cowboy lore, Dobie seems to have been particularly suspicious of western fiction that purported to tell the truth about range life. Alan Le May's *The Unforgiven* (1957), for example, received a brief negative assessment: "Not nearly so good as it's touted up to be. In a little while it will be forgotten, along with 1000's of other cow country fictions." His opinion of a more famous range novel, Walter Van Tilburg Clark's *The Ox-Bow Incident*, recorded in a paperback edition in 1954, expresses a similar view: "The novel is worthy of respect, but its celebration shows how hard up the West is for fiction." Dobie's hatred of formula Westerns, the Zane Grey school, seems to have contributed to his disposition to judge very severely indeed any attempts to write western fiction within the formulaic tradition, however serious or imaginative the writer might be.

Dobie also brought to his judgment of fiction a strong moralistic strain. Sometimes this tendency led to cursory and unfair judgments of the authors themselves. Texas author William Humphrey, for example, fared very poorly at the hands of Dobie. Here is Dobie on Humphrey's first novel, *Home from the Hill* (1958): "Much touted. Knopf's own word for the novel would go far with me. Still, Humphrey does not strike me as a whole man; I do not find time to read him." What on earth could Dobie have meant by calling Humphrey not a "whole man"?

Another review ad hominem was directed at the author of *The Rounders* (1960), of whom Dobie noted:

"This Max Evans did fairly well on John Dunn of Taos, though he had there no perspective. He has written me 2 or 3 times, the last time wanting to do my biography. He is a Philistine & a pretender to what he is not. Look at his mug on back of jacket." The letters Dobie refers to were breezy, first-name notes from Evans, and they obviously offended Dobie's sense of manners. But then so did Evans's photograph on the jacket.

Dobie's dismissal of Evans contains one kernel of valid principle—the notion of perspective, by which he seems to have meant something like mature, balanced judgment. In any case, his high regard for Michael W. Straight's *Carrington* (1960) combines this standard with others that reflect what Dobie wanted in fiction: "Whether this novel wins popularity or not, it was written by a civilized gentleman with perspective, a sense of values and the capacity for being morally outraged—a rarity among the producers of fiction of Western subjects." Dobie's honorific terms—perspective, values, morality—suggest a John Gardnerish preference for a fiction of moral seriousness. In his remarks on an obscure work by Texas writer Leonard Sanders, *The Wooden Horseshoe* (1964), Dobie says, "I like a novel with some decent people in it." Another thing he liked about this novel was the passage he bracketed on page 132, wherein an old man gives the following advice to the young hero: "Read J. Frank Dobie. His is the only books worth readin', 'cept the Bible, of course."

Some of Dobie's most vigorous opinions were directed at Texas writers, especially those belonging to the new post–World War II generation. The fiction of older writers, such as that of William A. Owens, Dobie liked a good deal, calling *Look to the River* (1963) "delightful." Friendship with a writer did not, however, mean that Dobie could not be critical. Here is how he evaluated the work of another friend, Fred Gipson's *Old Yeller* (1956): "I like Fred Gipson very much & find this pioneer narrative pleasant, but it is manifestly contrived and nowhere near being a Mark Twain classic as is claimed."

But Dobie's response to the work of younger Texas writers was distinctly not warm. In the early 1960s a new generation of novelists came on the scene, and none of them was welcomed by Dobie. In 1961, for example, William Brammer's *The Gay Place*, arguably one of the best works of fiction ever written about Texas, received very favorable national attention.

Gore Vidal called it one of the two best American political novels ever published, the other being Robert Penn Warren's *All the King's Men*. But Dobie had other ideas about the book's worth. For him it exhibited two grievous errors: excessive length and unseemly behavior. He summarized his impressions in some detail:

> Not a character in the thick novel who is not cheap. Some talk about what a great man Governor Fenstemaker is, but he never appears more than an astute fixer, babbling now & then a good phrase. We are in the middle of politics for 175,000 words and nobody actually every [*sic*] does anything but drink and drink & drink to boredom & screw, & screw & screw to death—the great governor's climax. I expected satire, inside views & a little wisdom at least. Bill Brammer has been with Senator Lyndon Johnson for some time.

This is a fascinating entry for a couple of reasons. First, it's shocking to see Dobie use a word like *screw*, rather like hearing one's grandfather utter an expletive. Second, one wonders how Dobie failed to appreciate the accuracy of the portrait of LBJ in the novel, a portrait praised by even such earnest types as Bill Moyers. Just three years later Dobie received the Medal of Freedom from then-president Lyndon Johnson.

Although Dobie didn't like *The Gay Place*, most younger Texas writers did. Edwin ("Bud") Shrake has said that Brammer's elegant urban novel came with the force of revelation, made it possible for young writers like himself and Gary Cartwright to write fiction about life in Texas cities.[7] Dobie didn't like Shrake's Brammer-inspired novel any better than he liked *The Gay Place*. He said of *But Not for Love*, which appeared in 1964: "Over drinking of everything but water. Prolonged drunk talk gets boresome. Shrake can keep talk going on any subject between any characters. Lacks art of omission. Pages & pages of talk that reveal nothing but more drinking, more smoking [*sic*], mere facility on part of the author, no character development, no integration with plot." In such reactions it is not easy to tell whether the basis of Dobie's dislike is primarily aesthetic—thus the complaints about length and lack of conciseness—or moral—the degenerate (or merely modern?) conduct of the characters.

The case of Larry McMurtry may shed light on the question. The most famous Texas writer since Dobie, McMurtry can easily lay claim to being the most important Texas writer since Dobie, too. Especially since the success of *Lonesome Dove*, a novel in which McMurtry invaded the romantic West of Dobie's favorite period, the cattle-drive era, and won three literary prizes in the process.[8] Like Brammer, McMurtry burst upon the Texas literary scene in 1961 with his tough and tender first novel about the end of an era, *Horseman, Pass By*. The publisher sent Dobie the galley proofs, hoping for a blurb, and Dobie read the novel and as usual recorded his impressions. They are brief: "If 'ripeness' were all, Larry McMurtry wouldn't get much of a grade. Picture of old cowman is good in places." By *ripeness* Dobie doubtless meant perspective. In any case, McMurtry was not yet twenty-five when this novel appeared. It is not surprising that the one thing Dobie admired about the book was the characterization of Homer Bannon, the old cowman.

Dobie's lifelong preference for and romanticization of the old ways, ranching versus any other means of getting a living, found a congenial corollary in McMurtry's most sentimental portrait in the novel. Dobie bracketed approvingly the impassioned speech that Homer delivers against the government, oil wells, and easy money, as opposed to the virtues of the old ranching pastoral tradition.

Why didn't Dobie respond more favorably to McMurtry's novel? There are possibly two reasons, both of which must be inferred. The first is that McMurtry was a potential rival, a young upstart writing about the ranching tradition to which Dobie had devoted no small part of his own life. The second, unarguably, was a matter of taste, of genteel recoil from McMurtry's explicit details of excretionary and sexual activity.

Dobie was not a literary prude except when it came to Texas. He liked *Lady Chatterly's Lover* and owned several copies; he was strongly opposed to its censorship or bowdlerization. Yet I think it is also true that similar material in Texas fiction bothered him, just as it bothered many of his generation. An older English professor at North Texas State University, not long after *Horseman, Pass By* appeared, told me that he wished his former student hadn't felt compelled to use the four-letter word for urination that rhymes with *hiss*. There is also the well-known story that Mabel Major, English professor at Texas Christian University and a leading bibliographical pioneer in the study of southwestern literature, kept *Horseman, Pass By* checked out on permanent faculty loan in order to prevent its falling into the hands of innocent TCU undergraduates.

My argument about Dobie's taste is circumstantial, but consider the two following pieces of documentation. Dobie admired very much a novel like McMurtry's in theme and narrative design, Edward Abbey's *Fire on the Mountain* (1962). Both novels employ youthful narrators to comment upon the values of grandfathers tied to the past, who resist progress, change, and the loss of the old frontier values of independence and freedom. Dobie's description of *Fire on the Mountain* points to precisely these qualities:

> Not a standardized Western. The center, the life, the tragedy of the novel is a rancher who refuses to be displaced by the Army, which wants his land to shoot on. I identify myself with him—am always against the army grabbing of land from human beings and displacing them. John Vogelin belonged to & on his plot of earth. Not great writing, but it has power.

This description would not have to be adjusted very much to fit *Horseman, Pass By*. But for some reason Dobie could not applaud McMurtry's novel as he could Abbey's. One reason may be language. Abbey's narrator is a boy untouched by the juices of puberty; McMurtry's is a boy (true, he is somewhat older) who is tormented by sexual longings and uses the language of street and cow lot to express them. Abbey's pristine, learned, and literary narrator contrasts sharply with McMurtry's realistic narrator, who uses four-letter words to describe the body's familiar functions. Finally, it is arguable that Abbey, whose book was set further west, outside of Texas, did not pose the same threat that fellow Texan McMurtry did.

Dobie's reaction to McMurtry's second novel, *Leaving Cheyenne* (1963), underscores what can only be regarded as a chilly reception of the younger writer's work. Placing the novel in a specifically Texas literary context, Dobie writes:

> I saw & heard Larry McMurtry at the meeting of the Texas Institute of Letters in Dallas when he received the Jesse Jones award of $1000 for *Horseman, Pass By* as the best Texas fiction of the year (1961). He re-

sponded to the award with a speech giving the Texas Institute of Letters hell. I did not get details of his dissatisfaction. I had looked at the book, not read it, without receiving the impression of reality in ranch life. McMurtry was at the time teaching English at Texas Christian University in Fort Worth. Some people were against the novel by taste & morals. I could read this but prefer *The World of Herodotus*.

Here again are the hallmarks of Dobie's limited perspective on fiction. He chooses not to read this novel, and says that he had not read the first one either (but he had, as clearly revealed by his marginalia and the inscription quoted above). Was Dobie fair in his appraisal of McMurtry? If reading a work is considered necessary for judicious criticism, the answer would have to be no.

One Texas novel that Dobie read during this period and liked a good deal was Benjamin Capps's *The Trail to Ogallala* (1964). Working within the formulaic tradition but committed to historical accuracy, Capps drew upon *The Longhorns*, freely acknowledging his indebtedness in a letter to Dobie.[9] Dobie's copy of *The Trail to Ogallala* bore more marginalia than most novels that he read. The unifying thread of his remarks is authenticity, a yardstick of limited aesthetic possibilities but one with which he felt comfortable. Most shoot-em-ups, of course, failed woefully in this regard. At the close of Dobie's impressions of Capp's novel there is a telling remark: "I read the novel with some interest, *not having any activity of mind* [italics added]." The key phrase clearly implies that novels are the pastimes of idle moments, that one's real mental energies must be reserved for nobler forms or for one's own creative work.

Because of Dobie's lifelong habit of reading books and recording his impressions, or in some cases *not* reading them and recording his impressions, we can thus piece together the history of his reaction to the increasing tide of southwestern fiction after 1952. Had Dobie revised the *Guide* a third time, he would certainly have had to expand the fiction section. For whether he liked fiction or not, he continued to read the novels of his time and place, and as the years passed there were more and more to read.

In the nearly two and a half decades since Dobie's death his own critical reputation has fallen, much like Carl Sandburg's. Regional sages, if they are to last, have to have a basis in good writing or in some form of art more lasting than the memories of those who knew them in the flesh. Will Rogers, for example, once regarded as a great national wit and treasure, has almost completely faded from sight. In Dobie's case, during all of his writing life, he enjoyed immense prestige; there were no serious challenges to the quality of his writing. Leaving aside the tributes that appeared upon the occasion of his death, many of which were brought together in a special issue of the *Texas Observer* in the late 1960s, while his memory was still very green, there have since appeared both encomia to his work and a famous dissenting opinion. In a pamphlet on Dobie published in 1967, folklorist Francis E. Abernethy expressed what many white liberals in Texas felt about Dobie's presence in the cultural life of his time and place. Abernethy championed Dobie's value as a spokesman for freedom: "His cry was a war whoop to the spirited throughout the world. . . . a battle cry and a call for a universal onslaught against any man or creed that tried to impose its claims on another." Reading many of Dobie's works as "parables of freedom written during the McCarthy sickness," Abernethy unabashedly proclaimed Dobie an "artist" without ever really demonstrating wherein lay his artistry.[10] Having the right (or in this case centrist liberal) ideas is hardly enough.

That same year Larry McMurtry, in his essay "Southwestern Literature?" shifted the focus from content and charisma to the writing itself. McMurtry thought that "much of [Dobie's] own prose reads as if it had bored him to write it." Specifically, he found Dobie too enamored of the anecdote, too hasty, too sloppy, too suspicious of the imagination to be anything but a pedestrian writer whose principal strength lay in the appeal of his subject matter. But to whom did it appeal, these stories of men who "would do to ride the river with," of men "out of the old rock," of men "with the bark on"—all signature turns of phrase that Dobie could hardly write a chapter without invoking? According to McMurtry, that audience was "composed primarily of middle-aged nostalgics, and it will probably not outlive him much more than a generation."[11]

In the 1970s there were more accolades. In a brief article praising Dobie's merits as a historian, T. Lindsay Baker accepts Dobie at his word when he told an Austin newspaper reporter in 1964, "I have written the best I could on what I wanted to write about." Baker finds Dobie's most scholarly book, *The Mustangs*, his best, and repeats the oft-cited remark that Dobie made to his friend Wilson M. Hudson, "I could get my Ph.D. with this book."[12]

Not surprisingly, Dobie's biographer, Lon Tinkle, accepts as a given the notion of Dobie's status as an artist. Relegating McMurtry's criticisms to a brief comment in his bibliographical notes, Tinkle concludes that the younger writer's negative judgments are simply "wrong." Tinkle praises Dobie's method of constant revision and finds in his work a "concern for form and structure."[13] But Tinkle is speaking almost exclusively of sentence rhythms, not of the kind of structure that binds books together. Certain that Dobie's work will endure, Tinkle, like Baker, rates *The Mustangs* as Dobie's best, most mature work. Throughout, Tinkle makes a more convincing case for Dobie as cultural lodestone than as artist.

The harshest deflation of Dobie in the seventies appeared in a novel, Andrew Jolly's *A Time of Soldiers*, published in 1976. In one scene Jolly presents the following dialogue between two students living in Austin in the 1960s:

"I work for J. Frank Dobie. Do you know him?"
"I know of him."
"He's a doll."
"He's a bore."
"You don't like him?"
"I don't like professional Texans of any sort."[14]

Calling Dobie a "professional Texan" would have been fighting words among Dobie's followers when he was alive.

In the 1980s Dobie's presence remains a factor in most discussions of Texas literature, and in a 1983 conference devoted to Texas writing John Graves, one of the heirs to the Dobie-Webb-Bedichek tradition, sought to assess the work of the Holy Trinity. Author of *Goodbye to a River*, a kind of amalgam of the best of the three pioneers in which history and nature are strung together in a successful narrative framework, Graves remains a perpetual favorite of the same audience that admires the Triumvirate. Though more appreciative of Dobie than the younger McMurtry was, Graves arrived at very similar conclusions about the bulk of Dobie's work. He believes that Dobie "distrusted form" and in only one book, *Tongues of the Monte* (the same one McMurtry most admired), came close to achieving a satisfactory aesthetic form for celebrating "that harsh landscape and the people it breeds"—always Dobie's fondest subjects.[15]

The still double-sided response to Dobie can be seen throughout the Texas critical community in the eighties. In *Texas Monthly*, for example, editor Greg Curtis dismissed Dobie as a creator of "bedtime stories for ten-year-olds."[16] One sees what Curtis meant, and Dobie's works are still assigned in secondary schools, but it hardly seems likely that many juveniles today would have the patience to follow Dobie's meandering organization and constant reliance upon anecdotes. McMurtry's description of an audience of middle-aged nostalgics seems closer to the mark. The best proof that somebody is reading him—or at any rate buying copies of his works—is that the University of Texas Press has virtually all of Dobie available in paperback.

Yet it is also in *Texas Monthly* that Dobie has received one of his most ringing defenses in recent years. Novelist Bryan Woolley, author of *November 22* and several other novels, took the occasion of the Sesquicentennial year to assess Dobie's contribution to Texas literature. Responding to those who have portrayed Dobie as "an embarrassingly primitive ancestor," Woolley summarizes Dobie's importance: "All writers make do with what they have, and what Dobie had was a Texas frontier ranch background, a keen intellect, a good education, strong opinions, a deep love of great literature, and—rare in the Texas of his day—an awareness that his native place contained all the materials necessary for the creation of art."[17]

In academic circles recent estimations exhibit a similar range and polarity. Tom Pilkington, writing in 1984, has made the best case for appreciating Dobie's literary artistry. Like Tinkle, he emphasizes Dobie's attention to revision and finds his style "conscious and sophisticated." Unlike most of Dobie's admirers, however, Pilkington rates *Coronado's Children*, Dobie's first big success, as his best *and* most characteristic work. Most importantly, Pilkington actually examines the structure of *Coronado's Children*. He defends the "rather chaotic" organization as a deliberate attempt by Dobie to imitate the random casualness of stories told in the oral tradition. Thus Pilkington's Dobie is a successful "mosaicist" who consciously structures his books and employs irony and symbolism to control a stylistic tendency toward romantic excess.[18] For Pilkington, Dobie is neither folklorist nor historian but rather a literary artist.

On the other hand, one recent critique of Dobie is harsher than anything McMurtry offered. In his essay "Arbiters of Texas Literary Taste," James W. Lee states that Dobie possessed a "genius" in only one regard: "as a promoter." Like Andrew Jolly, Lee finds elements of the poseur in Dobie's colorful persona, seeing him as a kind of Big Tex of Texas literature. He argues that "Dobie's career was the result of his cleverness as a self-promoter, his untiring ambition, some facility as a journalist, and the fact that Texas can always use an 'interpreter' to the nation." Calling Dobie the "Great Cham of Texas literature," Lee continues, "He became a literary dictator without taste and without serious study. He knew nothing about literature, but he knew what he liked. He liked books about cowboys, Indians, Texas Rangers, mustangs, humble Mexicans, ranch life, and buried treasure." Of the writing itself, Lee pronounces Dobie's style "stilted and awkward."[19]

A completely different estimation appears in *A Literary History of the American West*, a massive work of academic scholarship and hagiography. Henry L. Alsmeyer Jr., author of a dissertation on Dobie's view of nature, declares Dobie a "realmist rather than a regionalist." But like the other hagiographers, of whom Dobie has certainly had his share, Alsmeyer is content to make sweeping statements rather than demonstrate the grounds of Dobie's artistic accomplishment. He, too, believes that *The Mustangs* may "prove to be the most enduring of Dobie's works."[20] It is hard to accept such a judgment, though. *The Mustangs* has nothing to distinguish it from the other books on animals: it is meandering, sentimental, topically organized, and anecdotal.

Dobie's least rigorous critics prefer *The Mustangs*; others prefer, it seems, either *Tongues of the Monte* or *Coronado's Children*. My own preference lies elsewhere. For me, Dobie never wrote an entirely satisfying book. For me, he remains an essayist at heart, and the structure of all of his books bears the stamp of the essayist's fondness for anecdote, analysis, observation, and didacticism. Paradoxically, he never wrote a single essay that bears absolutely the stamp of greatness. Granted that Dobie worked hard on his style, what he concentrated on, it seems to me, was the sentence. Books, however, are composed of paragraphs and larger structures, and Dobie, for reasons that one can only speculate about, sometimes ignored the larger structures of prose. In any of his books such paragraphs as the following may be found; this one happens to be from *The Ben Lilly Legend*:

> Ben Lilly never asked anybody to show him a bear. To find sign was with him the same, except for the time element, as finding the bear itself. No horseman, East or West, ever kept up with him in bear country. Roosevelt wore spurs. He was the last American of public consequence on horseback.[21]

Clearly the writer who wrote this paragraph was not paying attention to even the most elementary concerns of unity. The appearance of Teddy Roosevelt in this passage is astonishing. And the last sentence is all too characteristic of Dobie's penchant for inserting solemn opinions in places where they don't belong.

For me, Dobie was at his best when he achieved focus and narrative unity. Among his most compelling work, then, I would place much of his posthumously autobiographical work, *Some Part of Myself*, and several of the pieces in the last book published during his life, *Cow People*, especially the essay "Charles Goodnight of Amplitude." When Dobie wrote narrative without assembling anecdotes and without wandering too far astray from his principal subject, he achieved the force of memorable prose. The best book Dobie might have written would have been a full-scale autobiography, but he wrote only part of it and only in bits and pieces.

Another potentially personal book, *A Texan in England*, turns out to be the biggest disappointment among his works precisely because he shied away from the personal and relied upon opinion and the generalized aside instead of crafting a carefully observed and reported English world. Dobie's confidence in his audience at home kept him content to repeat the usual sallies against industrialized civilization, jukeboxes, and other impedimenta of twentieth-century life without having to describe and narrate what he actually saw in England.

It is interesting, however, that there is so much disagreement as to which of Dobie's works is the best. Such variety of preferences suggests that among his twenty-five books there is something for nearly everyone, though increasingly the reader has to be interested first in the Southwest.

Dobie's importance in his home region, though, is assured. His books in the thirties, published by a major New York house, did much to direct national attention to Texas and the Southwest as a literary region. Katherine Anne Porter, the greater writer, cultivated both in her works and in her life a specifically southern image, and the Texas context got lost in appraisals of her work. But with Dobie, the Texas flavor was indisputable. Along with Walter P. Webb, Zane Grey, and a thousand western movies, Dobie helped define Texas to the nation as a western state.

He also was a tireless and sometimes eloquent polemicist for regionalism. What he said in his essay "How My Life Took Its Turn" is telling:

> If people are to enjoy their own lives, they must be aware of the significances of their own environments. The mesquite is, objectively, as good and as beautiful as the Grecian acanthus. It is a great deal better for people who live in the mesquite country. We in the southwest shall be civilized when the roadrunner as well as the nightingale has connotations.[22]

But Dobie didn't just make the case abstractly; he showed in his work the literary possibilities inherent in local materials. The next generation of Texas writers found in the older writer's works inspiration for their own. Benjamin Capps, for example, thanked Dobie for giving him "the first inkling that the West was not a never-never land away off somewhere but a real place close to home."[23] Billy Lee Brammer read Dobie's books as a boy in Dallas and, according to William Broyles, felt "that it was *possible* to write, that the Texas experience—whether high school basketball in Archer City or the social complexities of beer drinking at Scholz Garten—could be transformed into literature."[24] So did many other writers. In the Texas of his day, a state still close to the frontier, Dobie stood for literary aspiration and the life of the mind. His legacy as a literary pioneer seems secure.

NOTES

1. Ralph Yarborough, "Yarborough Talks on 'Don Pancho,'" *Corral Dust*, 12 (Spring, 1967), 5.

2. Lon Tinkle, *An American Original: The Life of J. Frank Dobie* (1978; reprint, Austin: University of Texas Press, 1983), 151–177.

3. J. Frank Dobie, *Guide to Life and Literature of the Southwest* (rev. ed.; Dallas: Southern Methodist University Press,

1952), ii–iii (quotation). The embryonic bibliography that eventually grew into the *Guide* was a twenty-seven-page piece called "Life and Literature in the Southwest"; it appeared in John William Rogers's *Finding Literature on the Texas Plains* (Dallas: Southwest Press, 1931), 31–57.

4. Francis Edward Abernethy, *J. Frank Dobie*, Southwest Writers Series No. 1 (Austin: Steck-Vaughn, 1967), 13.

5. Dobie's library is housed in the J. Frank Dobie Room in the Peter Flawn Academic Center of the University of Texas at Austin. All quotations from Dobie's inscriptions are taken from this collection. I am grateful to the Harry Ransom Humanities Research Center of the University of Texas at Austin, to Capital National Bank, and to Mr. Edgar Kincaid for permission to quote from these writings.

6. J. Frank Dobie, "Andy Adams, Cowboy Chronicler," in *Prefaces* (Boston: Little, Brown, 1975), 4. This essay originally appeared in *Southwest Review*, 11 (Jan., 1926), 92–101.

7. Edwin Shrake to D. G., Dec. 3, 1987, interview.

8. The prizes were the Spur Award of Western Writers of America, the Texas Institute of Letters Prize for Best Fiction, and the Pulitzer Prize.

9. Benjamin Capps to J. Frank Dobie, Mar. 24, 1964, J. Frank Dobie Collection (Harry Ransom Humanities Research Center, University of Texas, Austin; cited hereafter as HRHRC).

10. Abernethy, *J. Frank Dobie*, 1 (1st quotation), 36 (2nd quotation), 43 (3rd quotation).

11. Larry McMurtry, "Southwestern Literature?" in *In a Narrow Grave: Essays on Texas* (Austin: Encino Press, 1968), 44 (5th quotation), 46 (1st quotation).

12. T. Lindsay Baker, "'My Chief Pleasure Has Been in Telling Tales': J. Frank Dobie as Writer, Historian, and Man," *Studies in History* [Department of History, Texas Tech University], 6 (1976), 87 (1st quotation); Wilson M. Hudson, "Love of Life and Freedom," *Texas Observer*, 56 (July 24, 1964), 6 (2nd quotation).

13. Tinkle, *An American Original*, 242 (2nd quotation), 254 (1st quotation).

14. Andrew Jolly, *A Time of Soldiers* (New York: E. P. Dutton, 1976), 233.

15. John Graves, "The Old Guard: Dobie, Webb, and Bedichek," in *The Texas Literary Tradition: Fiction, Folklore, History*, ed. Don Graham, James W. Lee, and William T. Pilkington (Austin: College of Liberal Arts, University of Texas at Austin, and Texas State Historical Association, 1983), 23.

16. Quoted in Tom Pilkington, "Dobie Revisited," *Texas Books in Review*, 6 (1984), 25.

17. Bryan Woolley, "Voice of a Mythic Land," *Texas Monthly*, 14 (Jan., 1986), 176.

18. Pilkington, "Dobie Revisited," 26.

19. James W. Lee, "Arbiters of Texas Literary Taste" (in a collection of essays on Texas writing forthcoming from Southern Methodist University Press), 3 (4th and 5th quotations), 4 (3rd and 6th quotations), 5 (1st and 2nd quotations). [The essay was published in Craig Clifford and Tom Pilkington, eds., *Range Wars: Heated Debates, Sober Reflections, and Other Assessments of Texas Writing* (Dallas: Southern Methodist University Press, 1989), pp. 125–127—Ed.]

20. Henry L. Alsmeyer Jr., "J. Frank Dobie," in *A Literary History of the American West*, ed. J. Golden Taylor et al. (Fort Worth: Texas Christian University Press, 1987), 535 (1st quotation), 541 (2nd quotation).

21. J. Frank Dobie, *The Ben Lilly Legend* (1950; reprint, Austin: University of Texas Press, 1978), 95.

22. J. Frank Dobie, *Some Part of Myself* (Boston: Little, Brown & Co., 1967), 237.

23. Capps to Dobie, Mar. 24, 1964, Dobie Collection.

24. Billy Lee Brammer, *The Gay Place* (1961; reprint, Austin: Texas Monthly Press, 1978), iii.

HAROLD
BILLINGS

The Woman Who Ran Ransom's University

Checkered jacket over white ruffly blouse and checkered skirt, gray on gray, Frances Hudspeth routinely left the Tower around 6 p.m. after managing the University for the day. She carried a bulging briefcase that would occupy her during the evenings. She cared for her husband, who had a major degenerative disorder. I suspect that her telephone was also heavily used during that nonsocial and unselfishly spent time. Her back may just as well have been bent from the many loads she carried as it was from osteoporosis.

By 1970 Mrs. Hudspeth held the position of executive assistant to Chancellor Harry Huntt Ransom. For all practical purposes, however, as I saw her at her work, she carried an executive portfolio that far transcended any ordinary job description for that title. Indeed, she appeared to manage virtually everything relating to Dr. Ransom's responsibilities, including his obsessive interest in building one of the greatest intellectual edifices in the world. Her role towards that end had grown just as rapidly as had Ransom's after he became dean of the College of Arts and Sciences in 1954.

Frances Hellums Hudspeth was born in Hico, Texas, in 1907. She graduated from Austin High School and taught in the public schools of Lamesa and Rising Star before she completed a B.A. with honors at the University in 1933. While attending UT, and for some six years afterwards, she taught science in the Austin public schools. She married Jack Cheever Hudspeth in 1934. Jack Hudspeth was a science teacher and author of numerous science textbooks, several of which were coauthored with his wife. He would outlive her by less than a year, perhaps not understanding that she had died. They had no children.

Editorial work at Steck Publishing helped prepare Frances Hudspeth

---

Harold Billings was director of the General Libraries at the University of Texas for twenty-five years; he retired in August 2003. In the 1960s he worked closely with Harry Ransom during the formation of the Humanities Research Center. His books include Edward Dahlberg: American Ishmael of Letters, Magic & Hypersystems: Constructing the Information-Sharing Library, *and* M. P. Shiel: A Biography of His Early Years.

Pastel portrait of Frances Hudspeth by Mimi Jungbluth. *Frances Hudspeth Portrait, Center for American History, the University of Texas at Austin. (DI 02445)*

Plaque of Frances Hudspeth at the Harry Ransom Center. *Courtesy of the Harry Ransom Humanities Research Center, the University of Texas at Austin.*

for employment and her future role at the University. Her long career with UT started with her appointment as an attendance clerk in the Office of the Dean of Arts and Sciences in 1940. After fifteen years as a professor of English, Harry Huntt Ransom was named assistant dean of the College in 1951, where his close association with Frances Hudspeth began. His administrative promotions were rapid—dean (1954), vice-president and provost (1957), president (1960), and chancellor (1961). Mrs. Hudspeth's own advancements were from attendance clerk to statistical clerk, administrative secretary, executive assistant, and, finally, office manager and executive assistant. These positions kept her working virtually at Ransom's side for over twenty years.

Mrs. Hudspeth most frequently called Ransom *He*. Conversations in person or by telephone calls from her office generally began or included *"He wants . . ."* The expectation was clear that the person she was speaking to would do as she asked, with the full authority of the *He* behind the request.

Ransom became internationally known for es-

tablishing the Humanities Research Center (HRC), the magnificent rare book, special collections, and related programs located on the UT Austin campus. While many of the collections are housed in the building that bears his name, others rest elsewhere on campus. His influence also stretched far beyond his visionary library acquisitions program, reaching every corner of the University. The Undergraduate Library and Academic Center (now the Flawn Academic Center)—once called "Harry's Place"—is only one of many physical and programmatic representations of his ideas. Even now, the student-based innovations that he promoted, like the Plan II Program and the Junior Fellows Program, are considered part of what has made the University academically excellent.

Ransom's most dramatic and significant achievements were enabled by persuading the Board of Regents that Available University Fund (AUF) income derived from the Permanent University Fund (PUF) could be spent on capital items besides buildings—on books and manuscripts, and on academic "enrichment." For a time, special appropriations for collections he wanted to acquire were made as he requested them. Later, acquisition funds were routinely built into the HRC budget, reaching levels of $2.5 million or more, but they would decline significantly in the more distant future. It has been estimated that special materials perhaps worth $50 million were acquired during the Ransom Era, with some $16 million supported from excellence funds, the remainder from gifts or gift funds. A combined gift-purchase arrangement was especially popular with both the University and with donors. The University would pay for part of a collection; the owner would donate the remainder, gaining a significant tax benefit.

The lofty ambitions of Ransom's plans in the book and scholarly world became highly publicized in 1958 with the acquisition of the Parsons Collection and the T. E. Hanley Collection. To some extent, the Parsons Collection acquisition simply perpetuated the previous direction of UT's rare book collecting, with its emphasis on Americana, Classics, Dante, and the theater. The Hanley Collection acquisition, however, represented a thunderous declaration of where the HRC would direct most of its resources and energy in coming years—collecting the twentieth century in all of its literary and cultural representations.

The Hanley Collection was singularly rich in such holdings. A great pantheon of twentieth-century literary giants—D. H. Lawrence, Dylan Thomas, Samuel Beckett, George Bernard Shaw—was represented by thousands of manuscript pages, including the most recognized literary works of the century. An early version of Lawrence's *Sons and Lovers*, under its original title, "Paul Morel," was there, as were most other Lawrence novels—in Lawrence's own handwriting. All of Shaw's major plays were represented—in manuscript, typescript, shorthand, and proof, with over three thousand letters plus thousands of other documents included. (A small work in shorthand, "The Phonetic Play," would become *Pygmalion*, the basis for the classic American musical *My Fair Lady*.) Poems in holograph and typescript by Dylan Thomas included "Do Not Go Gentle Into That Good Night," "Fern Hill," and "In Country Sleep," along with a handwritten *Under Milk Wood* and many other works. Beckett's *Waiting for Godot*, in both French and English, was present, along with other of his works in both languages, and all in manuscript versions.

These constituted only the tip of the riches. In coming years they would be joined and extended by additions from the market place, auctions, gifts or purchases of archives from authors or their estates, and especially author and artistic archives assembled by private collectors. Correspondence between literary figures was gathered by the yard. There was a special attempt to ensure that ephemeral notes, memorabilia, and every related scrap of manuscript were acquired to document the complete auctorial record.

Mrs. Hudspeth served as direct liaison with many of the booksellers, authors, and other agents with whom the HRC worked. She once asked about a dealer new to HRC's business: "Is he a broker?" Early on, it was obvious that the practice was to look for agents who could front the initial purchases; compensation from HRC would come later. Lew David Feldman, the New York bookselling dandy who loved his cloak and cane, has long been identified as HRC's chief procurer during this period. His firm was known as the House of El Dieff.

With a growing largesse of funds for library and institutional excellence, Ransom also was able to recruit human talent just as vigorously as he pursued literary riches—and he stockpiled them both, regardless of whether there was an immediate place for them or not. It was up to Mrs. Hudspeth to translate his visions—and his offhand decisions—into reality. She had to find a place or position for the collections and the people acquired. She wielded every tool she could find to make it so, and if the measures sometimes seemed ruthless and strong-armed, the results still shine today, or perhaps in memory, like an illuminated intellectual palace. The means that built the HRC are no more apparent today than the sweat that lifted the pyramids.

I came to an involvement in all of this innocently enough. I had recently completed a master's degree in library science and was helping direct book cataloging operations for the Main Library. I had worked as a cataloger since I entered the University, both as a graduate student and as an employee, a library assistant, in the summer of 1954. In 1957, when the acquisition by Ransom of everything that he could persuade the regents to buy, or that he could persuade donors to give, was beginning to swell, I wrote him a note suggesting the acquisition of a group of books and manuscripts relating to the British *fin-de-siècle* fantasist M. P. Shiel. (Coincidentally, these were available from Feldman.)

Shortly afterward, Mrs. Hudspeth called to tell me

that the purchase was being made. Ransom himself wrote a note confirming the purchase; he asked me to tell him more about Shiel and where other significant collections of his works could be found.

As the decade continued, my relationship with the emerging programs that Ransom had conceived, and that Mrs. Hudspeth helped make happen, became more routine. For the most part, the Main Library administration remained as unengaged in Ransom's activity as possible. They were skittish about his ambitions and methods. What Ransom was attempting was completely antithetical to principles then taught by the Library School and shared by the library administration. No, no, I was told by the director of the Library School: cooperation among libraries was what was required, not the building of a research library from near scratch.

From the HRC point of view, the routine bureaucracies of library processes were hindrances to Ransom's need to move quickly when the opportunity for an important acquisition presented itself. In effect, a parallel library business office was established by Mrs. Hudspeth to enable the HRC to skirt as much routine red tape as possible, touching the Main Library system only enough for it to help meet state purchasing requirements.

I presume that I came to be considered one of a few allies receptive to Ransom's programs on the regular library staff. Further, my cataloging responsibilities for the materials being acquired for the several special collections of the Main Library—including the Latin American Collection and that of the Barker Texas History Center—became an increasing part of my duties. There was much to draw me to special collections, personal interests as well as work-based bibliographic questions.

The Rare Book Library—consisting of the Stark Library, the Wrenn Library, and the Aitken Collection—was still under Main Library management. Trips to the Rare Book Library on the fourth floor of the Main Building became frequent, as I explored the Shiel archives with plans (never fully realized) to write a biography of him. It was not at all unusual for Mrs. Hudspeth to call me, and say, "Another batch of Shiel materials has just arrived. Would you like to take them home to look at over the weekend?" Those early informalities in dealing with rare materials would become a problem in the future. The materi-

als that I handled all returned to their proper home, but later inventories could not account for everything that should have been in their places. A few works of art, including "Rembrandt's," as the *Daily Texan* described those particular misplaced engravings, were among the missing.

During the final years of the fifties, the Rare Book Library became as much a living literary garden as the fountained, outdoor terraces of greens and roses that served as east and west bookends to those collections on the Main Building's fourth floor. T. S. Eliot was a stately presence among the buzzing adulators that surrounded him in the crowded foyer. Edith Sitwell towered even more majestically among the crowd in her flowery hat. Katherine Anne Porter quickly slipped in and out—but not without running headlong into a terrible misunderstanding with the University. The University did not intend, she discovered, to name a library after her. Mrs. Hudspeth did her best to calm the literary diva. Dr. Ransom was in Houston during her visit and could never regain the lost relationship. The Porter papers went elsewhere.

Aldous Huxley came to speak, as did Robert Lowell and C. P. Snow. It seemed that prominent literary figures were becoming as common on campus as the arrival of collections.

Frederick Dannay (the more visible half of "Ellery Queen"), fluttering and intellectual, was especially gracious and entertaining. Following an exhibit opening of his detective and mystery collection in January 1959, he signed and embossed the "EQ" seal in red wax on the exhibit catalog. Dannay had accompanied his collection to Texas to lecture for a semester. He told me later that it was too bad that he did not know, until the time of his departure, of the common interest we shared in M. P. Shiel, whom Eudora Welty called "a sort of genius." (A. Reynolds Morse, a Cleveland industrialist and collector of Salvador Dali and Shiel, shared with me the same Shielian interest through correspondence for several dozen years. As a result, Morse considered Austin as a home for his Dali Collection in 1981, but arrangements could not be worked out. The Dali Collection, appraised in excess of $200 million, was given to the state of Florida.)

Prior to the establishment of the Humanities Research Center, Fannie Ratchford had long served as librarian of the Rare Books Library. After completing her B. A. degree from UT in 1919, she was appointed as an assistant to work on the recently acquired Wrenn Library while she pursued a master's degree. Following the addition of the Aitken and Stark libraries in the 1920s, and her appointment as head of the Rare Book Library, Miss Ratchford achieved almost legendary status on campus, but she returned from a vacation trip to Europe in 1957 to find that she had retired.

Miss Ratchford had become an established figure in the international rare book world. Her scholarly publications on the Family Brontë were notable. Important also was her work on the English forger Thomas J. Wise, the most respected bibliographer of his day, who counted John Henry Wrenn among the victims of his forgery sales. The full extent of Wise's twisted activities as a respected bookman and maker of imaginary rare nineteenth-century pamphlets was not known until well after the University's purchase of the Wrenn Library in 1918.

It is ironic that the most publicized portion of this fine collection of English literature would become the forgeries. Miss Ratchford's scholarly reputation was linked to her study and publication of the letters that Wise wrote to Wrenn, revealing how Wise duped the Chicago collector into purchasing his creative forgeries. More important to Wise than the sales of the pamphlets to Wrenn was the success that Wise achieved, a game won, by having the forgeries validated to the book world through their presence in Wrenn's library.

I respected Fannie Ratchford deeply. Her humanity greatly enlarged her slight figure. Despite rumors of occasional incivilities by Miss Ratchford, two events have always defined her character for me. It was the custom of the Ratchford library for all work to cease for tea at 10 a.m. During my first year at Texas, when for some reason I found myself in that library at teatime, Miss Ratchford approached me and graciously asked if I would join her and her staff for the occasion. It didn't matter what my rank was. A year of so later, library staff and others were invited to attend a lecture in the Stark Room by a visiting bookman. It became quickly apparent that the speaker was full of much more than tea. His slurred speech, his dancing from foot to foot, quickly embarrassed and unsettled the audience. Miss Ratchford stepped quietly to the podium and inserted an interesting bookish narrative as the speaker stumbled into the restroom across the hall.

But Miss Ratchford's expertise and energy had no place among projects dealing with contemporary literature that Ransom had decided to pursue. Beginning with Miss Ratchford's retirement in 1957, the Humanities Research Center, with Mrs. Hudspeth as the surrogate director for Dr. Ransom, effectively subsumed the Rare Book Library. Any pretense that it was part of the Main Library organization disappeared.

F. Warren Roberts, who had served as associate director of the HRC, was named director in February 1961, when Dr. Ransom became chancellor of the University. Effectively, Roberts and Ann Bowden (who had been rare book cataloger for the library) assumed daily responsibility for the collections and the HRC programs. Roberts, a professor of English, was a D. H. Lawrence scholar who had done his dissertation under Ransom's supervision. He was a nice, if pugnacious, fit for the primary directions that were eventually defined for the HRC.

Every space in the Main Building was beginning to bulge with Ransom's acquisitions. The several levels of stack space in the Rare Book Library—including a lower level in the richly paneled Aitken Study where future presidents would nap—were full of rare books and manuscripts. Collections were shoehorned into the upper floors of the Tower that were not occupied by Main Library book-stacks. The regular stacks themselves were becoming so full that books tumbled onto the floor. There were books stored in places that most of us did not even know about for several years. Even cats would have been pleased at the secret places that Mrs. Hudspeth found to lay away the truckloads of books as they arrived.

As soon as Ransom became president, and at his immediate urging, the regents approved the construction of a library dedicated to serving undergraduate students. It was a building, it should be added, that could provide additional storage and programmatic space for Ransom's specialized initiatives, although that was not the message. "If books have anything to do with education," Ransom had said as vice-president, "the undergraduate at Texas is being cheated." The proposed Undergraduate Library and Academic Center would permit open stack access for undergraduate students. They were not allowed in the stacks of the Main Library, a privilege reserved for faculty, graduate students, and a few undergraduate honors students.

Ransom's library for the undergraduates. *From the Prints and Photographs Collection—Peter T. Flawn Academic Center, Center for American History, the University of Texas at Austin. (DI 02383)*

Ransom's objective was to encourage students to mingle and be enriched—"startled into new awareness," he said—among many of the great books and manuscripts being acquired. The idea was that students could use ordinary books in the new library while studying among exhibit cases filled with literary treasures, not otherwise easily seen. Further, the top floor and the lower level of the new Center—to be identified as the Academic Center Library—would provide additional housing and public display for the more distinctive collections.

Books for the Undergraduate Library could be selected from the thousands of general books that Ransom had acquired by the simple expedient of buying, a parcel at a time, the contents of the Argosy Book Store in New York.

Critics had already started questioning what they considered the profligacy of Ransom's programs.

They argued that more of the money he was spending should be spent on routine academic library needs. They urged that the new collections should be more quickly cataloged and dispersed. Ransom's stated position during those collection-gathering days was "It's important to get the collections while we can. Scatteration can come later."

Ransom's full and consistent library vision has never been amply described. In retrospect, it is clear that his acquisitions program followed the plans that he proposed to the regents from the very beginning. "The only reasonable, intelligible, and workable view of a university library is one which takes into account totality resources," he said. "Totality resources," as he explained early in 1958, included the development of "three continuing projects: the undergraduate library, the special collections, and the main library."

"The steady purpose," he said, "should be to attain

eminence in unified library resources and to keep that eminence viable." The gathering of massive collections of more general library materials, with special funding, within the glow of the more glamorous acquisitions, offered an unusual opportunity to develop resources for this "totality" all at the same time.

In building a collection for the Undergraduate Library, it was planned that books in selected subject areas—biography, economics, history, travel, literary classics—would be pulled from their hiding places and cataloged and stored in the Tower awaiting construction of the new library. An entire additional floor of the Tower was emptied to provide space for this activity. It was Mrs. Hudspeth's responsibility to see that the new building was designed and constructed and that a collection appropriate for undergraduates was selected, processed, and ready for the opening of the building in 1963.

Initial exposure to the places that Mrs. Hudspeth had found to store many of the collections was as haunting as the locations were surprising. One was the extended, claustrophobic basement below the Main Building, where streams of water trickled, machinery vibrated, and darkness lay over most of this literal deep. It was reached through a locked door at the lowest level of the Main Building's small northeast elevator. I don't know how the books got there. The area seemed a more likely home for the Phantom of the Opera than for book storage. It would have been useful to have had a long piece of Ariadne's thread to find one's way through that ill-lit labyrinth.

Wooden shelving had been assembled in every empty area of the southwest basement, including shelves shoved into spaces where books would lean against the earth. Electrical wiring had been strung among the cheap pine shelves, with bare bulbs to light the books. Thousands of titles were pulled from the basement for the new Undergraduate Library. Additional funds were made available to purchase more current books and journals to mix with the older titles, and all were assembled for processing in upper floors of the Tower. Numerous out-of-date, out-of-fashion, and inappropriate books that should never have been part of the collection burdened that library until they were transferred or withdrawn in the early 1990s.

Excitement surrounded the 1963 opening of the new building, with its large, open-shelf collections, new audio-visual resources, study rooms, and library services aimed specifically at lower-division students.

Main Library stacks. *From the Prints and Photographs Collection–UT Buildings: Main and Tower, Center for American History, the University of Texas at Austin. (DI 02414)*

Ransom and Hudspeth were also establishing major display areas and reading rooms for the more bibliographic elite materials. These rooms would house collections named for individuals associated with them. The Knopf Room, the Dobie Room, the Hoblitzelle Room, the Tinker Room, and even a reconstruction of Erle Stanley Gardner's rustic study were located off the halls that encircled an unroofed atrium on the top floor of the new Academic Center. Several large wry-necked sisters of statuary by Charles Umlauf presided in the open-air atrium courtyard.

In addition to the areas devoted to storage and processing, special quarters were arranged on the fourth floor for the rapidly growing group of iconographic materials associated with the literary figures represented in the collections—portraits of the authors, their own artwork, literary drawings, related photographs. Other kinds of items were stored on the lower floor of the Center: the so-called Hall of the Horsemen of the Americas, with the saddles, spurs, and lariats of the gauchos; the grand, decorated double-doors removed from the Littlefield Building in downtown Austin; tiny pastel paintings of the American West, cattle, oxen by Frank Reaugh.

Offices were assigned on that lower floor to several of the persons whom Ransom had recruited right along with his other acquisitions. Several restless, world-class bibliographers, book designers, curators, and scholars were located there, increasingly uncertain of what their roles would be in the Ransom University. Mrs. Hudspeth had to keep them content.

The dedication of the Academic Center and Undergraduate Library was celebrated in 1964 with an extraordinary exhibit of contemporary literary materials assembled during the brief life of the Humanities Research Center development programs. If the world was not yet aware of what was occurring in Texas, the exhibit catalog, *A Creative Century: Selections from the Twentieth-Century Collections at the University of Texas*, would startle, amaze, and unsettle the international book world.

One hundred authors were selected for inclusion in the exhibit, each represented by both original manuscripts and published rarities. The authors and the manuscripts in the exhibit represented the rara avises of contemporary letters. Just a sample: James Agee, *A Death in the Family* (autograph Ms., including unpublished autograph notes); W. H. Auden, *The Age of Anxiety* (autograph Ms. with additional pages of autograph manuscript essays and poems); James Baldwin, *Another Country* (autograph Ms. and corrected typescript); Samuel Beckett, *Malloy* (autograph Ms.); Saul Bellow, *Seize the Day* (autograph Ms. and four corrected typescripts); Joseph Conrad, *Victory* (autograph Ms.); Hart Crane, *The Bridge* (corrected typescript with his own design for the title page); E. E. Cummings, *Poems 1923-1954* (corrected typescript with corrected galley and page proofs); J. Frank Dobie, *The Mustangs* (corrected typescript with corrected galley and page proofs); Arthur Conan Doyle, *A Scandal in Bohemia* (autograph Ms.); T. S. Eliot, *The Wasteland* (autograph Ms. with a line omitted from the published text); William Faulkner, *Absalom! Absalom!* (autograph Ms.); C. S. Forester, *Commodore Hornblower* (autograph Ms.); E. M. Forster, *A Passage to India* (autograph Ms. with early drafts and notes); Robert Graves, *Count Belisarius* (autograph Ms. and corrected typescript); Graham Greene, *The Power and the Glory* (autograph Ms.); Ernest Hemingway, *Death in the Afternoon* (autograph Ms. and corrected typescript); Aldous Huxley, *Brave New World* (corrected typescript and Ms. draft); James Joyce, *Ulysses* (master set of complete first edition proofs, with autograph corrections); D. H. Lawrence, *Sons and Lovers* (autograph Ms. with its original working title, "Paul Morel"); Sinclair Lewis, *Main Street* (corrected typescript); Somerset Maugham, *Cakes and Ale* (autograph Ms.); Arthur Miller, *Death of a Salesman* (autograph Ms. notebook and corrected typescript); Christopher Morley, *Kitty Foyle* (corrected typescript and early draft notes); Ezra Pound, *Ta Hio* (corrected typescript); George Bernard Shaw, *Pygmalion* (autograph shorthand Ms. with original working title, "The Phonetic Play"); C. P. Snow, *The Affair* (autograph Ms. notebooks); Lytton Strachey, *Queen Victoria* (autograph Ms. and corrected typescript); Dylan Thomas, *The Beach of Falesa* (autograph Ms. and corrected typescript); Eudora Welty, *The Ponder Heart* (corrected typescript); Oscar Wilde, *Lady Windemere's Fan* (corrected typescript); Tennessee Williams, *A Streetcar Named Desire* (corrected typescript and Ms. draft); William Butler Yeats, *The Winding Stair* (corrected typescript); Stark Young, *So Red the Rose* (autograph Ms.).

In addition to this horde of modern manuscripts—authors and manuscripts are only partially listed here—there were equally imposing exemplars of rare publications, correspondence, diaries, and other items representative of the creative lives of these authors of the half-century.

Bookish eyes in Britain were especially snared by this display. William Rees-Mogg, writing in the *London Sunday Times* (April 19, 1964) about the rare book market, said, "this is the last decade in which it is at all possible to form any sort of proper University collection of English literature, and the opportunity is already slipping fast away. The University of Texas has been taking it—we have not." Lee Minoff, writing in the *London Observer* (February 14, 1965), said, "Texas has become the world's greatest repository of source material in twentieth-century British and American literature . . . to pore over such treasures, scholars will travel anywhere—even to Texas." Bertram Rota, one of England's most respected booksellers (who had been selling to UT), commented more favorably, "they are building an edifice which will not be a mausoleum but a workshop."

Chancellor Ransom and his colleagues could glory in the attention. He proudly reported to the regents, early in 1965, on the activity leading up to the dedicatory exhibit: "It was an exciting time . . ." As the collecting world waked up to what was in Texas, the individual who had spent years bringing together a perfect collection of a man or a genre or a period began to be eager to have his things join others like them. By gift as well as purchase, the small collections came. It was an adventure for the Park Avenue sophisticate to send his collections to a 'frontier' library that really wanted the materials and needed them. (It was also pleasant to have the tax deductions.)

Collections, curators and catalogers were all over the place, and a new location was revealed for the continuing overrun of books. Two corrugated metal buildings at the Balcones Research Center (now the Pickle Research Campus), left behind from World War II days, were filled with wooden shelving. Several hundred thousand items were stored there—newly acquired collections, as well as many books moved from the Main Building's basement or from yet another storage place on Little Campus (where Custer had briefly billeted). Two former bookmen, paid to accompany their book stock to Austin, were assigned to list these thousands of items—an impossible task. They set about trying to do so, writing up descriptions by hand on 3x5 cards in bookseller fashion.

A first trip to Balcones, ten miles from campus, was just as startling as the descent into the basement of the Main Building. There had been little choice left regarding where to locate collections, but few books have ever likely suffered as those stored at these two places.

The Balcones buildings had concrete floors, their outer corrugated walls started several inches above ground, there was no air conditioning, and huge fans did little to relieve the heat and humidity. The rattlesnakes and vermin that found their way into those quarters from the brown fields of weeds just outside were disposed of as they were found. A massive antifungal operation was conducted when mold began to appear on book spines. Their backs were washed by hand. Fortunately, the titles stored there were from the more ordinary collections that Ransom believed would help strengthen Main Library holdings. Those airplane-hanger-like structures would hold these books until 1968.

Earlier, in 1965, I became Chief Acquisition Librarian of the University Library. Because of state-required purchasing procedures, every invoice for every Humanities Research Center purchase passed through my hands for payment. A full historical record of those purchases was present in our files. They indicated that materials acquired after the Hanley purchase had added significantly to the body of literary works displayed at the dedication of the Academic Center. New dimensions were added to the type of collections being purchased. Invoices disclosed that $120,800 had been paid for a "Collection of books

and pamphlets extending over the whole period of Catholic history"; $5,000 for a bronze bust of Ernest Hemingway; $24,000 for the Arturo Taracena Flores Library, a collection of five thousand volumes, broadsides, maps, and newspaper clippings that would enhance the Latin American Collection; $15,000 for a collection of ten thousand biographies (almost all placed in the Undergraduate Library); $5,000 for an original landscape drawing by Charlotte Brontë. And on and on. Processing these invoices established another routine link for me with Mrs. Hudspeth, HRC staff, and their business activities.

In 1967, I accepted more extended oversight for library acquisition programs, the Library's bookkeeping office, the central Cataloging Department, and the severally separated units that cataloged books for the HRC. Mrs. Hudspeth and Warren Roberts asked me for advice regarding the organizing of the collections stored at Balcones. There was increasing campus pressure to provide access to them. (Pulling the several cataloging units together on campus was something that I would not complete for another two years.)

We immediately stopped the handwritten book listing, placed photocopy machines in the coolest office area of the two metal buildings, and began an "xtp" (Xeroxed title page) project. This routine involved the placing of a numbered flag in each book and photocopying the book's title page with the numbered flag laid on it. Books were then returned to shelves in numerical order. The Xeroxed title pages were alphabetized by author or title, providing a primitive finding aid for each title in the many collections gathered at Balcones.

My increasingly closer association with Mrs. Hudspeth led to observations of her work that was not visible to most of the campus. By this time we both occupied offices in the Tower, up near where the weather begins, with gorgeous views of the western hills and the campus, a location that Charles Whitman and his rifle had used with deadly effect in August 1966. Mrs. Hudspeth would frequently call and say, "Can you come up?" The floor on which she maintained an exceedingly unorganized office area, a couple of floors above mine, was filled with evidence of the numerous campus activities that she was managing for Dr. Ransom. Each was reflected by its own stack of documents, manuscripts, letters, notes, building plans, located on and around her desk, competing for space with her ash trays and cigarettes. During a fire in the Tower in 1965, the chief of campus police had escorted Mrs. Hudspeth down from this workplace, virtually unreachable by fire hose.

Several bright young women assisted Mrs. Hudspeth with everything from secretarial work to unpacking new acquisitions. They gathered at noon to play bridge in the midst of trash and treasure. They were surrounded by packages, discarded wrapping paper, unopened crates of Houdini artifacts, framed Rembrandt engravings and other artwork leaning against the walls, and stacks and stacks of books and journals. Their working place in the Tower had been intended for book stacks, not for office work or as a receiving area. The floors were small, and activity had to be diverted around stanchions that formed the skeletal frames where shelving was meant to hang.

My business with Mrs. Hudspeth did not allow exploration of her office floor. There was only room for the conversation between us—I on a leather couch and she in a swivel chair, with her usual checkered suit, thick stockings, and flat shoes, and a constantly probing mind that caught me only once, as I recall, in a misstep. I don't remember the substance, but the memory remains strong that I didn't want the spearing that others had received. She was not bad tempered, but she demanded direct, accurate answers, and she was direct in turn.

Discussing the various book-related projects was one thing. Listening in on the business of the University was not always fun, especially when it dealt with personnel issues. An employee associated with one of the purchased collections, who had been on the staff for several years, was told that his work was not satisfactory, his job was being eliminated. A few days later, he committed suicide.

Trips around campus by automobile with Mrs. Hudspeth were not always aimed at solving space or bibliographic problems. Sometimes, they were simply intended to assess the status of the staff in a unit after some unfortunate incident or change. Basically, however, Mrs. Hudspeth avoided the public eye. She never attended social events, spending most of her time in her office, content with her cigarettes and the power of her telephone. I never heard laughter in her life. She was always business.

There seemed to be little that she did not touch—campus security issues, problems with the physical plant, the University's involvement in the construc-

tion of the Lyndon B. Johnson Presidential Library and its architectural foil, the thousand-foot-long Sid Richardson Hall. This structure would house the LBJ School of Public Affairs, the Barker Texas History Center, and the Latin American Collection. There were art collections for Mrs. Hudspeth to review for location with curators upon receipt. For want of other space for them, we worked to hang examples from the Mertz Collection of Contemporary Australian Paintings throughout the Undergraduate Library upon that collection's initial arrival in Austin. When the University acquired the Bauer House as a home for the chancellor—to first house Charles A. LeMaistre—Mrs. Hudspeth assumed responsibility for many of the preparations for occupancy of it. It included a large formal "library." Mrs. Hudspeth asked me and my colleague George Cogswell to assemble a suitable collection to fill its shelves. She had very specific ideas about what might best appeal to the LeMaistre family and also be appropriate for the setting.

She took President Johnson's daughter Lynda Bird under her wing when Lynda enrolled at UT. There was security, campus logistics, and academic counseling to be managed. Providing advice to young women students regarding their academic plans was apparently a practice that Mrs. Hudspeth had devoted much time to during her tenure in the College of Arts and Sciences.

Quietly, among all these other concerns, Mrs. Hudspeth was also helping manage the *Texas Quarterly*, a responsibility that began with its first issue in 1958. Eventually, she was named managing editor. Oversight of that enterprise alone, that she provided again as Ransom's surrogate, would have been sufficient work for most people.

A colleague recalls a meeting during which four of us were discussing the move of HRC collections from one location to another. Warren Roberts accepted a phone call, talked briefly, and told us: "Gentlemen, I must go. I've been summoned. Not to the throne room—just to the Prime Minister." We all understood what he meant.

Space needs were far from satisfied, and Ransom took a fresh idea to the regents. He suggested the construction of a new library storage facility, the Collections Deposit Library (CDL), at the southeast edge of the campus. General materials arriving for campus libraries could be received and processed there, he explained. Overflow from crowded branch libraries and rapidly growing general library collections from foreign countries, acquired through federal programs, could be made available to scholars there. It was no coincidence that the new structure would also allow the collections stored at Balcones to be moved quickly into it.

Mrs. Hudspeth directed the program planning for this new facility, just as she had for the Academic Center and as she would for the Humanities Research Center building still to come. Construction of CDL was completed in 1968.

Few storage facilities have a beautiful atrium, study carrels around the two upper floors, and spring-fed streams that too frequently flooded the three floors below ground level. But this one did. Every time there was a heavy rain, the lower levels would leak, as CDL virtually became a branch of Waller Creek that flowed under oaks and cypress just below it. A member of the Board of Regents had insisted that aesthetics for this storage facility should trump utility.

Numerous other items acquired by the HRC during its most vigorous acquisitions ecstasy joined the book collections that were moved to CDL from Balcones. Pianos, patent models, cameras, all the effluvium rising from one of the most aggressive collection-building programs in library history had to be housed or disposed of in some manner.

The Xeroxed title pages that had been produced for most of the books moved from Balcones to CDL offered at least minimal access to them in their new quarters. More formal processing of the collections, either by addition to the already-cataloged HRC collections or by location in other campus libraries, could begin. "Scatteration" had arrived.

In the meantime, however, other opportunities for adding to the HRC collections were presenting themselves. Early in 1969, Ransom was able to announce that the Sid Richardson Foundation of Dallas was making a $2 million gift to the University to pay for major additions to the HRC's history of science collections.

One of the additions, it was said, would "propel the Texas library in a single stroke into one of the most important repositories of architectural literature in the world." Other collections included manuscript items by Albert Einstein, a research collection relating to Sigmund Freud, a collection "in which many areas of developing science are represented from the 16th Century forward, with works by all the great scientists in the fields of biological as well as physical sciences." Several others were described as no less significant.

Truth to tell, I believe those collections were already on campus, waiting for Ransom to find monies to pay for them. He was beginning to make commitments beyond the financial resources available, and soon it would not be possible to continue the prodigious purchasing program that had been so constant over the previous ten-year period.

Dr. Ransom decided that it would be useful to have catalogs prepared for several of these history of science collections to display to the Richardson Foundation officers—of whom John Connally was one. Mrs. Hudspeth asked me to find a means to do so, and she diverted federal grant funds to establish a "History of Science Cataloging Project."

The immediate need for printed catalogs that Ransom wanted to show the Richardson Foundation executives was resolved by filming catalogs that dealers had already prepared for the collections, by producing Xeroxed title pages that were camera-reduced, reproduced fifteen to a page, and then bound into red buckram volumes with handsome title-pages included. The photocopies of the books' title pages, the size of catalog cards, were filed into a separate card catalog for the history of science collections holdings.

My personal interaction with Dr. Ransom increased. He asked me to speak to a visiting Harveian Society of London group about the cataloging projects, and generously introduced me as a renaissance librarian. There was a small dinner at his home to discuss book collecting with Gordon Ray, the president of the Guggenheim Foundation. I recognized several of the art works on the decoratively papered walls in the Ransom home as ones that I had seen earlier in the Tower. Dr. Ransom's extraordinarily lovely wife, Hazel, who had been a teaching assistant in English, welcomed us and departed, leaving the Ransom home feeling just as reserved as Ransom always appeared. At his warmest, there never seemed to be more than a thin tight smile. It was his words that were overwhelming.

Late in July 1970, when I was beginning a brief vacation, an early morning phone call asked me to hold for Dr. Ransom.

"Harold, I have a mission for you," he said. "I have a manuscript that I would like to have hand-carried to

New York. At the same time, you could explore some of the cataloging practices at various libraries in that city. Will you do this?"

I was curious as to what this manuscript was that made it important enough to carry by hand to New York. Was it a piece by Hemingway or an illuminated manuscript being delivered to a New York dealer or conservator? When I picked up a package from Ransom's office the next day—containing the manuscript, first-class plane tickets, and a reservation at the Algonquin Hotel, long known as a home for literati—there was a memorandum (July 30, 1970) of instructions from Dr. Ransom.

> Harold: The New York mission is triple: From NYPL, I need to get firsthand what they are doing with photographic (or other similar processes) in accession-listing, cataloguing, reproduction for loan, etc. I am less interested in the mere technology than in effectiveness, cost, etc. From Columbia, the same information. For Family Weekly, as addressed, delivery by hand of the Ms. H. R.

The manuscript for *Family Weekly*, whose editorial offices were squeezed into the eastern corridor on an upper floor of a Manhattan office building, was a brief article by Ransom about the HRC programs. It appeared in a fall issue of the Sunday newspaper supplement.

The trip provided also an opportunity to visit the Pierpont Morgan Library, as well as Columbia University and the New York Public Library, and to re-visit Edward Dahlberg, an American literary legend whose papers were at Austin. I had edited two books relating to Dahlberg, working from his archives, and was completing a bibliography of his works that would soon be published by the Humanities Research Center. None of this, however, seemed enough to justify the expense of the hand delivery of the manuscript.

It became apparent in time that the trip was simply a generous learning opportunity that Ransom had provided me. I was embarrassed, however. While I was asking about "photographic brief-listing" at the NYPL, that library was rapidly converting its card catalog to machine-readable format, a direction that we should have been pursuing.

Soon, Mrs. Hudspeth, Ransom, and I began discussing whether we might employ labor from the Texas Department of Corrections to create machine-readable records for a database of cataloged holdings of the HRC collections. By the following year, Texas had at least started the computer-generated production of catalog records, although fuller automation lay ten years ahead.

There were few occasions to observe Ransom and Hudspeth in conversation, but they were clearly relaxed, completely open with one another, as might have been expected from the many years of common interest and effort they shared. Conversation might be light; it was never light-hearted. Mrs. Hudspeth had assisted Ransom with his earlier responsibilities, as associate editor of both the *Southwestern Historical Quarterly* and *English Copyright Cases, 1660–1775*, as well as with his administrative duties in Arts and Sciences. That foundation of a working partnership permitted a simple extension of her own role as Ransom's responsibilities and influence grew. She knew his mind; she understood what needed to be done.

Plans for the grand culmination of library construction that would provide a home for Ransom's collections and programs had begun. In some ways, its genesis had been provoked at the time the Sid Richardson Foundation gifted the $2 million to Ransom for the history of science collections. In smaller newspaper type, at the time of the Richardson gift, there had appeared the news, "Novelist Michener Gives Art Collection to UT." James Michener was donating 252 paintings from his collection of Twentieth-Century American art to the University, and the curator of the collection, a friend of Michener, had been persuaded to join it in Austin. It would need quarters.

There was ample reason to construct a building in which could be gathered the most distinguished results of the Ransom enterprise. After completion of the Main Building in 1935, no library space was added to the campus until four buildings were erected during Ransom's tenure: the Undergraduate Library and Academic Center, the Collections Deposit Library, Sid Richardson Hall, and the Humanities Research Center. Mrs. Hudspeth had a hand in the work on all of them. The Humanities Research Center building was constructed as a mammoth, almost windowless fortress respecting the many fire-bombings of libraries, desecration of card catalogs, and other violent agitations that concerned universities at the time. Entry to the floors on which the book collections were housed would be tighter than through the proverbial eye of a needle.

On March 14, 1969, the UT news service announced that the regents had awarded a construction contract of $6,132,106 for the new Humanities Research Center. The total cost of approximately $7.1 million would be met by supplemental federal and other funds.

The seven-story center, it was announced, would house the contents of the Rare Books Library, many items from the fourth floor of the Academic Center, the more than one hundred special collections housed in various campus locations, the Michener Collection, and the Graduate School of Library Science. The belated addition of the paintings and the Library School meant that there was not space enough for all the Ransom collections in the building as initially planned. While staff had already occupied some of the Center, the move of collections into the building commenced shortly after Christmas in 1971. Others were left behind in the Academic Center.

Dr. Ransom occupied a large suite of rooms on the northeast side of the third floor of the new building, where a magnificent oak table with the usual bowl of red apples upon it was resting on a snow-white carpet. He called me over one morning, talked vaguely about the insufficiencies he felt existed in the HRC leadership, described the holy and exciting mission of library development, and asked if I would take an office as a consultant to him in the new Center.

I asked Mrs. Hudspeth—perhaps our final conversation—if she had any notion of what he had in mind. She said, "No, but I think it's a good idea."

I told Ransom that I would do anything I could to help, but reminded him that I now served another president. I knew instinctively at that moment that I was stepping outside his interest. He had shared too much, demanded absolute loyalty, and I had chosen reality over a falling dream.

For a time, it appeared that a brighter sun and a different moon hung above the Ransom University. Something special seemed to be occurring, although aspects of it smacked of excesses from *The Great Gatsby*. Hubris was not completely inappropriate, however, given the accomplishments. Never had a research library of such importance and magnitude been built in a mere fifteen-year span. The respected British bookman Anthony Hobson, in *Great Libraries*, called the UT Library one of the great libraries of the world. It was one of only five American libraries included in his book. The *Texas Quarterly* had achieved international recognition as a showcase for Austin's acquisitions and for wide-ranging scholarly reflections. Talent in research and librarianship, book design and bibliography was abundant. UT's academic corridors were crowded with the likes of William Arrowsmith, William Goetzmann, Vartan Gregorian, Roger Shattuck, and John Silber. It seemed as though the gods had returned to earth.

But a final accounting was gathering for Ransom. The Ransom University had always been an evanescent Cinderella of an institution, only minutes removed from midnight. Ransom's acquisition funds had become committed for several years ahead. The great faculty began to drift away, despairing of campus politics. Ransom's and Hudspeth's beloved College of Arts and Sciences was divided, its dean, John Silber, fired. The University of Texas was being rapidly expanded into a System that demanded a different kind of administrator. Ransom was named Chancellor Emeritus in 1971.

Frank C. Erwin Jr., chairman of the Board of Regents, whose ambition was simply to control the entire University, just put his thumb down on Ransom. Erwin told the *Houston Chronicle*, "When Ransom retired, he was promised another $1 million for the last few years, more or less to complete the project he had outlined to us." Ransom's library had been built, as far as Erwin was concerned. With his funds already obligated and with his strongest tool removed—access to the Board of Regents—Ransom was effectively without power. Another blow would wound him soon.

On January 29, 1972, Frances Hudspeth died after a short, heart-related illness. She was not yet 65. No more than Moses would she see the full promise filled. Honorary pallbearers at her funeral included President Johnson, Regent Erwin, Dr. Ransom, Chancellor LeMaistre, and other notables. The Board of Regents issued a resolution in recognition of Mrs. Hudspeth's exceptional service to the University. Ransom praised her loyalty. Her ashes were buried next to her mother's grave in Hico, Texas.

Ransom would live until a sudden heart attack killed him at his in-laws' home in Dripping Springs in 1976, but he had already become a ghost. His complexion grayed and his handshake was no longer warm. He had been relocated to an office in Sid Richardson Hall, where he was to gather materials for a history of the University. It might as well have been Elba or Siberia.

Without the strong arm of Hudspeth and the coordinating charm of Ransom, the HRC staff began to bicker over programs and priorities, and longtime critics found its operations more vulnerable to audit and attack. Soon, issues surrounding the HRC would help depose a new president, and additional breaches developed with each new University administration. Almost fifteen years of misadventure lay ahead.

For a few short years it appeared that the Ransom University—a magical shadow university much grander than the routine one in which we spent our more ordinary days—might achieve a permanence, a greatness that had narrowly eluded Austin in the past and would be just as hard to achieve in the future. I am convinced that the day that Frances Hudspeth died, the Ransom University died with her.

NOTES ON SOURCES

Brief biographical sketches of Frances Hudspeth can be found in *The Handbook of Texas* and in Carl Eckhardt, *One Hundred Faithful to the University of Texas at Austin* (pp. 48–49). Dr. Ransom's plans for library programs are gathered in a "Preliminary Memorandum on Library Development, July 31, 1970," delivered to the Board of Regents, "made now in a context of wide concern about libraries." This report appends statements and recommendations on UT Austin library programs that Ransom made in 1958 to the Committee on Expectations, Sub-committee on Library; to the Commission on Library Co-operation in 1965; to the regents in 1965; to the General Faculty in 1967; to the regents in 1969; and to "Representatives of Federal Agencies, February 20, 1970."

Excellent contemporary summaries of the acquisitions made during the Ransom Library Development Program can be found in Warren Roberts, *Twentieth-Century Research Materials: A Decade of Library Development & Utilization*" (Austin: Humanities Research Center, The University of Texas at Austin, 1972) and in Ann Holmes, "Late UT Chancellor Harry Ransom Made Collecting World's Eyes Pop," *Houston Chronicle*, Section 2 (May 2, 1976): 9–10. A more recent and dramatic description of some of the events behind collections acquired and collections missed is the chapter "Instant Ivy" in Nicholas A. Basbanes, *A Gentle Madness* (New York: Holt, 1995).

Statements made in my hearing by Mrs. Hudspeth and Dr. Ransom, as best I can recall them, as they might have been, are simply enclosed in quotation marks.

CHAD
OLIVER } **Some Blues for a Trio**

I came to the University in 1946. That was not quite as far back as the Paleolithic, but it was a time distant enough to belong to another world. Austin was a town of close horizons growing without urgency into a city. The University was less than half its present size. I am sure that a committee was already at work forecasting doom if enrollment ever reached the awesome figure of 20,000.

Mine was a postwar generation: a mixture of kids just out of high school and returning veterans of World War II. We were not as innocent as later generations seemed to believe we were. We were also not as boldly original as we thought we were.

We had the Bomb. It was our generation that had used it.

We had some other things. If you wanted a fancy hamburger, you could get a Frisco at the Night Hawk. However, for those addicted to quantity, you could go to boxes called Somewheres and buy—what else—a Someburger. (Remember?) The Princess was riding her bicycle then, not pushing it, and Gordon was selling newspapers everywhere simultaneously. (Remember?) Dirty Martin's was not an institution then; it was just there. You could put a canoe in the clean waters of Lake Travis, paddle all day without seeing another boat, and camp on the shore at night. Austin was not a Mecca for big names in the entertainment business in those days, but we had our moments. There was Harry James playing for a dance under the stars, Nat King Cole gracefully fielding requests from a lily-white audience, and one electric night when Louis Armstrong blew the roof off at what was supposed to be a segregated concert. (Remember?)

By the time Symmes Chadwick (Chad) Oliver died in August of 1993, he had spent more than forty years on the University of Texas campus. He was twice chairman of the Anthropology Department and was designated the Robert D. King Centennial Professor of Liberal Arts. In addition to his published works in anthropology, Oliver was the author of several acclaimed science fiction and western novels. His other non-academic accomplishments included jazz piano and fly fishing. This essay was first published in Texas Our Texas: Remembrances of The University, *edited by Bryan A. Garner (Eakin Press, 1984).*

We all have our memories of college years, and they are an indelible part of our youth. We all know that many of the most important things that happened to us did not take place in a classroom. The interactions between students and professors were of variable quality: some counted, and some didn't.

I want to share some memories of three professors who counted for me. They made a difference in my life. One of the weariest of all clichés is the one about the professor who made a lasting impression. Therefore, I am going to be very specific. I intend to spell out a few of the ways in which our lives intertwined.

Let us go back in time.

I had been accepted into Plan II out of a small high school in Crystal City, Texas. I arrived on the campus for my first registration quite literally without knowing a soul. Few of my high school classmates went to college. Of those who did, the boys headed for College Station and the girls went out of state.

It was a very hot day. (Some things haven't changed.) Sweating or not, I nevertheless wore my football letter jacket from high school. I still had a lot to learn.

I walked into the Plan II advising room on the second floor of the Main Building. I did not have a clue about what to do. There was a man seated at a table with a stack of books around him. He was not a big man but he had an air of relaxed friendliness about him that attracted me. He was dressed in a crisp blue suit, and I thought he had melancholy eyes behind his rather thick glasses. I recognized some of his books.

Very tentatively, I sat down across from him and introduced myself. The man smiled as though I had made his day by showing up. His eyes were no longer sad: they were bright and alive and interested.

"Hi," the man said. "I'm Harry Ransom. Let's talk about you."

More than an hour later, we shook hands and I left with several of Ransom's books under my arm. I had been "advised." We had talked about books and writing and football and education. I had explained why I wanted to take anthropology and astronomy instead of two required courses. Ransom was agreeable. "We'll work in the required courses later," he said. "The important thing now is to explore what interests you."

I knew that I had found a friend, and I knew something else: I wanted to take some courses from Harry Ransom. I didn't know what he had published, and

Harry Ransom in the classroom. *Courtesy of the Harry Ransom Humanities Research Center, the University of Texas at Austin.*

didn't care. I didn't know what his title was, and didn't care. I don't suppose that there were teaching evaluations in those days. If there had been, I wouldn't have looked at them. I knew that I had met a teacher.

I took freshman English from Dr. Ransom that year. (I never called him Harry, although he would not have objected. There was not a pompous bone in his body. He was Dr. Ransom to me to the day he died, and I intended it as a gesture of respect.) It was a world literature course and we started with Homer and ended with Sinclair Lewis. I would not have missed a class for anything short of Armageddon.

Ransom was young then and full of enthusiasm. The man loved books and he understood writers. He never preached and he never took cheap shots. He searched out what was good in any piece of writing and shared it with us.

He did not seem to lecture. He would come eagerly into class as though he could not wait to get started.

He had his targets all picked out: students who were bright but still green as grass. (He never exposed them to ridicule.) "Well, Mr. Smith," he would say, "what did you think of *Beowulf*?"

Mr. Smith would stammer along for a few minutes, and then the whole class was trying to talk. The "experts" all wanted to show Mr. Smith where he had gone wrong. By the end of that year, Mr. Smith—not his real name—could hold his own in any literary debate.

Ransom could lecture, of course. His Shakespeare class was legendary, and deservedly so. But he was at his best when he could work directly with an individual student. He had a knack for making you feel that you were better than you actually were, and his secret was simply that he *wanted* you to do well. He found the best that you had in you.

I was a few years away from selling my first fiction, and I wrote a number of things for Ransom. He would have been a superlative editor. Always, he spotted what was strong in a story. When he hit the soft spots, he made firm suggestions about rewriting. If he said a manuscript was hopeless, it was. He was never destructive in his criticism. His aim was to help and to encourage.

When my first novel was published, I took a copy to Ransom. I inscribed it: "To Dr. Ransom—for not laughing at the right time."

Although I had by then decided to go into anthropology, I delayed long enough to take an M.A. in English under Dr. Ransom's direction. In a way, we were back to that first meeting in the Plan II advising room. I wanted to write a thesis on magazine science fiction. Ransom did not say, "You can't do that. It's not on the approved list. I have my reputation to consider." No. He said: "That's interesting. I've read some of your science fiction stories. Let's do it!" As far as I know, that was the first study of modern science fiction done at a major university.

After Ransom was absorbed into the higher echelons of the University administration, I saw little of him. However, when I won the Harry Ransom Award for Teaching Excellence a few years ago I remembered him with renewed vividness.

There is a portrait of Ransom that hangs in the Harry Ransom Center. It is a very formal painting of a slightly forbidding man awash in academic regalia. That is not the Ransom I remember. I remember a man who never pulled rank, a man who always seemed relaxed and friendly, a man who was never afraid of a new idea. I remember a man with sad eyes who smiled at a raw, new student and said: "Hi. I'm Harry Ransom. Let's talk about you."

Clarence Ayres was a professor you heard about before you had been on the campus for very long. He had high visibility. He was either a god or a devil, depending on your source of information. He occupied a niche in the University community comparable to the one vacated by J. Frank Dobie. Dobie was still in Austin, but no longer on the faculty. The joke was that Texas had one of the most distinguished lists of former faculty members in the world. Ayres, however, remained on the faculty as a professor of economics.

By reputation, Ayres was a familiar faculty type: the Radical Professor who raised blood pressures in the Legislature. In his case, though, the reputation was a much smaller thing than the man himself. Ayres never pandered to the ephemeral shifts in student opinion. He climbed on no bandwagons. He neither sought nor avoided confrontations with higher authorities. He was simply there, like a block of granite.

Ayres taught a course called Social Science 601, which was required of Plan II sophomores. The thinking probably was that we could use a little intellectual shaking up at that point. I had no idea what to expect. I did know that it was a two-semester course, which can be an eternity with the wrong professor.

In came Dr. Ayres. He moved at a lope. He was never late for class, but he always conveyed the impression that he had just barely made it. He was a fairly tall, lanky man whose suits never quite fitted him. He had sharp features and hair that refused to stay combed. He had great bushy eyebrows that made him look like Foxy Grandpa.

There were no jokes. There was no attempt to establish rapport with the class. There were no preliminaries.

"I'm Ayres," he said flatly. "Start writing. Pay attention."

And he was off. Those two semesters constituted a virtuoso performance by Dr. Ayres. He fired off information and ideas like a machine gun. He never seemed to look at a note, but his lectures were so beautifully crafted that he even incorporated footnotes. He would stab his finger at the class and bark: "Footnote!" He

Clarence Ayres with students. *From the Prints and Photographs Collection—Clarence Edwin Ayres, Center for American History, the University of Texas at Austin. (DI 02415)*

would then take off on an elegant commentary, after which he would return to the main thread of the argument at the precise point he had abandoned it.

He was not after applause and he was not interested in conversion. He did not talk down to his class and he did not cloak his opinions in jargon. What he wanted was some sign of mental activity beyond the memory level. He was paying us the supreme compliment of assuming that we could think.

What was the course about? Well, it was approximately one-third economics (his point of view was about as "radical" as that of Franklin Roosevelt), one-third anthropology, and one-third Clarence Ayres. The common theme was the impact of technology on society, but Ayres talked about everything from classical music to the difference between mushrooms and toadstools. He was never dull, he would not tolerate sloppy reasoning, and he had apparently read everything ever written. He loved questions—the more obscure the better—and he relished lively disagreement.

His final exam consisted of one sentence chalked on the blackboard: "Tell me what you have learned in this class, if anything."

Some years later, when I was living not far from Ayres, my daughter wandered out into the yard and ate what was either a toadstool or a mushroom. I called Dr. Ayres. His advice was as sound as it had ever been: "Get her stomach pumped," he said. "Do that at once. *Then* bring me the plant. Footnote: the odds are in your favor."

Footnote: it was an edible mushroom.

For many years now, I have had the honor of teaching the lineal descendant of Dr. Ayres's Plan II course. It is a one-semester class, Social Science 301. (The loss of a semester, I suppose, reflects our relative abilities.) Very little of the content of the old course survives, but I hope that something of its spirit is still alive. Former students of mine may recognize the footnote motif.

I never teach the class without thinking of Dr. Ayres. I hope that he would approve of what I do. If not, I am confident that he would find some way of expressing his displeasure.

There was—and is—a very lively grapevine among students at the University. Students talk about professors, among other things, and I think that this is a vital part of the educational process. One of the professors my fellow students were talking about was a man named J. Gilbert McAllister of the Department of Anthropology.

Nobody ever referred to him as Dr. McAllister. It was always "Dr. Mac." The essence of what I heard was this: "Before you get out of this place, you really should take a course from Dr. Mac."

Why not? I was interested in anthropology, although it had never occurred to me that I might one day become a professional anthropologist myself. I had a spot for an elective my senior year. I decided to find out what this Dr. Mac was all about.

I found out. I walked into his class on "Social Organization" with a casual respect for anthropology. By the time it was over, I *was* an anthropologist. I was on fire with the stuff.

Dr. Mac was like no other teacher I have ever had. He was a somewhat frail-looking man who wore sport coats and handwoven Indian ties. (He had done fieldwork with the Kiowa-Apache, a Plains group.) He was intense, personal, and emotional. He was a man with a vision. The vision permeated everything that he taught. It was a belief—totally sincere and with no element of humbug about it—that this world could be a better place and that anthropology could do a lot to make that happen.

Within a week, he knew every student in the class by name. Within two weeks, he knew our life histories. Within three weeks, he had a personal battle going on with every single student. If you were with

Anthropology professor J. Gilbert McAllister. *From the Prints and Photographs Collection—J. Gilbert McAllister, Center for American History, the University of Texas at Austin. (DI 02384)*

him, he pushed you relentlessly to do more and better work. If you were against him, he hammered away to put a dent in your armor.

Years later, when we were colleagues, I would watch former students troop into Dr. Mac's office in Benedict Hall. Invariably, he would call them by name—and this with students he had not seen in a decade or more. "Well, Miss Jones," he would say with a twinkle in his eye, "about that question you missed on the second exam in the Polynesia course. What do you think about it now?"

Dr. Mac believed in what he was doing. He did not just "teach a class." He threw himself into it, heart and mind and soul. I have seen him leave a classroom so spent that he could hardly walk. I remember—and will remember as long as I live—one warm and humid day in his class on "Applied Anthropology." I was taking the course in summer session and had driven in from a lakeside cabin I was renting. I was in high good spirits. We were due to get a test back, and I knew that I had knocked that test dead in its tracks.

Dr. Mac returned the tests. I had a grade of 99.

Dr. Mac went to work on me. "Mr. Oliver," he said, "I'll bet you think you're really something."

I started to laugh in an aw-shucks manner, figuring that I was about to be singled out as an example. I was indeed, but not in the way I was anticipating.

"You are capable of making 100 on any test I give," Dr. Mac said. "This is an insult. I don't ever want it to happen again."

I began searching for a hole to crawl into. I could hardly believe my ears. I had missed one point on an exam, and this man was *angry.*

Dr. Mac was not kidding. He may have calculated his performance a bit, but he meant what he was saying. His point—which he made at considerable length—was that if I was thinking of going to graduate school in anthropology I had to learn to give my best. Anything less was unsatisfactory.

I left that class chagrined, angry, and determined. I never missed a point on one of Dr. Mac's exams again. I knew I never wanted to go through *that* experience again. The grade, of course, was not all that important. The lesson that he taught me, however, was invaluable; whatever you do, give it your best shot or don't do it at all.

I have no idea how many students Dr. Mac inspired to seek professional careers in anthropology or in related disciplines. There were a lot of us, and we all still make occasional pilgrimages to his home in Tarrytown. I do know that he gave us more than a vision. Dr. Mac had been trained at the University of Chicago under A. R. Radcliffe-Brown, one of the founders of modern social anthropology. When I went to graduate school at UCLA—which had a very high-powered department of anthropology—I found that I was as well prepared as students from anywhere else in the world. I attribute this largely to the training I received from Dr. Mac.

Oddly enough, I never had a chance to take one of his most popular courses, which was "Indians of the Plains." I wrote my Ph.D. dissertation on the Plains Indians, but after I joined the faculty at Texas I did not teach the course until Dr. Mac retired. It was not that he had any objection; Dr. Mac was always a generous colleague and friend. It was simply that "Indians of the Plains" was *his* course, and I was in no hurry to compete with a legend.

Dr. Mac's favorite question in class was, "So what?" He would summarize the contribution of some distinguished anthropologist and then ask his question. It meant: "What difference does it make? What did this person do that affects how you look at the world around you?"

Former students of mine may recognize the question. That is where it came from, along with my addiction to handwoven Indian ties.

Gilbert McAllister had—and has—a massive integrity about him. I do not believe that he ever did anything that he thought was wrong. I do not believe that he ever gave a dishonest answer to a question. We talk a lot about role models these days. He was one of the good ones.

This seems an appropriate place to say in public what I have said to him many times in private: "Thank you, Dr. Mac."

If I may borrow from McAllister one more time, I would like to conclude with his question.

So what?

I have told you a little of what I remember about three unusual professors I found at the University of Texas. They were all different, all unique, and all were mavericks in one way or another. (Yes, even Harry Ransom. He was not always on Mount Olympus. He had served his time in the trenches, and he never lost his basic decency.) What difference did they make? How important was it that they existed when and where they did?

We all change through the years, unless we are dead from the neck up. I am no longer the eager student who learned from Ransom, Ayres, and McAllister. (The blues in the title of this piece are partly for my own youth.) I no longer share all of their views.

Still, the spirit of their teaching remains. It is in me, and it is in the thousands of other students who came their way.

They were here when we needed them.

What about the students who are entering the University today? What about the students who will go through the University in the years to come? Whom will they find?

It is not clones of past professors that we should seek. Rather, we must keep our eyes fresh enough to see the exceptional new teachers when they appear. Teaching is not all that a university is about. Take it away, however, and the vital spark is gone.

There must always be room for the teachers of rare talent and dedication. Without them, we can have a respectable school but we cannot have a great university.

One hundred years from today, we don't want an essay like this one to read: "I went to the University. I got a degree. That's about all I can remember."

W I L L I A M
H A U P T M A N

A Particular Friend
of Shakespeare's

I was a drama major at the University from 1963 to 1966—a time when I was always searching for the truth. But everyone was searching then, except for B. Iden Payne, legendary director of the annual Shakespeare production, who had found the truth long ago and never lost it. The truth, of course, was Shakespeare, and *doing it right.*

Dr. Payne was walking history, a certified genius, and a great man of the theatre, the proudest possession of the Drama Department. He was also the oldest working director any of us had ever seen. At the time I met him, he was eighty-two but looked much older. His hair was frosty white, his eyes blue as glacial ice; he looked as if he had just been taken out of a cryologic tank. He had always had incredible energy though. Everyone knew the story of how, when he was directing at the Abbey Theater of Dublin, he had thrown George Bernard Shaw out of rehearsals.

We students were a mixed lot. Some wanted to become teachers. Others of us dreamed of becoming professionals. We could not decide what made one a good actor, or which plays were the great plays. But there was one thing we all agreed on: Dr. Payne's show mattered more than any other.

It was classical theatre—it was *Shakespeare,* directed by the man who we were sure was the world's greatest living authority, and we all wanted to please him.

I had entered the University in 1962 as an English major—a subject which had proved to be boring beyond belief. During the first semester I lived at a cockroach-infested dormitory called the A-Bar Hotel, where I soon fell into a strange malaise: instead of going to classes, I slept all

After William Hauptman graduated from the University of Texas, he attended Yale University's School of Drama, where he earned an M.F.A. in playwriting. His 1981 play for PBS, Denmark Vesey, *won an NAACP Foundation award and an Emmy nomination. In 1985 he won the Tony Award for Best Musical Book for* Big River, *his collaboration with Roger Miller based on Mark Twain's novel* The Adventures of Huckleberry Finn. *His books include* Good Rockin' Tonight and Other Stories *(1988) and a novel,* The Storm Season *(1992). He lives in Brooklyn.*

B. Iden Payne. *From the Prints and Photographs Collection—B. Iden Payne, Center for American History, the University of Texas at Austin.* (DI 02416)

day and stayed up all night shooting pool and reading Fantastic Four comic books—bored as a character in an Antonioni movie. In the middle of the second semester, I dropped out of school and returned home, pretending I had mononucleosis (a disease I still think was invented to explain the strange malaise of those days.) "When you go back," my father said, "why don't you study something you enjoy?"

I had enjoyed doing plays in high school, so when I returned I majored in drama and began studying acting, which I undertook as a search for the truth about my inner self—hoping the truth would be that I was a great actor.

But immediately I fell into confusion. My teachers told me I must be either a Method or a Technical actor. As I understood it, technical actors achieved complete control over their voice and body and could simulate any emotion. Method actors entered some sort of controlled psychosis, where for two hours they actually believed the play was *real*.

My efforts in acting class were met with complete indifference. But I thought I might still prove to have

a talent for classical acting, if I could just get myself cast in Dr. Payne's Shakespeare production—which, fortunately enough, I did.

B(en) Iden Payne's entry in *The Oxford Companion to the American Theater* doesn't tell me much, except that he was born in 1881, and actually spent most of his career in the United States. In 1944, he directed Ethel Barrymore on Broadway in *Embezzled Heaven*. After that, he taught at several schools, including Carnegie Tech and the University of Texas. It says nothing about his greatest artistic triumph, which was, when he was still in his twenties, to put himself in the shoes of an actor on the stage of the Globe. Through experience, he had learned how Shakespeare had actually been performed—how Shakespeare *should* be performed.

He was not a good director in the modern sense. He had already played almost every role in the plays he directed, so at auditions he gave lesser actors like me line-readings. The first role I performed for him was William in *As You Like It*. William is a sort of sub-mechanical, the village idiot who falls in love with the shepherdess Audrey. When I auditioned, he told me, "This is how you do it, dear boy"—then leaped up and began blundering around the stage with a fixed smile on his face, an Elizabethan Jerry Lewis. I copied him exactly, got the role, and never made a single change from that day to opening night.

Nor does his entry in the *Oxford Companion to the American Theater* say anything about his incredible resilience, which is what probably made the strongest impression on me. Dr. Payne was not only very old, but almost blind. When he directed Shakespeare, the shop built an extension onto the apron of the Hogg Auditorium stage so he could direct the actors from no more than ten feet away. This tribulation gave him the tragic dimensions of an Oedipus. But he also had this unpredictable energy: at any moment, he might leap up from his desk and bound into the action, *demonstrating* how the scene should be performed—the stage manager following a few steps behind him, trying to keep him from walking right off the stage, which he did during one of the first rehearsals for *As You Like It*. As we watched, he turned back from the actors and fell ten feet into the orchestra pit, where he bounced around like a rubber ball. A horrified silence fell.

Then he bounced up again, and said, "I'm perfectly all right, you see, because I know the secret of complete relaxation. If you start to fall, all you have to do is give up control of your body, and you won't be hurt."

It was this resilience which was the true source of his legend. He was as invulnerable as Carlos Castaneda's teacher, Don Juan. I have since seen more of this strange *good health* which seems to come with a life in the theater—but no one had more of it than Dr. Payne. I should also mention here, although I cannot explain it, that during the annual Shakespeare production, there were always a number of potentially fatal accidents. During *Julius Caesar*, a technician was adjusting the lighting instruments mounted on the wall of the auditorium when his extension ladder tipped over and he fell into the house. During *Measure For Measure*, another technician fell through an open stage trapdoor to the concrete basement floor of Hogg, and landed on his head.

But in each case, they were miraculously unhurt. It was almost as if Dr. Payne's propensity for accidents spread through the entire company and production staff—along with his magical ability to escape injury.

My performance as William was a qualified triumph. On opening night (Shakespeare's birthday) I got prolonged laughter and exit applause. Of course I thought: *this means I was born to be an actor.*

There was only one disappointment: the *Daily Texan* review said, "William Hauptman is frighteningly real as the village idiot, making you want to go backstage and see him without his makeup, just to make sure he's not really retarded." I had worn no makeup. But I decided to ignore this.

In the following years, Dr. Payne gave me bigger roles, although he never gave me a lead. Apparently he agreed with my acting teachers, who told me I lacked the "polish" necessary to play leads. I felt (with some justification) that "polish" was another term for being gay. And it was true that a group of gay students played most of the leads. But it was also true that they were much better actors than the heterosexuals. Still, there were times when I wondered why he could not see how good we were, and why he wouldn't give bigger parts.

Now I wonder how he could have worked with us at all. For I see we were uniformly wretched. I was still wondering who I was, lost in the confusion over Method and Technique, and liable to make all sorts of dumb choices. Then there were others like my friend (I shall call him Mike) who was absolutely sure—too sure—of who he was. Mike was from Amarillo, a diehard heterosexual who sounded exactly like Ben Johnson (the star of so many great John Ford movies and *The Last Picture Show*, not the Elizabethan playwright).

Dr. Payne cast Mike as the resentful Prince Oliver in *As You Like It*, and I can still hear him complaining about his treatment at the hands of his brother, Orlando: "Call you that keeping for a gentleman of my birth, that differs not from the stalling of an ox? His horses are bred better." Mike made this sound like the jealous declaration of an Aggie. He had no polish: it was his honor to play the scene as it might have taken place in an Amarillo stockyard. And I remember that I groaned inwardly, wondering how poor Dr. Payne could bear to listen to this—not realizing my own efforts at "classical diction" must have been equally painful to his ears.

But gradually, the shows I did for Dr. Payne knocked some sense into my thick head. There *was* some sort of absolute truth for actors in Shakespeare, with its combination of heightened language and the immediacy of presentational staging. I began to see the strict categories of Method and Technical acting were an illusion and that good acting was the meeting of both in one—began to see how to make it *work*.

In time, Dr. Payne and I began to talk. I learned he was not only a genius, but human: had a certain cynicism and even a love of gossip. From him I learned how to speak verse onstage—never to emphasize the negative word *not*. He told me some wonderful anecdotes and gave me good advice.

Once, I asked him about the gruff British actor Harry Andrews, whose work in the Sidney Lumet movie *The Hill* had greatly impressed me. "Oh, but he's a Nancy-Boy," Dr. Payne told me. "You can't tell by appearances, you know. Once I paid him a call, and he came to the door wearing a dress." (This revelation made me feel very adult.)

Another time, when I had blown my lines in *Julius Caesar*, he told me,

Oh, don't even think about it. The truth is, they don't listen, don't even care what you say. I remember seeing Godfrey Tearle in *Journey's End*. The setting was a trench on the Western Front. When he made his curtain speech, he said, "Why should we hate the Germans? We both speak the same blood, the same language flows in both our veins." And there was not a stir from the audience. So you see, they're not really listening to us. It's the action that counts: they don't really care what we say at all.

But what I, and everyone else, really loved about Dr. Payne were the little talks he gave the company before opening night, when he always told us, "I know your performance tomorrow night will be good, because I talked to Shakespeare last night in my dreams, as I do from time to time—he's a particular friend of mine, you know—and he gave me his blessing on your efforts." It was sentimental, it was contrived, but it never failed to bond us into that fabulous temporary family, the company—a ritual without which no show can succeed.

In my senior year, I discovered the plays of Harold Pinter and Sam Shepherd, and felt great historical changes were taking place. Then I graduated, and impulsively went off to New York to seek my fortune. It was the time of the Living Theater, of Café LaMa-Ma, of endless improvisation. To my astonishment, I worked. But what I discovered was that these new plays were actually more presentational than representational—they were about inner truth, and always involved delivering long monologues directly to the audience—were actually much more like Shakespeare than I had expected.

The year after that, I applied to the Yale School of Drama—as a playwright—and was accepted. But I insisted on attending the acting classes, feeling I had to keep touch with the sensation of performing.

In my first semester, we all went to New York to see Peter Brook's production of *A Midsummer Night's Dream*. What I saw, although it was bound by the confinement of a black box instead of the traditional Shakespearean stage, was something Dr. Payne would have approved of.

Peter Brook's postmodernist productions of Shakespeare were highly admired at Yale, and while I was there my class did several Elizabethan plays in this style, including *The Revenger's Tragedy*, *The White Devil*, and *The Duchess of Malfi*. The other students were uncomfortable, but I always felt at home on a presentational stage, and never had any problem speaking verse: I felt I had learned it already from Dr. Payne.

In the 1970s, I returned from New York to visit the drama school. First I went to the call board, looking for the note which still haunted my dreams—a note saying that I was called for the rehearsal of a play I had forgotten I was cast in, and never learned my lines (a rehearsal which was scheduled for the same Saturday on which I had to take the final in a course I had registered for and somehow forgotten.)

Dr. Payne was not in his office, but when I stepped out onto the little patio by the side door, I found him there, staring directly up at the sun, which was appearing and disappearing through the low, fast Austin morning clouds.

I spoke to him briefly—I think he remembered me—and told him I was grateful for what I had learned from him. He thanked me. Then I asked him why he was standing out here. "Staring at the sun, dear boy," he told me. "It's an exercise I learned long ago that strengthens the eyes.

It seemed to me more likely to burn a hole in his retinas. But Dr. Payne had his own methods. And if this worked for him, then it must be true, it must be so: he, more than any of my other teachers, knew what he was doing.

On Richard Fleming

Tribute to Richard T. Fleming at Memorial Services, March 16, 1973

JOE B. FRANTZ

On Monday morning I dropped by Dick Fleming's office to pick up this week's roster of enemies to be routed, bastions to be defended, and windmills to be tilted at. When his secretary, Maud Ann Armstrong, said he hadn't shown, we agreed that he had probably passed a bookstore en route and might not arrive till noon.

Shortly after, we learned that he had died earlier that morning sitting in his chair.

Checking back, we re-created his weekend—all day Friday at the annual meeting of the Texas State Historical Association visiting with friends of fifty years, all day Sunday playing with his adored, and adoring, grandchildren, talking with his son Jack, and then pottering about in the yard. Appropriately he had been active till the last. Dick Fleming was not born to let his last days ravel out. He left this world the way he must have entered it, and certainly the way he lived it—flank speed ahead, rudder hard over, all engines forward. No one was ever less intended for extended invalidism, for the pains and strains and diminutions of aging.

Dick did make a few concessions to time, but as few as possible, and each one grudgingly. The hands began to palsy a bit, the eyes watered more, the gold-headed cane which his grandfather brought from Ireland accompanied him everywhere. Lately he shuffled instead of spurted, but he still *got* there.

Once he *could* run. There was that melee in the latter days of the Johnson administration. Dick entered the Union, where an anti-military recruitment table had been set up.

Joe B. Frantz was a longtime faculty member in the Department of History at the University of Texas. From 1966 to 1977, he was director of the Texas State Historical Association, where he directed the Lyndon B. Johnson Oral History program. His books include The American Cowboy: The Myth and the Reality, Hard Times in Texas, *and* The Forty Acre Follies. *Frantz was the only historian to serve as president of both the Southern History Association and the Western History Association. He died in Houston in 1993. This essay first appeared in* The Library Chronicle of the University of Texas *(new series number 6, December 1973).*

Richard T. Fleming. *From the Prints and Photographs Collection–Richard T. Fleming, Center for American History, the University of Texas at Austin. (DI 02417)*

"Is that a Viet Cong flag?" he asked one of the students.

Assured that it was, Dick grabbed the flag, split its pole over his knee, and stalked out with it. A huge student, whose one therapy class left him ample time to reform the world, gave chase. Out from the Union, up the Mall, one round little body pursued by another a half-century younger and almost twice the height and breadth.

Youth won, the flag was grabbed away, and the victor started back to the Union. But Dick Fleming doesn't quit that easily. The chased—and with Dick the word would never be spelled c-h-a-s-t-e—ran after

Dick Fleming in his library. *From the UT Richard T. Fleming University Writings Collection Photographs, Center for American History, the University of Texas at Austin. (DI 02395)*

the chaser, caught him, and began to grapple again. The fight was uneven, but student bystanders intervened, captured the banner, and destroyed it.

A few minutes later, while Dick breathed like an accordion on a bench outside the Union, exuding a triumphantly apoplectic red halo, Dean Ed Price appeared on the run:

"I'm told there's a riot around here," he called.

"You're damned tooting there's a riot," Dick retorted between heaves. "And I'm it!"

When somehow President Johnson heard of the incident, he wrote Dick that his was a courage that matched any soldier's in the field.

The students cherished him, even when they thought he was wrong. No further witness is needed than the space they gave him this past week in successive *Daily Texans*. As Andy Yemma, a *Texan* editor a couple of years ago, pointed out, he taught more students what life and the University were about than do most formal teachers.

It's difficult to talk about Dick Fleming without resorting to profanity, for he orchestrated strong language with all the sensitivity of a Toscanini or Bernstein, setting his audience up with a strong crescendo, and then, when it seemed their ears would burst, suddenly dropping off into a *pianissimo* of almost filigreed delicacy. On indignant notes, the only time when he ever settled for less than High C came occasionally in mixed company when he'd reduce his oath to a pallid

"Oh, Garden Seed!" or "for corn sake!" But even that concession carried no hint of fakery.

But Dick did abhor unnecessary obscenity, and he railed at the casual use of four-letter words by the Now Generation. And a splendid feature of his blithe, happy turbulence was that he always acted or reacted as if he had invented the term "Direct Action."

On one memorable occasion Dick was returning from a favorite watering hole, the Forty Acres. Scrawled in paint on the sidewalk outside Hemphill's-on-the-Drag was the ultimate obscenity. How many disapproving nice persons must have tut-tutted the words as they had walked by that day. But not Dick!

With one of the fastest-heating motors in the mobile world, he flashed into Hemphill's, waving his short arms and screaming for the manager. In a moment he was almost dragging a startled manager of Hemphill's out on the sidewalk, bucket of paint in one hand and brush in the other, and with Dick superintending, the offending words were painted into oblivion. Twenty minutes later some pedestrians must have been wondering why that big blotch of fresh red paint was defacing the busy sidewalk. As for Dick's friends, they were wondering how many more daily confrontations his system could take without blowing every gasket in his chunky body.

Dick also had no use for the gay liberation movement, though he confined his distaste to talk until on another day he saw the group handing out literature to some youth of high school age or younger. If he had written what he said to the gay group on that occasion, the whole Drag would have had to be blotted with red.

Not all the memories are contemporary, but Dick could reminisce with vividness and fidelity mixed with intelligent sentimentality. He never reproduced static tableaux; rather, his memories resembled kinetic art, all animated and full of pulls and twists and squashings. And explosions.

Although none of us here was there, Dick could transport us to the time he was jailed in Nuevo Laredo because of a technicality involving his papers. For the Mexicans it must have been "The Ransom of Red Chief" re-enacted. "Oh, how I shook those bars and cussed," he would recall. "I used words I didn't know I knew."

Released, he tramped angrily across the international bridge into Laredo and hailed a taxi.

"Take me to Temple," he directed.

"Temple Avenue?" the driver asked.

"No, damn it! Temple, Texas!"

Six hundred and fifty miles later a tired, bewildered, but rewarded taxi driver re-entered Laredo, probably wondering whether his family would believe where he had been.

Or recall those gloomy political days in the 1920's when the Ku Klux Klan held power in Texas. One can see a young, dapper little man on the sidewalks of downtown Houston, inveighing so loudly against the hooded brethren that finally the city police hauled him off to jail. It was the only way they could figure to silence his protest against bigotry.

It's easy to resurrect in memory the Democratic National Convention in 1928 in Houston, bent on nominating Alfred E. Smith [a Roman Catholic] as the Democratic candidate. Equally determined were the evangelical Protestant denominations, holding round-the-clock prayer meetings to ward off this alleged disaster. And the secretary of the State Democratic Executive Committee, one Richard T. Fleming, marshaled all his eloquence and knowledge of both backroom and street maneuvering to nullify the churchmen. Although he lost that round, the opposition must have felt his sting.

Or that morbid, terrifying 1966 day of the Charles Whitman massacre from atop the University's Main Building. Just a few moments after Whitman started spraying bullets on the noon crowd, Dick's secretary received a call from her husband in the Tower. Since neither he nor anyone else was sure at that moment whether a single gunman or a whole platoon had taken over, her husband cautioned her not to leave the Academic Center. She warned Dick.

With his instinctive high gear he ran out of the office and up the stairs to wave away the departing students and staff from the exits. Then he thought of the second floor reading room with all of its glass. He almost leaped up the stairs and burst into the room, yelling at the top of his voice for everyone to get away from the windows: "They're killing people out there!"

From behind a desk a pleasant little librarian came rushing at him, fingers to her lips, shushing him.

"Damn it, woman," he cried out, "there's a madman loose in the Tower."

Then he started shouting again: "Get back! Get down! You'll be shot, damn you all!"

By this time she had caught up to him, and in a

desperate whisper, finger still to her lips, admonished: "You'll have to leave. You can't talk like that in here. This is a LIBRARY!"

Later, under less serious circumstances, Dick, finger exaggeratedly at his lips, liked to tell this story, terminating invariably with a bit of philosophizing— "It's reassuring as all hell to know that some people maintain standards. We could have had bodies and blood all over the floor, but by damn, she'd keep her library quiet!"

Or that great week in Manhattan when he was supping at another favorite bistro, Le Cheval Blanc. Glancing up from his companions, he noticed that the place lacked any painting of a white horse, Gauguin's masterpiece or otherwise. According to his account, and I checked it out two decades later with the proprietor and the bartender, he pounded the bar and demanded as only Dick Fleming could demand when his outrage was triggered. The bartender, taken back, charged:

"If you're so hot for a white horse, why don't you paint it yourself?"

"I will; by gad, I will indeed," Dick shouted—and left forthwith. For nights on end he painted furiously. From this freshet of creativity emerged the Richard T. Fleming delineation of *Le Cheval Blanc*, derivative perhaps, but good enough that a quarter century later it still hangs there, dead center above and behind the bar, with a bold and unmistakable Fleming signature.

"I'm really Grandpa Moses," he used to say with an admixture of pride and deprecation. "But if Churchill and Eisenhower can get away with it, why can't I?"

Then there is the picture of Richard and Harriet Fleming, denizens of the silk stocking, rock-ribbed Republican community of Rye, New York, deciding that the time had come for the local Democratic party, in more disarray than usual, to assert itself. They learned what political types had failed to notice—Rye has strong ethnic minorities, particularly Italians. And so Dick and Harriet stuffed themselves at spaghetti-and-Chianti suppers night after stupefying night until on election day the city chose the first Democratic mayor in memory, perhaps in history. According to Dick, "After that, it was some years before we could tolerate spaghetti again, and Rye reverted to the Grand Old Party." The way he flattened his lips on those last three words was hardly complimentary.

There is that autumn in 1931 when Dick arranged a special train and cudgeled all possible Texas alumni

Student protests against the Establishment continued through the early 1970s. *From the Prints and Photographs Collection—UT Demonstrations, Center for American History, the University of Texas at Austin. (DI 02385)*

in the New York sector to carry the torch of Southwestern football honor to the gates of Harvard Stadium. But alas, the Longhorns, weary from almost three days on the train, lost by four touchdowns, and in Dick's words, "I was so humiliated that for days I felt that every shoeshine boy and every waitress in midtown Manhattan was looking down on me." Actually I don't believe that, for it is my observation that Dick's effervescence would bubble through in a matter of moments. Lasting humiliation did not harmonize with his belligerent zest.

Dick Fleming was a character—individual and sometimes outrageous and irrepressible and often unmanageable. But in a world in which we seem increasingly stamped out like interchangeable parts, he was unique. His interests were wide-ranging, as one glance at his cluttered office and library, which spills over into every room in his three-story house, will demonstrate. Although he loved to travel, he refused to learn to drive, which meant that his wife logged

Demonstration at the University. *From the Prints and Photographs Collection–UT Demonstrations, Center for American History, the University of Texas at Austin. (DI 02418)*

more hours on European and Mexican highways than an airline pilot. He loved sports and art and music and ballet. But mostly he loved to read and talk and persuade.

The combination of knowledge, articulateness, and persuasiveness carried him a long way. From being the son of a railroad engineer in Temple; through a distinguished student career at the University of Texas and a love affair with that institution that endured to the end; to the First Officers Training Corps at Leon Springs and eventual rank as a major; to becoming one of the organizers of the Houston Oil Company, a major independent for forty years; and on to serving as vice-president and general counsel of Texas Gulf Sulphur.

"Dick, how did you ever survive as the lone Democrat on Texas Gulf's board of directors?"

"Oh," he'd reply, "those characters"—and "characters" is a euphemism—"those characters never knew what I was talking about! Besides, they panicked

when the New Deal came on, and I was the only one who kept my head!"

When on one December night in Washington, D.C., in 1958, Walter Prescott Webb gave the presidential address to the American Historical Association, Dick Fleming came down on the train to hear it, the first time I met him. Parenthetically, I was struck that any corporation vice-president would travel to Washington to hear a historian—I would have been impressed if he had traveled crosstown in Austin!

It turned out to be like many a late lunch and evening together over the next fifteen years. At midnight Walter Webb dropped out, almost with Dick's blessing, since Webb had asked for a glass of milk in a Washington bar. At 3 o'clock in the morning I begged off, with Dick shouting about the softness of the younger generation and demanding to know whatever had happened to the sturdy spirit of the American pioneer.

But he forgave my defection, and we grew closer together through visits in Austin and New York. And then one day he queried me from New York: would the University be interested in 250 packing boxes of books and pamphlets by University ex-students that he had been collecting over the years? Harry Ransom settled that question before I could finish asking him, and shortly Dick Fleming was installed as a nothing-a-year man in the Main Building and then later in the Academic Center.

Over the next dozen years he begged, threatened, cajoled, and otherwise conned ex-students and faculty out of their creations—and as a group they don't give easily. If his pay had been at his accustomed level, the cost would have been astronomical. Even at librarian's scale he contributed possibly a couple of hundred thousand dollars' worth of time. Once I asked him how much of the collection he had bought personally: "Joe," he said, "I realize I'm passing up a tax break, but I've never kept records. I didn't want to know how much I was spending for these books, because I was afraid it might inhibit me." But one thing I can assert—his personal expenditures ran into the tens of thousands.

He was always a little hurt, though not surprised, that he was never named a Distinguished Alumnus. Mainly the award goes to distinguished Establishment types. By accomplishment Richard Fleming belonged to the Establishment, but by nature he was a rebel.

But he knew that many appreciated him, as witness this excerpt from a 1970 note which Harry Ransom wrote: "I stand in admiration, of course, when I think of your career; but in deeper, more personal, more lasting ways I stand in gratitude for your gift of your life to this University. I wish I could tell you how much sense and determination and clarity your being 'with us' has brought to these last years . . ."

Thus he rode the Austin city buses, arguing and agreeing with the maids and the yardmen; he fought furiously with the administration and many alumni over burnt orange *versus* regular orange, a battle that he lost, though like Goldwater in 1964, he never conceded; he fired off letters and shouted over the telephone at every sinner; and he attended regents' meetings, where he exercised his right of free speech. Just last week in Dallas, Rabbi Levi Olan, a former regent, talked about Dick to me: "He was a nuisance, but you know, we sometimes needed a nuisance."

Dick loved a worthy antagonist, and he found one in Frank Erwin, with whom he tangled at every opportunity. Actually the two scrappers were very alike, an observation which both would deny vehemently and profanely. And nothing pleased Dick more than when, after one particularly acerbic interchange, Erwin sent him a handwritten apology. He must have shown it to me at least once every two months, along with his fat walletful of speakeasy cards that he had carried daily since 1933, "just in case."

Three more short, final glimpses of this remarkable spirit, this rampaging fighter against cant and hypocrisy and covert actions, this creature of extreme dignity and sometimes Victorian courtesy and genteelness, this bundle of emotion and pride and drive.

One portrait takes place at the Forty Acres Club, where he threw his own 80th birthday party three years ago this coming April 12. Although he invited old friends to lunch at noon, we didn't begin to eat till almost mid-afternoon. He was eloquent, and he was not the least ashamed to tell each and every one how dearly he loved us. On his next two birthdays he and I ate alone, because as he said, "I can't go through that sort of emotional wringer for another eighty years!"

Another occurred this past December when the Philosophical Society of Texas met at the Hilton Inn at Dallas. Like all meetings, it was a bit of an endurance contest, and most people were ready to turn in after the dinner speech. As Mrs. Frantz and I walked through the lobby en route to the elevator, there sat Dick looking bellicose.

"Something wrong, Dick?"

"Spurned!" he said. (He made the word sound somehow obscene.) "Spurned! I'm never coming to another of these—everyone but me has gotten too everlasting old to enjoy himself!"

So we went with Dick to the hotel lounge, picking up Ed and Anne Clark on the way, thereby enhancing the prospect of good, competitive talk. About midnight the Clarks and the Frantzes were frankly tired, and excused themselves. But by then Dick had gathered a fresh group of auditors and hardly seemed to notice our going.

Through all this hyperactivity Dick had a wife and son who understood him—his faults, which he almost paraded; and his strengths, about which he was frequently diffident. Later, from his own remarks, I gather that both his daughter-in-law and grandchildren recognized that he was more than a little special.

When he and Harriet married, Dick said they agreed that they would never tell the same story twice about either their backgrounds or about how they met. From the Fleming folklore that I have gathered from their casual acquaintances, they undoubtedly kept their vows.

They married after a post–World War I romance that saw her in Alaska and him in the District of Columbia, and evidently they had only one or two dates over a three-year period. But they agreed to meet and marry in New Orleans. Typically, on the train over from Houston Dick met a couple of men, strangers both, told them where he was heading, and they took charge of the wedding arrangements on arrival. During the service at the Hotel Roosevelt a tiny tad of a lad stole into the ceremony, took Dick by the hand, and stood between the bride and groom throughout the entire rites, with Dick squeezing the boy's hand tightly.

He held a lot of our hands over the years, and less often we held his. He had his heroes—like Edmund Heinsohn, H. J. Ettlinger, Robert L. Moore, J. R. Parten, Charles Sparenberg, Leonard Kreisle, Frances Hudspeth, Leon Green, Donald Weismann, and most especially, Harry Ransom. And he had others who preceded him, like Walter Webb, Stanley Walker, Edmunds Travis, Will Hogg, Frank Dobie, John W. Thomason, John A. Lomax, and Harry Benge Crozier. All were men who have or had ranged widely, but never attained the weariness of cynicism nor enjoyed the luxury of negativism.

Looking back, it's not Dick Fleming's fault that he

didn't save the world from its folly. He spent eighty-three indignant years trying, and never once did he falter in his faith nor surrender his dream.

Just last week he and Mrs. Fleming had their wedding anniversary, and though the facts were against it, Dick talked to her about how as soon as she was able, they would take one more long trip and just enjoy each other. Although such talk may not be realistic, it expresses the truth of his life.

So now the loud voice has grown quiet and the restless, questing, questioning spirit serene. And no longer can a boring day be salvaged by fueling Dick's indignation. And no more will the belligerent, jaunty figure in the Harris tweed and old-fashioned railroaders' watch and Sherlock Holmes hat wait outside the Co-op for the evening bus.

For the feasts and frolics of old days together will have vanished. And these good times and these good battles and these defeats and these occasional victories will never come back again. But Richard T. Fleming burned his spirit deep into our souls, and when tomorrow we ride out again on a new morning's wind, we'll carry him with us right to our own journey's end. And the world will be less grey because of the greenness of his once-presence and now the salt and savor of his memory.

RICHARD A.
HOLLAND

Thirteen Ways of Looking at Chairman Frank

1. 1969

Baby boomers who packed the Texas campus during the fall of 1969 retain two vivid memories of that dramatic semester. The first is Texas' football win over Arkansas in the "game of the century." This unlikely come-from-behind victory matched the number-one-ranked 'Horns and the number two Razorbacks—the game was played in remotest Arkansas, where multitudes of hog-hat–wearing fans bayed "Soooeeee Pig." Texas was behind in the last quarter, but everything turned on an improbable fourth-down forward pass called by Coach Darrell Royal and executed by Texas quarterback James Street and receiver Randy Peschel. The game is thought to have had the biggest viewing audience in the history of college football—50 percent of the reporting television watchers. When the struggle was over (Texas prevailed 15–14), President Richard Nixon appeared delighted to present Royal and Street with the national championship trophy.

The other riveting contest during that fall was the "Battle of Waller Creek," a bizarre confrontation that pitted environmentally committed students and other concerned citizens against the most vivid and divisive character in the long and tumultuous history of the University: the bigger-than-life chairman of the Texas Board of Regents, Frank C. Erwin Jr. The outcome of *this* battle was never in doubt—in those days Chairman Frank always won; it was later that he did himself in.

Love him or hate him, Frank Erwin was inescapable and his legacy to the University is still very much alive. During his glory days as chairman of the Board of Regents (fewer than five years—December 1966 through February 1971), he dominated events at the University like no one had before or has since. No one could deny the intensity with which he advanced his goals for the Austin campus and the burgeoning UT System; howev-

---

Richard Holland was in graduate school at the University of Texas during the Frank Erwin years. He stood on the portico of the Main Building in the fall of 1969 and watched Chairman Frank issue hostilities to a large gathering of angry students.

er, his detractors have questioned his overall legacy and everyone has questioned his methods, which were a combination of subtle strategy based on hard-earned knowledge and execution about as subtle as a bulldozer.

Faced with potential rebellions similar to those at other prestigious universities in the late 1960s, Erwin took on all comers, respecting no boundaries when it came to questions of University governance, faculty review, student affairs, or campus architecture. He seemed to glory in the spotlight but was widely perceived as a belligerent, red-faced bully who in his last years was seen flamboyantly drunk in public, sometimes weaving up the wrong side of Guadalupe Street in his orange and white Cadillac—a cartoon image of the unbridled, powerful Texan. At the same time, no powerful figure in the state had more loyal friends—even many of the students and faculty who opposed his actions grudgingly admitted his intellect and charm. Frank Erwin was, in the words of the old song, devil or angel—or perhaps more aptly, devil *and* angel.

II. THE COURTHOUSE

If the child is father to the man, we must travel to Waxahachie, Texas, to study our subject in his formative years. By 1920, when Frank Jr. was born to Frank Craig and Margaret Edwards Erwin, Waxahachie was a booming community of 8,000, with three banks, five cotton gins, and two weekly and two daily newspapers. Manufacturing in the cotton town included textile mills, a garment factory, and an ice cream factory. Frank Sr. supervised a turkey-processing plant located between Waxahachie (a name thought to be derived from the Tonkawa word for "cow") and Midlothian. Margaret Edwards' family was recognized in Waxahachie as being important to the town during the Great Depression by extending credit in their family business, a dry goods emporium called the Bridge Store.

When Frank Jr. was an adolescent, his family moved into his mother's big family home on Marvin Street, both then and now dotted with handsome nineteenth-century houses. As a youngster, Frank Jr. was known to be proud of living in the gray two-story Victorian house with white gingerbread-style trim. On his father's side, Erwin was descended from a long line of

Ellis County Courthouse, Waxahachie, Texas. *From the Prints and Photographs Collection-Waxahachie, Texas, Center for American History, the University of Texas at Austin. (DI 02386)*

North and South Carolina judges and legislators, including Colonel Alexander Erwin, a fierce leader in the American colonies' fight for independence from the British.

Waxahachie is a seat of county government and the town plan is based on a courthouse square. Occupying the center of the square is one of Texas' finest public buildings—the Ellis County Courthouse, designed by the notable San Antonio architect James Riely Gordon. His Waxahachie building, Romanesque in style, is a huge pile of red stone and brick, with masonry turrets, narrow vertical windows, and on the corners, widely arched doorways. Adding to the looming presence of the building is its scale in relation to the town's buildings that surround it on four sides. Not only is the courthouse much taller and more substantial than the town's other buildings, it also feels as if the big red courthouse dwarfs nature itself—like most of J. Riely Gordon's courthouses, it is built close to the curb, as if asserting its importance to the community it regulates.

Frank Erwin's father was elected county clerk of Ellis County in 1934. Young Frank was a freshman in high school, and he immediately became enthralled with local politics as practiced in the big courthouse. Frank not only helped campaign for his father by handing out leaflets and flyers, he spent much of his time downtown, talking politics with the older Ellis County courthouse regulars. Some thought that Frank Jr. spent too much time at the courthouse instead of concentrating on his studies, but this proved not to be the case since he finished second in his class. His favorite high school subject was journalism, and as a music student, he developed a love of conducting. It is not hard to imagine him "conducting" in the living room of his parents' handsome home, waving his arms in time to the music playing on classical 78s.

Down at the courthouse, he held a part-time job doing clerical work in the office of Alvis Vandygriff, then clerk of the District Court. Decades later, when Vandygriff was interviewed about the young Frank Erwin, the old district clerk described Frank Jr.'s style at the courthouse when he was a high school boy: "He loved to converse with different ones and would inject himself into arguments. He was a strategist—a definite leader. He wasn't satisfied to sit back and let someone else do it all. He was in the forefront."

In 1970, when Erwin was riding high as the University's chairman of the Board of Regents, his devoted mother was interviewed about his character growing up. Contrasting Frank Jr. with his younger brother, Mrs. Erwin said, "He doesn't like the common herd. My younger son, Tom, knew every black and white in Waxahachie, and liked them all. But Frank picked his friends."

III. BIG MAN ON CAMPUS

In later years, Erwin commented that he was "very green" as an incoming freshman at the University of Texas in the fall of 1937, but it did not take him long to get into the thick of campus activities. Just as in his hometown, Erwin picked his friends carefully, though this time it was a group that he used as a power base for the rest of his life: the Kappa Sig fraternity. He quickly quit the Longhorn Band, later saying that the social circles on campus he saw running things were occupied by athletes and fraternity men. By his sophomore year, Erwin was a student politico, managing the campaign

of Tom Law (a future regent) for student body president. Law (and Erwin) lost to a handsome non-fraternity candidate from South Texas named John Connally. Frank Erwin did not often find himself on the losing side after that 1938 student campaign. In later years, when there was no doubt about his power in the state, Erwin remained a fraternity loyalist, tapping many young Kappa Sigs to occupy positions in state government. Long after his student days, Erwin was always on call as a powerful alum to help out the membership of the wildest campus fraternity when it got itself into scrapes with the UT administration or with the law.

Frank Erwin graduated in four years, commencing in May 1941 as an honors graduate in government. He had excelled academically, finishing as a member of Phi Beta Kappa. Like many other graduates that year, Erwin joined in the war effort as soon as he could after Pearl Harbor; he spent the bulk of his Navy service in Norfolk, Virginia.

Soon the mood of the campus shifted dramatically. During Erwin's four years at UT, the atmosphere had been one of quiet complacency, but by 1942 trouble was brewing between the University president, Homer Rainey, and an ultra-conservative Board of Regents, who, among other things, censored reading lists in English courses and began firing professors they thought harbored dangerous ideas. Then in 1944 the regents fired President Rainey. This led to one of the most passionate student protests in the history of the University, comparable to that of a generation earlier when UT students played a large part in the downfall of Governor Pa Ferguson.

In the fall of 1944, Erwin wrote several letters to friends on the campus, including the long-time Dean of Student Life Arno Nowotny, strongly expressing his opinions on the Rainey fight. In this correspondence, Erwin not only placed himself firmly on the side of the student protestors, he also "looked askance at the wealth of certain members of the Board of Regents." A quarter of a century later, with the shoe now on the other foot, Chairman Frank renounced his youthful radicalism: "I ran across a letter the other day I had written damning the Regents. It just shows how mistaken you can be." In the 1960s, Erwin the regent embellished his role in the Rainey protests by bragging that he led marches to the Capitol from the campus, when in fact he was over a thousand miles away in Virginia during all of the upset. But Chairman Frank always did like a good story.

After the war, Erwin got back to Texas as quickly as possible, enrolled in the law school, and resumed what would become his almost lifelong role as a big man on campus. He was active in the fraternal life of the law school—his favorite teacher was torts professor Page Keeton, with whom he would bitterly feud decades later when Keeton had become an independent and stubborn dean.

IV. HIS RISE

Upon graduation from law school in 1948, Erwin moved seamlessly into practicing law in Austin with the firm of Hart, Brown, and Sparks. His civic involvements included being named vice-president of the city commission charged with drafting a new city charter in 1952. In 1959 and 1960 Erwin argued a major case before the U.S. Supreme Court and received high praise from the young Larry Temple, who was then clerking for Supreme Court justice Tom Clark. Temple later described Erwin's appearance in the high court as "absolutely brilliant."

By the time he entered the world of Texas politics, Erwin had already established himself in Austin as an outstanding trial lawyer with a reputation as a tough courtroom brawler. In the late fifties, he worked as a lobbyist/lawyer in Washington, D.C., moving back to Austin in 1961 when he cast his lot with John B. Connally (then President Kennedy's secretary of the Navy) in Connally's effort to run for the Texas governorship.

Frank's personal life was a major concern of his mother since he was still single well into his thirties. He joked that all the available girls that he had gone to college with were already taken. In 1954, he married June Houston, recently divorced from her husband. She was described as a powerhouse with red hair who was fully Frank's equal. When they married she had a twelve-year-old daughter and a nine-year-old son. The couple had a son, Frank III, in October 1955.

Governor Connally appointed Erwin to the University Board of Regents in 1963, after W. St. John Garwood's nomination to the Board was rejected by the Texas senate. The chairman of the Board when Erwin joined it was W. W. Heath. Other regents during Erwin's twelve-year run on the Board included Wales Madden, Frank Ikard, Jack Josey, Rabbi Levi A. Olan, Joe Kilgore, John Peace, Jenkins Garrett, Lady Bird

Johnson, and former Texas governor Allan Shivers. No one would argue that this was not a capable and forceful assemblage, but because of his high profile, it was Erwin who received most of the credit and all of the blame for the Board's actions during the dozen crucial years that he served.

V. THE SCHOLAR AND THE CEO

In 1963, the Ransom revolution was in full bloom. Harry Ransom, the charming and elusive professor of English whose specialty was the history of copyright, had risen through the ranks and by the mid-fifties was vice-president and provost of the University. From this position, Ransom established the Humanities Research Center, in its origins an almost invisible entity that hid in plain sight on a floor above the Main Library stacks in the Tower. Ransom's heroic collection-building in the field of modern literature is described elsewhere, but the spillover onto the rest of the campus marked the flowering of Ransom's vision.

By the time Frank Erwin came along, the humanities on campus had stepped up to a level previously occupied only by the School of Engineering, the departments of Geology, Biochemistry, and Mathematics, and football. Intrigued by what they heard about Texas, the cream of international culture began to stream into Austin. The image of T. S. Eliot delightedly accepting a Stetson hat before his reading in Gregory Gym was indelible. Rumor had it that Aldous Huxley, who lectured in Batts Auditorium, was drawn to Austin because of his deep interest in the work of Roger J. Williams, the brilliant scientist who pioneered the idea of biochemical individuality. By the early sixties, the elite of English and American letters frequently camped out at UT: Lord C. P. Snow lectured on the "two cultures," Stephen Spender read poems in the Knopf Room in Ransom's Academic Center, and in the less-rarefied confines of the Texas Union Ballroom there were readings and talks by the likes of Tennessee Williams, Robert Penn Warren, and Norman Mailer. Cynics might have said that any place that threw as much money as Harry Ransom did at literary acquisitions would attract a crowd, but the educated world did notice that Ransom was creating something new and significant down in football country. The dark days of the Rainey controversy that tainted the academic reputation of the University throughout the 1940s were now just a memory.

On some level, Ransom built his great library at the expense of the ones already in place on campus. By setting up a separate operation, he could work with some of the younger and forward-thinking librarians, and create his own budgets to pursue treasures in New York and England. Chances are good that Ransom bought something forty years ago that still hasn't quite been paid for.

He approached faculty recruiting the same way, creating a new level of "University Professors," who were appointed by him and were entirely free of the promotion and tenure requirements of the other faculty in the university. Ransom took the opportunity to have one shot at faculty improvement, and the result was a handful of gifted teachers and scholars who might not have come to Texas through regular faculty recruitment. This famous assemblage was led by William Arrowsmith in Classics and Roger Shattuck in French. Others with this designation were Donald Weissman, a wittily sarcastic art professor, and D. S. Carne-Ross, who set up what was to become an internationally important center for literary translations. Last, but in no means least, was the brilliant John Silber, whose Plan II philosophy course was dreaded by every smart kid in that elite program. University politics being what they were (this would be true at any university), much of what Ransom did in this area was disliked in the departments. But the creation of an elite always threatens those who perceive that they are left out.

Forty years ago, the legislature provided virtually the entire budget for the University, and Erwin was superb at getting what he thought the growing campus needed. His influence can be attributed to his political connections at the Capitol. He also cultivated promising younger men, including Ben Barnes and Larry Temple—the three of them were known to burn the midnight oil writing legislative bills that directly benefited the University. Underlying all this success was Erwin's encyclopedic knowledge of all aspects of the University, and his ability to discuss its programs in language that the legislators understood.

One undeniable result was an unbelievable 800 percent increase in University appropriations, from \$40.4 million in the 1963–64 appropriations year to \$349.7 million in 1975–76. Building and enrollment increased proportionately: building contracts totaled \$762 million during Erwin's reign and enrollments exploded as waves of baby boomers reached college age. Higher education had become a big business, and Frank Erwin dedicated himself to running every aspect of the campus like a CEO. Part of Erwin understood Ransom and was in awe of his accomplishments, and in the sixties there appeared to be enough money to fund both Ransom's vision and Erwin's plans for the expanding campus.

VI. DIRTY NOTHIN'S

By the time Erwin was in the middle of his tenure as a regent, his beloved wife, June, was very ill with cancer, and after she died in 1967 he seemingly spent all of his time on campus. Sunday worshipers at the University Methodist Church, on the corner of Guadalupe and 24th, became accustomed to seeing Erwin walking the campus at noontime on Sunday, inspecting buildings with a notepad in his hand. His attention to detail, always focused, now extended to having a network of contacts all over the University, particularly among some of the higher ranking staff whom he trusted to truthfully inform him of problem areas. He did not hesitate to drop in on any office on campus, feeling that his high perch as Board of Regents chairman gave him access to everyone in every office at the University. He made it his business to know everything that was going on—good, bad, and indifferent—and frequently expressed the idea that it was this knowledge that established his power.

It has not gone unnoticed that Erwin's five-year term as chairman exactly coincided with the greatest period of unrest on American college campuses in the twentieth century. The University of Texas had a robust history of progressivism, and by the middle of the sixties the campus had an identifiable contingent of student radicals, capably led by two charismatic members of the UT chapter of Students for a Democratic Society: Jeff Shero and Alice Embry. Although the Austin SDSers shared many of the viewpoints and goals of their counterparts at Columbia, Michigan, and Cal Berkeley, historian Doug Rossinow characterized the Texas group as "grassroots radicals" in his 1998 study *The Politics of Authenticity* (Columbia University Press). Whatever kind they were, they had effective leadership, a widely read publication (*The Rag*), and a successful track record in some of their

Lyndon Johnson and Frank Erwin. *From the Prints and Photographs Collection–Frank Craig Erwin, Center for American History, the University of Texas at Austin. (DI 02387)*

efforts like desegregating businesses in the University neighborhood.

Frank Erwin would doubtless have placed himself in opposition to these groups even if he had not been close to Connally and Barnes and Johnson, but he *was* close to the governor, the lieutenant governor, and the president, and, upon assuming the chairmanship of the Board of Regents, he felt that it was his role to personally turn back the tide of unruly and unkempt students that were threatening to turn his beloved campus into a battleground similar to those that made the evening news.

Early in 1968, about six weeks before President Johnson announced that he would not be a candidate for re-election, Erwin planned a birthday bash for John Connally in the heart of the UT campus, Gregory Gym. LBJ was invited and came. Of course there were protestors, but one has to wonder at Chairman Frank's *hubris* in staging such an event on the campus at that time. It was as if he was asking for an opportunity to confront the elements he had begun to dislike. As the invited guests left the old gym, walking through crowds of war protestors, Erwin grabbed a microphone and said: "I am disturbed because a bunch of dirty nothin's can disrupt the workings of a great university in the name of academic freedom. When it comes to the point where 300 armed policemen are needed to keep from embarrassing the President, we need to reexamine the goals of higher education." In no time at all, students were wearing "dirty nothin'" pins—and Chairman Frank himself was known to wear the button, grinning broadly.

VII. THE BATTLE OF GRANT PARK

All along Erwin kept his hand in politics. He felt that it was his solid credentials as a conservative Democrat and his hands-on involvement at the Capitol that guaranteed his success as a leader of the regents. At the height of his power in the sixties, he observed:

> My political friends and affiliations have given some people who were opposed to me anyway something to talk about. Personally, I think they have been a great asset to the University. It has enabled me to do many things for the University, both in the way of appropriations by the legislature, obtaining federal grants, obtaining additional land for University expansion. In all sorts of ways, I have been able to do all sorts of things for the University I never could have done, had I not had those political friendships.

It was Erwin's close friendships with Governor John Connally and with Ben Barnes, who had been elected lieutenant governor, that formed his view of politics as a pragmatic exercise. His effectiveness as a politician was reflected in his serving as vice-chairman of the Texas delegation to the 1964 Democratic Convention that nominated Lyndon Johnson. He then became chairman of the Texas State Democratic Executive Committee and a Texas committeeman to the national Democratic organization.

In 1968 he chaired the Texas delegation at the ill-fated Democratic Convention in Chicago, where he made a nationally televised speech defending the unit rule, a procedural means of stifling dissent within state delegations. In terms of his own delegation, this was a way that Erwin forced his divided Texas group to back John Connally's "favorite son" presidential nomination.

Certainly, 1968 was one of the most discouraging years in American history, and by the third week in August, Chicago was braced for potentially deadly violence on its streets. A summary of the year's events would include:

- January 30—The Tet Offensive begins on the part of coordinated North Vietnamese and Viet Cong armies,

reaching almost into Saigon. For the first time, American opinion turns against the war.
- February 8—Alabama governor George Wallace enters the presidential race as an Independent; on the same day state troopers in Orangeburg, South Carolina, fire at civil rights demonstrators, killing three and wounding twenty-seven.
- March 12—President Lyndon Johnson wins a narrow victory over antiwar candidate Eugene McCarthy in the New Hampshire Primary.
- March 16—Senator Robert Kennedy announces his candidacy for the Democratic nomination; on the same day, Lt. William Calley leads his infantry company into the Vietnamese village of My Lai, where they kill over 300 civilians. The massacre is not reported for over a year.
- March 31—President Lyndon Johnson withdraws from the Democratic primary race.
- April 4—Reverend Martin Luther King Jr. is assassinated in Memphis, Tennessee. Riots break out in over 100 American cities, including Chicago, where nine blacks are killed and twenty blocks are burned.
- April 15—Chicago mayor Richard Daley gives his police orders to "shoot to kill any arsonist and to shoot to maim anyone looting."
- June 5—Robert Kennedy is assassinated in Los Angeles after declaring victory in the California Democratic primary.
- August 8—Richard Nixon is nominated for president by the Republican Convention in Miami. Close by, in Miami's black neighborhoods, riots result in hundreds of arrests and four deaths.
- August 22—Four days before the opening of the convention, Dean Johnson, a seventeen-year-old Sioux Indian from South Dakota is shot dead by Chicago police.
- August 23—At Chicago's Civic Center Plaza, the Yippie Party (so-named by Abbie Hoffman and Paul Krassner during a 1967 New Year's Eve party) nominates its presidential candidate: Pigasus the pig. Seven Yippies and Pigasus are arrested.
- August 25—On the day before the convention begins, 800 protestors organized by MOBE (Mobilization to End the War in Vietnam) march on the convention hotel, the Hilton, in a "meet the delegates" march. By curfew, 11 p.m., police are battling over 5,000 in the streets of Old Town.

A feeling of inescapable dread surrounded the opening of the Chicago convention. The Democrats had lost their president when LBJ chose not to run, their leading candidate to replace him when Bobby Kennedy was shot in Los Angeles, and most likely the South in the upcoming election, because of the insurgent candidacy of George Wallace.

On the second day of the convention, Black Panther Party leader Bobby Seale spoke in Lincoln Park. He urged his followers to defend themselves "by any means necessary" if attacked by the police. By the middle of the week, a crowd estimated at 15,000 gathered in Grant Park for the MOBE's antiwar rally. There were around the clock speeches by nationally prominent antiwar leaders, including Dave Dellinger, Rennie Davis, Abbie Hoffman, Tom Hayden, and the pediatrician Dr. Benjamin Spock. There were nightly clashes between the assembled crowd and the tough Chicago police, who had been augmented by Illinois National Guardsmen.

Inside the convention, things were hardly less contentious. On Wednesday, August 28, the "peace plank," sponsored by liberal Democrats to be part of the party platform, is voted down. This news caused immediate unrest among the protestors at Grant Park. That evening, Senator Abraham Ribicoff, in a speech nominating George McGovern, denounces the police's "gestapo tactics on the streets of Chicago," setting off screams of outrage on the part of Mayor Daley and other mainline Democratic delegates, including Frank Erwin.

Back on the streets, a group of MOBE marshals try to protect the protestors from the police—peace leader Rennie Davis is beaten unconscious. The bulk of the protestors try to march from the park to Michigan Avenue, only to find the bridges sealed off by National Guardsmen with .30 caliber machine guns and grenade launchers.

Miraculously, no one was killed during the week, but hundreds of demonstrators were beaten, maced, and tear-gassed. There were close to 700 arrests. Months later, the official Walker Report on the Chicago riots referred to the conflicts as "a police riot."

Frank Erwin and the rest of the Texas delegation stayed in the Hilton Hotel, which had an excellent view of Grant Park just across the street, providing them with ringside seats to the battles surging just below. Nick Kralj, who was a young staff member working with Lt. Governor Ben Barnes, told me that from where Erwin and the other Texans enjoyed their nightly cocktails, the park and streets looked as if they had been taken over by coordinated mobs who were close to overwhelming the police. Kralj vividly remembers all of the Texans draining quarts of Cutty Sark scotch (Erwin's favorite) while watching the almost psychedelic chaos over in Grant Park. Looking down at the civil mayhem from his hotel room made a lasting impression on the Board of Regents chairman and helped solidify his opinion of protestors of any kind.

VIII. "GET THE BIG ONES FIRST"

"Arrest all the people you have to. Once the trees are down, there won't be anything to protest."
—FRANK ERWIN AT WALLER CREEK, OCTOBER 1969

By the beginning of the 1969–70 academic year, the stage was set for the public events that finally began to discredit Erwin. There were all the ingredients for a perfect storm. It began with a secret plan to expand Memorial Stadium at the expense of meandering Waller Creek that had run through what was then the center of campus since the days when Comanches occupied the waters of Austin.

The most eloquent rendition of the "Battle of Waller Creek" was written by a retired professor of English, Joseph Jones, in his 1982 study titled *Life On Waller Creek*. Jones sets the scene with a description of Erwin:

Not unlike some of his predecessors in state politics, Mr. Erwin felt that power should be exercised—decisions made—by those who held it; that consultations and explanations were weak-spirited and wasteful of time. Openly contemptuous of student liberals, he was generous with invective and with what he knew they considered insult. Opinion has remained divided as to his final usefulness to the University, although most fair-minded observers agree that in his own way, on his own terms, he was singularly devoted to it. At the same time, however, he seemed to many to be singularly ill fitted to play any public role short of the already obsolescent Texano-Napoleonic, with gestures. (*Life,* 215–16)

During the middle of the football season, the plans for an expansion of Memorial Stadium were leaked. The ambitious plan (to cost $15 to $20 million) called for moving San Jacinto Street west into the creek bed—several large oaks and other trees would be pulled down. Remarkably, by the fall of 1969, the University of Texas had never had a confrontation between students and police where there was the threat of violence.

Joseph Jones describes what happened next:

The students came forth with their own plan to save the trees and protect the Creek by providing a tunnel-arch through a corner of the stadium. This compromise the board (Mr. Erwin) refused to consider; and with the contractor under pressure to proceed, it was clearly necessary to block off the boulevard and begin to destroy the trees. On Monday, October 20, bulldozers, chainsaws, and other equipment, along with workmen to operate them, were ready for action. So were the students. Led by Architecture students, sign-bearers picketed the area in protest, requesting time for an alternative to be considered. Some of the signs read: TREES ARE IRREPLACEABLE, NO BULLDOZING HERE, DON'T RAPE MOTHER NATURE, SAVE OUR TREES AND WATER, and simply, SAVE OUR TREES. No trees were felled that day, but preparations were obviously being made.

Tuesday morning the protestors stood in the way of bulldozers in the Creek bed as workmen attempted to carry on as best they could, lopping tree foliage to dress the trunks for final slaughter. Along with the students, almost certainly, there was a sprinkling of both local and out-of-town semiprofessional dissidents; few protests on any campus during this period were ever without them; but overwhelmingly the majority were bona fide University of Texas men and women who felt nausea and outrage at what was going on. "The cry," reported the *Austin American-Statesman*, "was also taken up by moderates and conservatives saddened by the loss of man's fast-receding natural environment and frustrated by what they believe is inflexible decision making which does not respond to pleas, requests, or demands." (*Life*, 217)

On Tuesday night, October 21, scores of students and other protestors spent the night in the bed of Waller Creek. They knew that a coalition of student leaders, concerned faculty, and the Sierra Club were working on getting a restraining order to have the workers cease and desist in cutting down the trees.

Frank Erwin also knew this, and early Wednesday morning, he came to the creek only to find an amaz-ing sight: the biggest trees were all occupied by students, and the workers, all armed with chain saws, appeared frozen in their tracks. Not knowing when the restraining order would be issued, Erwin took charge as only he could: volubly cursing both the protestors and the tree-cutters, he demanded the removal of both the persons and the plants. The persons were removed from the trees, the trees were quickly dispatched, and the Chairman, having no direct authority whatsoever, bullied his way through a swarm of protestors. As the trees were cut and the protestors taken away, Erwin smiled in satisfaction and clapped his hands. Some present heard the Chairman say, "Get the big ones first." This phrase came back to haunt Erwin in a few years as student protests increased.

The story of the confrontation immediately made news all over the country, including the *New York Times*. The newspaper stories appeared not to be as much about remodeling an athletic facility as it was about the renegade regent who decided to take charge without consulting his colleagues on the Board of Regents, not to mention the president of the University or anyone else. Being Chairman Frank was enough.

As to the defeated students, they carried limbs and branches and leaves up to the portico of the Main Building and just placed them there, as a reminder. The fact that no one attempted to burn the brush pile demonstrated the essentially nonviolent nature of the Texas protestors. Joseph Jones contemplates the lasting impact of the episode on the defeated creek defenders:

All of us, as young people, do things we live to regret and wouldn't wish to repeat, but I wonder if there is even one ex-student survivor of the Waller Creek episode who now regrets being pulled out of a tree by policemen and arrested, or helping to carry and pile brush into the loggia of the Main Building. In the perspective of time, which party had right on its side? No medals were struck, no ribbons awarded, no monuments or plaques set up; but let us hope nevertheless that in the appropriate anniversary year, whether fifteenth, twentieth, or whatever it may be, the Defeated Druids, the Waller Creek chapter of the Veterans of Domestic Wars, may see fit to hold a reunion. Whatever, by then, life may have done to them, they will still have something to remember with pride. And let us hope, that if they choose to meet on the Creek, it will by then have moved a little farther in the direction of their youthful dreams . . . (*Life*, 220–221)

On Friday, October 24, Erwin was at a gathering to present the annual distinguished alumnus awards. During the proceedings, Master of Ceremonies Wally Pryor presented Erwin with the "Distinguished Axe Award" (an actual double-bladed axe) and read the following poem, titled "Trees, 1969."

Above: Chairman Frank at Waller Creek. *From the Prints and Photographs Collection–UT Demonstrations, Center for American History, the University of Texas at Austin. (DI 01352)*

Opposite page: The Waller Creek conflict progressed from marching to confrontation. *From the Prints and Photographs Collection–UT Demonstrations, Center for American History, the University of Texas at Austin. (DI 01810 [young man with placard]; DI 02388 [protester being pulled from tree]; DI 02419 [protester perched on stump])*

I think that I shall never see
Construction lovely as a tree.
A tree whose hungry mouth is pressed
Because the street must angle west.
A tree that lifted its leafy arms to pray
That Chairman Erwin would go away.
A tree that did in autumn wear
A nest of students in her hair.
Upon whose bosom axes are lain
While pickets utter words profane.
Poems are made by fools like me
But only Frank can kill a tree.

Not everyone was as light-hearted about the Waller Creek clash as Wally Pryor. Twenty-six protestors were pulled out of the trees and arrested. Years later, one protester expressed the common feeling to a *Texas Monthly* writer: "In the entire history of Texas, a place where being an S.O.B. is a respected art form, there are few finer examples of arrogance on a rampage than Erwin clapping his hands as the trees fell."

Some of Erwin's colleagues on the Board of Regents were beginning to question the Chairman's methods. Erwin quickly justified his actions at the creek to them on legal grounds, pointing out that the important expansion of the stadium could have been stymied for months if the restraining order had been delivered. Although there was little open opposition to Erwin on the Board of Regents, it was clear that his directed efforts to run the campus did not sit well with some of them. One particularly strong-minded board member was Regent Jenkins Garrett, a distinguished Fort Worth attorney, who appears to have been not in the least intimidated by Chairman Erwin. Months before the Waller Creek episode, Regent Garrett had written a formal letter of complaint to Erwin, calling him on his habit of making end runs around both his fellow regents and especially university administrators. The letter was dated March 19, 1969, and was as direct as Erwin himself was:

Dear Frank:

In the mail today I received copies of two letters written by you to the Chancellor, each dated March 18, in which you have demanded of the administration an investigation and a report to you personally with respect to incidents which have been reported to you on the campus. It appears to me that you intend to forward these reports to the respective individuals whose complaints have come to your attention.

I have a firm conviction that these are administrative matters which a Regent should refer to the administrative officers to investigate and work directly with the complaints . . .

Incidents of this sort should not be personally handled by members of the Board of Regents, but rather referred to our administrative people. I have complete confidence in the administration to handle this type matter. I am sure that every year they take care of literally hundreds of various complaints without the intervention of any of the Regents.

If a Regent wants a report on any matter involving the University System from the administration, I feel he has the clear right to so request. If a matter is not handled properly by the administration, it can be discussed at a Board of Regents meeting and a collective decision made as to the competency of the administration to handle such matters.

I trust that you will not handle these matters unilaterally without the concurrence of the majority of the Board of Regents. If you intend to persist without such concurrence, I wish to request the call of a special meeting of the Regents to discuss procedures in matters of this sort.

I am sending copies of this letter only to the Regents because I feel it touches upon a very serious matter of policy.

Sincerely,

Jenkins Garrett

There is no record of Erwin's response, either to Garrett or his other colleagues, but the concern over his operating style was clear.

In a *Texas Observer* obituary written after Erwin died in 1980 it was reported that on the evening after the trees fell Erwin may not have relished the day as much as it appeared, drinking even more Cutty Sark than usual at the Forty Acres Club, and repeatedly listening to "I Did It My Way" on the jukebox.

IX. ENEMIES AND FRIENDS

There was no doubt that the Battle of Waller Creek had given the University a black eye and that Erwin was the center of heated negative attention. Earlier in 1969, Governor John Connally reappointed Erwin to

a second six-year term as regent, but the process did not have smooth sailing in the legislature. Erwin enemies, including Oscar Mauzy of Dallas, finally came around, and the reappointment was confirmed. However, the fact that there was public opposition at all meant that Erwin's future as a regent had become a topic of discussion around the state.

The Waller Creek riot was seven months later and the reaction on campus was immediate. Within a week, the faculty, by a vote of 242 to 197, called for Erwin's resignation and for the Texas House of Representatives to impeach him if he refused to quit. Erwin quickly responded, linking the faculty vote to previous actions by the campus SDS:

The S.D.S. has repeatedly demanded that I resign as Chairman of the Board of Regents of the University of Texas System. I sincerely regret that this afternoon with less than 30% of the U.T. Austin general faculty present, less than 20% of that faculty adopted a resolution which makes a similar demand upon me.

However, my answer to that small minority of the faculty is the same that I have always made to the S.D.S: I was not appointed by them and I have no intention whatever of resigning in response to any demand made by them.

I am persuaded that the people of Texas are sick and tired of paying taxes to support this kind of conduct on the part of both faculty and students.

Unlike many faculty in the College of Arts and Sciences (as it was then called), who thought of Chairman Frank as the local personification of evil, historian Joe B. Frantz held a guarded admiration for Erwin. In his off-the-reservation book *The Forty Acre Follies*, Frantz tells a couple of revelatory tales:

As chairman of the regents, Erwin was easily available, always. I could wait a month to see some university administrator, but Erwin was just a telephone call away. Unlike the good Lord, he never rested. There were other dissimilarities. Once the University of Southern California sent a delegation to talk with UT officials about establishing a Richard M. Nixon presidential library on the Southern Cal campus. I shepherded them around to the university administrators and to Harry Middleton, director of the LBJ Library. Then we went to see Frank Erwin.

We met in Erwin's office in the Brown Building

downtown. I explained, then they explained. They wanted the library; they didn't really want a museum. Museums are expensive, require expert staffing, and cause parking and security problems. If they had to have a museum to have a library, they preferred to place the museum separately, perhaps on land twenty miles outside Los Angeles. What did Mr. Erwin think?

"Goddamn," said Erwin for openers. "If you don't put a museum with that library, you don't have shit!" That was the milder part of his response. He tore them from end to end, drew them and quartered them, and then held them up by their hind legs and whacked them. Then he gave that big grin he could sometimes summons, stuck out his hand, and bade them good luck. "You tell that president of yours out there," he said in the doorway, "to either get that museum or look like a damned fool." I could see them giving a direct quote. In the elevator one of them said to me, "Our regents don't talk to us like that." Although I didn't know their regents, I allowed as how they were probably correct. (pp. 274–75)

Frantz's other story reveals the ways that Erwin worked around the president and chancellor when he saw fit:

In the early 1970s I fell heir to the job of coordinating the Webb Symposium, the lecture series for which C. B. Smith and J. R. Parten had given $25,000 apiece. Smith, who can hover with the best of them, told me to put together the best possible roster of speakers. I aimed high, which meant offering some sizable fees. If everyone accepted, I would go about $5,000 over budget. I had a meeting with President [Stephen] Spurr and Chancellor [Mickey] LeMaistre, who greeted me as if I had a social disease. We must have talked for an hour. I argued that if someone puts in $50,000 from the outside, the university should be willing to augment it with $5,000. They argued that if I was over budget, I had committed a sin. We got nowhere.

I went to see Erwin, repeating the arguments I'd made to Spurr and LeMaistre and saying that I could not believe that an institution with all the millions that UT has could not dredge up $5,000 somewhere. I showed him the roster of speakers and told him that I was tying to make this first-class all the way. I didn't want ten elevenths of a symposium. Could I drain the money out of Smith and Parten? he asked. I told him

that I had no intention of milking good cows to death. He mused a moment, then said, "Do the best you can. I'll cover any overage. But don't say anything about it. Just do it."

You could feel good about Erwin after such encounters and then you would read in *The Daily Texan* and just about every other paper in the state that he had ordered campus security into the Chuck Wagon to pick up an underage girl suspected of running away from home. (p. 275)

X. THE EMPEROR'S NEW CLOTHES

More trouble was brewing on campus for Erwin, and this time it came from an unexpected source: philosophy professor John Silber. While Erwin blithely ignored or subverted the offices of president or chancellor, when occupied by the likes of Harry Ransom and Norman Hackerman, and later Stephen Spurr and Charles (Mickey) LeMaistre, the powerful chairman seemed brought up short by the audacious philosopher whom he had promoted to the powerful job of Dean of Arts and Sciences. During the sixties, Silber had made his mark on the campus as a demanding teacher and, as chairman of Philosophy, an unusually direct administrator. Off campus, Silber was known as a passionate believer in liberal causes, including a well-articulated and often-debated opposition to the death penalty.

Erwin was known to admire Silber, particularly for the way he unambiguously dismissed the young leftist philosophy professor Larry Caroline, for Silber's support of building the LBJ Library on campus, and for the hiring of the Johnson Vietnam advisor Walt Rostow and his wife, Elspeth. But, as dean of a combined Arts and Sciences College, Silber controlled the majority of the faculty, the student body, and the teaching and research budget. In *The Forty Acre Follies*, Joe Frantz, no fan of Silber's, describes his ambition:

Meanwhile Silber had perceived that the road to power in the university was controlled by Frank Erwin. These two unlikely partners became blood brothers, as Silber figuratively carried Erwin's bags and opened his doors. Silber dazzled Erwin in his terribly eloquent way, explaining what all the university could become if it just got someone in office who understood excellence. Eventually even Erwin succumbed to the Silber

Arts and Sciences dean John Silber. *From the Prints and Photographs Collection–John Silber, Center for American History, the University of Texas at Austin. (DI 02389)*

treatment, and Silber became Dean of the College of Arts and Sciences.

Previous Arts and Sciences deans, like H. T. Parlin and John Alton Burdine, had been true administrative types. Content to run a college that houses more students under its wing than any other. More students, more professors, more money. Silber was the first to see that the Dean of Arts and Sciences could wield more power than the president of the university, particularly if he had the chairman of the Board of Regents in his pocket. Silber cut a wide swath. He fired the chairman of the largest department, English, and placed a professor of philosophy in charge. English lost its temper . . . Silber reminded the irate English faculty that their appropriations came from the office of the Dean of Arts and Sciences and if they proved

themselves worthy, they might get one of their own kind as chairman some day, as well as increased appropriations. (pp. 276–77)

It appears that Erwin did appreciate Silber's dynamic leadership on campus, but became deeply alarmed when Silber began fund-raising off campus, charming checks out of mainstream, wealthy audiences in cities across the state. Silber himself later told a story about Erwin and Ben Barnes driving up to Dallas to witness an after-dinner talk he gave to a packed room of millionaires at the Mansion on Turtle Creek. Frantz continues:

In time, Erwin began to think he had raised a monster by promoting Silber. He started a movement from the top to divide the College of Arts and Sciences into three separate colleges: Liberal Arts, Behavioral Sciences, and Natural Sciences. The College of Arts and Sciences had become so large that it was unmanageable, was the word that went out. Translation: Erwin thought Silber was getting too powerful to manage. Silber didn't agree in the least. He fought back with his best weapons, the dedicated portion of his faculty and students and his power of persuasive speech. The contest between the two power brokers was joined. (p. 277)

By the time Erwin fired Silber as dean in the summer of 1970, Norman Hackerman had gone to be president of Rice University and the acting president was Bryce Jordan. Ronnie Dugger, in his opinionated book on UT, *Our Invaded Universities*, gives close to an eyewitness version of the firing that Dugger says occurred in the office of the Silber ally and University professor Donald Weismann:

Much had passed between Erwin and Silber. The dean had saved the situation for the chairman in the Caroline case, had defended Johnson, had spoken up for order, had gone to the legislature with Erwin prepared to testify for his reconfirmation as a regent, had cleared the way for the hiring of the Rostows. Erwin, he figured, was in his debt. Erwin was, and he knew it, but the purposes and interests he represented were more powerful in the course of events than his personal regard for a worthy adversary . . .

The three of them sat facing each other in the middle of the room in front of the desk, dour Erwin, peering over the tops of his half-glasses as he talked and listened, the short-tempered, edgy Dean Silber, and Weismann, a professor of art knowing he was the victim's companion in a deathful act of power. They came together into a locked concentration, direct, person-to-person, forgetting themselves.

"I just want you to know, John," Erwin said, "this is a very unpleasant subject." He had had a lot of trouble as regent, but John had done him favors, had given him a lot of essentially sound advice. "I am indebted to you, and consequently I want to talk to you not as chairman of the board of regents . . . I hope you've just come as John . . . and what I want to say to you is, it's all over. The war is over, and there's nothing more to be done about it. There's no point in your seeing any more regents and going around this state or doing anything else. It's all over. You're going to be dismissed as dean . . . Actually, this is going to be worse than the Rainey affair. You're going to be a famous man, but it's not going to do you a damn bit of good, and it's not going to do the university any good." (Dugger, p. 217)

Joe B. Frantz completes the story of the firing:

Silber asked Erwin to wait until Monday. Erwin, figuring that given a weekend, Silber could build backfires as hot as the fires of hell, said no, get out right now. This minute. Give me your keys. As happens too often, the aftermath was savage. Since Silber had no choice, he went straight to the media. The wires and headlines crackled all weekend. Students and faculty lined up. Silber built his fires, but Erwin had robbed him of his forum. Silber was now an outsider looking in.

The *Daily Texan* and the *Texas Observer* and half the eastern press tried to make a martyr of Silber, but he was poor timber for such a role. Two runaway locomotives had gotten on a collision course, and the heavier was sure to prevail. Soberer observers felt that Silber would have been just as merciless in firing Erwin if he had the chance, so what did it matter? Silber left shortly to become president of Boston University, a huge institution in the shadow of Harvard and MIT. He brought Boston out of the shadow, ran off a large portion of the faculty in the name of excellence, promoted himself in national magazines like *Life* and *Esquire*, and received a close and not altogether favorable examination on CBS's *60 Minutes*. Erwin did indeed make him famous. (Frantz, 277-78)

More to the point, Erwin had fired the only person on campus he felt was his equal.

The most telling reaction to Silber's dismissal was that of University professor Roger Shattuck. Shattuck was the most solid of Harry Ransom's "boys" both from the standpoint of his fine French literature scholarship but also because of his quietly committed political views. If Roger Shattuck took a stand it was always subtle and persuasive and everyone else on the Texas campus noticed. Shattuck composed an open letter to Regent Erwin, Chancellor LeMaistre, and Interim President Bryce Jordan protesting the dismissal of his good friend John Silber:

3 August 1970

Frank C. Erwin, Chairman of the Board of Regents
Charles A. Lemaistre, M.D., Chancellor Elect
Dr. Bryce Jordan, President ad interim
The University of Texas at Austin

Sirs:

There are certain fundamental principles, written and unwritten, for the just governance of a university. Major administrative decisions must not be made without faculty consultation and without full public accountability. Basic educational policy belongs to the faculty. Your recent actions dismissing Dean John R. Silber and dismembering the College of Arts and Sciences gravely violate those principles. The University stands dishonored. As a member of the faculty at the University of Texas, I feel compelled to protest.

Dr. Silber's unexplained dismissal cannot tarnish his magnificent record as dean and as teacher. What he stands to lose, like many other citizens of the state, is his faith in Texas as the home of a great university. By carving up the College of Arts and Sciences you have destroyed one of the last unifying forces which might hold the swollen university together as a community of minds and of men. Only some form of panic could have produced such hasty and benighted decisions. . . .

All too often, at the end of the story of the Emperor's new clothes, we are told that only the child was wise enough to see that the Emperor had nothing on. Yet there's more to the story than that. The Emperor may have been duped by clever tailors, but the people were right not to laugh. He was still fully clothed. He was wearing naked power—nothing more. The Emperor in the story was benign. I fear that the power the three of you yield is malignant. I hope you will prove me wrong by reconsidering your actions before irreparable damage has been done.

Sincerely yours,
Roger Shattuck
Chairman, Department of French and Italian

Professor Shattuck's eloquent letter was widely distributed to the local and national media as well as to the University faculty and Texas governor Preston Smith. Erwin's response was to slur Shattuck's impeccable reputation by referring to a recent research leave as an indication that he, like other high-powered faculty critics like William Arrowsmith, lived "in a lucrative playhouse." From Harry Ransom, who had handpicked Shattuck to lead his elite arts and letters faculty, there was nothing but silence. When Shattuck resigned from the University five months later, most campus observers felt that the Ransom era was done with.

XI. THE NIGHTS THE BOTTLE LET HIM DOWN

After the dramas of 1969 and 1970, Erwin's behavior grew more confrontational and erratic and not all of it could be attributed to his campus opposition: many noticed that he was drinking even more heavily. After June's death, he usually could be found at one of his favorite late-night drinking spots, such as the Forty Acres Club or Quorum Club, where he consumed rivers of scotch whiskey and held forth on history, politics, and his viewpoints on his enemies of the moment. He was also the house intellectual in the watering holes that he frequented. Nick Kralj, by then the proprietor of the Quorum Club, recalls Erwin setting up a huge map of the Middle East in the club, and lecturing to all assembled on the locations and importance of the various oilfields in Saudi Arabia and Iraq.

In 1974, when Ronnie Dugger published *Our Invaded Universities*, the Chairman crashed his party. Dugger's polemical study painted a dark portrait of Erwin, who refused to be interviewed for his book. But at the gala book-signing party held at the liberal's favorite gathering place, *Scholz Beer Garten*, Erwin walked in, surrounded by a contingent of young men (his posse of Kappa Sigs), sat down in the front room

with his bottle, and began signing Dugger's book for anyone who recognized him. Everyone did. It was great theater, and a perfect way to steal attention away from one of his avowed enemies.

Examples of Erwin's colorful style, carefully calculated to inflame his critics on the campus, are many. Although a lover of opera and a supporter of Harry Ransom's ambitious literary acquisitions, the Chairman sometimes found it to his liking to play the buffoon. Nothing illustrates this better than his press conference after a meeting of the regents up in the parquet-floored room on the second floor of the Main Building. After years of lobbying and planning, the regents finally voted to build a huge new open-shelf library (it was to become the Perry-Castañada Library). Another regent's chair might have quietly commented on the importance of libraries and books to the University community—but not Frank Erwin. He simply smiled, and with a twinkle in his eye, announced: "We're going to build us a library bigger than five K-Marts."

There were two well-publicized DWI arrests—in both Erwin was found weaving on the wrong side of Central Austin streets in his orange and white Cadillac. Both times he beat the rap: his attorney, Roy Minton, managed to attain a change of venue for both trials, an unheard-of accomplishment in a DWI case. The trials, even though not held in Travis County, were followed closely. Everyone in Austin loved the lawyer's characterization of Erwin to a small-town jury as "a lonely widower in search of Mexican food" during the trial of the incident when Erwin was charged with pulling out of the parking lot of Austin's El Patio going the wrong way on Guadalupe Street. Yet there was some truth and poignancy to the phrase that even Erwin-haters acknowledged.

XII. THE LUCRATIVE PLAYHOUSE

Frank Erwin was leery of most of the press—an example of this is his refusal to return the calls of Jack Keever, the respected AP political reporter located in Austin. He did make an occasional exception, however, and one of these was Brenda Bell, a young political reporter that Erwin took a liking to. Years later, Bell wrote a fascinating account of one of Erwin's few vulnerable moments as Board of Regents chairman (*Texas Observer*, August 17, 2001). This embarrassing

Frank Erwin late in his chairmanship. *From the Prints and Photographs Collection–Frank Craig Erwin, Center for American History, the University of Texas at Austin. (DI 02390)*

episode had to do with the University's acquisition of the Bauer House.

Bell points out that by 1970, it appeared to insiders that Harry Ransom and Frank Erwin had reached some kind of compromise that might be summarized this way: Erwin gave Ransom full permission to build his rare book center with virtually a blank checkbook in exchange for Ransom letting Erwin run other aspects of the University as he saw fit. Fairly minor, in the scheme of things, was the purchase and remodeling of the Bauer House, a West Austin home designed to be a residence for the UT chancellor and his family. As Brenda Bell puts it, "it was supposed to be Harry's house," but Ransom retired from his chancellor position before work on the big house was completed. Various unexpected costs made the allotted budget for the mansion run over by more than $600,000. One

early donor to the project was retired regent W. H. Bauer, for whom the house was named.

Faced with the overruns, Erwin began looking for other donors to make up the deficit. The funding problem hit the pages of the *Daily Texan*, just then having a vicious battle with Erwin for survival. The student paper delighted in calling the mansion a "lucrative playhouse," using the phrase that Erwin had employed about some of the privileged faculty that Ransom had recruited, most of whom left the University after the Silber firing.

In February 1971, Erwin stepped down as chair of the Board, not entirely at his own choosing. The next month the red-faced former chairman was called before a Texas Senate subcommittee to testify about the Bauer House's cost problems. Bell reports:

Harry Ransom with the model for the HRC building. *Courtesy of the Harry Ransom Humanities Research Center, the University of Texas at Austin.*

Conspicuously missing from his testimony were important facts about a mysterious $600,000 check supposedly donated by an "anonymous foundation" four days earlier to pay for the cost overruns. Erwin insisted that under terms of the gift, the donor's name could not be revealed. That implausible account drove the news media wild. Reporters hounded UT officials for the name (LBJ was a popular rumor) and chased down tips that led nowhere. Three weeks later, under pressure from the legislature to make the name public, the regents returned the gift and used public funds to pay for the Bauer House.

Bell met with Erwin and finally asked him about the mysterious $600,000.

"Eugene McDermott wrote the check," said Erwin. The late McDermott was a founder of Texas Instruments; he and his wife formed a charitable foundation in Dallas which has given a fortune to the university over the years. "We had to keep it secret because he didn't want his wife to know. So when they tried to get us to make it public, we destroyed the check. It was a check for $600,000. We burned it in an ashtray one night at the Quorum Club."

After Erwin left the chair's position on the Board of Regents, he served on the Board for four more years, but his days of hands-on power were over and everyone in Austin who cared for him knew that he missed calling the shots at UT.

Erwin's battles with the media continued for the remainder of his term and, on the day that he announced that he was leaving the Board, his public statement bitterly attacked the press. On that day (November 7, 1974), a reporter for the *Austin American-Statesman* named Steve Wisch accompanied Erwin to his accustomed watering hole, the Quorum Club.

Wisch put Erwin's announcement in context by pointing out that Erwin's reappointment was thought to be highly unlikely. His particular beef with press just then was the report that he was behind on the taxes on the estate of his dead wife, June. Erwin feuded with all of Austin's television stations except for KTBC, owned by the Johnson family, and accordingly had allowed only Channel 7 to film his statement. He then retreated to the private Quorum Club to watch himself on the evening news. Ironically, his final big moment was lost when the television equipment did not work—so Chairman Frank's final blast was lost. Then, as Erwin watched the national news at the bar, Wisch reported the following remarkable scene:

Earlier, on the national news, he had heard Walter Cronkite report that Yale law professor Alexander M. Bickel, who had successfully defended the *New York Times* against the Nixon administration's attempt to bar publication of the Pentagon papers, had died of cancer.

Hearing Cronkite report this, a look of joy suffused Erwin's face. He grinned and applauded.

One was forced to ask a close friend of Erwin why Bickel's death drew such a reaction. When Erwin probably had never met him and surely could not have known him well.

The friend, shrugging his shoulders, struggled for an answer, but could not find one. "I guess he knows that someday, when his enemies hear of his death, they will do the same thing."

XIII. THE CONDUCTOR

Without Erwin to protect his library acquisitions, Ransom appeared lost. His last assignment on the campus was to write a history of the University that he never completed. Everyone who saw the great man on campus in his last years felt that he seemed somehow defeated. On April 19, 1976, Harry Ransom died at his wife's parents' home in Dripping Springs. Frank Erwin spoke at Ransom's memorial service held in the LBJ Library Auditorium. In his high, croaking voice, Erwin reminisced about knowing Ransom as a student in the 1940s, and read a Tennyson poem. Then he summed up Ransom's final days on campus, when he had a lowered status that many felt Erwin helped create: "It is my opinion that following his retirement, Harry was at peace with himself and with the persons and things around him. He was well aware

of his already considerable accomplishments and was quite content to be judged by them."

During the remainder of the seventies, Erwin appeared to be healthier and had even dried out. Then he suddenly died of a heart attack on October 1, 1980, while visiting the University's John Sealey Hospital in Galveston for a checkup. He was sixty years old. The funeral was huge. It was held in what was then called the Special Events Center, now the Frank Erwin Center. Joe Frantz observed that, like the Hollywood funeral of Louis B. Mayer, half the crowd at the ceremony singing "The Eyes of Texas" with the Longhorn Band just wanted to make sure Erwin was really dead.

One thing that remained all of his life was Erwin's love of classical music and opera. Many think that the wrong building was named after him—that it should have been the Bass Concert Hall, designed to stage grand opera. Late in his life, Chairman Frank was known to call friends to come over to his big house with the white columns in Austin's exclusive Pemberton Heights neighborhood, the house where he had lived alone since June's death a decade earlier. Some time after the drinks were flowing, he would put classical music on the record player, playing it so loud that it drowned out conversation. He would then stand in the middle of the room, waving his arms as if he were conducting. He always knew all the parts.

NOTES ON SOURCES

There is no book-length study of Frank Erwin. The only comprehensive look at Erwin's life and career is Deborah Lynn Bay's 1988 University of Texas dissertation, "The Influence of Frank Erwin on Texas Higher Education." This 521-page unpublished work is full of praise for Erwin's accomplishments on behalf of the University but is balanced overall. It is especially strong on Erwin's younger years, his career as an attorney, and his many behind-the-scenes connections in Texas politics.

Both Ronnie Duggers's *Our Invaded Universities: Form, Reform, and New Starts* (W. W. Norton, 1974) and Joe B. Frantz's *The Forty Acre Follies* (Texas Monthly Press, 1983) contain articulate character sketches of Erwin and others on campus during his term as Texas regent. Dugger's account presents Erwin as a villain, and Frantz is more or less amused by the Chairman's antics, but both books contain compelling portraits.

Joseph Jones' *Life on Waller Creek: A Palaver About History as Pure and Applied Education* (AAR/Tantalus, Inc., 1982) is a charming meditation on nature in an urban setting. Jones writes about several aspects of University history, and specifically about Erwin in his chapter titled "Anatomy of a Riot."

Erwin figures in Douglas C. Rossinow's *The Politics of Authenticity: Liberalism, Christianity, and the New Left in America* (Columbia University Press, 1998) but only in the context of the history of faculty and student radicalism at the University. Brenda Bell's fascinating essay appeared as "Harry, Frank, and the Bauer House: A History Lesson on the University of Texas," in the August 17, 2001, *Texas Observer*. Erwin's friendly entry in *The New Handbook of Texas* was written by Mitchell Lerner. Central to any Erwin research is *Quotations From Chairman Frank* (Druid Productions, 1970).

The University Archives in the Center for American History at UT contain dozens of clippings on Erwin in their "vertical file," and their archive of Board of Regent minutes, 1963–1975, is not limited to the official record. By far the largest archive on Frank C. Erwin Jr. resides in private hands. It is the Frank Erwin History Project, a large collection of oral history interviews transcribed and stored by Austin businessman Jeff Sandefer and his staff.

My conversations with the Austin lobbyist Nick Kralj took place in his office in the spring of 2003 and on the telephone in June 2004.

JOSÉ
LIMÓN }

Américo Paredes and
Rancho UT Austin

In 1990 Américo Paredes retired as the Raymond, Dickson, Allan Professor of English and Anthropology at the University. On May 5, 1999, he died in a hospice not too far from the University, his professional and intellectual home since 1950, although earlier in his life he had crafted a fascinating imagined relationship to the institution. During his final days, I tried to lend some assistance to his small family by taking a turn sitting with him so that they could get a break. Mrs. Paredes was herself ill and would die very shortly after him in that way that couples sometimes do who have spent over half a century with each other. On one of those occasions, in a weak but still audible voice, he asked me in Spanish, "Como van las cosas en el rancho?" (How are things at the ranch?). Neither Dr. Paredes nor I had anything to do with ranches at this time nor for most of our lives. Although he himself had been born and raised in South Texas, he had spent some time on an uncle's northern Mexican ranch. For my part, I could offer only cowboy movies from my boyhood. Yet, without any hesitation, I replied something like, "Todo va bien, señor" (Things are fine, sir).

For the two of us, the "*rancho*" was a clearly understood reference to the University. Frankly, I don't remember when Professor Paredes and I started using this reference in the thirty-two years we knew each other, but I do seem to recall that he, and not I, originated the phrase. I wish I could definitely say that it was some sort of parodic takeoff on "the Forty Acres," itself a takeoff on General Littlefield *qua* rancher and his contribution of land to begin building the University. I wish I could say that perhaps Professor Paredes was drawing on the memory of his very pleasant boyhood moments on his uncle's Mexican ranch, a memory now somehow transposed to the University, the University now perhaps representing some version of the academic pastoral—a beautiful campus and a site

José Limón is professor of English and director of the Center for Mexican American Studies at the University of Texas. His books include Dancing With the Devil: Society and Cultural Poetics in Mexican-American South Texas *(1994)* and American Encounters: Greater Mexico, the United States, and the Erotics of Culture *(1998).*

Professor Américo Paredes. *Courtesy of the Nettie Lee Benson Latin American Collection, University Libraries, the University of Texas at Austin.*

of uncontaminated learning—but I think this would be disingenuous. Mr. Paredes knew about working ranches and working universities, neither particularly pastoral.

I think it more likely that the reference was yet another example of his well-known ironic and deep wit. Because, after all, the *ranchos* were of course the kind of site that Spanish/Mexicans had first established in Texas, some of which continue in Mexican-American hands to the present day. But not as many as during the Spanish-Mexican period, because many such *ranchos* became *ranches*, the lands that Mexicans lost—in ways fair or foul—to the Anglo-Texan newcomers after 1848 even as they taught the newcomers ranching culture and became *vaqueros* on these new ranches. The *ranch(o)*—both Mexican and Anglo—is a site which then entered into Texas mythology as the last site of critical difference, the last to resist the forces of modernization in the twentieth century, most centrally symbolized by oil but also by a spreading

suburbia (witness Edna Ferber's written and George Stevens' film version of *Giant* and Larry McMurtry's *Horseman Pass By*). And today, in our twenty-first century, what successful individual in today's Texas, Anglo or Mexican, doesn't immediately want to buy a ranch as if to affirm while disowning their urban-acquired wealth?

But in similar fashion, the University, especially its liberal arts, has often been construed in critical counterpoint to the unchecked forces of capitalist modernization, especially in the rather raw articulation of such forces in Texas. In part, was this not one of the fundamental issues in the titanic struggle between John Silber and Frank Erwin in 1969? Was this not the issue that, in an earlier period, also guided J. Frank Dobie's care and concern for the University? For indeed, it was Dobie who, in his writings and other public statements, brought the University as a site of liberal learning into conjunction with his beloved ranching culture, both in mutual critical difference to a new oil- and petrochemical-driven Texas.

I suspect that Américo Paredes may have shared more of Dobie's vision than he might have cared to admit for reasons that we shall note below, although his *rancho* metaphor for the University would complicate this contrapuntal vision between the liberal-arts/ranches and modernity by inserting the particular history of Mexicans in Texas and their *ranchos* of yesteryear. To make perhaps more sense of Paredes' use of this metaphor, we need to chart the fruitful yet complicated relationship that Paredes had to the University.

This relationship had begun long before he set foot on the campus. Born in 1915 in Brownsville, Texas, by the thirties and forties he had become a reporter for the *Brownsville Herald* even as he was also becoming a creative writer. He had won a statewide high school poetry contest and also published his first book of verse as a teenager. By the late thirties, he ventured into fiction, writing and publishing some short stories even as he also worked on a long novel called *George Washington Goméz: A Mexico-Texan Novel.*[1] Its central protagonist is a Mexican-American young man in South Texas named George Washington Gómez who lives a culturally conflicted life, having to mediate Anglo and Mexican cultures. To some degree his tortured movement into "Anglo" culture is congruent with his family's move from the *rancho* life of Mexican South Texas to the city of Brownsville, where an

Anglo-American educational system awaits. In one scene his Mexican side emerges in opposition to the Mexican-condescending sentiments expressed by the commencement speaker for his high school graduation, a prominent folklorist and raconteur from the University of Texas. In the novel he is called K. Hank Harvey, a thinly satirical if not sarcastic rendering of J. Frank Dobie. Harvey/Dobie appears as something of a benign anti-Mexican racist who only *thinks* he knows something about Mexican-American ranching folkloric life. Ironically, young George decides to go the University, where his cultural conflict manifestly ends as his fate is sealed. He emerges from the University as a seemingly wholly Americanized, assimilated Mexican-American, albeit one with certain cultural repressions articulated only in bad dreams. Oddly enough this passage through the University itself receives no treatment in Paredes' narrative. When asked years later why he left out George's University experience, Paredes is reported to have said that he could not realistically recount something that he himself never experienced at George's age.

That in his early years Paredes would have had such a fictional view of the University as a threatening assimilative site might be understandable given the paucity of Mexican-American students, faculty, and staff on the campus in those years. But on the other hand, Paredes also knew that the University was the intellectual home of Professor Carlos Castañeda, the eminent historian/archivist of Spanish-Mexican Texas for whom the Perry-Castañeda Library is, in part, named and who, like Paredes, was a native of Brownsville, Texas. By the 1940s, Professor George Sánchez from New Mexico had also joined the faculty and become a distinguished professor and civil rights leader for whom the Sánchez Education Building is now named. Also, the well-known South Texas folklorist and writer Jovita González had received her M.A. in history under Eugene Barker in 1930 even as the eminent civil rights attorneys Gus Garcia and Ed Idar Jr.—among others—had earned their law degrees at the University Law School in the 1940s. Perhaps it was the latter tradition but also the University's growing intellectual reputation and its proximity to South Texas that finally brought Américo Paredes himself to the University in 1950 after serving in the U.S. Army as a journalist in World War II, followed by a continuing career in journalism in the Far East after the war. As a correspondent for *Stars and Stripes*, he interviewed the imprisoned Japanese general Hideki Tojo for *Stars and Stripes* shortly before Tojo was executed for war crimes. In the later 1940s, as a journalist for the American Red Cross publications, he covered the civil war in China and the eventual victory of Mao Tse-tung and the Communists. From this six-year stay abroad, Paredes gained considerable fluency in Japanese even as he also met and married his wife, Amelia, who, though a Japanese national, had spent some time in Latin America with her father in the Japanese diplomatic service.

They decided to return to the United States and to the University of Texas at Austin, with the choice of going to Berkeley if he had wanted to. But he was thirty-five in 1950, with only two years of junior college to his credit. A mature man with a wife and family, he set out to make up for lost time as they took up residence in the Brackenridge married student housing. By taking course overloads, going to summer school, and working very, very hard, he completed the B.A. in 1951 in one year (Phi Beta Kappa) but then stayed on at the University to complete the M.A. in 1953 and the Ph.D. in 1956, all three degrees in the Department of English, while supporting his family as a teaching assistant in English. (During this period he also wrote *The Shadow*, a short prize-winning novel about the Mexican Revolution, as well as his first scholarly articles).[2] Whatever misgivings he had expressed fictionally about the University were seemingly set aside by this real native of South Texas who clearly found the University of great educational value. To be sure, the old racial animosities and conflicts that still characterized Texas society could and did make their way onto the Forty Acres. Mexicans found it difficult to get a haircut along the Drag, and Paredes would take a bus—a car was a luxury—over to East Austin twice a month for this necessity. More troubling yet, he told me that when he taught his first day of English composition as a graduate teaching assistant, in 1952, a number of the Anglo students walked out of class, refusing to be taught English by a "Mexican." But Paredes overcame such slights with characteristic dignity even as he achieved an even more profound and long-lasting victory over racial-cultural xenophobia. In effect he took a cautionary lesson from his fictional character, George Washington Gomez. The University that assimilated the fictional character did quite the opposite for Paredes but largely as a result of his own proactive agency. Even as he was embracing a fundamentally American education, especially in an English department, he was also actively shaping that education in the direction of his native Mexican-American culture and society and, in doing so, he decisively accelerated a half-century of change in the University itself, change not without its problems but also not without its precedents. As we have already noted, the University had already been put into the service of Mexicans in Texas by individuals such as Carlos Castañeda, Jovita González, and even Dobie, but Américo Paredes enlarged, extended, and institutionalized these precedents.

To begin with, he put together what was for those times an extraordinary program of cross-disciplinary, cross-cultural course work for his graduate program, which, although officially in the Department of English, included not only the required courses in English/American literature but also encompassed course work in Spanish, history, and anthropology. (His undergraduate work in English had also included Spanish, as well as philosophy). Perhaps even more extraordinary, his English Department doctoral dissertation on the life, legend, and folksong of the Mexican-American ballad hero Gregorio Cortez dealt predominantly with Spanish-language folklore, particularly the ballads, or *corridos*, as Mexicans call them. For, whatever other academic identities Paredes came to have, his primary identity was as a scholar of the folklore of the Mexican-origin community, principally in South Texas. That such folklore was itself primarily sited on the Mexican-American ranching culture of that region is to the point of these remarks. Paredes had the intellectual vision to cross disciplinary and cultural boundaries, but something also needs to be said favorably about an English department and a university that not only let him craft such a program but encouraged him. We need to recall that we are speaking of the McCarthy-tainted 1950s and, in my estimation, one of the University's better moments as it fought off the forces of the local articulations of right-wing racism and reaction and continued to do so through the early 1960s.

With his Ph.D. in his hand, Paredes left the University for his first full-time academic position, at the old Texas Western College of Mines in El Paso, now the University of Texas at El Paso. But the same English department and university that had fostered his interdisciplinary and cross-cultural style of inquiry now had the further enlightened good sense to invite him back to the faculty after an absence of only one year, a rare honor for any Ph.D. from the University. Here he would teach courses in American literature and, without protest from University authorities, newly designed courses both in general folklore and in what he called the folklore of "Greater Mexico," to encompass the folkloric contributions of people on both sides of the U.S.–Mexico border. After returning to the University, Paredes was also successful in publishing his doctoral dissertation as a book, thereby winning early tenure. His now-classic book is titled *"With His Pistol in His Hand": A Border Ballad and Its Hero.*[3]

As many know, the book concerns a Mexican-American man named Gregorio Cortez. On June 12, 1901, near Karnes City, Texas, not far from Austin, Anglo-American lawmen confronted Cortez and his brother Romaldo on charges of horse thievery. As it turns out, the charges were baseless, but in the ensuing confrontation words in Spanish and English were misunderstood and a gunfight erupted, leaving Romaldo and one sheriff dead. Probably imagining that his Mexican life would not be worth much, Gregorio began a long horse ride for the Mexican border, only to give up near Laredo with Mexico in plain view when he heard that his wife and children had been arrested and were languishing in the Karnes City jail. Paredes then recounts the trial that followed Cortez's sentencing and eventual pardoning. However, folklorist Américo Paredes' principal concern in the book is a study of the traditional ballads or *corridos* that the Mexican folk created about Gregorio Cortez, making him into a hero for the racially and economically besieged Mexican community in Texas, a hero who, "with his pistol in his hand," as one of the ballad lines says, had resisted Anglo authority, particularly the hated Texas Rangers.

The publication of *"With His Pistol in His Hand": A Border Ballad and Its Hero* by the University of Texas Press in 1958 was not without controversy and conflict that seemed like a continuation of the old *rancho*/ranch wars. The story bears repeating. Initially UT Press tried to persuade Paredes, this beginning assistant professor, to tone down both his criticisms of the Texas Rangers and their callous treatment of Mexican-Americans and his criticism of those two major University academic figures Walter Prescott Webb and J. Frank Dobie, the latter on issues already noted, the former for his glorification of the Texas

Rangers and his disparagement of Mexican culture. Paredes refused to change the manuscript, and UT Press relented after he threatened to take it to another press. The publication of the book generated further controversy, especially when a former Texas Ranger threatened to pistol-whip the SOB who wrote that book.

In the 1960s Paredes' program to bring salutary change to the University received important support from the Mexican-American student movement on campus, in which I played some part. These students, with Paredes as our faculty spokesperson, proposed new curricular and research agendas focused on the Mexican-origin peoples of the United States. These proposals soon resulted in the creation of the Center for Mexican-American Studies at the University, for which the University deserves overdue credit. Américo Paredes was the Center's first director, and I am honored to hold this position today.

Indeed, it was in 1967 that I first met Mr. Paredes, when, as a second-year graduate student in the English Department, he selected me as his teaching assistant for his sophomore literature classes and his survey of American literature. No one was walking out of his classes by then; indeed, they were consistently over-subscribed. He gradually persuaded me away from the Ph.D. in English that I was then pursuing to work instead on the Ph.D. in folklore and anthropology in the newly created Center for the Study of Folklore and Ethnomusicology, which he directed for several years. And I was not alone. Several such students completed their Ph.D.s under his able direction and are now serving in universities across the country. (I got the best job of all, teaching and writing here at the ranch.) But these activities did not detract from more fundamental research and writing even as he struggled with cancer and heart problems for the better part of his University career and also with the challenge of helping Mrs. Paredes raise her two sons and also his beloved daughter, Julie, who was born with multiple birth defects.

With His Pistol in His Hand from 1958 was soon followed by numerous scholarly articles and six more books, assuring his early promotion to full professor and eventually his appointment to a distinguished University Chair.[4] Some of the research time for his work was funded by a Guggenheim fellowship, arguably the most prestigious fellowship that can be awarded to a scholar in the humanities. But *With His*

Pistol in His Hand remains his *magnum opus*, the classic by which many scholars and the socially conscious public will always remember him.

"Como van las cosas en el rancho?" he asked me. What *did* he mean by that? Why did I take so easily to the metaphor? We might gain insight from *With His Pistol in His Hand.*

As noted earlier, critics of various persuasions have placed a great deal of emphasis on what Paredes had to say about the Texas Rangers, Walter Prescott Webb, and so on, as well as what the Cortez *corridos* have to say critically about Anglo-Texana at that time. But I have often felt that a more profound appraisal of Anglo-Mexican relations in Texas resides in *With His Pistol in His Hand.* When the Anglo lawmen confronted Cortez, he and his brother were engaged in stoop labor on a farm near Karnes City. But it soon became evident that Cortez could both shoot quickly and accurately with a pistol and ride, both so successfully as to fight off or evade capture by many lawmen pursuing him toward Mexico, especially the Rangers. Although we know relatively little of the early part of Gregorio's life, it seems reasonably evident that he had been a skillful horseman and an able hand with a gun somewhere in his native northern Mexico and South Texas. These were skills acquired at another time in Texas, perhaps as a result of working on a Mexican-owned ranch or, for that matter, a new one whose deed of ownership now had an English name. Now, in 1901, with the closing of the cattle kingdom and the expansion of cash-crop agriculture in Texas, Mexicans were being subjected not only to racial and economic exploitation but also to a reduction in status from *vaqueros* to "cowboys," now more increasingly identified with Anglo culture but themselves really only working hands subject to their own eventual agonizing reduction in identity, the subject of early and later Larry McMurtry. One suspects that the Mexican community celebrated this hero, not only for confronting and escaping a dubious Anglo law, but for restoring the primacy of the Mexican *vaquero* and the now-fading institution of the Mexican *rancho* in Texas, at least for one symbolic moment. It was less the escape itself than the escape as an accomplished rider and a man competent with his pistol in his hand.

I would like to believe that both *vaqueros* and cowboys who have rendered long service to the ranch come to identify closely with it even if it is not their own, even if the "real" owner lives in corporate Dallas. I am led to wonder if Américo Paredes did not construe his life at the University like that of some hard-working Mexican *vaquero* such as his own hero, Gregorio Cortez had been. Through his prodigious, ground-breaking, cross-cultural scholarship, his exemplary teaching and mentoring, and his dedicated service to so many University committees, Américo Paredes contributed greatly to the University. Even as the *vaquero* recognizes that the ranch is not quite his, yet devotes his life to it, like some *vaquero*, Paredes was at home on this *rancho*, this "Anglo-owned" ranch, and like any ranch, the only real home *vaqueros* and cowboys ever come to know. A place of demanding labor to be sure, and some insult, conflict, and alienation, but still home and, over time, with increasing affiliation, hard work, dedication, and service, one comes to make it one's own and perhaps even transforms it in one's own way to make it a better *rancho*, with its own life-giving source of identity, even though its ownership is always elsewhere. There are infinitely worse- and better-paying ways to make a living.

"Como van las cosas en el rancho?" he might ask me now.

Mejor, señor, mucho mejor, I would have to say, because he helped mightily to make them that way.

NOTES

1. Paredes' early literary work has been republished by Arte Público Press, Houston, as *George Washington Goméz: A Mexico-Texan Novel* (1990); *Between Two Worlds* (1991); and *The Hammon and the Beans and Other Stories* (1994). Forthcoming from Arte Público Press is an early collection of his adolescent poetry in Spanish titled *Cantos de Adolescencia (Songs of Youth)*, edited and translated by B. V. Olguin and Omar Vasquez Barbosa.

2. Since published as *The Shadow* (Houston: Arte Público Press, 1998).

3. Américo Paredes, *"With His Pistol in His Hand": A Border Ballad and Its Hero* (Austin: University of Texas Press, 1958).

4. Américo Paredes, *The Folktales of Mexico* (Chicago: University of Chicago Press, 1974) and *A Texas-Mexican Cancionero: Folksongs of the Lower Border* (Champaign-Urbana: University of Illinois Press, 1981). His major articles have been collected as *Folklore and Culture on the Texas-Mexican Border* (Austin: Center for Mexican-American Studies, 1993).

JAMES
MAGNUSON

The Week James Michener Died

The day after the first newspaper articles appeared announcing James Michener's decision to go off kidney dialysis, the students began to call me. Was there anything they could do? Could they bring him a cup of tea? Could they make him a dessert (they all knew that he loved sweets)? One former Michener Fellow, now a successful screenwriter in Los Angeles, phoned, nearly in tears. She was flying into Austin on the weekend. Was there any way she could see him or speak to him, even for a minute? There wasn't. He died on a Thursday night, twelve hours before she arrived.

Back in the early eighties, when James Michener came to work on the novel *Texas*, he was given the red-carpet treatment. He was wined and dined by Governor Bill Clements, flown to private airstrips in Marfa, taken on jeep tours of the biggest ranches. He was also given a ten by ten office at the University. It was a particularly astute move, because one thing you quickly learned about Michener was that he was a lover of universities. Soon thereafter he bought a house in Austin and every so often a rumor would waft through the halls of the English Department that he was considering endowing a creative writing program. I had just come to teach at the University myself, so when I was approached by an administrator who wanted to know if Michener could sit in on my graduate fiction workshop, it didn't seem wise to say no.

The students were in awe of him, and he took their work very seriously. He was like a stern Dutch uncle, encouraging but concerned that no one got too big for their britches. "I'm just your T.A.," he told me, and he was a remarkable T.A. He attended every class and gave detailed notes on their stories. He passed out lists of the most common grammatical errors: the differences between *lie* and *lay*, between *there*, *their*, and *they're*. If he could

---

After a long career as a playwright in New York City and at Princeton University, James Magnuson came to Austin, where he is director of the James A. Michener Center for Writers at the University of Texas. His novels include Open Season *(1982),* Money Mountain *(1984),* Ghost Dancing *(1989),* Windfall *(1999), and* The Hounds of Winter *(2005). A version of this essay appeared in the December 1997 issue of* Texas Monthly.

Jim Magnuson and James Michener. *Courtesy of the James A. Michener Center for Writers.*

be intimidating, it also quickly became apparent what an old-fashioned idealist and an enthusiast he was and that he had a lot more nerve than the students. One afternoon a group of young writers was talking about their plans after graduation. One woman said she was thinking about going to Bosnia to work with the rape victims of the war. Michener jumped right on it. "Go," he said. "Do it now. Drop out of school if you have to." Her eyes went wide. She stammered something about needing to finish her thesis, but Michener didn't seem to really understand that. There was an opportunity. It needed to be seized. He did not believe in half-measures.

In 1988 it was announced that James Michener was giving $2 million to create an interdisciplinary M.F.A. at the University of Texas. It would not only train students as screenwriters, poets, playwrights, and fiction writers, it would ask them to work in more than one genre, "to give them another arrow in their quiver," Michener said.

I remember how dubious I was. Having fellowships for our students would utterly revive our program, but wasn't it hard enough to teach students in one writing discipline? How could we possibly do it in two? Wouldn't our students be spreading themselves too thin? It sounded very grand and Michenerean in its ambition, but it also sounded as if we'd just bitten off a lot more than we could chew.

In 1991 I went on leave, taking off for Los Angeles to write for television. While I was there I began to

receive faxes from Joe Kruppa in the English Department, proposals for how this new MFA would work. Then in the summer of 1992, just before I came back to Austin, the announcement was made that Michener had endowed an additional $16 million to fully fund the program. I was stunned; it was far and away the largest gift ever made to support creative writing anywhere.

The year after I returned I became director of the Texas Center for Writers, succeeding Rolando Hinojosa-Smith. I soon discovered that James Michener was not a man who was going to give you $18 million and then forget about it. Each fall he would invite every member of the entering class to his home. He would offer to read their work, give them advice about their work, tell them stories.

When we held our annual barbecue at the Salt Lick, he would always be there in his bolo tie, his Hobo Times baseball cap, and his tennis shoes with the Velcro straps, sitting at the center table, greeting everyone. He was well into his eighties and not in good health. He was not a meddler, but he was a man used to seeing results and there was not much time.

The students had a genuine admiration for him as well as an understandable gratitude. Yet they were often shy around him. There was something in him that didn't invite intimacy, and he could be gruff. "Young lady," he once told an aspiring fiction writer in front of the class, "your teachers have told me that you have talent, but I didn't see it until this story." At another gathering, when he was feeling particularly glum, he said, "All my life I've wanted to support a talented young writer, but I've never found one."

But his darker moods would always be answered by bursts of enthusiasm. I remember when he decided to throw a party for the students at Louie's Mexican Restaurant in Dripping Springs, a spot that had become a favorite of his. He spent two days on the invitations, typing out the menu on his typewriter ("crispy taco, rice and beans, guacamole . . .") and gluing various pieces of it to a big piece of construction paper.

He was deluged with requests. One person wrote declaring that, with a little financial backing from Mr. Michener, they were prepared to write an American novel in the style of Nikolai Gogol. Someone else was more direct; he wrote saying he knew he couldn't get into the program, but he needed the money; he had included a deposit slip. A third wrote requesting money for a sweet-potato farm that would help save the starving populations of Africa. Every one of these got a polite, considered reply.

It seemed as if he had known everyone, from the Pope to Arthur Miller to every president since Truman. When I asked him once what he thought about Marilyn Monroe, he said, "We all thought we could save her." He had sailed with Walter Cronkite and corresponded with bullfighters.

But for all his fame, if there was one key to his character it was the fact that he had been an orphan. In the last couple years of his life, it seemed to come up a lot. He could be quick to feel rejection and would write letters to his friends saying that he was thinking of moving again. One of his last books was entitled *The World Home*, yet I had the sense that he never felt utterly at home anywhere.

The first full class of ten was admitted to the Texas Center for Writers in the fall of 1993. Within two years there would be forty students supported by $12,000 fellowships. Michener's endowment would make it possible to bring in some of the finest writers in the world to teach and give seminars: J. M. Coetzee, David Hare, W. S. Merwin, and Michael Ondaatje.

Our program was certainly not the only one to benefit from Michener's generosity. Over the last decades of his life he gave an estimated $165 million to universities and museums, as well as individuals. No writer had ever amassed such a fortune and now it seemed as if he had set about, in his characteristically methodical way, to be sure that every penny would be used.

The question I was never able to bring myself to ask Michener was why. What would motivate a person to give in such an unprecedented way? My guess is that a lot of it had to do with his Quaker background and that he grew up in a time and place where you could utter words like service and duty with a straight face. Constitutionally he was a man incapable of squandering anything. He had lived through the Depression and known hard times. He loved to eat at the Marimont Cafeteria and if there were leftovers he would have the waitress wrap them for his lunch the next day. If he saw an Arby's two-for-one coupon fluttering across the sidewalk, he would pin it to the concrete with his rubber-tipped cane and announce, "Skipper, this is where we're going to eat lunch."

Part of it too was that he had been, throughout his life, in love with the grand enterprise. He was a man who enjoyed being feted. Even as he grew more feeble, he had an incredible ability to rally for an interview on *Good Morning America* or an appearance at Barnes and Noble where two thousand people stood patiently for up to four hours to have their books stamped.

In the winter of 1997 the University gave him a gala birthday party. It began with the inevitable and interminable receiving line. Governors, publishers, and college presidents spoke, and Stan "The Man" Musial played "It's a Small World" on his harmonica. Michener read from a book of one hundred sonnets he published the month before. After it was over I walked out into the lobby of the Alumni Center and there he was, inexplicably sitting alone. "Happy Birthday," I said. He looked up at me. He seemed incredibly tired. He gave me the thinnest of smiles and, as always, his chin was up.

By autumn, he was too ill to meet the incoming students. There were so many things to tell him—two years after the first class had graduated, three had published books, one had a full-page rave review in the *New York Times*, another had a film at Sundance, another had her play produced Off Broadway—but the last couple of times I called his house, he was sleeping. He had taken himself off dialysis and the end was near.

At the funeral one of the students told me, "He was such a chronicler. Wherever he went, he would always come back and tell us everything he learned, everything he found. This is the first time he's gone someplace where he can't tell us what it was like."

Once again this fall, forty young writers will meet at the Salt Lick. A lot of it you can count on being the same: the vegetarians will complain about having to eat all that meat, the professor of poetry will get lost on her way out, someone will break up with a boyfriend in the parking lot. The only difference is that the center table will be empty.

History

RICHARD A.
HOLLAND

George W. Brackenridge, George W. Littlefield, and the Shadow of the Past

If you were on the Texas campus sometime around 1911, you might have seen two prosperous-looking old men walking toward the original Main Building—but never together. They were George W. Brackenridge and George W. Littlefield, arguably the most generous and visionary University donors in its first hundred years. Both were regents in the second decade of the last century and both backed up their regard for the University with large portions of the fortunes they had made, yet neither could stand to be in the company of the other. They had the visages of well-to-do Edwardian gentlemen—both bearded, each wearing a hat and a three-piece suit. From a block away, you couldn't tell one from the other.

The source of the two powerful regents' conflict reaches back into the bloody America of the 1860s, and although Brackenridge and Littlefield have now been gone for over eighty years, in some ways the issues that divided them are still with us and with the University.

GEORGE WASHINGTON BRACKENRIDGE

When Texas governor John Ireland appointed George W. Brackenridge to be a University of Texas regent in 1886, the college in Austin was barely underway and its eventual success was a matter of some doubt. Five years after its founding, and in its third year of actual operation, the campus consisted of two hundred fifty students, a handful of newly hired faculty, and one unfinished building sitting forlornly on a barren hill stripped of its trees.

Governor Ireland was thought to be indifferent to the new university in Austin, placing him in the company of most other Texans at the time who cared about education—a relatively small number in an uneducated state just emerging from the traumas of war and reconstruction. Baylor (founded in 1846) satisfied the advocates of denominational education, and

Richard Holland was the history bibliographer in the UT General Libraries for seventeen years. During that time he helped develop the library's southern history collections through the Littlefield Fund for Southern History.

Texas A&M, only seven years old, already command-ed fierce loyalty across a state whose economy was overwhelmingly based on agriculture.

Brackenridge's appointment as regent illustrated the clash of historical cultures that developed in Texas and the South in the period immediately following the Civil War. Two decades after the Old South fell, mem-ories of Reconstruction had only deepened sectional resentments—and a Union officer, like Brackenridge, who had returned to Texas just after the war would au-tomatically be distrusted. Furthermore, Regent Brack-enridge would oversee an 1880s campus crawling with Confederates, including several distinguished faculty: among them were English professor Leslie Waggener, who had been wounded at Shiloh and Chickamauga; philosophy professor Robert Dabney, who served as Stonewall Jackson's chief of staff; and law professor Oran M. Roberts, who had presided over Texas' seces-sionist convention. Ireland's appointment of Bracken-ridge must have seemed an eccentric decision, but one that was perhaps little noticed since the Austin cam-pus had such poor prospects.

The second son born to a comfortable family in southern Indiana, George Brackenridge really did ap-pear to get to Texas as soon as he could. In George's late teens, his father recognized his business prow-ess and sent him to Port Lavaca in 1850 with a load of goods to trade. Young Brackenridge had just com-pleted his freshman year at Hanover College. Based on his quick success, the family moved down to Jackson County, where George's father, John Adams Brack-enridge, quickly established a mercantile business in Texana, a community on the Navidad River. Texas in the early 1850s was a land speculator's dream, and soon enough George commenced buying land. He suffered some setbacks in his land investments, but it was clear that he had a gift for making money.

The defining moments in Brackenridge's crucial al-liance with the Union in the Civil War were made up of equal parts belief, accident, and business opportuni-ty. Always an independent thinker, during secessionist arguments Brackenridge was drawn to the position of Sam Houston, the most notable pro-Union politician in Texas. On the other hand, he now felt that he was a Texan, and after the fighting began, his brothers (pro-Union voters in the Jackson County secession vote, yet owners of slaves) joined in to resist the expected Yan-kee naval blockade on the Texas coast. In the end, it may have been pure logistics that helped Brackenridge

decide to align himself against his adopted state. At the advanced age of twenty-eight he enrolled himself in Harvard Law School, and it was just then, when he was living in Massachusetts, that hostilities began in South Carolina. Another factor in Brackenridge's pro-Union leanings was his boyhood memory of Abraham Lincoln visiting his father at their home in Indiana.

The vote to secede in Texas was hotly contested, and one result was that passing the secession declaration instantly created a new class of identifiably seditious Union sympathizers. The new war also brought forth opportunities for some who could take advantage of the chaos, and no nineteenth-century American place was more chaotic or more steeped in international in-trigue than the lower Rio Grande Valley.

George Brackenridge dropped out of Harvard and returned to his family in Texas. It was then that he fell in with one of the most fascinating scoundrels in Texas history, Charles Stillman. Since the days of the Republic, South Texas had been awash in land grabs, shady transactions and, because of the river, a thriv-ing smuggling trade with Mexico. One of the maestros of this dark and profitable business was Stillman, an adventurer who had come to Durango, Mexico, from his home in Connecticut in 1828. By the time hostili-ties commenced in 1861, Stillman had helped lay out the city of Brownsville, just across the river from the old Spanish-style Mexican town of Matamoros. Still-man's partners in a Rio Grande steamboat company were the future South Texas land barons Richard King and Mifflin Kenedy, themselves no strangers to border intrigue.

The early months of the war were marked by Union attempts to enforce a naval blockade all the way from Virginia on the East Coast, around the Florida pen-insula, and along the entire Gulf Coast, ending in Brownsville. Charles Stillman, like other South Texas entrepreneurs, maintained business locations on both sides of the Rio Grande; the way he used the politically neutral river as a transfer point depended on the way political winds were blowing in Texas and Mexico. The sudden shutdown of the Texas coast by the Union navy brought into play a brand new dangerous set of oppor-tunities that can most charitably be described as mor-ally ambiguous. This opportunity lasted for only two years or so—but it became the basis of George Brack-enridge's fortune and reputation.

At the beginning of the war, the Confederate gov-ernment cut off the export of its most cherished agricultural product: cotton. Its hopes were that England and France, at best weak friends of the United States, would back the Confederacy in order to maintain their imports of the South's cash crop. The simple laws of supply and demand dictated that the parties who controlled and brokered this now-scarce commodity could become immensely wealthy.

George Brackenridge's introduction to this heady possibility came in the fall of 1861, when he visited the Rio Grande Valley, crossed over to Mexico, and understood the leverage that the trader Charles Stillman could bring to bear. This trip convinced Brackenridge that he and his business partners should acquire quantities of cotton immediately. George's closest partner was his brother Tom, who had enlisted in an inactive Confederate cavalry company that some thought George would join as well. But, as his biographer Marilyn Sibley points out, Brackenridge abandoned any idea he had of joining Tom's cavalry company. Instead, he began his business relationship with Stillman, which would make him a rich man.[1]

Brackenridge began purchasing cotton from growers by the end of 1861, stashing most of it on Charles Stillman's large coastal ranch. The Union blockaders soon noticed that sleepy Matamoros was booming with activity, as Stillman's ships left for New York loaded with Texas exports. Even after the waterway smuggling routes were shut down, the old established land routes were employed. It was like trying to stop hemorrhaging with a Band-Aid. By December of 1862 some of the proceeds were distributed—one of Stillman's payments to Brackenridge and his partners totaled $30,000 in gold. By the time profits were realized, two of Brackenridge's partners were dead—his father, who had furnished the investment capital, and James Bates, his sister's suitor. Brackenridge was the executor of Bates's estate and many questioned what happened to the dead partner's assets after his death.[2]

The war hit home in Jackson County in the spring of 1862 when casualty reports from the battles of Shiloh and Corinth came in. In a county of 2000 inhabitants where only 224 men had cast votes on secession, there were over a dozen war casualties, a tremendous blow. Brackenridge's Confederate brother Tom had already gone to war, and all of a sudden George's Union proclivities were no longer tolerable. After a close call with a lynching party, Brackenridge escaped from Jackson County on a July night in 1863. He made it down to the by-then-familiar Rio Grande and, traveling on the Mexican side of the river, made it to the coast, where he was picked up by a Union gunboat. By the end of the month he was in Washington, and quickly he had an appointment with President Abraham Lincoln, who fondly remembered Brackenridge's father. Soon enough after he left the war-beleaguered president's office, Brackenridge was appointed to a position in the Union treasury.

Although he was now formally aligned with the United States government and this allegiance appeared to be based on sincere belief, George Brackenridge stayed in character as a businessman who could play two sides to his own advantage. After a period in Washington, Brackenridge was assigned to New Orleans as an assistant special agent in the Treasury. Quickly he was moved on to Brownsville, where the commodities smuggling that he had participated in before his hasty departure was still thriving. His commanding officer, Charles Dana, must have been a quick study, because he immediately suspected Brackenridge of double dealing when the new agent brought his old business partner Charles Stillman into Union headquarters. In all fairness, Brackenridge was not unique and Dana knew this—cotton was still king along the Texas and Mexico Gulf coasts and many Union officers were tempted by the uniquely profitable juxtaposition of a surplus of a valued commodity, a war, and a series of short-lived governments and constant upheaval in Mexico. Adding to Brackenridge's personal war complications was the fact that a few weeks before he arrived in Brownsville, one of his brothers who fought for the Confederacy had been captured and sent to a Louisiana prisoner of war camp. His other two brothers continued fighting for the South and George helped free the imprisoned brother. Never seeing battle himself, George Brackenridge ended the war with his pockets full.

Brackenridge wasted no time after the war ended—by 1866 he was in San Antonio operating a successful bank. One of his biggest customers was Charles Stillman, who throughout the war had continued making fortunes all the while eluding the Yankees and maintaining alliances with the Confederate army. Brackenridge's postwar career fell into place in the 1870s when his bank invested money in the new cattle industry, and his natural talent for making money was further demonstrated when he purchased the San Antonio Water Works Company. He soon built a mansion at the headwaters of the San Antonio River for himself and his mother. Brackenridge remained aloof when faced with charges of war profiteering or traitorous conduct during the war, but those issues followed him until his death. In his personal life he was an atheist, a bachelor, an intellectual, and a natural philanthropist who was obsessed with education. His study in the mansion was full of history and philosophy books that he constantly read and reread. By the time his regental appointment came along in 1886, Brackenridge was fifty-four years old.

Although he maintained the San Antonio residences, the new regent's close ties to the struggling Austin campus were immediately apparent, and he quickly made himself indispensable. Early evidence of his unusual generosity became obvious when he personally funded the construction of the male residence building that he insisted be named University Hall, but that quickly became known on campus as "B. Hall," the "B" standing for Brackenridge. In its placement just east of the original Main Building and its symbolic importance as home for several generations of self-governing "poor boys," the structure was much beloved and the source of University lore for decades. Perhaps of more lasting importance were Brackenridge's interest in the University Medical School, located in Galveston, and the close attention that he paid to the University's arid lands in West Texas.

The regent's specific interest in the Galveston campus was in attracting female students to the medical profession. When told that the new medical branch had no housing for women students, he immediately donated $41,000 to build a combination food facility and women's house that would accommodate 29 students. The female enrollment was disappointing for years, but his dedication to educating women doctors never waned and his attention to the education of professional women resulted in several pioneering women in the medical profession choosing to live in San Antonio.

As to the empty University lands in West Texas, Brackenridge was the first regent to pay much attention to the holdings that totaled something over two million acres. To characterize these lands as neglected is an understatement: not only did they produce just a pittance of income, there was not even a reliable survey that reported the extent of the holdings. With his customary efficiency, Brackenridge applied a working solution to the problem: he personally arranged a survey and estimated that, properly managed, the desert lands could bring in $80,000 a year. His avid interest

George Washington Brackenridge. *From the Prints and Photographs Collection—George W. Brackenridge, Center for American History, the University of Texas at Austin. (DI 02398)*

in this neglected property extended to his trying to get his fellow regents to travel with him to examine the land, but none of them took him up on the offer. His efforts paid off in 1895 when the legislature transferred direct management to the University. With his own money, Brackenridge hired West Texas land managers and completed an abstract. All of this hard work was far-reaching—three decades later when the sea of oil was discovered in the Permian Basin, Brackenridge's greatest contribution to the University manifested itself.

If his original regental appointment had been an anomaly, George Brackenridge's several reappointments were no-brainers. By the time he retired from the Board of Regents he had become a symbol of the heart and soul of the University. Not only had his personal generosity quietly created living quarters for "poor boys" in Austin and women students in Galveston, he single-handedly, it seemed, upheld academic standards, particularly when it came to the appointment of his colleagues on the Board of Regents. The University's bitter enemy, Governor James Ferguson, railed against "the University crowd," and Brackenridge was that crowd's first citizen. In an *Alcalde* article profiling him, Roy Bedichek called the San Antonio regent the University's "patron saint,"[3] a designation that Marilyn Sibley suggests would have amused the agnostic Brackenridge, "who never pretended to be a saint and who was never really sure there were saints or a heaven to house them."[4] Bedichek's illustration of Brackenridge's virtue demonstrates how he stood up to political pressure:

> When one of "the really great Governors of Texas" approached Brackenridge, suggesting the appointment of two of his friends to the university faculty, Brackenridge replied expressing satisfaction in the governor's interest. But noting that it was unusual for such a busy man as the chief executive of Texas to take time to investigate thoroughly the qualifications of potential faculty members, "he went on quite incidentally to detail the qualifications that such men should possess," said Bedichek, "and wound up by intimating that the regents would take it for granted that the Governor had assured himself upon all the points so outlined, and that the regents would give, therefore, the Governor's recommendations the most serious consideration." The governor got the point. By return mail he showed "evident anxiety to get out from under the responsibility" placed on him; the appointments were not made; and there was no further pressure from the executive office.[5]

No one could have anticipated that the businessman/intellectual from San Antonio would end his higher education career at the University as the regent with the longest term, honored on the campus as a beloved figure. Brackenridge continuously served on the Board for twenty-five years, from 1886 to 1911, and then-governor William P. Hobby reappointed him in 1917 for two years more. During this long stretch, Texas elected six different governors, and Brackenridge remained the sole Republican appointment in a solidly southern Democratic state.

GEORGE WASHINGTON LITTLEFIELD

George Washington Littlefield is usually portrayed as Brackenridge's opposite number. The two were temperamental opposites, and it is certainly true that their backgrounds and each man's experience in the cauldron of war in the 1860s could not have been more different. Looking at Littlefield's family history from our standpoint, the starkest fact is his familiarity with slavery as a child and young man.

George Littlefield's mother, Mildred Terrell Satterwhite, had been left a widow in her first marriage. In 1838 she lived near Como, Mississippi, on her late husband's plantation, with forty slaves. Her slave overseer's brother was Fleming Littlefield, who met her while visiting the plantation. They soon fell in love and married, much to the disapproval of both her family and her dead husband's family. The marriage took place in 1841 and George W. was born on the plantation in 1842. Another boy and girl were born before hostilities between Fleming Littlefield and his in-laws grew intolerable and he decided to relocate his family to Texas. In 1850 the feud culminated in Fleming's shooting a man who had been sent to challenge him to a duel. George Littlefield's father left on a horse in the night and settled on the Texas land, on the Guadalupe River above Gonzales. Soon Fleming was joined by his wife, young George, his brother and sister, and one of their older half-brothers. Fleming Littlefield expanded his farm, buying more acres on the river, and then opened a store in the town of Gonzales. He died of pneumonia in January 1853 and left his estate to be divided among his wife and their three children. In his hagiographic *George W. Littlefield, Texan*, the historian J. Evetts Haley chillingly describes Fleming Littlefield's estate:

> The inventory of the estate listed 1,760 acres of land, 22 Negroes, 65 bales of cotton, more than 100 head of Spanish and American horses, besides mules, oxen, 300 cattle, 100 hogs, 1 Page's sawmill, 4,000 bushels of corn, 11 stacks of fodder, ox and horse wagons, 1 old carriage, 20 plows, 16 pairs of gear, farming tools, $23 in cash and $1,825 in notes. Everything except the land, which was held intact because of the difficulty of division, was partitioned. One fourth of the estate, to the value of $5785, went to each member of the family. George received four mules named Jack, Lagan, Harry and Pall; eight horses and colts, among them Simon,

Prince and Black Hawk; and five slaves—Byatt, valued at $1,000, George at $1,050, Jack at $700, Frank at $550, and Susan at $900. Besides these legacies, George W. Littlefield received cattle, oxen, hogs, tools, and "the old carriage."[6]

George Littlefield was eleven when his father died.

Fleming Littlefield's farm remained intact, with Mildred Littlefield managing all of the property and the slaves. By the middle of the 1850s, she was aided by several other Littlefields who had moved from Mississippi to Gonzalez to join her and the children. By the time George Littlefield joined the Confederate Eighth Texas Cavalry (also known as Terry's Texas Rangers) in 1861, his mother and her extended family owned three plantations along the Guadalupe and San Marcos river bottoms, all worked by slaves. Littlefield was nineteen when he joined up and soon was battle-experienced—he fought at Chickamauga and with General Albert Sidney Johnston, the legendary Texan who was killed at the Battle of Shiloh. Littlefield himself was seriously wounded in 1863 at the Battle of Mossy Creek and almost died. He received a battlefield promotion to major, a title that followed him after the war. Before his war wound, Littlefield had briefly returned to Texas, where he married Alice Payne Tillar, a native of Houston. The couple had two children, both of whom died during infancy.

After the war, George Littlefield worked on the family land as he gradually recuperated, but a drought followed by two years of floods in 1869 and 1870 wiped out any farming profits. By 1871 Littlefield began to establish himself in the burgeoning Texas cattle industry—but in a way that set him apart. The common pattern for a cowman in "the trailing business" was to drive other ranchers' cattle, charging by the head. But young Littlefield took the riskier path of buying the cattle that he drove, guaranteeing great profit if the drive were successful and disaster if it were not. His first ranching activities were in the Central Texas counties of Hays and Caldwell, but he soon turned his opportunistic eye to the west. In 1877 he bought water rights along the Canadian River near the panhandle town of Tascosa, and established the LIT Ranch. Four years later he sold the LIT for the astonishing sum of $248,000, making the thirty-nine-year-old a rich man.

Littlefield's ranching associates were loyal family and friends whom he had brought with him from Gonzalez, a tough and opportunistic crew who built

George Washington Littlefield. *From the Prints and Photographs Collection—G. W. Littlefield, Center for American History, the University of Texas at Austin. (DI 02399)*

on their West Texas success for the next thirty years. Key ranching acquisitions came about in eastern New Mexico, where they purchased 15,000 acres. But by purchasing water interests and pioneering the use of windmills to gather water for the stock, Major Littlefield and his associates had effective control of over four million acres of ranch land west of the Pecos River by 1882, the bulk of it lying between Fort Sumner and Roswell. His cattle there carried the LFD brand. His ranching activities in Texas culminated in 1901 with the purchase of the 312,000-acre "Yellow Horse" division of the XIT Ranch in Lamb and Hockley counties. Further major land acquisitions in Mason, Kimble, and Menard counties marked his return to the Hill Country.[7]

Littlefield moved to Austin in 1883, and like Brackenridge in San Antonio, the Major established a bank, this one the American National, originally located in a wing of the Driskill Hotel. The bank moved in 1890 after Littlefield built what is still one of the handsomest buildings in downtown Austin, on the northeast corner of Sixth and Congress. Among the building's notable features were a pair of oversized bronze doors, cast by Tiffany, that depicted cattle and ranch scenes. As successful at banking as he was at ranching, by the end of the century he was one of the wealthiest men in Texas. Although the Major built himself and his wife an imposing red stone mansion right on the edge of campus (the Littlefield home is still a campus landmark), he had little interest in the affairs of the University until a fateful juxtaposition of Board actions by his San Antonio rival-to-be, George Brackenridge, caught his attention.

A CAMPUS ON THE RIVER

By 1910, Brackenridge had been a regent for twenty-four years and the nature of the campus had fundamentally changed. Thanks in part to his dedication and high standards for the University, it was now starting to be competitive with other good southern colleges. An able faculty was being assembled and an important new building designed by the New York architect Cass Gilbert was being built to house the University library. The biggest change was a by-product of this success—by the turn of the century enrollment was edging up close to two thousand. The original plot of land had seemed like an immense space in 1883 when there were fewer than three hundred students and twenty faculty, but now the Forty Acres were becoming packed and residential neighborhoods had grown up on all sides.

George Brackenridge had a bold and generous solution: move the campus to land he would donate to the University down on the banks of the Colorado River. By the first decade of the new century, he had put together five hundred acres on both sides of the river, considerably west of town. Any plans he had for developing this lush acreage for other purposes were changed when the Lake Austin dam broke in 1900, to this day the most destructive natural occurrence in Austin's history. On the other hand, Brackenridge was always quick to see a real estate opportunity and river land was now suddenly very affordable. As the years passed, however, his vision outran his land. Marilyn Sibley describes what happened next:

If he added a few hundred acres and other landowners

could be persuaded to make contributions, the university could have a park-like setting large enough to answer its needs for all time to come. Brackenridge pored over the maps, and the plan for a big campus took more definite shape in his mind. Between his tract and the university lay the estate and antebellum mansion of his old friend Elisha M. Pease. The three heirs of the late governor then owned the property. With their cooperation the campus could become a memorial to the man who as Governor had given life to the idea of the university in 1858 and who, because of his Unionist sympathies, had been denied the honor of serving on the first Board of Regents.[8]

Brackenridge pursued his idea by drawing up plans that combined the existing forty acres with the river acreage. The Pease mansion formed the fulcrum of the extended campus that would run from the present site through what is now Pemberton Heights and all the way down to Town Lake where Exposition Boulevard runs into Lake Austin Boulevard and then west to where Red Bud Trail is now. Eventually a sprawling campus would be centered on a commodious leafy area facing the river. The original forty acres would fade away as the new campus grew, remaining symbolic at best.

George Brackenridge enjoyed his wealth and was determined to advance his idea. When the time came, he brought two of the Pease heirs down to San Antonio in his private rail car. The regent's coachman met Julia Pease and her nephew R. Niles Graham at the railroad station and took them to Brackenridge's mansion, where they enjoyed a formal dinner—the only others present were Brackenridge and his sister Eleanor. Then Brackenridge presented his ambitious idea, spreading out on a big table the blueprints for an imaginary campus. The presentation had its desired effect: "Even after nearly half a century I marvel at the vision he unfolded before us," Graham recalled when he told the story. "The blueprints he exhibited to us revealed the most wonderful vision of what the University campus could be."[9]

Explaining that he planned to give his acreage to initiate the plan and leave the bulk of his fortune to the University in order to develop it, he bluntly asked Pease and Graham if they would donate their legendary family acres to adjoin his own. The regent must have been disappointed when Graham pointed out that both he and his sister were contemplating marriage and that the extensive property was the family's principal asset. Then they flatly turned down Brackenridge's offer to buy the Pease property in order to memorialize the former Texas governor. Undeterred, Brackenridge made a verbal offer of his land at the December 1909 Board of Regents meeting, with the proviso that his river tract could be used only as a new campus. This preliminary idea was favorably received, and at the next meeting, in June 1910, Brackenridge's lawyer presented the Board with a deed to his river land, albeit a deed covered up in restrictions concerning future use—his tract would revert to "the people of Jackson County" if not used by the University for educational purposes. When asked by his lawyer, Leroy Denman, about his reason for the unusual reversionary clause, Brackenridge told the following story that dated back to the middle of the Civil War.

A group of men apprehended Brackenridge late one day during the decline of the Confederacy. They rode him to a lonely place, put a rope around his neck, threw the rope over the limb of a tree, and were preparing to draw the rope tight and drive the horse out from under him.

At that point, one man stepped out and said, "Boys, Brack is a Unionist and he's against sesesh but I ain't ever heard him say he was abolish. I don't believe he's an abolish."

The men discussed this for a while and admitted that no one had ever heard him say he was an abolitionist. With that, they slackened the rope and agreed to let him go provided he left Jackson County before sunup.

> "I left on a good dark horse before dawn and pushed forward with all due haste to the Rio Grande," concluded Brackenridge, "and I have placed this reversionary clause in the deed out of appreciation for the good judgment of the citizens of Jackson County in not drawing that rope taut and not driving the horse out from under me."[10]

Austin was a small town in 1910 (it did not reach 35,000 until the 1920 census) and a prominent citizen like George Littlefield would have heard of Brackenridge's relocation idea immediately. What, you may ask, would Littlefield not like about the plan? The answer is: everything—including losing his close neighbor across 24th Street. Most of all, however, Brackenridge's scheme would have fit perfectly into Littlefield's

southern suspicions about what the University was becoming. First and foremost he would have abhorred any idea that originated as a way to honor Texas governor Elisha M. Pease, a distinguished Texas transplant from Connecticut who was instrumental in establishing the Republic of Texas but who (in Littlefield's world view) became a traitor when he sympathized with the Union, even remaining in the state during the conflict. Adding to Pease's tainted résumé in the eyes of Littlefield and other believers in "the Lost Cause" was his brief appointment as governor during Reconstruction—this at the hands of none other than the victorious Yankee general Philip H. Sheridan. If that were not enough, Pease, along with Brackenridge, was one of the founders of the hated Republican Party.

Much more incendiary to Littlefield in the summer of 1910 was a dissenting Brackenridge vote on a minor matter. The University, always interested in financial support of any kind from any direction, had been approached by the Albert Sidney Johnston Chapter of the United Daughters of the Confederacy about giving an annual prize of twenty-five dollars to the student who wrote the best paper on a southern history topic. This kind of vote, usually automatically approved, received one vote of "no," this from Brackenridge, who commented that he would like the University to not "keep alive" Civil War subjects. Beside the fact that the small bequest by the Daughters could presumably have been awarded to a paper considering any period of southern history, it appears that Brackenridge was at last tired of being the odd Republican Union sympathizer quietly coexisting with the prevailing Democrats to whom the Lost Cause was very real. This "coming out" on his part, however, was to have a galvanizing effect on the University's wealthy neighbor on the northwestern edge of campus.

REGENT LITTLEFIELD AND PROFESSOR BARKER

A new Texas governor, O. B. Colquitt, named George Littlefield to the University of Texas Board of Regents, with his term to commence with the January 1911 meeting. Littlefield's biographer, J. Evetts Haley, describes what happened next:

> Littlefield came to the Governor's office and told Colquitt that while he would very much like to serve

he would have to decline, as he could not serve with Brackenridge, whom the Governor had reappointed. Colquitt countered with the University's need for him, mentioned the fact that the institution had a great potential endowment in land from which it had been receiving little return, and insisted that, as Littlefield was a cowman versed in the values of land, he wanted him on the board particularly for this reason. Likewise Colquitt must have explained then, as he did later, that he did not want to reappoint Brackenridge, but that "the University bunch wanted him very much." Perhaps this raised the Major's temperature a little, and he must have reasoned that Texans should not surrender, even to a peaceful infiltration of Yankees, without a struggle, and he accepted the appointment. (*George W. Littlefield,* pp. 219–220)

Meanwhile Brackenridge, the hero to the University bunch, realized his awkward position, and having just celebrated his twenty-fifth year on the Board, tendered his resignation, much to the relief of Governor Colquitt and the delight of the Major. In another year Brackenridge would turn eighty.

True to Governor Colquitt's promise, Littlefield was given the assignment of looking after the University's West Texas lands, replacing Brackenridge as head of the Land Committee. Having no particular interest in general campus matters, Littlefield began to examine closely the way that the University taught the subject he cared about deeply: the history of the American sectional conflicts that led to the Civil War, the War itself, and the hated period of Reconstruction. Littlefield was active in Texas' Confederate veterans organizations, and a major concern of these focused groups was the way that history books presented "the recent unpleasantness," by then almost fifty years past. Specifically, what obsessed Littlefield and other old Confederates were the versions of the Civil War and its aftermath that appeared in high school and college textbooks. It took a clever professor of history to transform the Major's potentially meddling interest in academic content into an act of philanthropy that still benefits the University of Texas.

The story goes that almost immediately upon taking his position on the board, Major Littlefield wrote a letter of inquiry to Eugene C. Barker, the new chair of the History Department, bluntly expressing his concern that prejudiced northern historians wrote the history of the Confederacy and the Civil War that was be-

Professor Eugene C. Barker. *From the Prints and Photographs Collection—Eugene C. Barker, Center for American History, the University of Texas at Austin. (DI 02406)*

ing taught in Texas. Another professor, so approached, might have deflected the question, or otherwise avoided the issue. But that was not Professor Barker's way. On December 5, 1912, Barker wrote Major Littlefield a letter that not only responded to his concern but suggested a clear solution: to create a research repository at Texas for the study of the South that would be unequaled.

The accumulation of historical material in northern libraries has attracted to the universities of the North the greatest historical scholars and teachers of America. And the teachers and libraries have drawn the students. From the period of the Revolution to the Civil War Yale and Harvard were the finishing schools of educated southern men; and today, fifty years after the close of the Civil War, Johns Hopkins University of Baltimore is the only southern institution whose graduate degrees command the respect of well informed students and scholars. It is worthy of thought that Johns Hopkins University is the offspring of a private benefaction and not of the civic pride of the South.

The historians of the younger generation are honest. Many of them are absolutely without conscious sectional bias. They try to discover the truth and write it fairly and accurately. But the historian must draw his conclusions from the material that he has at hand. Generally he has not the financial means to travel through all the states searching for scraps of information here and there; and even if he has the money to do so he certainly hasn't the time. As a result, he goes to the libraries which have the largest collections and does most of his studying there.

The remedy for the situation is perfectly simple. In the last analysis it is merely a matter of money to collect the historical materials of the South, and time to use them. Until this collection is made the resolutions and protests of patriotic societies against the misrepresentation of the South are "as sounding brass and tinkling cymbals."

I write this to you because I know your interest in the subject, and because you are a Regent of the University. I believe that there are wealthy men in the South—in Texas—who would be glad to provide the means for making an adequate collection of southern materials if the matter were properly brought to their attention. Frankly, I hope that this subject will appeal to you.[11]

Barker's eloquent plea ended with a suggestion for an endowed professorship in addition to funds to seed a research collection "so that Texas would then begin to remove from the South the reproach of neglecting its own history."

Perhaps Barker sensed that Littlefield would appreciate plain talk—it does appear that by not underestimating the Major, Barker carried the day. He must have also sensed that the new regent always preferred action to complaining. Littlefield was nothing if not competitive and he soon wanted figures from the professor and the librarians about how to catch up with the northern libraries. What Barker reported back to Littlefield confirmed his letter. He learned that the University of Wisconsin spent $8,000 a year on American history materials for their collections, whereas UT was spending $500 "for books in all fields of history." In a survey of southern schools, he reported on other state universities: North Carolina spent about $300 on

southern history; Mississippi, $400; Georgia and LSU about $100; and Florida, only $10 to $15 a year on all of American history. By March 1914, Littlefield was ready to proceed, writing Barker:

No one would appreciate the building up of a Southern History collection more than myself. My whole life has been in the South, having given four of the best years of my life for the protection of our Southland. I am anxious to see something done that will begin the foundation for acquiring a history, in which the South will be accorded her just rights.[12]

In a final display of prescience, Professor Barker persuaded Littlefield to not just donate $25,000 to be spent over a five-year period, but to present the money gift to the Board of Regents as a trust, with the income used to purchase southern materials.

Much has been written about the accumulated riches of the Littlefield Collection, but for the purposes of our story, we can say that from the very beginning the library collecting using the fund was aggressive and broad-gauged, in the sense that a wide definition was given to the accumulation of materials relevant to the study of the South. In an early report on the uses of the fund, the University librarian remarked: "The literature for the history of the South is only in part a separate literature, and in building up a research library to satisfy the needs of the investigator the history of the whole country is quickly involved."[13] Regent Littlefield would have read this report that suggested that the study of the South at Texas would not be a parochial enterprise.

The first seven years of the fund have been characterized as a heroic period in collecting. This was true for two reasons: first, because the University had a superb "University Bibliographer," E. W. Winkler, who knew the book trade inside and out; second, because this was a perfect time to have some money to buy books and archives. Winkler estimated that over eleven thousand volumes were purchased using the fund between 1914 and 1921. Individual items were cheap—one 1917 invoice of forty-nine books and pamphlets totaled $53.20. But it was the other items that gave distinction to the Collection—these included a tremendous run of Charleston newspapers that sold for $5,750 and, surprisingly, runs of papers from the northern United States that trace the onset of war from the non-southern perspective. As might be anticipated, this swift

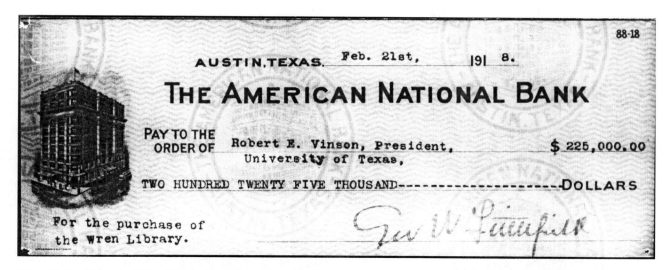

Littlefield's personal check that purchased the Wrenn Collection. *From the Prints and Photographs Collection–UT Libraries: Rare Books, Center for American History, the University of Texas at Austin. (DI 02420)*

beginning called for more money, and the Major was happy to oblige. During this period he personally came forth with an additional $40,000.

To administer the trust, Littlefield named a committee that consisted of an officer of the American National Bank, a professor of history (Barker), the state librarian, the University librarian, and the president of the University, "or their successors in office." The board of the Littlefield Fund for Southern History has a similar configuration today. In 1918, it must have seemed as though Eugene Barker's conversion of the tough businessman to the cause of books had become evangelical when Major Littlefield wrote a $225,000 personal check to buy for the University the library of John Henry Wrenn, a Chicago banker who had accumulated a choice collection of over six thousand rare English and American books and pamphlets. Littlefield contributed an additional $5,000 to build a paneled library to house the Wrenn books.[14]

Major Littlefield's tenure as regent lasted a decade, and half of those years were marked by the greatest disruptions in the University's history. The man who appointed Littlefield in 1911, Governor O. B. Colquitt, had begun to turn against higher education, partly as a result of a bitter feud with the president of Texas A&M. Colquitt's housecleaning of the regents at both state schools appeared to lead him to think that his control over the campuses would follow, but the governor was surprised at the resistance to his actions both at A&M and at the University of Texas, just down the street

from the Governor's Mansion. In the end-game of his feud with A&M, Colquitt vetoed the entire higher education appropriations bill in June 1913. The UT president at that time was Sidney Mezes, who was away in Washington, working with his brother-in-law Edward M. House to plan Woodrow Wilson's presidential campaign. Mezes immediately began a circular letter to his colleagues on the Austin campus and to friends of the University across the state, pointing out that if the funds did indeed disappear, the University would have to close its doors by 1915. Although the cause of the University had wide support across the state and the Colquitt veto failed, Mezes stepped down from his presidency, just as A&M's president had. Mezes went on to serve with distinction as president of the City College of New York until 1927.

ROBERT A. VINSON

If University politics were simmering under Governor Colquitt, the pot began to boil over when his successor, James E. Ferguson, was elected. George Littlefield had helped elect the Bell County populist, fully subscribing to his anti-prohibitionist and economic positions designed to help the farmers and working men against landlords and other symbols of oppression.

In meeting the acting president of the University, Dr. W. J. Battle, Farmer Jim encountered his opposite number in every way. Dr. Battle, a gentlemanly scholar

James E. Ferguson. *From the Prints and Photographs Collection—James Edward Ferguson, Center for American History, the University of Texas at Austin. (DI 02430)*

Robert E. Vinson. *From the Prints and Photographs Collection—Rev. R. E. Vinson, Center for American History, the University of Texas at Austin. (DI 02400)*

of classics, might have confused the blustery Ferguson with his quiet approach to negotiating the University's budget, but he did not back down. When Ferguson commenced his full assault on the University, he expected support from George Littlefield, but in the end, Littlefield appears to have taken his oath as a regent quite seriously. Nothing illustrates this loyalty better than the Board's independent decision that named Robert Vinson president of the University.

When Battle did not yield to the governor's wishes, Ferguson demanded his resignation. Battle refused to submit his resignation, but let it be known to the regents that he would not be a candidate for the permanent position when their search began. Governor Ferguson had a candidate: R. L. Batts, who at the moment was living in Pennsylvania and was general counsel for the Gulf Oil Corporation. Ferguson made this contact through another Woodrow Wilson connection, T. W. Gregory, who was attorney general of the United States. But while Ferguson was trying to line up Batts, the Texas regents went ahead and named Robert E.

Vinson as president, much to Ferguson's displeasure.

It is hard to imagine a more unlikely hero to step into a very hot political environment than Robert E. Vinson. He was a University outsider who had served eight years as president of Austin Theological Seminary, just north of the University campus. A Presbyterian minister, Vinson was the unanimous choice of the regents and a particular favorite of Major Littlefield, who knew him as a neighbor and as an eloquent preacher. Vinson's pitched battle with Jim Ferguson is not our story here, but the bottom line of that narrative is that Vinson, backed by a strong Board of Regents and an organized group of Texas ex-students, prevailed when the governor faltered.[15] What should be pointed out, however, is that Vinson would not have been strong enough to engage in what became known as the "bear fight" with the governor (who dismissed Vinson as "a silver-tongued preacher") without the help of Regent Littlefield and a reactivated George Brackenridge, who by 1916 was eighty-four years old.

Although he was Littlefield's choice to be president,

Marilyn Sibley points out that "Vinson took care not to be marked by the Littlefield brand."[16] As if to demonstrate this, Vinson quickly accepted George Brackenridge's summons to meet him in San Antonio. After being reassured that Vinson had no narrow Presbyterian designs on the University, the two hit it off famously, speculating on philosophical matters for hours at a time. Vinson returned often to spend time with Brackenridge, becoming one of the old man's favorite companions. The University president also became a believer in Brackenridge's vision to move the campus down to the Colorado River.

When it came to the University, Jim Ferguson was something of a one-trick pony. After an initial meeting with Vinson (accompanied by Littlefield) before the new president was inaugurated, the governor presented him with an enemies list of campus men that he wanted fired. Leading the list was Professor Battle, who had stood up to Ferguson when he was acting president, and John Lomax, who headed an ex-students association that the governor regarded as a threat. Vinson did not act on the governor's demand, and several months later he requested that the governor bring specific charges against the half-dozen faculty and staff. Ferguson retorted, "I am the governor of Texas, I don't have to give reasons." Relations between the governor and the campus continued to deteriorate, and by the fall of 1916, Ferguson was calling for Vinson's dismissal, just as he had Battle's. Once again, the governor's big stick was a threatened veto of the entire University budget. Marilyn Sibley describes a tense meeting of a small group of regents with Vinson, in which Vinson turned to George Littlefield and asked him what he would do in his place:

> But as both Littlefield and Vinson recalled, Littlefield did not urge a course of action. Rather he stated the alternatives. If Vinson resigned, the governor would not file the veto of the appropriation bill; if Vinson remained, then the university faced the prospect of closing its doors for lack of funds.
>
> "Major, put yourself in my place and tell me frankly what sort of answer you would make if faced with the same alternative," Vinson said after hearing Littlefield out.
>
> "I would tell him to go to hell," Littlefield responded . . .

Vinson's answer was a spirited, "Major Littlefield

. . . the only way that you'll get me out of the presidency of the University is to plant your foot between my coattails and kick me out."[17]

Faced with almost certain defunding of the University, Vinson then turned to the old hero of the University bunch, George Brackenridge. Without hesitation, Vinson called on Brackenridge to ask him if he could step up if Ferguson followed through on his threat. Vinson also bluntly asked Brackenridge if he could underwrite the University's budget for the next two years. Vinson later remembered that Brackenridge promised to do so "even to the extent of his entire fortune." Brackenridge then had a wicked suggestion: that Vinson also approach Littlefield to see if he would share the burden with his old Yankee antagonist. By then, Brackenridge must have been well aware that Littlefield's assets far exceeded his own—decades of philanthropy had taken their toll on the San Antonio banker's fortune. In the end, Littlefield welcomed the challenge, picking his University president over his governor, but in the end, neither regents' offer was necessary—the Texas attorney general ruled Ferguson's veto illegal on a technicality.

So in the end it was Robert E. Vinson who perhaps knew the personalities of Brackenridge and Littlefield best, or at least he wrote about them best. In December 1939, Vinson spoke to the Texas Philosophical Society at the Hall of State in Dallas. Vinson had left Austin in 1923 to become president of Case Western Reserve University in Cleveland and had retired from there in 1933. His talk in Dallas, titled "The University Crosses the Bar," was a look back at his presidency of UT, his conflict with Ferguson, and also a warm portrait of his two heroes, George Brackenridge and George Littlefield. He began speaking of his debt to the two, describing them as "on or off the Board my confidants, advisers and helpers."

> Both were strong men, self-reliant, capable. Both grew up with the State of Texas, had far-sighted vision of and confidence in its progress and profited, materially, to an unusual degree from their shrewd judgments of its values. They were exact opposites. I trust it may not be indelicate for me to say now, that their dislike for each other was profound. There was between them a personal antagonism which I can only explain by saying it had its roots in the Civil War and the period of reconstruction that followed. Each of them seemed

to regard the other as the representative, if not the embodiment, of the principles which had once driven the nation asunder. Any yielding of one to the other would have been regarded by both as a surrender of the principles for which they had stood and fought. It was not easy to know these men . . . Once their defenses were penetrated one found in both of them a wealth of sentiment and richness of personality more than sufficient to compensate for the efforts expended in their discovery. It fell to my fortunate lot to know them both well.

Then Vinson summarized the two personalities:

One was primarily a man of thought, the other a man of action. One always wanted to know the explanation and meaning of things, the other the best method to do things. Mr. Brackenridge was by instinct a scholar. His mental companions were Charles Darwin, Alfred Russell Wallace, Thomas Henry Huxley, Herbert Spencer, John Tyndall, and curiously enough, Isaiah and Paul. He read them and as he used to say "quarreled with them" every day . . . In his later years he impressed me as laboring under a feeling of disappointment, if not frustration, as though life had played a trick upon him and had by some means kept him from the fulfillment of his most cherished desires. He was a good business man, but business was a side issue with him, apart from the world in which he really lived.

Major Littlefield, on the other hand, lived and died in the world and in the work he loved. The men who were Mr. Brackenridge's familiars were but names to Major Littlefield, if that. He is rather to be classed with men who carve empires out of the wilderness, who make the desert to rejoice and blossom as the rose, who push against the horizon. He was busy to the last, always conscious of the generations pressing up behind him, for whom he was making preparation. When Mr. Brackenridge spoke of the University of Texas he always emphasized the word University. Major Littlefield emphasized the word Texas. One was primarily concerned with the policies of the institution, the other with the people whom it served.[18]

The final act of their great rivalry would also be presided over by Robert Vinson.

TWO WILLS

Robert Vinson and the University survived the Ferguson scare, due in some large part to the loyalty and force of George Littlefield and to the always generous-minded George Brackenridge. Vinson's other great test as University president overlapped with the Ferguson crisis—this was America's entrance into World War I. By 1917, the campus was being transformed in two ways: first by the exodus of male students joining up, and secondly by the construction of military barracks to house military trainees. Littlefield, the unreconstructed rebel, was totally behind his country in the Great War, and, when Vinson faced delays in building the barracks, Littlefield personally loaned the University construction money. The University's dedication to the war effort was so strong that Walter Long of the Austin Chamber of Commerce observed, "Had the Kaiser known that Major Littlefield and Bob Vinson were going to gang up against him, he would perhaps never have invaded Belgium" (Walter Long, *For All Time to Come*, p. 40).

Governor William P. Hobby reappointed George Brackenridge as a Texas regent in 1917, and in his meetings with Vinson the old regent talked of little else but moving the campus to the river tract. If anything, his idea had grown over the years—he now envisioned a campus of fifteen hundred acres, five hundred of which would be his plot by the river. He proposed using his own money to piece together the rest of the property. Brackenridge's dream fell on receptive ears: Vinson was acutely aware of the physical limitations of the forty acres, particularly after the construction of the military barracks. However, both men knew that Littlefield was dead set against the plan. Brackenridge was fixed on the idea of the Pease property being the center of his campus, and Littlefield still viewed Pease as a traitor to the Lost Cause and grouped this idea together with Brackenridge's slight of southern history. More important, Brackenridge realized that Major Littlefield was reaching ever greater heights as a University donor (remember, Littlefield bought the Wrenn Collection in 1918) and decided that he and Vinson should discuss the river tract move discreetly. It was at this point that Littlefield began to talk publicly about his own dream for the campus, which was to have an archway at the entrance to the South Mall, with the mall itself lined with sculptures of some of his personal heroes.

In 1919 Brackenridge retired from the Board a second time and Littlefield also left because his health was failing. In her biography of Brackenridge, Marilyn Sibley makes it clear that President Vinson and George Brackenridge were essentially waiting for Littlefield's death before they formally proceeded with initiating the big campus move. Vinson was so confident in the move's eventual success that he commissioned Austin Chamber of Commerce head Walter Long to purchase options on the properties adjoining Brackenridge's river tract. When Littlefield did die in his mansion on November 10, 1920, Vinson and Brackenridge were prepared:

> Littlefield's death was the signal for which Vinson and Brackenridge had waited. Littlefield died on Wednesday, was buried on Friday, and on Monday, in something that approached indecent haste, Brackenridge again took his seat on the Board of Regents. A meeting of the board was promptly scheduled to meet at Brackenridge's home on 5 January, and it was an ill-kept secret that foremost on the agenda was the proposal to move the university to the river tract.[19]

What neither the president nor the surviving regent anticipated was the language contained in the Major's will, revealed a few days later. According to the Haley biography, Littlefield had drafted his will in July 1918, replacing a 1912 document that very likely had not left important assets to the University. Sibley describes the principal features of the Major's will as it would affect the University. It appears to have been airtight:

> But Brackenridge and Vinson had reckoned without Major Littlefield . . . Obviously anticipating their action after his departure, he had taken effective means to thwart them. He left over $1 million in assets to the University that either would be lost entirely or reduced in usefulness if the campus were moved.
>
> He willed $500,000 for the construction of a main building, "same to be constructed on the campus now used and occupied by the said University and nowhere else." This gift, moreover, was to be made only on the condition that the Board of Regents pass a resolution "that the location of the University should not be removed from its present position in the City of Austin,

Texas." In addition, he provided for a girls' dormitory, costing as much as $300,000, to be constructed on lots he owned adjoining the campus. The dormitory was to be built and then deeded to the university, "such deed to provide that the property shall revert to my estate if the Main University shall within 21 years after my death be changed from its present location near my home in Austin, Texas." He left $200,000 for the erection of "a massive bronze arch over the south entrance to the campus of the University of Texas"; and only hours before he died he threw in one last incentive to peg down the university on its original site. He gave his mansion adjoining the campus to the university, subject to Mrs. Littlefield's life interest.[20]

And Littlefield did not forget his wife and extended family nor the southern history fund—he left an additional $100,000 "for the purpose of the preparation and publication of a history of the United States with the plain facts concerning the South." J. Evetts Haley describes Littlefield's will as being a kind of summation:

> No document among the tens of thousands he was responsible for preserving so thoroughly illustrates the measure of Littlefield's character and mind as his last will and testament. His careful regard for a future that he would not share, his concern for the many children who were nearest to being his own, his loyalty to people and to province, his hope for the perpetuity of the story of the South, his desire for the immortality of the Littlefield name, and his refusal to risk anything of his own, even though he was dead, to the faulty judgment, frailty, perverseness, or cupidity of others—all of these are illustrated in this remarkable document.[21]

The revelation of the contents of Littlefield's will appears to have precipitated a sinking spell in George Brackenridge. Only he knew that his fortune had dwindled, and that his estate would perhaps total only $1.5 million, including his mansion, its furnishings, and such luxury items as his private rail car. By the first week in December, Brackenridge became very ill himself. His close friend Robert Vinson visited him in San Antonio for three days in the middle of the month, and their conversations always led back to Brackenridge's own will, a dated document that included several codicils handwritten by Brackenridge. Although Bracken- ridge was in turmoil about his diminished means, he did not share this with Vinson, who was still brim- ming with enthusiasm over the prospects of a river campus, in spite of Major Littlefield's parting wishes. Vinson left San Antonio thinking that Brackenridge would have a new will in place.

George Brackenridge died quietly on December 28, less than two months after George Littlefield. Presi- dent Vinson's plan for the new campus continued apace—the plan was now public knowledge and many of the legislators convening in Austin in January also knew of it. On January 5, 1921, there was a totally er- roneous story in the Austin paper that ran under the headline "University Gets Brackenridge Fortune." The story speculated that the size of the fortune was more than $3 million. But when the will was probated on January 17, there was no mention of the Univer- sity at all, just vague language about some monies left for "educational purposes." The handwritten changes that Brackenridge had made over the years were con- tradictory in some instances—this only added to the confusion.

Robert Vinson flew in the face of these portents and became the spokesman for the campus move at the legislature. There was a lot of support for the idea, and then, as is often the way with Texas politics, the plan started to backfire. It wasn't long before traditional en- emies of the university began broadening the concept of the campus moving to the Brackenridge Tract to the concept of the University moving from Austin. The impeached former governor Jim Ferguson was delight- ed to chime in, suggesting that the University move up to Bosque County. This unforeseen development backed Vinson into a corner as the spokesman for leav- ing the forty acres, and soon the president became the most hated man in Austin, whose citizens very much wanted to hold on to the University. Vinson was even blamed for the erroneous story that ran in the Austin newspaper. In truth, Vinson believed in the idea of the move and believed that Brackenridge would be coming forth with millions to make it possible. Many thought that Vinson accepted the presidency of Case Western Reserve University because he had worn out his wel- come at UT.

TWO LEGACIES

If you look at the rivalry between George Bracken- ridge and George Littlefield as a competition to de- termine the location of the campus, there is no doubt that Littlefield won, leaving Brackenridge's dream of a leafy campus on the lake as the University's greatest "what if." There is also no doubt that the University after 1920 carries Littlefield's mark the deepest, with the Littlefield Dormitory, Littlefield Mansion, and the Main Building still important campus landmarks. The Major's dream of a grand entrance to the campus facing south was partially realized by the construction of the Littlefield Fountain on 21st Street (a surreal World War I memorial designed by Pompeo Coppini) and by the large statues of notable men lining either side of the South Mall. These are of some of Littlefield's heroes: President of the Confederacy Jefferson Davis, Confed- erate generals Albert Sidney Johnston and Robert E. Lee, Texas senator John H. Reagan and governor James Stephen Hogg, and President Woodrow Wilson. The University chose George Washington to be represented at the top center of the grouping.

Littlefield's on-going contribution, however, is one that is at the heart of the scholarly enterprise: his sup- port of the University libraries. His stunning purchase, in 1918, of the Wrenn Collection laid the foundation for the University's deep and distinguished rare books programs, brought to fruition forty years later by Harry Ransom. Reaching even further, though, has been the on-going Littlefield Fund for Southern History. The library career of E. W. Winkler continued until his partial retirement in 1945, but he continued working as University Bibliographer until close to his death in 1960. His forty-five years of collection-building in American and Latin American history[22] stretched back to working with G. W. Littlefield and Eugene Barker in the second decade of the century and marked the University with excellence.

Fifty years after the passing of Littlefield and Brack- enridge, the Main Library was squeezed into the stacks in the Tower and bursting at the seams. In 1971 I joined a group of brand-new librarians who were given the assignments of building the collections in the Main Library and tending to them in a number of ways (in some real sense this might be seen as needing six peo- ple to replace E. W. Winkler). My biggest area was his- tory, and this placed me in proximate distance of the Littlefield Fund for Southern History. Gradually the richness of the Littlefield Collection dawned on me, but its power as a collection was muted by its invisibility. This was due to a specific request on the part of Major Littlefield, namely, that the contents of the southern history collection be distributed throughout the campus libraries so that the average student could come across them in the course of his or her studies. This populist idea was faithfully carried out by generations of Littlefield Fund board members and librarians, with the result being that there is no Littlefield Collection as a physical entity. The only thing that identifies a book or document as one purchased by the fund is a book plate and a separate cataloging entry that is not available to the public. The overriding result is that the Littlefield Collection is hiding in plain sight: materials on southern literature were cataloged in the American literature sections, while the same is true for the southern history materials—the quirks of the cataloging systems determined where even a very rare item might be. Even more cryptic is the practice of locating other southern subjects around the different campus libraries—southern music and southern art in the Fine Arts Library, a biography of a southern botanist in the Biology Library, and so on.

Some of the abundance of Littlefield's library legacy became clear to me in 1976 and 1977 when the Tower library prepared to move to the new Perry-Castañeda Library. Since the PCL was to have open stacks, some thought was given to identifying rare materials in the closed-stack Tower library, which would be relocated before the move. Just in the ranges of library call numbers dealing with slavery, I came across a treasure trove of rare items that had been bought during the Winkler years using the Littlefield Fund. The literature of slavery is largely the literature of antislavery—the hundreds and hundreds of pamphlets, broadsides, periodicals, and books written by anonymous and named individuals in Great Britain and America that argued against "the peculiar institution" during the eighteenth and nineteenth centuries. Nestled in the Dewey Decimal shelves were scores of beautifully printed English pamphlets published in the 1760s, 1770s, and 1780s—for the most part, they were abolitionist tracts. Not far away on the shelf was this item:

Argument of John Quincy Adams: before the Supreme Court of the United States, in the case of the United States, appellants, vs. Cinque, and others, Africans, captured in the Schooner Armistad, by Lieut. Ged-

A

LETTER

ADDRESSED TO

THE LIVERPOOL SOCIETY

FOR PROMOTING

THE ABOLITION OF SLAVERY,

ON

THE INJURIOUS EFFECTS OF HIGH PRICES OF PRODUCE,

AND

THE BENEFICIAL EFFECTS OF LOW PRICES,

ON

THE CONDITION OF SLAVES.

By JAMES CROPPER.

LIVERPOOL:

Printed by James Smith:

PUBLISHED BY HATCHARD & SON, PICCADILLY, AND J. & J. ARCH, CORNHILL, LONDON; SOLD BY W. GRAPEL, CHURCH-STREET, AND G. & J. ROBINSON, CASTLE-STREET, LIVERPOOL.

1823.

Title page of an antislavery pamphlet purchased using the Littlefield Fund for Southern History. *From the Littlefield Southern History Collection, Center for American History, the University of Texas at Austin. (DI 02394) ney, delivered on the 24th of February and 1st of March, 1841; with a review of the case of the Antelope, reported in the 10th, 11th, and 12th volumes of Wheaton's reports. (New York. S. W. Benedict, 1841)*

Close by this small landmark in American jurisprudence were many representative Fourth of July orations, all with antislavery messages, published in places like Philadelphia, Boston, and Syracuse, New York. All of the pieces were marked with the bookplate of the Littlefield Collection. What amounted to one of the strongest American collections of antislavery rarities was made possible by the use of monies provided by Major Littlefield, who as a boy was raised on a plantation, a boy who had inherited slaves himself.

When I began adding to the Littlefield Collection, my quandary was that the library already had virtually every scarce southern book, pamphlet, and broadside. But the southern history fund had an annual income of over $10,000 and buying an occasional privately printed book of Georgia poetry or a small-town church cookbook from South Carolina wasn't putting much of a dent in such a handsome balance. The 1970s and early 1980s were an ambitious period for academic libraries and there were a number of reprints and archives available on microfilm that fit the collection. Some of the records of the Civil Rights groups were now available and we managed to add extensive archives on microforms from groups like the National Association for the Advancement of Colored People (NAACP) and the Student Non-Violent Coordinating Committee (SNNC) to Major Littlefield's collection. This was the cutting edge of the political history of the South during the previous twenty years, and it seemed no more counter to the intentions of what George Littlefield was about than the riches I saw when looking through the antislavery literature that had been gathered in previous decades. The distinguished southern historian and bibliographer Barnes Lathrop was on the faculty during my tenure in the UT libraries and we worked in close collaboration.

The University's most notable library purchase in American history since that move was the acquisition of the Natchez Trace Collection in 1986. This great accumulation of Mississippi Valley plantation records, hand-drawn maps, extensive runs of newspapers, personal and family letters, and governmental and official publications that had been stored in Natchez slave cabins and moved to the Center for American History

complemented what was already in place, put together through the auspices of the Littlefield Fund. The Natchez Trace Collection was like a capstone placed on top of a great construction.[23]

George Brackenridge's tangible legacy on the twenty-first-century campus has all but disappeared, but in a real sense Brackenridge was a figure of the founding years of the University that preceded Littlefield. There was no place on campus more important to the spirit of the University during its years than B. Hall, and like many other of Brackenridge's ideas, his support of female students was decades ahead of its time. There was a reason he was beloved by the progressive elements that governors Colquitt and Ferguson derisively called "the University bunch." It was George Brackenridge's steady hand and quiet example that had helped create a college of excellence by the later era when Major Littlefield began to participate in campus matters. Brackenridge's confusing will was contested by some of his nephews and nieces and a 1913 draft with its handwritten changes was not fully probated until after his sister Mary Eleanor's death in 1924. The will finally resulted in the creation of the Brackenridge Foundation, the first major family foundation in Texas and one that focuses on college scholarships for high school graduates of Bexar County. As to the land by the Colorado River, it is still there, still maintained by the University. It is a great irony that two years after Brackenridge's death, the first rumblings of West Texas oil in the Permian Basin were heard. Brackenridge's steady stewardship of the remote lands finally began to pay off. If Brackenridge (and Vinson) had been able to hang on a few more years, his dream of moving the campus might have become a reality.

Indeed, ironies abound in this story of the two powerful regents. George Littlefield, the man of action, leaves as his lasting legacies two different library projects that have cast a long shadow, building the University a national and international reputation as a research center. George Brackenridge, who ran out of money before he could effectuate his dream, set in motion the University's lands program that enabled it to take full advantage of the oil discoveries when they began. Littlefield, an unlettered man, leaves as his last will a closely written masterpiece. The bookish and thorough George Brackenridge leaves a will that is a hodge-podge of handwritten codicils that led to confusion.

Both men attempted to control the future, always

a doubtful enterprise. Brackenridge's property restrictions are still talked about by UT System attorneys. Not only does the Brackenridge Tract on Town Lake revert to the citizens of Jackson County if not used for University purposes, Brackenridge Park, in the heart of San Antonio, reverts to the University of Texas if there is any evidence of liquor being consumed on its huge grounds. Brackenridge, in line with his Republican Party, was a strict prohibitionist, although he maintained a fine wine cellar and entertained his guests with whiskey drinks. The anti-prohibitionist Littlefield was known to drink a ceremonial glass of champagne, but other than that was a teetotaler.

If character is fate, our two George Washingtons present quite a study. Littlefield grew up in a plantation culture that incorporated slave labor, and in his last years supported both the memory of the Lost Cause and was known as a soft touch for many aging Confederates. If you completely subscribe to J. Evetts Haley's portrait of the Major (I don't recommend doing so) you see a man who never overcame a sentimental attachment to a plantation owner's fairy tale of happy slaves who were left bereft by emancipation. If you look at the evidence, however, Littlefield appears to have become a westerner more than a southerner at the end, with his fortune being accumulated in West Texas and New Mexico. Although there was a Klan presence on the Texas campus in the second decade of the twentieth century,[24] there is no evidence that Littlefield was a member. Moreover, his openness to the solid ideas of scholarship as presented to him by Eugene Barker and Robert Vinson show us a man ready to embrace the future.

If Littlefield appears free of self-doubt and steadily moving forward at all times, his counterpart Brackenridge is a study in introspection and, in the end, entropy. If Littlefield embraced his trial by fire as a young officer in the Confederacy, Brackenridge never freed himself from the label of war profiteer—in fact his warmest memory of that tumultuous time appears to have been that of not being strung up by a lynch mob so that he could run away. The depression that Robert Vinson sensed in him shortly before he died may have been a final acknowledgement that if he had lost the battle for the future of the campus, there was no sense in changing his will. The University did name a new men's residence for him in 1932: Brackenridge Hall. Just about the only other trace of Brackenridge left on the present campus is an oil painting of him hanging outside the old regents meeting room on the second floor of the Main Building. Beneath the portrait are these words:

George Washington Brackenridge, 1832–1920
First Great Benefactor
Champion of Educative Progress
Free of Partisan Politics and Sectarian Religion
Long Time Regent

Although the portrait is handsomely painted and framed, it is hung in a dimly lit alcove that visitors seldom visit.

NOTES

1. See Marilyn Sibley's *George W. Brackenridge, Maverick Philanthropist* (University of Texas Press, pp. 37–71).

2. The mystery surrounding James Bates' estate and burial is discussed in Sibley's *George W. Brackenridge*, pp. 49–50. It does appear that Bates, who was the love of Eleanor Brackenridge's life, may have misplaced his trust in the Brackenridge family.

3. *Alcalde* 5 (April 1927), 480–86.

4. *Brackenridge*, p. 175.

5. Ibid.

6. J. Evetts Haley, *George W. Littlefield, Texan* (University of Oklahoma Press), 1943, p. 8.

7. For a thorough discussion of Littlefield's ranching career, see David B. Gracy II, "George Washington Littlefield: Portrait of a Cattleman," *Southwestern Historical Quarterly*, 68, no. 2 (Oct., 1964): 237–258.

8. *George W. Brackenridge*, p. 188.

9. Ibid., p. 189.

10. Ibid., p. 54.

11. E. C. Barker to G. W. Littlefield, December 5, 1912, Barker Papers, Center for American History. As quoted in Haley's *George W. Littlefield, Texan*, pp. 259–260.

12. Littlefield to Barker, March 17, 1914, Barker Papers, Center for American History, quoted in Haley, *George W. Littlefield*, p. 261.

13. "For the Study of the South," by Barnes F. Lathrop, *Texas Quarterly*, 1, no. 2: 158.

14. Soon the Wrenn Collection became better known for its literary forgeries than for its fine bindings. The forger was an English bookseller named T. J. Wise, and John Henry Wrenn was the victim. In 1944, the University's rare books librarian Fannie E. Ratchford published *Letters of Thomas J. Wise to John Henry Wrenn: A Further Inquiry Into the Guilt of Certain Nineteenth Century Forgers* (New York, Alfred A. Knopf, 1944). The first chapter describes Littlefield's role in the purchase of the Wrenn Collection.

15. For a detailed account of Ferguson's battles with the University, see Lewis L. Gould, "The University Becomes Politicized: The War With Jim Ferguson, 1915–1918," *Southwestern Historical Quarterly*, 86, no. 2 (October 1982): pp. 255–276.

16. *George W. Brackenridge*, p. 227.

17. Ibid., pp. 233–34.

18. "The University Crosses the Bar," *Southwestern Historical Quarterly*, vol. 43, no. 3 (January 1940), pp. 283–84.

19. Sibley, *George W. Brackenridge*, p. 244

20. Ibid., pp. 244–45.

21. Haley, *George W. Littlefield*, p. 271.

22. In addition to his groundbreaking collection-building in southern and U.S. history, in 1921 Winkler appraised and purchased the Genaro Garcia Collection, the fundamental building block for what is now the Nettie Lee Benson Latin American Collection.

23. For descriptions of the contents of the Littlefield Collection through the mid-twentieth century, see Barnes F. Lathrop, "For the Study of the South," *The Texas Quarterly*, 1, no. 2 (spring, 1958): 157–166. See also "The Littlefield Fund for Southern History: Cataloged Books and Pamphlets on the Negro, Slavery and the Civil War," by Thomas Frank Harwood, *The Library Chronicle of the University of Texas*, 6, no. 2 (spring, 1958: 3–15.)

For a partial checklist of Littlefield Collection pamphlets, see *Slavery and the American War; Pamphlets in the Littlefield Collection for Southern History, University of Texas at Austin*, compiled by Mary Sue Neilson and Richard Holland (1987). There are two cataloged copies in the Perry-Castañeda Library and two in the Center for American History.

For the best overview of southern history at the University libraries, see "Southern History Resources at the Center For American History," at: www.cah.utexas.edu/guides/southern.html. This on-line guide includes a good description of both the archival contents of the Littlefield Collection and of the Natchez Trace Collection.

24. UT law professor William S. Simkins had founded the Florida KKK and joined the Texas faculty in 1899. He delivered an address praising the Klan on the Texas campus every year on Thanksgiving Day. Judge Simkins' entry in *The Handbook of Texas* describes him as "the most colorful character ever connected with the law school."

DAVID
DETTMER

When the Poor Boys Ruled the Campus
A Requiem for B. Hall

Those who labour in the earth are the chosen people of God, if ever he had a chosen people, whose breasts he has made his peculiar deposit for substantial and genuine virtue. It is the focus in which he keeps alive that sacred fire, which otherwise might escape from the face of the earth.

THOMAS JEFFERSON, *NOTES ON THE STATE OF VIRGINIA,*
QUERY XIX "MANUFACTURES"

B. Hall, the self-styled "citadel of Jeffersonian democracy," is now silent as the grave.

Perhaps in our own transience on the Forty Acres the occasional one of us has, while rushing busily and importantly across campus, paused on the east side of the Main Building, either on the steps atop the subterranean Computation Center or on the broad, shaded walkway in the space bounded by Garrison Hall, the Will C. Hogg Building, and Inner Campus Drive, and felt the lingering ghosts of the men of B. Hall. Perhaps some of us have heard the faint cries of "Freshman in the Hall—get 'im!" reverberating from the past, or seen hazy outlines of the cupolas and strange architecture of old B. Hall. But apart from extra-sensory perception—or historical documentation or the memories of the small group of people remaining who experienced it firsthand—B. Hall has its quietus made.

Today B. Hall is largely forgotten. There is no plaque to memorialize it. There are no ruins or outlines of a foundation at which to pause and ponder. If one were to stop people at random on campus today and ask them about B. Hall, only one in a hundred—no, only one in a thousand—would have any idea what the question was about. Yet B. Hall has been, arguably, one of the most important buildings ever to exist on the University of Texas campus. It was a place that was uniquely Texan—yet its death and disappearance speak as loudly about what kind of place Texas is as its life ever did.

David Dettmer is assistant to the director at the Center for American History, University of Texas. He received an M.A. in English from the University and for many years taught literature and English composition at Austin Community College.

The original B. Hall. *From the Prints and Photographs Collection—UT Buildings: B. Hall, Center for American History, the University of Texas at Austin. (DI 02427)*

B. Hall was an all-male dormitory and campus mess hall. Built in 1890, the original portion of the building was the second permanent structure on the University of Texas campus, facing the east side of the yet-unfinished Main Building. It served as a dormitory until 1926, and survived from 1926 as a hodgepodge of office and museum space until its demolition in 1952. As a dorm, it was by design the place where the poor boys on campus lived.

THE WILD WEST: COTTON-CHOPPIN', PELLAGRA, AND NOTHIN' TO READ

B. Hall represents a world far removed from the one we inhabit today. When B. Hall was constructed, virtually all of the original UT campus—the famous "Forty Acres"—was little more than imaginary lines on a plat map. To the east and north of the Forty Acres

were mostly open fields—dotted with an occasional farmhouse and its owner's cattle, the beeves grazing on bluestem grass among the goldenrod, Texas bluebells, ironweed, and perhaps a few pecan or persimmon trees—and beyond those fields lay a state that was still guided largely by a frontier mentality. The young men and women who came by train, horse, or foot to Austin with the dust and sand and cockleburs and manure of their rural homes on their boots and bits of hayseed from the harvest in their pockets knew mostly hard work, provincialism, ignorance, and a standard of living that most of us today would describe as poverty.

Who were these poor boys? They were Roy Bedichek, reared in rural Falls County, near Eddy (pop. 500), who left B. Hall and formed a famous friendship with Frank Dobie and Walter Webb. They were William F. Buckley, Sr., born in tiny, albeit historic, Washington-on-the-Brazos and reared in San Diego, Texas

B. Hall following the 1899 expansion. *From the Lewis Fisher Photographs Collection, Center for American History, the University of Texas at Austin. (DI 02396)*

(pop. 2,500), who left B. Hall and developed real estate and oil interests in Mexico and Venezuela. They were Morris Sheppard, reared on the family farm in Morris County near the unincorporated village of Wheatville, who left B. Hall and served twenty-eight years in the U.S. Senate. They were T. V. Smith, reared in a two-room cabin near Blanket (pop. 300), who left B. Hall and took a professorship in philosophy at the University of Chicago. They were Byrne Baucom, reared in Milford (pop. 650), who left B. Hall and became an American Ace in the Great War, earning the Croix de Guerre and the Distinguished Service Cross. They were Hines Baker, reared in rural Mills County near the village of Big Valley, who left B. Hall and became president and CEO of Humble Oil and Refining, which we know today as ExxonMobil.

Texans are world-famous for their bravado about the virtues of their state, and this bravado comes in spite of—or perhaps, ironically enough, because of—the state's humble and difficult origins. A reminiscence by J. W. Mallet appears in the very first issue of the University's magazine for former students, *The Alcalde* (April 15, 1913). For its first twelve years, the University's organization was modeled after that of Jefferson's University of Virginia, with a chairman of the faculty rather than a president, and Dr. Mallet, a Virginian, was the first chairman. When he remembered his students from that first year, two impressions came to mind:

In the first place, comparing them with such students as I had known in the older States, these young Texans were characterized by great lack of formal school training—a condition much modified no doubt since those early days—combined with a certain quite notable maturity of mind derived from early contact with and participation in the activities of adult life. Boys whose spelling and arithmetic were much behind their years talked and thought like grown men of house building out on the prairie, of cattle driving, even of social and political movements.

Secondly, I was struck with the immense value to a people of a State history, and a State pride in that history as influencing even the very young. I remember well an interview (in private) as Chairman of the Faculty with a boy who was rather disposed to scout the force of college law, and his quick change of attitude when I said something of the value of discipline among soldiers and spoke with hearty admiration of Hood's Texas Brigade as I had known it in the Army of Northern Virginia. Those were days when not only Confederate recollections were comparatively recent but when there were still survivors to be pointed out in the street of the men who had achieved the independence of Texas, and it remains a source of gratification to have seen and known a few of them.

Nineteenth-century Texas was a place where people, by necessity, grew up in a hurry.

The nineteenth-century Texas economy was based on cotton and cattle, dependent on the vagaries of weather, soil conditions, and the markets. There were certainly times of prosperity, but a drought or market decisions made in New York or Chicago or New Orleans could be devastating, especially to the poor. Vast areas of Texas territory were still controlled only nominally by mounted Texas Rangers and local sheriffs, posses, and picket riders, or not at all. Most of the tribes of Comanche, Tonkawa, and Kiowa had already been exterminated or removed to the Indian Territory by the late 1870s, though their memory would still have been fresh and remnants of their people and culture still present as University hopefuls made their way to Austin in the 1890s. At the turn of the century, when B. Hall had already been in operation for a decade, Texas still shared half of its total land border with organized but open territory. To the north, the Oklahoma Territory and Indian Territory did not become the state of Oklahoma until 1907; to the west, the New Mexico Territory did not achieve statehood until 1912. The recognized states that adjoined the other half of Texas' land border were, at best, only slightly more advanced than the territories: the Mexico-Texas borderlands to the south were controlled during the University's first years by the dictatorial Mexican president Porfirio Díaz and later by the likes of revolutionists Pancho Villa and President Victoriano Huerta, with much blood spilled legally and illegally by parties on both sides of the Rio Grande, while to the east of Texas the American states of Louisiana and Arkansas were moving torpidly into twentieth-century modernity.

Dr. Mallet concludes his recollections by commenting on his delight in, but also subsequent consternation at, being a newcomer to the "Great West," a place of great distances and new geography:

It seemed that when one crossed the Mississippi and got into Texas one had become a denizen of a new and expanded world, in which it was hundreds of miles to anywhere, and in which one was by distance alone cut off to a large extent from the regions to which one had formerly belonged. [. . .] Very striking was the difference in the Texas landscape due to drought or abundant rainfall. The autumn of 1883 was a very long, hot and dry one, the heat continuing practically unbroken from August, when I reached Austin, until almost Christmas. When rains came in the spring one was able to realize the truth of both parts of a wise saying which I heard from a dealer in real estate during the seemingly endless heat and dust that had preceded—viz, that "Texas can send a man up higher, and let him down lower, than any other region on the face of the earth."

The boys—no, the men—who lived in B. Hall knew firsthand the ups and downs of rural Texas farm life. When they decided to attend the University, they came to Austin, a very small city that was itself just emerging from its rural roots. The University of Texas was founded in 1881, and by constitutional mandate it was to be "a University of the first class," so its founders looked to the schools of the Old South and the eastern seaboard for its models of success as they started, basically from scratch, to build a university whose founding had been tabled since the 1830s. Its founding had been thwarted since the days of the Republic by foreign and domestic wars, Reconstruction, economic depression, and vulgar indifference, if not hostility, toward higher education. Yet we can see through Dr. Mallet's remarks that the schools of the East Coast and Old South and the University of Texas were not quite analogous: the University of Texas had to deal, in the early days, with many inherent disadvantages not as well known by the eastern and southern establishments. One of the greatest disadvantages facing the University was the extreme privation from which most of its students emerged. B. Hall was a tool the University used in the early days to ameliorate this disadvantage.

BOYS WILL BE BOYS: LIFE AND NEAR-DEATH IN B. HALL

By all accounts (and accounts of B. Hall lore are legion), B. Hall was a wild place, occupied by wild boys recently emerged from wild environments across a still-wild state. It was a fact of life that students, professors, and administrators who approached B. Hall or interfered with B. Hall activities did so at their own peril.

For example, B. Hall boys would patrol the roof of the old pile, pelting with water bombs (20-pound brown sugar sacks filled with water) those below whom they felt were deserving of such treatment. When the administration outlawed "spooning" on campus and hired a police officer to patrol the campus after hours to enforce the ban, a couple of B. Hallers (one in drag) faked a romantic escapade on a campus bench in order to draw the attention of the police officer. He chased them as they dashed into B. Hall and as he reached the steps he was pummeled with torrents of water from above, knocking him nearly unconscious. In 1903 when hatchet-wielding Kansan Carrie Nation—the temperance leader who was half reformer and half sideshow act—came to Austin to root out sin at the University, gleeful B. Hallers egged her on, escorting her around campus and pointing out which faculty were boozers (of course, the ones to whom the B. Hallers directed Ms. Nation's tirades were the teetotal faculty members). During the 1911 faculty–senior baseball game on a blistering June afternoon, famous B. Hall prankster Gene Harris spiked the faculty water bucket with citrate of magnesia, causing the faculty to forfeit the game abruptly and cancel their classes the next day. Students of all sorts would be hauled to the fourth floor of B. Hall, given a firm paddling, then thrown down one of the tin fire-escape silos on the side of the building, where, upon emerging, they would have to run a gauntlet of paddles and punches. On one occasion B. Hallers stole (temporarily) the 300-pound bell from the Fulmore School in South Austin and installed it in B. Hall; they also once stole a giant metal milk bottle from a local creamery and mounted it prominently on the roof of B. Hall between the front cupolas with the graffito "Nursery of Jeffersonian Democracy" scrawled in big letters on it. On another occasion, a serious, straight-laced B. Hall resident (future U.S. senator Ralph Yarborough) was

Temperance leader Carrie Nation during her visit to Austin. *From the Lewis Fisher Photographs Collection, Center for American History, the University of Texas at Austin. (DI 02397)*

made to run in his underwear from B. Hall to the Capitol and back. B. Hallers would stage elaborate practical jokes, some of which would take weeks to develop, such as the month several residents conditioned B. Hall manager Harry Birk Beck to believe that a particular resident was deeply depressed, then one day gave a call of alarm to Beck that something was wrong; he came running to find the "depressed" student appearing to be hanging from a noose, and the accomplices suppressed their chuckles as Beck desperately cut the noose of the "expiring" resident and frantically revived him.

As one reads about these antics in sources such as Nugent Brown's sentimental patchwork book of anecdotes titled *B Hall, Texas* (1938), Walter Long's article "B Hall of Texas" in *The Southwestern Historical Quarterly* (April 1959), and the chapter on B. Hall titled "The Last Cry of the Innocents" in Joe B. Frantz's *The Forty-Acre Follies* (1983), one gets the sense that B. Hall was in a constant state of warfare. The rivalries were internal (the jousting for dominance between the law students and the engineering students in B. Hall seems to have been the strongest rivalry), unless an outside force tried to impose its will on B. Hall, which always resulted in a unified B. Hall response. The strongest threats from the outside came from the freshmen, the fraternities, and the University administration (comprised largely of men who had joined fraternities during their student days at their East Coast colleges). For most of B. Hall's history, freshmen were, with a few exceptions, disqualified from living there. Entrance into B. Hall had to be earned, and over time B. Hall became the coveted domain of the non-fraternity upperclassmen. As the freshman ban solidified over the years, a tradition began in which the freshman would annually conduct an organized assault on B. Hall, attempting to "take" it from the upperclassmen.

The Freshmen Fight of 1925 precipitated the closing of B. Hall as a dorm. On Sunday evening, March 1, while most of the B. Hall upperclassmen were "returning from church," the freshmen came in three organized mobs, armed with ladders, a fire hose, fire axes and fire extinguishers, clubs, paddles, bricks, and a plan of attack that had been weeks in the making. The few residents who were inside B. Hall yanked balusters from the stair railings and used them as clubs to beat back the freshmen long enough for more upperclassmen to enter the building and assist with the fighting. The fighting became so fierce that almost $2,000 damage was done, as became clear in the ensuing days through a hailstorm of administrative reprimands, newspaper reports and editorials, and discussion on the floor of the statehouse concerning future University appropriations. The fire hose had brought down some ceilings, and one freshman had suffered a broken skull. In Brown's book, one of the participants recounts how he had rushed toward "a big Frosh" who was charging at him with a fireman's axe, rushing in so close that the full swing of the axe went around and behind him; he snatched the axe from the Frosh and years later, as a middle-aged man, still possessed it as a souvenir.

The upperclassmen prevailed, though, as they always had in the past. They held the Hall and captured many of the freshmen by luring them in through a window. Once captured, the freshmen's hands were bound with rope, on which the upperclassmen poured water to tighten the knots; then they were led to the upper floor and the roof, where they were made to stand all night, enduring thirst, fatigue, and paddlings. In the morning the heads of the freshmen—especially the "Jelly Beans" who sported elaborate pompadours—were given grotesque haircuts, with epithets painted in red mercurochrome on the parts that were shaved bald. They were then thrown down the silos and made to run the gauntlet. For several weeks afterward, their mangled heads revealed to their professors, girlfriends, and parents what had transpired.

The upperclassmen of B. Hall had other, more subtle, methods for torturing the freshmen as well, one of which, unfortunately, reveals that the Hall's famous Jeffersonian egalitarianism did not extend beyond the "white race" in turn-of-the-century Texas. A brief notice in the March 1914 *Alcalde* announces the death of "Morris Givens, the old negro cook who was for many years at B Hall." The single accomplishment listed in the notice was that Givens was elected ten times as president of various freshmen classes. There is further evidence of the unmitigated terror that the fourth-floor commons area and the roof of B. Hall must have inspired in the hearts of the unfortunates who were taken up there. In a section in Brown's book titled "The Official Butt Beaters Court," contributor Alf Toombs tells how "this inquisitorial body" would punish its convicts by throwing them "off" the roof:

> [T]he victims were led to the parapet and allowed to peer down below and see, on the ground [four stories below], the crew with a blanket in which they were to be caught. They were then blindfolded, rolled in a sheet and securely bound, after which they were carried to a division wall on the roof which was mounted by the bearers and, after three prodigious swings, were launched into what must have seemed eternity but proved to be another blanket held by another crew standing on the roof not more than four feet from them.

From virtually its beginning, B. Hall became invested with the reputation as a place of an independent spirit. It was a very Texan place—which means that it was a place of opportunity, that it was a fun place, but that it could also be a mean, violent place for those who were not able to hold their own. It was a very Texan place, and it inspired Texas-sized loyalty. Those who begin with few material possessions and even less power enjoy a kind of freedom of body and mind less well-known to those burdened with the privileges and expectations of wealth and status. Poor boys need to make no apologies for what they don't have or how they didn't get it—not yet, anyway.

The pranks and practical jokes of B. Hall are legendary, though every B. Hall storyteller is careful to point out that all the shenanigans were good-natured and constructive, never hurtful—or, if they were hurtful, the joker was immediately ostracized. In Brown's book, contributor Victor "Dutch" Lieb observes that

> [t]he humor of B Hall was distinctly American, and TEXAN; a product of the soil from which it sprang. "Country boy humor," without uncouthness, and I take pride in the remembrance thereof. [Engineering] Dean [T. U.] Taylor, in a reminiscent mood, speaks of it as an important contribution to what he so fondly terms "the golden age of the University." In the quips, pranks, and "tall tales" there was much of originality of application, native wit and good sense and appreciation surprisingly in advance of our age in years. Obscenity and cruelty were seldom heard, and there was always a "point"—otherwise the teller or perpetrator found few listeners or sympathy.

Any prankish punishment generally would be appropriate for the transgression: the resident who had the means—not to mention the inconsideration of the relative poverty of his fellow residents—to overdecorate his room would return from class to find his furniture and belongings "stacked." Likewise, the engineering student who awakened others with his realistic mule-braying would be paddled with a T-square, while the law student who disrupted residents' studies by dropping bricks down the metal fire escape silos would be paddled with Volume One of Blackstone (a law textbook) the next day. Elsewhere in Brown's book, Dutch Lieb tells the story of Paul Rochs, who

> was quite a lady's man, his privilege and right. No one objected to the fact that when the B Hall telephone rang it started a universal cry of "Paul Rochs, telephone" even before anyone answered it. But after Paul

came in many times after midnight singing at the top of his voice—loud enough to waken everyone—then it was high time to do something about it.

Indulging in the pleasures of the flesh (apparently that sort of thing happened even back in 1907) was the occasion for an admiring (and probably envious) smile, but a man's pleasure could cross the line by interfering with the others' sleep or studies; in Mr. Rochs's case, his fellow residents hid alarm clocks, set to go off at different times all night long, throughout his room, and presumably he kept his singing to himself after that. All the residents shared in a fellow's success, but if a prank were nothing more than maliciousness—such as the time a student poured molasses in another resident's new shoes, ruining the only pair of fancy shoes the impoverished student perhaps had ever owned—it would be met with universal condemnation.

The significance of a good joke runs deep: it allows the joker to plumb the depths of his victim, gauge his response, and see his true mettle. To survive a good B. Hall practical joke enabled the victim to demonstrate to the joker and everyone else that he had a sympathetic understanding of his fellow residents and their plight, and surviving it with aplomb strengthened the bonds of the precarious community in which they had all found themselves and maintained its equilibrium. The leaders of the B. Hall community were always some of the most motivated students on campus—they were "have nots" who hoped someday to be "haves." Why else would a poor boy come to the University?

GREEKS AND BARBARIANS: THE AMERICAN FRONTIER AND THE DILEMMA OF DEMOCRACY

By today's standards, B. Hall would have been a grim place to live—Spartan rooms that would be infernally hot in September and drafty in January—but to many of its residents it was a definite improvement over the homes they had left out in the provinces. It had gas lamps, running hot and cold water, and water closets on each floor. The mess hall was right below their rooms in the basement, and beginning in 1903 the new Women's Building (the "Women's Mansion") stood right on the other side of Old Main. In its original configuration, it housed forty-eight men, who paid $2.50 per month for rent.

B. Hall was a gift of "Col." George Washington Brackenridge, a regent of and major benefactor to the early University. Brackenridge was a war profiteer in the cotton trade and a Union sympathizer, and after the war became a banker and prominent business leader in San Antonio. Throughout its existence the building's official name was always University Hall, though common usage in the early days preferred "Brackenridge Hall," against the Colonel's wishes, so the appellation "B. Hall" was the eventual compromise. Brackenridge and the regents' original intent in planning for a second building on campus even before the final, east wing of Old Main was finished was to satisfy the immediate practical need for an on-campus mess hall for male students. In 1890 Austin was a town of only 15,000 residents, and students were from the beginning scrambling for adequate and affordable room and board. Brackenridge's $17,000 gift provided a four-story, flat-roofed brick building, with both a fully outfitted mess hall and three floors of dorm rooms, of stunning rectangular ordinariness. But despite the building's almost complete lack of ornamentation, it fulfilled Col. Brackenridge's strongly held conviction that the University and its opportunities should be available to all students, not just the wealthy.

Because of its in-house mess hall and the fact that it was at the center of campus, and thus far away from the dust, stench, and noise of nineteenth-century city streets, B. Hall had an advantage over the ninety or so boarding houses about town. However, it did not enjoy the same advantage over the fraternities. From the beginning, the students who came to campus with something already going for them—economically, socially, and politically—tended to seek each other out and bind together in fraternities; these fraternities then struggled amongst themselves for control of campus politics and institutions, whether the fraternities were officially affiliated with the University or not. As the years passed and the University grew, B. Hall earned a reputation as the residence of the students who could not afford a boarding house and in whom the fraternities were not interested—the nobodies with no money and no prospects. "Barbarians," or "barbs," the fraternity "Greeks" called those not in fraternities, and B. Hall residents were least likely to be candidates for Greek life.

In the 1890s, however, many B. Hall residents joined fraternities. None of the frats had its own house yet, and with the male population growing from a miniscule 225 students to only 650 in the 1890s, there was not yet the sense of rivalry and competition for resources that crowding induces. But in the first decade of the twentieth century, as the student population expanded and the social and political life within the student body matured and grew increasingly entrenched, a deep rift began to develop between the frats and the barbs. In 1904 the Pan-Hellenic Association was formed as a campus organization, though the fraternities could carry out many of their activities independent of the University, and from 1900 onward much of the power of campus politics resided behind the private doors of fraternity houses scattered beyond the "perip" of the Forty Acres.

How ironic, then, that the home of the nobodies would be in a fortified building right at the navel of campus. Poor boys found their way to B. Hall from every nook and cranny of a poor state located (then as now) within both the South and the West, with Austin at the very nexus of the two—a state that was still struggling to find its way after years of Reconstruction and the ups and downs of a statewide economy based almost solely on cotton and cattle. Once those boys got to B. Hall they did what poor but motivated people are wont to do: they lived by their wits, they formed alliances and friendships, and through skill, cunning, and hard work set out as individuals to make the most of the little they had been given. The B. Hall residents represented, both to themselves and to the "Greeks," a world that everyone was working feverishly to destroy—a world of privation and struggle, the world of the frontier. However, the frontier is precisely what made America unique, and has made Texas a special place, even to us today. To fulfill its special role in history, America has always needed the frontier and the outlaws and rubes who inhabited it.

In 1893, three years after the opening of B. Hall, Frederick Jackson Turner, a professor of history at the University of Wisconsin, declared in his famous essay "The Significance of the Frontier in American History" that the 1890 census data showed that the American frontier as a single, continuous line had recently ceased to be. The thesis of Turner's essay is that the existence of the frontier has been the most prominent influence in shaping the development of democracy and its institutions in America. A constant cycle of change initiated by the frontier continually renews and reinvigorates that which lies settled and civilized behind it, reaching all the way back to Europe itself, and provides fertile soil for a democratic spirit. Turner writes:

> [F]or a moment at the frontier the bonds of custom are broken, and unrestraint is triumphant. There is not tabula rasa. The stubborn American environment is there with its imperious summons to accept its conditions; the inherited ways of doing things are also there; and yet, in spite of environment, and in spite of custom, each frontier did indeed furnish a new field of opportunity, a gate of escape from the bondage of the past; and freshness, and confidence, and scorn of older society, impatience of its restraints and its ideas, and indifference to its lessons, have accompanied the frontier. What the Mediterranean Sea was to the Greeks, breaking the bond of custom, offering new experiences, calling out new institutions and activities, that, and more, the ever retreating frontier has been to the United States directly, and to the nations of Europe more remotely.

When the foundations of B. Hall were laid in 1890, most of Texas was still very much within the remaining pockets of the American frontier, and many of the institutions that are the hallmarks of advanced civilization—diversified manufacturing and trade, transportation, internal policing, formal education—were undeveloped if not altogether nonexistent. It is from this environment that many students somehow made their way to the University, and they brought their frontier mindset—with both its strengths and its weaknesses—with them. There were some Texan students from families of means who came to the University for their advanced education, but to send their sons and daughters to Austin those families would have had to resist the powerful lure of the ivy-covered halls to the east.

In the first two decades of B. Hall's existence, the University of Texas strove to imitate the ivy-covered halls to the east, figuratively and literally. The regents imported most of the early faculty from East Coast schools. The fraternities proudly traced their origins back to the universities in Ohio, Virginia, Alabama, and New Jersey where the fraternities were founded.

Even the architecture of the early campus paid banal homage to the old-line schools, with its College Gothic designs that were already out of style as they were being built and the imported English ivy that was coaxed up the walls of Old Main but soon dispatched by the unforgiving Texas heat.

In 1899, the year the final wing of Old Main was completed, a project to enlarge and "dress up" B. Hall was undertaken. Two wings were added to either side of B. Hall, giving it an "H" shape and adding thirty-nine dorm rooms. At the expense of square-footage to the original twenty-four rooms, the division wall between the north and south stacks of rooms was removed, creating north-south hallways that made each floor fully traversable, thereby encouraging a greater level of unrestrained behavior than before. The basement mess hall was expanded and staff living quarters were added. Also, the façade was transformed: a large room with open loggias and four towers was added to the roof; cupolas were placed above each of the four rises of bay windows; and, curiously, the bay window projections and the wings were interconnected, from window to window, by small iron balconies. The roof was now no longer flat, but its slope low and Mediterranean, arguably the first foretelling of the design of the architecture to come in the Paul Cret era which defines today's campus. There was even space made available to house any of the regents when they came to visit campus.

One wonders whether the architect, James L. O'Connor, realized the full significance of the changes he made. The room on the roof was the only commons area in the building other than the mess hall and was accessible only by running the gauntlet of three floors of dorm rooms. It quickly became a tree house and kangaroo courthouse of sorts for the residents. The iron balconies were probably added for decoration or perhaps for fire safety, but all of these factors existing in toto—iron balconies connecting rooms by their windows, open loggias on the roof, a gently sloping roof, a young and all-male residency, and the advent of air conditioning still several decades away—naturally caused much of the life *inside* the building actually to occur on the *outside* of the building. It is very difficult to find a photograph of B. Hall in which the balconies are not crowded with young men and without at least a few people cavorting on (and dropping things off) the roof. This externality of the building, along with the

B. Hall with its residents assembled on the grounds below it and standing on the roof, with the central steeple and recently completed east wing of the Main Building in the background. *From the Prints and Photographs Collection—UT Buildings: B. Hall, Center for American History, the University of Texas at Austin. (DI 02428)*

wings that made the yards on the east and west sides partially enclosed, gave B. Hall the sense of a fortress, defendable from all angles and approaches. Virtually nothing could happen anywhere on the small campus without falling within the purview of the energetic and ambitious—and ornery—residents of B. Hall.

SELF-RULE IN B. HALL: THE REGENTS HAND THE CLODHOPPERS THE REINS

B. Hall was the embodiment of the great American dilemma: the "common rabble" has and must have a political voice, but how can that voice be permitted without descending into mob rule by the ignorant and unqualified?

The Board of Regents, with assistance from a University Hall committee of faculty, maintained a relatively direct but nominal authority over B. Hall. The regents and faculty committee placed a steward in the Hall as the agent of their authority. Harry Birk Beck (who was the University's long-time groundskeeper

and namesake of Beck's Pond near the old Library Building, today's Battle Hall) was the original B. Hall manager, but his tenure was shaky at best. Part of Beck's difficulty, despite the misfortune of being a convenient lightning rod for the residents' boundless and ornery creative energy, was the red ink that dominated the mess hall's ledgers.

The problem of financial insolvency was solved in a profoundly American way: self-government. As an act of trust, desperation, or resignation, the regents backed off their intentions to close the Hall as a mess hall/dormitory, and in February 1896 a committee of faculty and regents approved the following agreement:

It is agreed between the Brackenridge Hall committee appointed by the Regents of the University and the committee on behalf of student boarders at Brackenridge Hall (as indicated by the superscriptions) that the students through their committees are to have complete control of the financial management of the Hall, including room and restaurant, for the current month; the hall committees will retain their control of the conduct of student boarders, and others, at the hall. Net gains of the management for the month may be retained by the students; net losses, if any, must be paid by them, and to secure payment of losses a deposit to the amount of at least $100 must be made by them; the students will not become responsible for any debt contracted prior to Feb. 1st; the Hall Committee will retain control of the two rooms now occupied by Mr. [Lester] Bugbee [a recent graduate who was on the faculty as Tutor in History]; the hall and all property appurtenant to it is turned over to the students indicated without charge or rent, but must be returned upon the termination of this agreement in the same condition, necessary wear + tear excepted, as received. It is also agreed that if this arrangement is continued after Feb. that the net profits on the basis of the present prices, shall be applied to liquidating the past indebtedness; and it is further agreed that Mr. Bugbee shall represent the Brackenridge Hall Comm. in matters of discipline.

One could consider this document to be the University's "Magna Charta," the seed from which germinated the notion of "Jeffersonian democracy" in B. Hall—a government instituted among men, deriving its just powers from the consent of the governed—and true to the spirit of Jefferson (as he wrote, more than the way he lived, at least), the reins of the government were handed to the yeoman farmers—in this case, the poorest of the poor. It was a decision that made great sense: the poor boys, by the time they were able to work their way off the farm and come to Austin, were usually several years older than the average student and accustomed to genuine responsibility and hard work. When a father trusted his fourteen-year-old son to care for the livestock or help harvest the crop, the entire family's security was at stake. After years of responsibility on the farm, running a college dorm was a piece of cake. The experiment did not fail, as the students were able to break even for the remainder of the year.

With little fanfare, for the next two years the students ran B. Hall successfully. In his report to the regents on June 16, 1897, President George Winston informed them that the present management had actually earned a surplus for the year, and then posited that this profit had been earned in spite of an inherent deficiency—the Hall's small number of rooms did

not provide economies of scale sufficient to justify the mess hall—and recommended the regents build another dorm to share the mess hall. He concludes his report optimistically by stating that they "hope however by the most careful economy and skillful management to make the Hall a success, even under the present inherent difficulties, and by means of it to keep down the price of living for University students who are rooming and boarding elsewhere."

Is it possible even to imagine today's regents and president turning the entire operations of Jester or San Jacinto dormitories over to the students who live there?

The spirit of democracy, healthy economic competition, and egalitarianism had found a home at the University. In January 1898 another gift from Col. Brackenridge came to fruition: University Hall opened on the medical campus in Galveston, operating under a constitution and a board of managers comprising a number of "ladies of Galveston." The Galveston University Hall provided room and board for women and board for men, and was expressly designed, as was B. Hall, to provide the opportunity for higher education that students of lesser means could otherwise not afford.

Despite the success, changes also came to B. Hall in Austin. A woman, Mrs. M. E. Hicks, was made steward of the Hall in 1898, perhaps because the Galveston Hall was succeeding under female leadership. But there was conflict between Mrs. Hicks and the residents. Following the 1898–1899 school year, the regents addressed the faculty committee's report on residents' complaints about alleged favoritism by Mrs. Hicks. The regents concluded that her misconduct was more perceived than real, but then laid ground rules for her that she was to supervise the mess hall's operations, that she was not to hold her own table or distribute arbitrarily foods she had received as perquisites from the Hall's suppliers, and that guests were to sit at separate tables. In short, the residents demanded that she participate in the spirit of egalitarianism they had so proudly established the preceding two years. At that same meeting, President Winston made an urgent plea for a women's building to be constructed on campus, for more male dorm rooms to be provided, and for monthly rents to be lowered from $15 to $10. He had prefaced his plea by pointing out that six students—four women and two men—had died during the school year, and concluded by urging that these

B. Hall residents in 1905, at the height of their influence on campus. *From the Prints and Photographs Collection–UT Buildings: B. Hall, Center for American History, the University of Texas at Austin. (DI 02421)*

changes would greatly improve the physical and moral health of the student body. One month later the regents passed a resolution that residents of University Hall would be required to pledge themselves not to play cards, drink intoxicating liquors, or gamble in the Hall, and also appropriated money to expand the Hall. Construction began months later, disrupting the life of B. Hall for the 1899–1900 school year. At the end of the year, the regents bought out Mrs. Hicks' contract.

THE GOLDEN AGE OF RUSTI-CUSS: "DOWN WITH ALL TRUSTS; OPPOSE ALL MUSTS; AVOID ALL BUSTS"

In 1900 self-government returned to B. Hall. A governing committee was established, with the offices of president, secretary, and steward. The steward had the greatest effect on the day-to-day operations of the

Hall, so old Beck's position retained its power. The steward was John A. Lomax, a recent graduate, who would go on to serve the University for the better part of his life and earn a place in history as a pioneer in preserving American music.

Then in 1902 the Golden Age of B. Hall was ushered in when Adrian Pool began his five-year tenure as the Hall's most capable steward. Pool, a law student who was beloved by almost all the residents, ran B. Hall's operations with a selfless efficiency. But even beyond the nuts and bolts of running the facility, Pool mastered the social and political aspects of B. Hall as well. By the end of his tenure B. Hall had become the Tammany Hall of campus, wresting significant power away from the fraternities. Like Cortéz plotting against Montezuma, Pool understood the factions that existed in the already existing power structure, and played rival fraternities against each other, cutting deals to get those on B. Hall tickets elected to important student offices. With its self-government,

The members of the inaugural class of Rusticusses, with representatives from the rival P.E.C.s and Goo Roos, strike a barnyard pose for their page in the student organizations section of the yearbook. *From the* Cactus *yearbook (1904, p. 143), Center for American History, the University of Texas at Austin. (DI 02391)*

its fortress-like building at the center of campus, and an increasingly level political playing field, B. Hall became a real threat to the fraternities and increasingly more difficult to control for the University's administrators, who left campus for home every evening.

In this Golden Age of B. Hall, Steward Pool tended to the factions outside B. Hall and to the ones inside as well. It was during Pool's tenure that several competing organizations within B. Hall—anti-frat fraternities—coalesced. The first of these anti-frats was the P.E.C.s. According to Brown, the P.E.C.s held power by administering beatings with clubs. In time, a rival faction formed simply to offer protection in B. Hall to non-P.E.C.s. As Brown states, "Under these conditions life to those who did not belong [to] the P.E.C.'s became somewhat burdensome and those who had felt the mighty stroke of the powerful club began to seek means of redress and mutual protection. [. . .] Thus the Rusti Cusses came into existence."

The Rustic Order of Ancient and Honorable Rusty Cusses soon emerged as the leading force within B. Hall. Other factions came and went—the Goo Roos, the Moo Cow Moos, the Yellow Dogs, the Secret Six, and the predictable I Felta Thi's—but the Rusticusses reigned. In them we can see clearly the mindset of the poor boy who had found his way to the University. The organization mocked the fraternities,

both their pretensions and their power. There were a multitude of Rusticuss officers, including Landlord, Overseer, Cotton Weigher, Hen Setter, Cow Juicer, and Plow Shaker; the members were known as Reubens, and they referred to B. Hall as the Barnyard. Each year the members would pose for their yearbook photo in a real barnyard with outlandishly corn-pone outfits, props, and poses. They embraced their poverty-stricken rural roots and used them with irony to their own advantage.

A pretension of the "Greek" system is to trace its lineages back to ancient occult European societies that have maintained cosmopolitan power over the uninitiated for centuries and to trace its lineages, more recently, to the East Coast and Old South schools at which the particular fraternities were founded. That pretension was squarely in the sights of the Rusticusses. Their inaugural entry in the 1904 *Cactus* gives the following history of the group:

> Farming is the oldest, most honorable, and most essential vocation in the world. As an organization, the Rusty Cusses could trace an unbroken descent from Adam and Eve; but they make no such claim. Indeed it is their proudest boast that they are newly organized; their plantation is all fresh land; their appliances and their farming utensils of the latest invention. Even the plow-handles of old Beck are of the newest design. [. . .] The Rusty Cusses propose to ignore the effete old-line fraternities, and be a moving power in the University of Texas.

In light of Turner's thesis, the frontier and its renewing spirit had found its way into the University. As a political power, the Reubens provided competition—both in its beauty and its violence—for the old orders. Yet we can also see in the history of the Rusticusses the complexities that the poor boys must have felt when they left home to take a satisfying bite of the world beyond their hometown, as is the case with any group that feels excluded or disenfranchised, even today. "Historically underrepresented" people are caught in a dilemma, caught between wanting to be a success and feeling like a sell-out. They also risk feeling alienated from the community that they have left behind—or, even more problematic, becoming oppressors themselves. Rural and small-town life has a powerful gravity toward the economic center; both poverty and wealth tend to upset the social balance.

The history that the Rusticusses wrote for their page in the 1908 *Cactus*, satirical in its self-conscious stupidity and written at the height of the B. Hall Golden Age, embodies this dilemma:

History

The Order of the Rusty Cusses is goin on its fifth year. seventeen of the old Reubs er back agin. this means thet the Barnyard gate wuz opened and nine new'uns admitted as Reubs. we selebrated by givin a swell supper at the driskill. it wuz a grand affair. some uv the Reubens made therselves sick eatin and tastin uv the new fangled things.

Somebody might hav a hankerin to know what a Rusty Cuss is and what goes on in the Barnyard. a Reuben is a feller who hez bin scent to austin by his pa to git a little book-larnin at the big school-house. our pas kaushuned us not to let our hed git turned by a little book-scents, or to forgit how ter foller old beck in the corn field, and not ter bring back to the country sich idees as the waring uv those bean shaped shoes thet yer kin see yerself in, or how ter crease yer pants in the right place. Now to protekt ourselves agin sich evils we hev organized and established our Barnyard here. the Sports who sometimes but in on our Barnyard and soon after extract therselves in the way the boy did who krawled into a holler log and struck a hornets nist, never git the proper consepshun uv what goes on in the place. well I aint got time to explain what goes on—besides saying thet there is a good deal uv yarnin and fiddle-playin. our object is to make lots uv friends and larn all we kin. one of our Reubs knows how to draw real pictures, another knows how to play foot-ball, and one, and I think mebe two (but I'm not sartain), called on the gals at the woman's manshun once. so yer see we aint squanderin our time. school aint sich a bad thing when these winter days keep us away from the farm.

Most B. Hall residents did not return to the farm, though. A few became senators, ambassadors, millionaires, and ivy-league professors, and a great many of them returned to their home counties armed with law degrees, teaching certificates, engineering skills, and business acumen that enabled them to make a good living in ways other than following a mule up and down the windrows. Why else would a rube come to the University, even if it meant running the risk of wearing left and right shoes and having a nice crease in one's pants?

THE EFFETE OLD-LINERS FIGHT BACK: DID B. HALL BECOME "MOLLYCODDLEIZED"?

To most outsiders, B. Hall appeared to be controlled by mob rule, and by 1910 much of the faculty, not to mention the majority of the fraternities, had had enough. In addition, the magnificent new Library (today's Battle Hall) was being completed, and the building it faced, B. Hall, was increasingly being perceived by much of the University as a danger and an embarrassment, especially following Pool's departure. In the summer of 1911 President Sidney Mezes (who was an active Chi Phi member and a graduate of the University of California and Harvard University and who resigned in 1914 to become president of the College of the City of New York) reported to the regents that University Hall was a problem, and the problem stemmed from the following roots: the removal of the central dividing wall and the addition of the two wings during the 1899 expansion project had placed too many students in one place and made the building too communal; students ran their own affairs; and it was a dormitory on the Forty Acres proper. There were some faculty and regents whose sympathies lay with B. Hall—most notably Col. Brackenridge himself; dean of Engineering T. U. Taylor (who writes in his book *Fifty Years on Forty Acres*, "The B. Hallers were and are the tenth legion of University democracy and college spirit. They were as poor as poverty and as patriotic as Patrick Henry."); and new dean of Arts and Sciences and future University president H. Y. Benedict (who as a student had won the lottery drawing and been the first boarder to choose a room when the Hall opened in 1890). But opposition was mounting.

To make their point clearly, the faculty and regents who were anti–B. Hall began the erosion of B. Hall's independence by hiring a *woman* from *Boston* to be the new steward. Walter Long writes in 1959 that "[t]he opinion still prevails that this change was made because of jealousy on the part of some faculty members and fraternities toward B Hall leaders." Mrs. Katherine C. Smith was universally despised within B. Hall, and the scheming against her power probably surpassed even that which Beck had had to endure. Many of those who schemed against her and were inept enough to get caught were summarily removed from the Hall, but the experiment failed miserably

A typical B. Hall fracas, viewed from the steps of Old Main. *From the Prints and Photographs Collection— UT Buildings: B. Hall, Center for American History, the University of Texas at Austin. (DI 02429)*

and Mrs. Kate Smith lasted only one year as B. Hall manager.

The regents' action was the beginning of the end for B. Hall. Three more damaging blows followed. The first came when the office of steward was occupied by student residents once again but the basement mess hall was closed, meaning the denizens could no longer break bread together en masse and enjoy the camaraderie—the communion—that eating together provides. Despite its effort to oppose the forces conspiring against it, B. Hall was vulnerable to the Siren song of success and respectability, evidenced by the following satire that appeared in the November 1916 *Alcalde*:

B. Hall.

Each year it is said, B. Hall has become civilized, all of which seems to point to one of two things: either B. Hall has never been civilized, that [it] is thor-

oughly civilized, or it has never been uncivilized, for in either case it could not annually enter into the state of civilization. It cannot be denied, however, by the most zealous champion of the University traditions, that B. Hall is as it used to be. There have been no killings whatever there in years. No students of late years have lost their lives in hazing escapades. It can even be shown that there has not passed the portal of the ancient pile a person breathing of spiritous, vinous, or malt liquors during the remembrance of the oldest student in school. Some say, in fact, that B. Hall is becoming molly-coddleized, and many there are who believe the allegation. Freshmen now pass in and out, and experience not the least perturbation. Recently a co-ed, new in school, mistook the place for a seminary or something of a like nature, and had mounted to the third floor before she was informed that she was in a men's dormitory.

The fact remains, however distasteful it may be to the former denizens, that B. Hall has again been renovated. In fact, renovation of B. Hall has got to be an annual occurrence. It is gradually evolving into a millionaires' retreat.

The University provided a new commons and cafeteria, open to both men and women, in one of the many temporary wooden shacks that surrounded B. Hall in 1912, with Mrs. Katherine Smith as its manager. Its civilizing effect can be seen in the December 1916 *Alcalde* report that

> the number of women who patronize the "Caf" is almost double what it was last year. Someone has even gone so far as to introduce potted plants of divers sorts for the ornamentation of the tables, and the prominence on the menu of sundry salads and mayonnaise concoctions indicates that the management has not overlooked entirely the new contingent.

The *Daily Texan* during the 1912–1913 school year reports on the several attempts the administration made to fabricate elaborate social occasions in B. Hall, sending the boys to Eastwoods Park to collect garlands and flowers to decorate the commons room on the fourth floor, after which they would clean up and "call on" the residents of the Women's Building and formally escort them to B. Hall for an evening of genteel socializing. Some B. Hall denizens may have even begun wearing bean-shaped shoes and creasing their pants. However, by the middle of the spring semester the Caf was in serious financial trouble and Mrs. Smith resigned. As a counterattack to the erosion of B. Hall's vulgar influence, the "barbs" initiated in the 1913 spring semester a serious political movement to abolish all Greek-letter fraternities and sororities and "all other secret societies." The administration formed a faculty investigating committee, and the struggle lasted most of the semester. The movement gained support when former B. Haller Gene Harris, by then a state representative from El Paso, introduced a bill in the House requesting abolition, though both his bill and the University's investigation died in committee.

The second great blow to B. Hall came when the United States entered the Great War in Europe. On March 27, 1917, the inmates of B. Hall received twenty-four-hour notice to evacuate the Hall to allow 108 enlisted men to take residence. The armistice of 1919 allowed the students and their self-government to return to B. Hall, but it was never quite what it once was. Perhaps in those years following the "war to end all wars" the B. Hall denizens carried out their antics more to fulfill their sense of duty and homage to the already legendary traditions of the sacred pile than simply to act out what should have come naturally to them. But the years after the Great War were some of the most violent—the meanest and most contrived—in B. Hall's history.

The final stubborn, prolonged blow to B. Hall began in 1923 and ended in 1926. In 1923 the Permanent University Fund began to swell with oil revenues, and with the construction of Memorial Stadium the next year down on Waller Creek, the campus leapt across Speedway and escaped the provinciality of the Forty Acres. Having a crude, all-male dormitory on campus proper was becoming less and less tolerable. Additionally, the standard of living students were willing to accept was evolving. Since the construction of the Women's Building in 1903, the female students had always been better cared for (meaning, more closely protected and supervised) than the males had, and posh off-campus women's dorms were becoming available. The Episcopal Church offered Grace Hall as a wholesome and secure home for thirty female students beginning in 1897; in 1917 the Dominican Sisters opened Newman Hall on the Drag; and in 1924 the Methodist Church constructed Kirby Hall on 29th Street to house 112 women. But the crowning achievement for the women was the construction in 1922 of the Scottish Rite Dormitory on 27th Street, which was opulent even by today's standards and certainly more genteel than anything that exists today. Soon the men would be expecting the same amenities that the women were already enjoying, though probably not the strict supervision.

When the Freshman Fight of 1925 got out of hand, the anti–B. Hall faction had the justification it had been waiting for, and over the next several weeks, despite expulsions, apologies, and financial remuneration from the guilty students, the wheels were set in motion within the conference rooms of the regents, the faculty, and the state legislature and on the pages of the local newspapers to close B. Hall once and for all. Yet, perhaps even more critical than the Freshman Fight in sealing B. Hall's doom was the planned construction of Garrison Hall just a few yards south of B. Hall and the fact that the Hall's early placement was now blocking the East Mall as provided for in the campus master plan that had been gradually evolving since the era of Cass Gilbert's magnificent Library Building. The windows of Garrison Hall's classrooms, which would contain both men and women, would look directly into the upper dorm rooms of B. Hall, where who-knows-what could be going on at any moment.

In addition, the University had recently acquired from the state the original site of the Blind Asylum, whose first building appeared in 1859 at what today is the intersection of I-35 and Martin Luther King Boulevard. In 1917, when the expanding Institute for the Blind moved to its present location on 45th Street, the School of Military Aeronautics took over the site and its buildings, and after the war the State Hospital used them for senile patients. The University's plan was to use the complex of aging buildings as dormitory space for students of limited means. Located several blocks southeast of campus, it was dubbed Little Campus. Intentionally or not, it would segregate the poorer students at a considerable distance from the hive of campus activies. (Decades later, the contiguous main campus eventually absorbed the site, renamed the Heman Sweatt Campus in 1987; today its southern perimeter lies in the shadow of the massive Frank Erwin Special Events Center). A series of more upscale dormitories for men and women (Hill, Roberts, and Prather dormitories, and the new Brackenridge dormitory) was being conceived for an area just off the Forty Acres proper, down the slope toward Memorial Stadium.

Howls of protest and actual legal threats over the closing of B. Hall poured in to the University administration. Walter Long reports that "[t]he crux of the court battle [*Woodward vs. Splawn*] was whether B Hall was a trust created by Brackenridge for poor boys or a gift." The courts ruled it had been a gift. No doubt a great many of the protests came from the denizens who lived in B. Hall during its Golden Age, who by this time had made their way into the world and found fortune and political clout and who perceived the romantic beginnings of their transformation from "have nots" to "haves" as having sprung to life in the idealized old Hall. In the 1950s Walter Long solicited memories from former B. Hall residents, but, as Long states, perhaps the best-expressed sentiment he received came from someone who had not

> I AM ONE OF THE OLD GANG
> ADMIT ME
> TO
> # The B HALL REUNION BANQUET
> Texas Union Building, Texas University
> Saturday, April 17th, 1937
> Rusti-Cusses or Moo Cow Moos—
> To Hell with the FRATS—
> The Spirit of B Hall Lives On and On

Evidence of the sentimental attachment to B. Hall that persisted long after it ceased being a men's dormitory. *From the University of Texas Memorabilia Collection, Center for American History, the University of Texas at Austin. (Box 4P158)*

initially gotten a room there; Rex Baker, brother of Hines Baker, wrote: "I really wanted to stay in B Hall, and think that if the opportunity were afforded again, I would still wish to do so. The men in B Hall had a tremendous attachment to it; more than they had to the University." This sentiment was, however, not universal. During the summer of the B. Hall controversy, President Splawn received the following letter:

Carnegie Institution of Washington
Department of Embryology
Carnegie Laboratory of Embryology
Johns Hopkins Medical School
Baltimore, Maryland

July 5, 1926

Dr. W. M. W. Splawn, President, The University of Texas, Austin

Dear Dr. Splawn,—

Speaking as an alumnus, count me as most emphatically endorsing your decision to make an office building out of B. Hall. This ancient and honored domicile would be a blot upon the campus were the filth of that beastly place well known. As a member of the "Sick Committee" I inspected the Hall twice—even a student couldn't live there except for the fact that he leaves the shack at sunrise & doesn't see it again till after dark.

There is one difficulty about making an office out of the "Hall"—it's too filthy & too full of vermine.

B. Hall residents performing daily chores. *From the Prints and Photographs Collection—UT Buildings: B. Hall, Center for American History, the University of Texas at Austin. (DI 02422)*

It should be fumigated with Sulphur Dioxid, thoroly before putting in an office force—that process will kill all the host of bed bugs of the crevices—or are these animals sacred because lo! their revered ancestors happened to suck the life blood of now famous and perhaps deceased alumni?

Cordially
Carl Hartman.

P.S.—I hope the place burns down during fumigation!

C. H.
(Ex. B.-Hallite)

CODA: SHINY-CLEAN PICKUP TRUCKS AND FIVE-HUNDRED-DOLLAR SHIT-KICKERS

Today, as I write this essay, my office is on the second floor of Sid Richardson Hall, a structure built in the early 1970s whose stark, modern lines look like they came from the set of a Stanley Kubrick movie and which stands parallel to no fewer than seventeen lanes of traffic (I-35, frontage roads, and Red River Street) crammed together on a hill on the eastern edge of campus. When I cast my glance over the top of my computer and out the window, I look directly down the center of the East Mall with my view unobstructed until it reaches the Main Building. (Sometimes I feel, with great irony, like Louis XIV sitting in his bed at the center of Versailles.) My gaze from this height goes over the tiptop of the pulsating LBJ fountain, over the East Mall fountain, over the top of the elegant, newly installed statue of Martin Luther King Jr. (facing triumphantly eastward toward the rising sun) and, then, just before it gets to the Main Building and the famous Tower with its four gold-leaf clock faces, my gaze passes through the empty place where B. Hall once stood.

The poor boys of B. Hall would have had trouble comprehending this vista. To my left is the expanded Darrell K Royal–Texas Memorial Stadium; on Longhorn game days scores of luxury European imports with tinted windows drop off people representing immense wealth, who mingle in the VIP tents on the grassy area below my window before they rise to the new luxury boxes to watch the game in air-conditioned comfort. Behind the stadium is a complex of towering dormitories, including new San Jacinto Hall, whose amenities include private bathrooms, high-speed Internet connections, in-room microwaves and refrigerators, a recreational amphitheater, lounges and a game room, a computer center, a convenience store, and meals designed by a registered dietician; students provide their own stereo systems, televisions, and in-room computers. Yesterday, while I was at a standstill in Austin's rush-hour traffic on MLK Blvd., facing me in the oncoming lane was a $60,000 BMW, whose contents included a student parking permit and an attractive nineteen-year-old woman who had just pulled out of the seven-level parking garage adjacent to the Jester Dormitory complex. (The students, though, no doubt still find things to gripe about—or still "kick," to use the analogy used by B. Hall men who grew up with mules and cranky milk cows.) To my right looking out my window is the sprawling performing arts complex, where expensive nationally touring shows cater to Austin's voracious appetite for entertainment, and behind it is a forest of box-like buildings for applied science research that serves as a mighty engine to help drive Texas' diversified manufacturing, agriculture, energy, and high-tech economy.

The space where B. Hall stood is now an empty sidewalk, and the beeves that grazed and bluebells that grew wild in the fields behind B. Hall 115 years ago have been replaced by an empire of material wealth. In the chapter on manufactures in his *Notes on the State of Virginia*, Thomas Jefferson opines that manufacturing would best remain back in the old world of Europe, where the frontierless landscape forces people by necessity into such jobs. He argues that America would best remain a nation of independent farmers: "Dependence begets subservience and venality, suffocates the germ of virtue, and prepares fit tools for the designs of ambition. [. . .] While we have land to labour then, let us never wish to see our citizens occupied at a work-bench, or twirling a distaff." But Jefferson's yeoman farmer lost out to Alexander Hamilton's industrialist a long time ago; in fact, because of political exigencies in Europe and on the high seas Jefferson himself late in his life admitted in a letter to Benjamin Austin that America could not depend on Europe for its finished goods. Michael Dell, the young entrepreneur and multibillionaire who owns more than a few factory assembly lines in the Austin area and around the world, famously began his business by assembling computer components in his room in Jester Dormitory. Even in Texas, the seat of American frontier mythology, the "citadel of Jeffersonian democracy" is now gone.

Nevertheless, we subconsciously labor to keep the old Texas alive on UT's sprawling and increasingly dense and luxurious campus. The poor boys had something in their possession—something we can't name but that we yearn for. Perhaps because of that sense of loss we feel, vestigial remnants of the old-Texas mythology hang on tenaciously as part of the University identity. For example, though not used to ward off cattle hooves or the elements or fit easily into a stirrup, expensive cowboy boots and Stetson hats can still be seen on campus, virtually lost among the shorts and T-shirts and saris and business suits and turbans and tie-dyes and dashikis crowding today's sidewalks. At football games the Longhorn Band can be seen decked out in gaudy Western fringe and piping, and the Silver Spurs sport faux cowboy garb from head to toe. A few male students crawl through the urban traffic in enormous, immaculate pickup trucks, some of which get driven during holidays and breaks to their fathers' coveted and increasingly scarce and expensive deer leases in South or West Texas. Amidst the noise and exhaust, the earthen banks along I-35 bloom with sown bluebonnets. Statues and terra cotta sculpture of longhorns—cattle bred to survive in dry and hostile conditions—are ubiquitous on campus. The old Texas still exists on the Forty Acres, but it would be unfair to say that that presence is merely kitsch.

Students today, even the ones with the cowboy boots and pickups, are much more likely to have been reared in cozy, upper-middle-class suburbs like Plano or The Woodlands than on subsistence farms on a forlorn, windswept Texas plain. Those suburbs and the first-class university that today's students enjoy are precisely what their great-great-grandfathers who survived the days of B. Hall desired for them—and worked hard to bequeath to them. Today's students come to Austin hoping to make the University—and perhaps even a romanticized atavism of the Texas the poor boys of B. Hall lived in—a part of their own personal identities. But the irony of cities (and today's campus is itself a small city within a city) is that as people's surroundings become more crowded and comfortable, their social circles become smaller and harder to maintain. People today must "invent" themselves through their free choices of appearance, possessions, and friends.

Today's student can be profoundly lonely, even within the inevitable daily crush of people and material things on the UT campus, or at home in a towering campus dorm or in an antiseptic, cookie-cutter apartment complex on the downscale fringes of suburbia miles from campus. In the intimate, Spartan confines of B. Hall, the poor boys must have been much less prone to suffering from loneliness or crisis of identity: they knew they were poor, owned only one suit, that they had dirt under their fingernails and hayseed in their pockets, and that they had to champion both their own and their fellow students' aspirations by working hard and succeeding cooperatively in Austin if they wanted to avoid their otherwise preordained occupation of subsistence farmer. With comforts such as private bathrooms and high-speed Internet connections, today's student faces a much greater challenge to understand who he or she is and his or her responsibilities to others. Nevertheless, despite the realization of Jefferson's fear of the encroaching factory, Texans still consider themselves to be invested with an enviable, rugged individualism, and much of the rest of the world, for better or worse, sees Texans that way, too.

When we stand in that empty spot where B. Hall stood and feel the presence of its reposed souls, we are caught in a dilemma. Today we envy the poor boys' genuine independence and communal bond. That sacred fire—that "substantial and genuine virtue" called to mind by Jefferson—still flickers within us. For that sense of independence and community to be genuine, however, it must be purchased, and the purchase price is the humility and sense of urgency one develops in the face of true adversity. In his first *Crisis* pamphlet, Jefferson's contemporary Thomas Paine observes with typical vulgar clarity: "What we obtain too cheap, we esteem too lightly; it is dearness only that gives everything its value." Despite our yearning for something Texan, for something dear, we are relieved that our material wealth and the comforts it provides us are not proper currency and that we cannot afford the price of real independence and community—a price the men of B. Hall had ample means to pay.

WORKS CITED

Benedict, Harry Yandell, ed. *A Source Book Relating to the History of the University of Texas: Legislative, Legal, Bibliographical, and Statistical.* Austin: University of Texas, 1917.

Berry, Margaret C. *Brick by Golden Brick: A History of Campus Buildings at the University of Texas at Austin: 1883–1993.* Austin: LBCo. Publishing, 1993.

———. "Student Life and Customs, 1883–1933, at The University of Texas." 2 vols. PhD diss., Columbia University, 1965.

Brackenridge Hall. Vertical file. Center for American History, The University of Texas at Austin.

Brown, Nugent E. *B Hall, Texas: Stories of and about the Famous Dormitory, Brackenridge Hall, Texas University.* San Antonio: The Naylor Company, 1938.

Cactus yearbooks, 1894–1927. Center for American History, The University of Texas at Austin.

Daily Texan, Austin, Texas, 1912–1913, 1925–1926. Center for American History, The University of Texas at Austin.

Drawings of Brackenridge Hall in the University of Texas Buildings Collection. Alexander Architectural Archive, Architecture and Planning Library, The University of Texas at Austin.

Frantz, Joe B. *The Forty-Acre Follies: An Opinionated History of the University of Texas.* Austin: Texas Monthly Press, 1983.

Jefferson, Thomas. Letter to Benjamin Austin, January 9, 1816. In *Thomas Jefferson, Writings*, ed. Merrill Peterson. New York: The Library of America, 1984.

———. *Notes on the State of Virginia.* In *Thomas Jefferson, Writings*, ed. Merrill Peterson. New York: The Library of America, 1984.

Long, Walter E. "B Hall of Texas." *Southwestern Historical Quarterly* 62 (April, 1959): 413–441.

Smith, T. V. *A Non-Existent Man: An Autobiography.* Austin: University of Texas Press, 1962.

Splawn, W. M. W. *The University of Texas: Its Origin and Growth to 1928.* 2 vols. Austin: The University of Texas, 1956. Unpublished typescript. Walter Marshall William Splawn Papers. Box 2R189. Center for American History, The University of Texas at Austin.

Taylor, T. U. *Fifty Years on Forty Acres.* Austin: Alec Book Company, 1938.

Texas Almanac and State Industrial Guide, 1978–1979. Ed. Fred Pass. Dallas: A. H. Belo Corp, 1977.

Turner, Frederick Jackson. "The Significance of the Frontier." In *History, Frontier, and Section: Three Essays by Frederick Jackson Turner.* With an introduction by Martin Ridge. Albuquerque: New Mexico University Press, 1993.

Tyler, Ron, ed. in chief. *The New Handbook of Texas.* 6 vols. Austin: Texas State Historical Association, 1996.

University of Texas Board of Regents minutes, 1890–1910. Microfilm 808.21, 808.22. Center for American History, The University of Texas at Austin.

University of Texas Memorabilia Collection. Box 4P158. Center for American History, The University of Texas at Austin.

University Residence Halls Application, 2001–2002. Brochure from the Division of Housing and Food Service, The University of Texas at Austin, 2000.

UT Brackenridge Hall Records. Box 4P98. Center for American History, The University of Texas at Austin.

UT—Buildings: B. Hall. Photo file. Center for American History, The University of Texas at Austin.

UT—Housing. Vertical file. Center for American History, The University of Texas at Austin.

UT: "Push Ball." Photo file. Center for American History, The University of Texas at Austin.

Williamson, Roxanne Kuter. *A History of the Campus and Buildings of The University of Texas, with Emphasis on the Sources for the Architectural Styles.* Unpublished thesis, 1965. Center for American History, The University of Texas at Austin.

LAWRENCE
SPECK

Campus Architecture
The Heroic Decades

From 1910 to 1942 the University of Texas at Austin built an extraordinary ensemble of buildings which demonstrated palpably to its public the ambitions of an emerging institution. In a relatively short period of time, the image of the University was transformed from a sleepy, small-town college housed in a hodgepodge of mismatched buildings into a powerful, sophisticated institution whose campus exuded confidence and a memorable identity. During this period, a core of 33 buildings were constructed by three different architects of significant distinction (Cass Gilbert, 1910–1922; Herbert M. Greene, 1922–1930; Paul Cret, 1930–1942). It is remarkable both that all work done through this era was directed by architects with very strong credentials and that the architects used were firmly committed to building a real *campus* and not just a collection of individual buildings. In planning, massing, character, material selection, and detail this core campus and its components offer an instructive model for how to create a rich, lively, yet coherent urban place.

When this era began, the University's 27-year-old campus consisted of a motley collection of makeshift structures on the crest of a hill just north of the city's center. In the late 1880s the State of Texas had replaced the original Greek Revival Capitol Building with an impressive new granite edifice designed by Detroit architect Elijah Myers. The mammoth structure with its vertical cast-iron dome (taller than the nation's capitol in Washington) sat atop a hill at the termination of Congress Avenue—the main street of Austin, the modest city below. The city's grid, which had been laid out in 1839, provided the basis for a coherent urban ensemble with the Colorado River forming a southern boundary, prominent bluffs creating east and

---

Lawrence Speck is the W. L. Moody, Jr., Centennial Professor in Architecture. He has been a professor in the University of Texas School of Architecture since 1975 and served as its dean from 1993 to 1999. As a working architect, Speck designed the Austin-Bergstrom International Airport terminal building, the Austin Convention Center, and the Umlauf Sculpture Garden. He has written or co-written a number of books and is preparing a guide to the architecture of the University of Texas campus.

west edges, and the Capitol on its hilltop crowning the city to the north. With the new Capitol Building reinforcing the symmetry and grandeur of the original plan, the fledgling capital city had a memorable presence and a striking skyline.

The University's image in 1910 was significantly less impressive. Its first structure, a portion of Old Main Building, was located thoughtfully by architect Frederick E. Ruffini in 1882 on the highest point of the forty-acre campus, near its center. It faced the Capitol Building to the southeast, establishing an axis between the two hills which was slightly skewed to the city's grid. But the initial structure remained an odd fragment for years until the building was finally completed in 1899 after three construction phases directed by three different architects. By the time it was finished, its collegiate Gothic style was dated and old-fashioned. Even so, in 1900, the only other building on the campus, a simple brick men's dormitory (Brackenridge Hall), just to the east of Old Main, was remodeled to add a series of highly decorated towers in a somewhat futile effort to make the adjacent structures complement each other.

The buildings that followed in the first decade of the twentieth century discarded the spiky towers and elaborate ornamentation of their predecessors but failed to establish any new order of their own. Although San Antonio architects Atlee B. Ayers and Charles A. Coughlin were hired to do a formal development plan for the campus in 1903, little regard was given to the very ordinary plan, even in the placement of the three buildings constructed over the next few years. The Women's Building of 1903 by Coughlin and Ayers was a Neo-Romanesque structure which, if enlarged, could have complied with the master plan. The neoclassical Engineering Building by the same architects in 1904 and the Neo-Palladian Law Building by Atlee B. Ayers of 1908, however, were located clearly at odds with the master plan.

Rejecting the disappointing results they were getting from their local consultants, President David Houston and Regent George Brackenridge began in early 1907 to search for a nationally respected architect to create a new campus master plan and to establish a greater cohesion for the growing university. They selected Frederick M. Mann, head of the Department of Architecture at Washington University in St. Louis, to prepare a new development plan in 1909.

Mann had established a strong reputation as an advocate for quality campus design largely through his involvement with the implementation of Cope and Stewardson's competition-winning 1899 master plan for his home campus.

Mann's plan essentially recommended starting over from scratch. It advocated demolition of all but the two most recent buildings on a campus, barely a quarter-century old. The massive but stylistically regressive Old Main Building was to be replaced by a smaller building of similar T-shaped footprint capped by a polygonal lantern. A broad green lawn with a double row of trees down its center would link the new building to the Capitol Building, creating a grand, open gesture to the south. The rest of the campus buildings were tightly clustered in a U-shaped ensemble wrapping the west, north, and east sides of the forty acres. Consistent rows of fairly uniform buildings lined Guadalupe Street, 24th Street, and Lampasas Street (later Speedway), walling the campus off on three sides.

THE CASS GILBERT ERA, 1910–1922

Even before Mann's plan was complete, University of Texas regents and administrators had contacted New York architect Cass Gilbert for advice. They were disappointed, as they had been earlier, with Frederick Mann's failure to create a compelling vision for the University's future. Cass Gilbert was just the architect to project a more powerful and ambitious direction. Schooled at M.I.T. and later in France, Gilbert had worked for McKim, Mead and White, the most prominent American architectural firm of the era. He had won prestigious competitions for the design of the Minnesota State Capitol and the U.S. Customs House in New York. At the time, he was working on a comprehensive development plan for the University of Minnesota. At fifty years old, he had reached a peak of maturity in his career with recent projects in Ohio, Minnesota, Michigan, and Missouri as well as on the East Coast. Beginning in 1908 he had served a term as president of the American Institute of Architects. The University of Texas had finally found a nationally known architect with ambitious vision capable of creating an enduring image for the campus and the institution.

Cass Gilbert, from his very early sketches, imagined a campus for the University of Texas that was grand and monumental. Even before actually receiving the commission, he produced sketches of the UT campus with a powerful scale and clarity well beyond the work of Coughlin and Ayers or Frederick Mann. In these images, buildings conspired together to frame dominant vistas and to create memorable exterior spaces. Gilbert imagined an *urban* campus with well-defined malls, courts, and plazas. The rural-feeling green lawns of previous schemes were replaced by rigorously ordered outdoor spaces defined by arcades and formal planting as well as the buildings themselves.

Four powerful features set Gilbert's plan apart from its predecessors. First, it replaced Old Main with a much larger and grander classical building called University Hall at the very center of the campus. Three distinctly different architectural approaches were envisioned for University Hall over Gilbert's 10-year tenure as University architect. It was a grand domed node in sketches as early as February 1909, and as late as October 1920. It was a large pedimented temple with a dominant gable-front facing the State Capitol Building to the south in sketches as early as January 1910, and much later as well. In a sketch from 1920 University Hall was comprised of a single very tall tower rising from a low, flat base. (By the 1920s Cass Gilbert had become famous for designing towers—his Woolworth Building in New York of 1913 being the tallest building in the world at the time.) Gilbert was the seminal voice that established the idea of a very large building, prominent on the Austin skyline, that would serve as an iconic symbol for the emerging university.

A second powerful feature that distinguished Gilbert's plan involved the creation of four axes which led down the hill from University Hall in roughly cardinal directions. The South Mall was the most prominent of the four, linking the front of University Hall forcefully to the Capitol Building at the other end of the axis. A broad main plaza flanked by symmetrical buildings introduced the South Mall, which was articulated by double rows of trees flanked by continuous arcades. This grand urban ensemble of University Hall, Main Plaza, South Mall, and State Capitol stretched the realm of the campus beyond the forty acres to make it a dominant player in the larger context of the city. It established a parallel between the University and state government and al-

lowed the campus to borrow some of the grandeur of the State Capitol. As it eventually came to fruition twenty years later, it established a signature presence of the University of Texas as a strong, confident institution commanding a powerful physical presence in the city.

The other three axes, though less grand, established important connections and contributed significantly to a sense of clarity and coherence for the campus. The East Mall and West Mall focused on the short ends of University Hall and were terminated by a well-defined gateway on Guadalupe and Lampasas streets respectively. The somewhat shorter North Mall was about as broad as it was long, giving it a less-directional character. But its axial walkway with flanking pavilions at the northern terminus focused it clearly back to University Hall. Contrary to the schemes of earlier architects, Gilbert's axes indicated multiple connections to the city around and provided ready options for expansion beyond the forty acres. At the same time the axes exuded an aura of strength and confidence, of order and stability. They set a tone for the public image of the campus that made a lasting mark on the character of the University.

A third feature of Gilbert's plan, which would have lasting significance, focused on the creation of a more intimate, personal scale for the campus. Within the four quadrants created by the cardinal axes, Gilbert envisioned well-defined quadrangles. Each of the four spaces had its own distinct character, but all of them were loosely contained by an assemblage of carefully aligned, mostly linear buildings. It was in these less-formal courts that the everyday academic life of faculty and students could thrive. They, along with the four malls, acknowledged the dual role of the University as both a powerful institution and a nurturing place of learning.

The fourth feature of Gilbert's plan which gave it appeal to University leaders over previous efforts had to do with its attitude toward consistency versus inclusiveness in the architectural character of buildings on the campus. Whereas Frederick Mann had proposed demolishing all but two of the extant buildings in order to create strong cohesion, Gilbert projected retaining all of the existing structures except Old Main. He very cleverly integrated Brackenridge Hall, the Women's Building, the Engineering Building, and the Law Building, all with very diverse architectural expressions, into his grand scheme. Even in the two buildings he completed for the campus, the Library (now Battle Hall) and the Education Building (now Sutton Hall), he worked with two very different architectural vocabularies. In the schemes he projected for other projects—sketches for University Hall, a gymnasium, and an outdoor theatre—the range of architectural character he imagined for the campus was quite broad. Gilbert's vision embraced existing campus buildings of diverse styles as well as a range of new architectural expressions designed to fit various functions and sites. This approach is consistent with his contemporaneous campus work at Oberlin College, where the five structures he built represent a striking architectural range. Gilbert clearly imagined a university campus, not as a military-style assemblage of uniform buildings, but as a community of diverse structures. He believed buildings should be carefully coordinated with each other, but not restricted by an imposed stylistic code.

Battle Hall, which Gilbert began conceiving in 1909, was to be the westernmost of the two symmetrical buildings flanking the Main Plaza in the Master Plan. Its design was based loosely on the form of a Renaissance *palazzo* with office and administrative functions located on the ground floor behind heavy walls with plain, spare openings. The gracious reading room was raised to the upper *piano nobile* and graced with high ceilings, arched windows, and a monumental façade treatment. This approach owed much to late-nineteenth-century library precedents such as Henri Labrouste's Bibliothéque Ste.-Genevieve in Paris and McKim, Mead and White's Boston Public Library as well as to Gilbert's own St. Louis Public Library, the commission for which he had won in a competition in 1907.

But the library for University of Texas had its own distinct character apart from its precedents. It was much smaller and simpler than the very urban libraries in Paris, Boston, and St. Louis. Its campus location gave it a softer, gentler context and allowed it to be more an object building than urban in-fill. Its hipped tile roof with deep, shadowy overhangs differentiated its massing and placed it firmly as a southern building distinct from its more-northern counterparts. Battle Hall also had a more festive, lively character, built as it was from the cream-colored Central Texas limestone rather than a more dour granite and decorated with exuberant, brightly colored terra cotta ornamentation.

Design of Gilbert's second building, Sutton Hall, began in 1915 with construction completed in 1918. It was a general purpose academic building conceived by Gilbert to be the first step in creating the purest of the four quadrangles in the Master Plan at the southeast corner of the campus. Although planning documents had indicated flanking projections on the north face of the building at each end, the structure as completed became a long, simple rectangle in plan with a double-loaded center corridor and an entry hall facing south at its midpoint. Ironically, even though Sutton Hall was immediately adjacent to Battle Hall, there was very little relationship between the two either formally or functionally. Battle Hall created the west face of what was to be the new Main Plaza. Sutton Hall delineated the northern face of what was to be a new southeast quadrangle. They each seeded development for the future, but, because of the twelve-foot topographical change between the two, they were initially rather isolated from each other.

In terms of architectural character, Sutton Hall was also strongly differentiated from Battle Hall. Though each building relied on the Renaissance *palazzo* as a precedent, their material usage, scale, color, and ornament were substantially different. Sutton Hall was much darker and less monumentally scaled than Battle Hall. Predominantly faced in a rough textured brick in browns, tans, oranges, and ochers, Sutton Hall had a ruddier, less refined building character. Even the stone used for its base was a grayer color than the creamy hues of Battle Hall. Paint colors were much darker and even the roof tiles were a deeper red and more variegated in color than the Library.

Though Gilbert did not complete as many buildings as might have been anticipated during the twelve years he served as University Architect, he left an indelible mark on the campus' future. Both through his Master Plan and through the diverse architectural vocabularies of his two completed buildings he established an inspiring vision for what the University of Texas might become. Gilbert helped the University administration and regents make the leap from seeing their institution as a small-town college to envisioning it as a sophisticated institution "of the first class." Though his successors would create more buildings, Cass Gilbert was the seminal and visionary force in the development of the core UT campus as it exists today.

THE HERBERT M. GREENE ERA, 1922–1930

In 1922 the regents decided not to renew Gilbert's contract. For the next eight years the role of University Architect was filled by Dallas architect Herbert M. Greene, whose firm later became Greene, La Roche and Dahl. Greene was born in Pennsylvania, received his education in architecture at University of Illinois, and moved to Dallas in 1897 at the age of twenty-six. By the early 1920s his successful practice had spread beyond Dallas and included the Scottish Rite Dormitory just north of the UT campus as well as work for the University of Texas Medical Branch in Galveston. At about the same time as he received the appointment as University Architect, he became the first Texas architect to be named a Fellow in the American Institute of Architects. He was a very talented and capable architect who was a good friend of Sam Cochran, then chair of the UT Board of Regents.

In the early years of his tenure as University Architect, Greene worked closely with James M. White of the University of Illinois, who did two new development plans for the campus, neither of which had much lasting significance. The first, done in 1923, envisioned the demolitions of all existing buildings except the two most recent ones by Cass Gilbert. Though not influential as a whole, this scheme over the next few years did locate several buildings—most notably, a new stadium and a new gymnasium—off the original forty acres. White revised his plan in 1926, responding, in particular, to criticism by William Battle, the head of the Faculty Building Advisory Committee. The new scheme for the forty acres retained more buildings than the earlier one and had a stronger sense of formal order. Even the buildings completed by Greene in the core campus over the next few years, however, did not follow White's development plan.

Herbert Greene's first project built after his appointment was the Biology Building (later called the Biological Laboratory) of 1926. Though not entirely in compliance with Cass Gilbert's Master Plan of 1914, it came close. It created a long, hard boundary on the northern side of the forty acres as well as a western edge for a tightened axis projecting north from the Main Building. The architectural character of the Biological Laboratory also owed much to Gilbert—especially to the vocabulary he established in Sutton Hall. Though the budget was clearly much lower than for the Gilbert precedent, the general conformation of the Biological Laboratory was the same. The long, thin rectangular volume had a stone base made of Leuders limestone, two brick-faced floors above pierced by regular windows, and a red tile roof. Because of the significant slope of the site, the building's basement was exposed on the east end and faced with a rusticated version of the stone used on the first level. Windows for an attic floor also pierced the frieze under the eave, so that the building actually had five floors with natural light, although it generally looked like a three-story building.

Concerns for maximum economy, which may have driven this extraordinary utilization of the building volume, did not have such a positive effect on exterior finishes. The use of terra cotta ornament was far more parsimonious than in Sutton Hall, restricted as it was to a band under the eaves, turned columns flanking a few special windows, and occasional decorative panels. Themes depicted in the ornament included both classical motifs and local botanical elements such as bluebonnets and oak branches. The building's duller, less variegated brown brick and flat tile panels did not have nearly the same richness and liveliness as Sutton Hall.

But Greene's second building, Garrison Hall, of 1926, demonstrated his capability to produce the same kind of strong character and texture that Gilbert had accomplished. Sited in a very prominent location on the east side of the Main Plaza opposite Battle Hall, the new building, which would house the History Department, was, again, generally located in compliance with Gilbert's 1914 plan. Its L-shaped massing, with the shorter leg facing the plaza and the longer leg running down the hill to the east, enabled Greene to get four usable floors with generous basement windows in a building that looked to be three floors (and about the same height as Battle Hall) on the plaza side. The Leuder's limestone base—rusticated at the basement level, smooth above—is pierced by arched windows on the first floor, like Sutton Hall. The brown/tan/orange/ochre brick colors and quantity of terra cotta ornament are also much more like Sutton than like the Biological Laboratory.

But the theme of the ornament was, distinct from Gilbert, tied very strongly to the building's use and locale. The ornament evokes scenarios of Texas history in the form of longhorn skulls, Lone Stars, bluebonnets, and cactus and by means of the names of state heroes like Austin, Travis, and Lamar emblazoned above focal windows. Rondels feature brands of famous Texas ranches over more than a century. In Garrison Hall Greene successfully transformed Cass Gilbert's general building vocabulary into an expression quite uniquely his own and strikingly Texan.

Greene designed two other academic buildings employing Gilbert's Renaissance *palazzo* format and generally in compliance with the 1914 Master Plan—Waggener Hall and the Chemistry Building, both completed in 1931. Waggener Hall was distinguished by its greater height—five full floors—as well as by the creation of a very deep limestone frieze under the eave which makes its top floor seem more a part of the cap than of the midsection of the building. Again, Greene manages to increase the density of building on campus without losing the basic motif of the stone base, brick midsection, and prominent cap. As in the Biological Laboratory and Garrison Hall, the ornament of Waggener Hall, which housed classes in Business, was themed to its use and locale. Emblems around the frieze under the building's bracketed concrete eave depict the industries of Texas. The dominance of agriculture (corn, cotton, citrus fruit, pecans, peaches, onions, cabbage, etc.) is striking, though livestock (cattle, sheep, goats) is well represented, as are oil and construction.

The design of the Chemistry Building differed from the others of this genre by its extraordinary length—almost twice as long as Sutton Hall or the Biological Laboratory. With its three short wings projecting on the south side, it had a much larger building footprint than these precedents. The Chemistry Building anchored the northeast corner of the forty acres and, with Waggener Hall and the Biological Laboratory, began to create a strong edge to the academic part of the campus along 24th Street and what is now Speedway. A very elaborate stone portal in the center of the north face divided the building's most dominant façade into two segments of more pleasing proportion. Outside of the limestone portal, which contained emblems depicting beakers and other equipment related to chemistry, Greene employed far less color and ornament on the building than he had on Garrison and Waggener. Again, Greene demonstrates ingenuity and finesse in adapting the original Sutton Hall model to very different programmatic needs, site situations, and budgets.

Greene's greatest contribution may well have been in the series of buildings he did just off the forty acres, extending the campus domain to the north and east and broadening campus functions to include athletic facilities and a women's residence hall. His Littlefield Dormitory of 1927 staked out a residential precinct to the north of the forty acres and became seminal in the subsequent development of an entire women's quadrangle a decade later. Located about halfway between the Biological Laboratory and the Scottish Rite Dormitory for girls that Greene had completed in 1921, the Littlefield Dormitory generally had a U-shaped plan with a forecourt facing south like the Scottish Rite facility. However, whereas his earlier dormitory had been a red brick Georgian building with three-story limestone columns and a slate roof, the newer University-sponsored dorm had a strong stylistic connection to other campus buildings. Above its split-face ashlar stone base, it was a primarily brick building of roughly the same coloration as Sutton Hall. There was no terra cotta ornament, but windows on the ground floor were lined with vaguely Moorish carved stone ornament. Turned columns and heavy wood framing on a small loggia gave a feeling of southern Spain without placing the building within any doctrinaire architecture style.

In terms of athletic facilities, Greene completed a new stadium in 1926 (now much expanded to become Darrell K Royal–Texas Memorial Stadium), a baseball field in 1927 (later Clark Field), a men's gymnasium in 1930 (later Gregory Gym), and a women's gymnasium in 1931 (later Anna Hiss Gym). Through these athletics buildings Greene stretched both the architectural and the materials vocabulary for the campus, enriching its range of color, texture, and scale. In the stadium he created a grand curved concrete arcade with massive, very plain arches providing generous light to the spaces below the raked seats. In the women's gym he produced a diminutive ensemble of single-story volumes around an intimately scaled courtyard. But it was in the men's gym that Greene made the strongest departure from the vocabulary employed in the academic buildings on the forty acres and established the important precedent for sympathetic but very distinctive special-function buildings at the outer ranges of the campus.

Gregory Gym was sited generally in the same location as had been indicated in James M. White's development plan of 1923—just east of the street that became Speedway at the southeast corner of the cam-

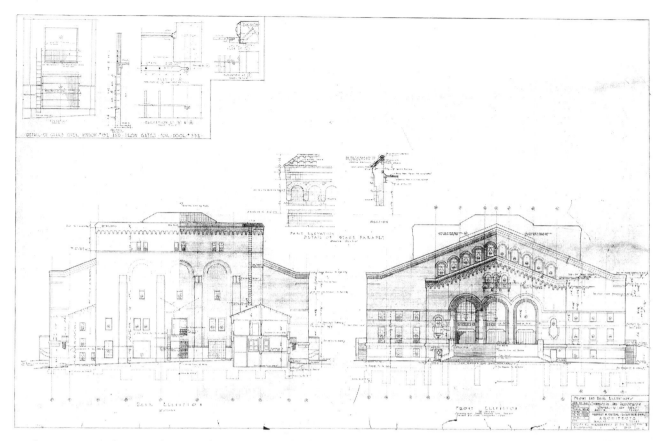

Herbert Greene's elevation drawings for the Gregory Gymnasium, 1929. *Courtesy of the Alexander Architectural Archive, University of Texas Libraries, the University of Texas at Austin. (University of Texas Buildings Collection, Gregory Gym sh. #5)*

pus. (Gilbert's 1914 plan made no provision for building off the forty acres.) Its tall, flat front faced the academic campus to the west. This monumental façade with its great central flight of steps and nested gables presented a very strong contrast to the horizontal, hipped-roof volumes of the newer academic buildings on the forty acres. The gymnasium sat on a rather raw concrete base and had concrete spandrels articulated by bold geometric designs traversing grand arches on its north, west, and south facades. The shiny, colorful terra cotta ornament of other campus buildings was strikingly absent. The gymnasium was robust and muscular compared to its more delicate neighbors.

Stylistically, Gregory Gym eschewed the Renaissance precedent set by Battle Hall and Sutton Hall in favor of the more ancient Romanesque. This dramatic shift may have been provoked in part by an extended trip which Greene took to Europe in 1928, just prior to designing the gym. The building adopted a vaguely Lombard flavor, particularly in its distinctive relieving arches and corbel tables. Dominantly brick, the gym utilized limestone only sparingly in a few decorative balconies. It was the brick, similar in color and texture to that used in Sutton and Garrison halls, that tied Gregory Gym back to the rest of the campus. Even here, however, Greene employed more exotic configurations than had been used previously—abstracted dentils, herringbone and diaper patterns.

Inside, the lower floor of the building contained a maze of handball courts, dressing rooms, and exercise spaces. Above was a single grand room with a basketball court surrounded on three sides by bleachers elevated a full level above the gym floor. Interior walls were faced in the local Austin Common brick, which was lighter and softer than that on the exterior. Dramatic steel trusses in a tapered gable configuration spanned the space, which had a stage with fly-loft on the east, allowing the gym to double as a performance venue.

Perhaps because of its distinctiveness and its de-

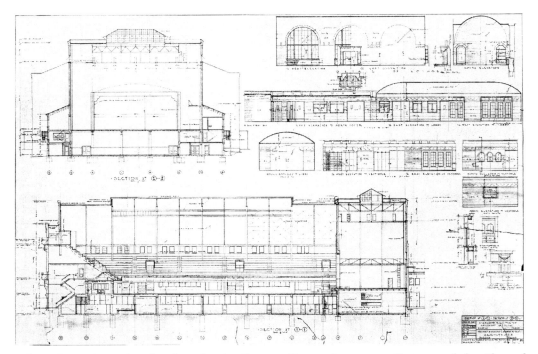

Herbert Greene's section drawings for the Gregory Gymnasium, 1929. *Courtesy of the Alexander Architectural Archive, University of Texas Libraries, the University of Texas at Austin. (University of Texas Buildings Collection, Gregory Gym sh. #10)*

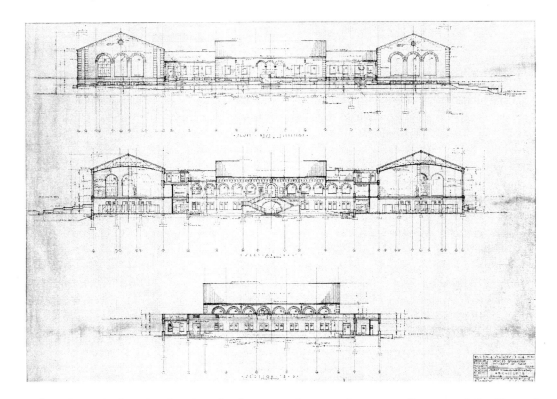

Herbert Greene's elevation drawings for the women's gymnasium, 1929. *Courtesy of the Alexander Architectural Archive, University of Texas Libraries, the University of Texas at Austin. (University of Texas Buildings Collection, Anna Hiss sh. #6)*

parture from the dominant surrounding vocabulary, Gregory Gym soon became a favorite building on the campus. It demonstrated the importance of both Gilbert's and Greene's notion that there should be a variety of styles and materials in campus buildings, especially as utilized to create landmarks and to particularize exceptional functions. The building also demonstrates Greene's capabilities as an outstanding architect who could generate appropriate expressions independent of precedents set by Cass Gilbert before him.

Greene designed a total of twelve buildings on the UT campus during his tenure as University Architect and left an indelible mark on its character. His respect for the planning and architectural acumen of his predecessor as well as his own creative capabilities made him an excellent architect for this era of the University's growth. His knowledge of the state and his commitment to it generated references to regional characteristics in the ruggedness and toughness of structures like Gregory Gym and in the erudite detail of buildings like Garrison Hall. By early 1930, with the design of most of his UT buildings complete, Greene's health began to fail. Although his contract as University Architect was not due to expire until 1933, his direct role in the work became greatly curtailed. Greene died in February 1932, leaving his firm to complete the last year of the UT contract.

THE PAUL CRET ERA, 1930–1942

In March of 1930 the Board of Regents signed a contact with Paul Phillippe Cret to become consulting architect for the university and to create a new vision for the next era of campus building. Initially engaged to conceive only a development plan, Cret was awarded a second contract by the Board of Regents in June 1931 to design ten new buildings. This extraordinary flurry of construction activity was provoked by the creation of the Permanent University Fund by the Texas Legislature in April 1931. This mechanism authorized the University to pledge its income from oil production on lands in West Texas to secure long-term loans. The regents, fearful that the legislature might rescind the loan authorization when it met again in 1932, took the architect they had at hand and moved forward quickly.

In these initial ten buildings Cret designed for UT he established four distinctive architectural vocabularies which he would extend to all 19 buildings he eventually designed for the campus. Like Gilbert and Greene before him, Cret knew a campus the size that the University would eventually need required diversity. In a report written to the regents in 1933, Cret advocated buildings "related, to be sure, but independent, and requiring a certain variety of treatment, to avoid the monotony and the 'institutional' character inherent to the repetition of similar units."

The first of the vocabularies Cret employed was a clear outgrowth from the *palazzo*-based work of Gilbert and Greene in academic buildings like Sutton Hall, the Biological Laboratory, Garrison Hall, Waggener Hall, and the Chemistry Building. Cret's Physics Building of 1933 (now Painter Hall) had the same limestone base, brick midsection, and elaborate bracketed eaves with red tile roof that was, by then, well established on the campus. In this version, the four-story height was reduced in scale by treating the top floor as a broken frieze rendered in limestone, much like Greene had employed at Waggener Hall. Several elements in Painter Hall were new, however. A perpendicular tower at the western end of the building broke the otherwise simple massing of the long hipped roof, acknowledging the location of that end of the building on the north axis of the campus. In addition, a much lighter, yellower brick was used as well as smooth limestone edging at vertical corners. Both of these gestures created a somewhat cooler, cleaner, less rugged feeling to Painter Hall in comparison to its predecessors.

The Geology Building of 1933 (now Will C. Hogg Building) also extended the familiar vocabulary of other Forty Acres academic buildings. More elaborately ornamented than Painter Hall, the Hogg Building gave Cret the opportunity to use the same sort of department-specific theme that Greene had employed earlier. A horizontal carved limestone band that wrapped the structure utilized seashells, starfish, dinosaurs, and other prehistoric creatures as symbols for geology. Thick concrete brackets under the eaves were comparable to those employed by Greene in Waggener Hall. But, here again, there were some new touches as well. Blank slate panels were inserted between vertically stacked windows, and brick pilasters with carved limestone ionic capitals rose between the window stacks to give a more classicized character to

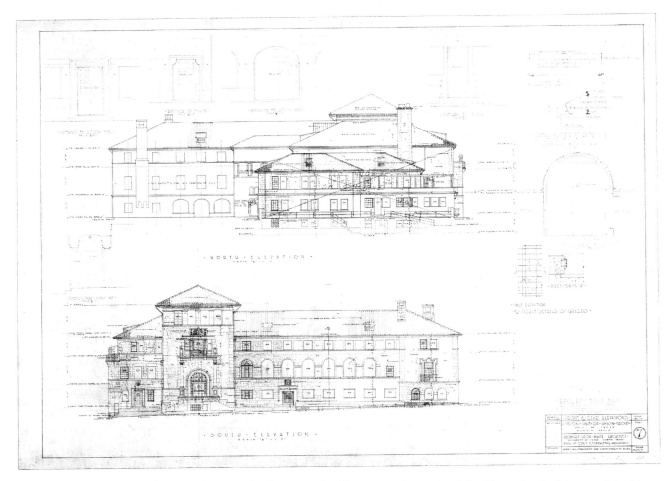

Paul Cret's front and rear elevation drawings for the Union building, 1931. *Courtesy of the Alexander Architectural Archive, University of Texas Libraries, the University of Texas at Austin. (University of Texas Buildings Collection, Student Union sh. #7)*

the building. Rusticated quoins were applied to corners extending the direction begun at Painter of using brick as infill panels in a stone frame. Over the following decade, Cret utilized this first vocabulary with some significant variations on six other campus buildings, ranging from residence halls like Carothers Dormitory of 1937 to academic buildings for Chemical Engineering and Petroleum Engineering in 1942.

The second vocabulary Cret employed was more rugged and varied in massing like Gregory Gym, Anna Hiss Gym, and Littlefield Dormitory from the Greene era. Cret used it in the vicinity of Gregory Gym and for functions comparable to Littlefield Dormitory. The first building of this genre was Brackenridge Hall of 1932, a men's dormitory located on 21st Street just southeast of the men's gym. The building's conformation was looser than the vocabulary generated from

the rectangular *palazzo* format. Its long, thin volumes were broken in plan and featured a prominent tower at the west end. A rusticated base was created by corbeling out every ninth course of the brick on the first floor, lending a very rugged character in striking contrast to the Physics Building or the Hogg Building. Clearly an economy-minded project, Brackenridge Hall had coffered plaster eaves rather than bracketed ones with a simple stucco frieze below. The sparse ornament in the frieze picked up regional themes similar to the sort Greene had used in Garrison Hall and Waggener Hall. Western and cowboy images were predominant—cacti, lone wolves, shotguns, broncos, pistols, and knives. Cret did two other buildings in this genre on the campus—Roberts Hall of 1936 and Prather Hall of 1937.

The third vocabulary utilized by Cret was also

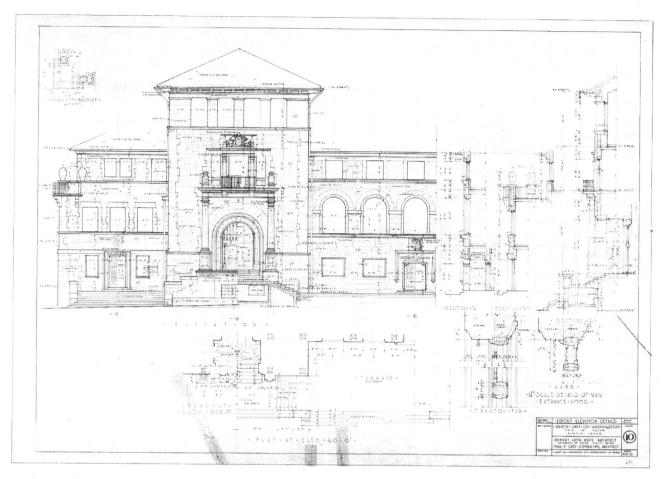

Paul Cret's front elevation details for the Union building, 1931. *Courtesy of the Alexander Architectural Archive, University of Texas Libraries, the University of Texas at Austin. (University of Texas Buildings Collection, Student Union sh. #10)*

characterized by informal massing with buildings assembled as collections of separate, sometimes juxtaposed, volumes. These buildings, however, eschewed brick, which had become a dominant material in every new campus building since Battle Hall, in favor of creating all-stone buildings. Three of Cret's best works, the Home Economics Building (now Mary E. Gearing Hall), the Architecture Building (now Goldsmith Hall), and the Student Union—all of 1933—defined this genre. They were all composed of one, two, three, and four-story elements sheathed in a combination of smooth limestone and random ashlar fossiliferous limestone. Together, they created a fresh new look for the campus, quite distinct from any previous projects.

Mary E. Gearing Hall was created as a combination of a four-story north-facing central block with a hipped roof, two flanking three-story wings with flat roofs, two dominant towers at the intersection of the central block and the wings, and a lovely one-story loggia surrounding a courtyard with a fountain on the south side. The building's composition was symmetrical, appropriate to its location on the north axis of the campus, but was, nonetheless, extremely varied and romantic. Window rhythms were syncopated and seldom aligned floor to floor. Cret originally conceived the building to be clad in rubble stone, which would have made it even more rustic and distinctive in its context. He used heavy timber beams and purlins in the loggia and turned-wood handrails on balconies projecting from the building to contribute a far more informal, rural character than existed in the Gilbert and Greene buildings.

Goldsmith Hall similarly incorporated a tower, a

loggia, and a courtyard, along with volumes of varied heights to create a loose composition reflective, like Mary E. Gearing Hall, of its varied internal functions. Two thin wings with long north/south faces housed well-lit design studios. A thicker, taller block with windows oriented east and west stacked a lecture hall on the first floor, a library on the second floor, and classrooms on the top to create the third side of a well-scaled courtyard. Unlike Gearing Hall, Goldsmith was dominantly asymmetrical with the eccentric four-story tower anchoring the northwest corner of the building and a flat-roof two-story volume trailing off the southwest edge. Local symmetries, as in the entry portal or the west façade of the lecture hall/library/classroom wing, contributed partial order but also served to differentiate the various parts from each other.

The Student Union was composed of two wings with a corner tower at their intersection that matched Goldsmith Hall's tower across the West Mall. Together the two towers created a prominent gateway to the campus from Guadalupe Street. The long wing of the Union on Guadalupe Street was two stories and accommodated the most-public building functions, like the cafeteria and ballroom. The shorter wing along the West Mall housed less formal activities like meeting rooms.

The Union and Goldsmith Hall formed a striking ensemble at the major pedestrian entry point to the campus. They were similar to each other in compositional character and materials, but quite different in fenestration and detail. Together, they created a totally new architectural character very different from Cass Gilbert's seminal landmarks nearby. The simple stereometric volumes, *palazzo* compositional format, and materials treatments of Battle Hall and Sutton Hall were rejected in favor of a fresh but compatible new expression. These were looser, less formal, more dynamic buildings than their predecessors. They reinvented, twenty years later, a vocabulary for the campus which Cret imagined would eventually be generously represented on the forty acres.

The fourth vocabulary Cret employed was also a new invention for the campus. Reserved for the most monumental buildings and ensembles, Cret called this vocabulary "New Classicism," dominated as it was by traditional architectural elements like columns, pilasters, architraves, keystones, quoins, cartouches, and so forth. The most prominent example of this vo-

cabulary was the Main Building, constructed in two phases in 1933 and 1937. Planned to house both the library and the University administration, Cret located the Main Building on the top of the hill at the center of the forty acres just as Cass Gilbert had envisioned. Even its composition of tower atop a broad base had been conceived by Gilbert more than a decade before its construction.

The role of the Main Building as the center of what was rapidly becoming a very large urban campus demanded a monumentality and scale much greater than any prior campus project. Cret rose to the occasion with building forms that were gigantic and impressive in their context. As in the Union and Goldsmith and Gearing halls, the previously ubiquitous UT brick was avoided in favor of lavish expanses of creamy limestone. But unlike these three gentler buildings, the stone in the Main Building was cut, carved, and refined to embody a feeling of power and dominance. Huge stones with highly articulated joints formed a monumental base. Giant columnar orders accentuated by deeply recessed balconies inflated the scale of upper floors. The comparatively plain, but massive, shaft of the tower was capped by classically ornamented clocks on four sides, with a grand temple housing nothing but bells at the very top. Both in massing and in architectural character the Main Building lorded over the campus and created a striking counterpoint to the dome of the Capitol Building on the Austin skyline.

Cret designed three other buildings in the "New Classicism" vocabulary, though in far less grandiose versions than the Main Building. Hogg Auditorium, completed in 1933, drew both its symmetrical composition and its ornamental articulation from classical sources. But the interpretation was more severe, blocky, and abstracted than in the Main Building. Texas Memorial Museum of 1937 was simpler and cleaner still. Modern and progressive in general feeling, the museum emphasized the "New" in Cret's "New Classicism." Its flat roof, glass-block windows, and large unrelieved surfaces made it fresh and striking. But its symmetrical composition as well as its abstracted pilasters with "longhorn" capitols kept it comfortable within the larger campus context. The Music Building of 1942 (now Homer Rainey Hall) was among the last buildings done under Cret's influence, his involvement at UT being significantly reduced after his surgery for cancer in 1939. Its "New Classi-

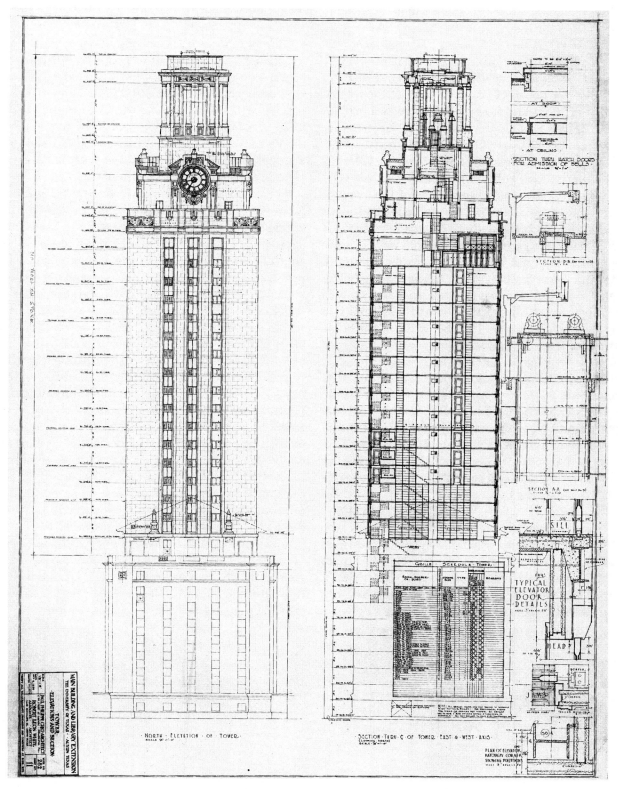

Paul Cret's elevation and detail drawings for the Tower, 1934. *Courtesy of the Alexander Architectural Archive, University of Texas Libraries, the University of Texas at Austin. (University of Texas Buildings Collection, UT Tower sh. #11)*

cism" set the tone for a formal six-building ensemble which would line both sides of the South Mall.

In addition to the 19 buildings for which he was supervising architect from 1930 to 1942, Cret's legacy includes the preparation of a comprehensive development plan for the whole campus in 1933. Completed after ten of his buildings were already pretty much finished, the plan knit Cret's own work to date together with the work of Cass Gilbert and Herbert Greene. The scheme was remarkably respectful of Gilbert's master plan of 1914 with north, south, east, and west malls defining four varied quadrants of the campus, where long simple building forms defined pleasant outdoor rooms. Cret's South Mall was about the same width as Gilbert's with similar double rows of trees along each side and buildings connected by colonnades. But Cret's buildings were arranged perpendicular to the mall, more like those Gilbert had planned for University of Minnesota (and had suggested in a 1909 sketch for UT) than like the arrangement in his 1914 master plan.

Cret's development plan of 1933 also paid great homage to Greene's work of the 1920s. Anna Hiss Gymnasium and Littlefield Dormitory became key delineators of a Women's Group to the north of the forty acres in Cret's plan. The women's gym became the focus of a grand symmetrical composition of buildings in the district. Gregory Gym and Greene's buildings for engineering similarly became the centerpieces for formal open spaces masterfully woven around them by Cret.

The holistic development of the campus from 1910 to 1942 represents an exemplary balance between contextual considerations and fresh, new innovation. All three key architects—Cass Gilbert, Herbert W. Greene, and Paul Phillipe Cret—as well as their collaborators who often bridged the transitions between them (including Ayers and Ayers; Greene, La Roche and Dahl after Herbert Greene's death; Robert Leon White; John Staub; and Page Brothers) demonstrated a remarkable commitment to creating a powerful, coherent, and dynamic place. The Board of Regents, the University administrations, and key faculty members like Dr. William Battle, who was chair of the Faculty Building Committee through much of this era, had the vision to select extraordinary designers and then to support them in the pursuit of both enlightened planning and architectural innovation.

The resulting physical environment has played a prominent role in shaping the best aspects of the University of Texas at Austin today. Winston Churchill's often-quoted dictum, "We shape our buildings; thereafter our buildings shape us," is certainly applicable in this instance. The power, prestige, and dignity embodied in UT buildings when the institution was still fledgling predicted its future. The campus *felt* big and strong long before it actually was. The environment of the University set a benchmark that the institution grew to achieve over time. Generations of prospective students have looked up the South Mall toward the Main Building and have sensed an ambition and aspiration that matched their own. Thousands of freshmen over seven decades have discovered the intimate courtyards and warm interiors of buildings like the Union or Goldsmith Hall and have felt welcome and "at home." Faculty, staff, and students from all over the globe and with diverse and conflicting values have mingled and engaged in meaningful dialogue amidst the civility and graciousness of the West Mall. The campus has become the crucible in which the ethos of the University of Texas is best contained. For many people this physical environment *is* UT and is a place they return to over and over to connect to the institution and to its role in transforming their lives.

MICHAEL L.
GILLETTE

Blacks Challenge the White University

For a few days in October 1938, the history of segregation at the University of Texas might have been different. When George L. Allen, an African American, appeared at the geological auditorium to enroll in an extension business course, confused officials admitted him. With his fees paid, his registration completed, and class tickets in hand, he began attending the seminar in business psychology and salesmanship. His presence posed a problem for the University, since statute and the state constitution stipulated that "separate schools shall be provided for the white and colored children, and impartial provision shall be made for both." Although Texas lacked a graduate and professional school for blacks, never before had an African American applied to the University. Now the state's tradition of segregation was in jeopardy because a clerk and a professor had allowed Allen to enroll and attend classes.[1]

The situation also posed some difficulty for Allen. The Austin district manager of Excelsior Life Insurance Company had only applied to the University in order to be refused admission. NAACP officials in Dallas, who had arranged his attempt, believed that Allen's rejection and the prospect of a court action would pressure the legislature into providing scholarships for Texas blacks to attend out-of-state schools. "The only wrench in the whole machine," Allen remarked, "was that they admitted me."[2]

But the NAACP's plan ultimately worked as the organization had intended. Ten days after registration, Professor C. P. Brewer called Allen to a conference in the Driskill Hotel and informed him that he would have to withdraw from the course. When Allen declined to do so, officials

Michael L. Gillette has been executive director of Humanities Texas (formerly the Texas Council for the Humanities) since 2003. He moved to Austin from Washington, D.C., where he was director of the Center for Legislative Archives at the National Archives. Before living in Washington, Dr. Gillette was director of the LBJ Library's Oral History Program for fifteen years. This essay was first published in the October 1982 issue of Southwestern Historical Quarterly.

Heman Sweatt registers at the University. *From the Prints and Photographs Collection—Heman Marion Sweatt, Center for American History, the University of Texas at Austin. (DI 01127)*

cancelled his enrollment and prevented his return to class. Within nine months the scholarship provision became law.[3]

Seven years later a second African American, Heman Marion Sweatt, attempted to register on the Austin campus. The NAACP sponsored his application to the University's law school as part of a carefully conceived attack on segregated education in the South. After President Theophilus S. Painter refused to admit Sweatt because of his race, a legal struggle raged for four and a half years. Determined to maintain segregation despite extravagant costs, the state did not stop at establishing a separate law school for Sweatt. It created an entire Negro university. When the United States Supreme Court decided *Sweatt v. Painter* in June 1950, the ruling in effect barred segregation in the nation's law schools. It also undermined the legality of segregated graduate and professional education generally, and served as an important precedent for later cases involving lower educational levels.[4] In Texas, *Sweatt* enabled the first black graduate and

professional students to attend the University. It also marked the first major setback in a series of defeats for segregated education. One is inclined to speculate how different the state's educational development and legal history might have been if University officials had allowed George Allen to remain in class in October 1938.

Those who controlled the University had no intention of admitting black students. Satisfied with the constitutional and statutory prohibitions, the Board of Regents that selected Homer P. Rainey as president in 1938 gave little thought to the matter. As the Board became increasingly dominated by conservatives in the 1940s, the issue came under discussion but with an air of defiance. "There is not the slightest danger of any negro attending the University of Texas," wrote Regent Orville Bullington in January 1944, "regardless of what Franklin D[.], Eleanor, or the Supreme Court says, so long as you have a Board of Regents with as much intestinal fortitude as the present one has." When the Board removed Rainey as president, his views on race relations surfaced as an issue. The fact that he had addressed interracial audiences and encouraged the development of African American educational facilities led his adversaries to suggest that he favored social equality and a desegregated university. But the racial issue was not among the regents' formal reasons for Rainey's firing, nor was there any evidence that he entertained such notions. In fact Rainey firmly repudiated the claim, testifying that he had never advocated racial equality but rather favored separate educational institutions. When the same accusations plagued his gubernatorial campaign in 1946, he again refuted them. His successor as president, Theophilus S. Painter, was less inclined to arouse the regents' suspicion on racial issues. The eminent geneticist, selected over faculty opposition as well as his own pledge not to accept the position, proved to be a cooperative lieutenant in reflecting the Board's views and disciplining wayward professors.[5]

By the mid-1940s, many blacks had realized the various inadequacies of the scholarship program. Not only did it fail to compensate students fully for the added expense of attending out-of-state universities, it was also insufficient to provide aid to all qualified blacks who applied. Greater distances and travel costs separated students from their families for longer periods than their in-state counterparts. Often those students who had left did not return to the state afterward to live, thus depriving Texas blacks of the benefit of this professional training.[6]

Whites also were becoming aware of the scholarship fund's drawbacks for different reasons. State officials had viewed the program as a means of forestalling attempts to enter the white university. While there was an informal understanding with Negro leaders that money would be available if they did not force the issue in the courts, the agreement was only tentative and not binding. It did not prevent an individual African American from pressing his claim with a lawsuit. Some officials also realized that the scholarship plan could not withstand litigation, for it had been legally obsolete since its enactment. In 1938, the year before the scholarships were created, the Supreme Court had ruled in *Missouri ex rel. Gaines v. Canada* that a state had to provide within its borders equivalent educational facilities for blacks or else admit them to the existing white institution.[7]

Plans for expanding Negro educational opportunities within the state gained support in 1945 amid increased speculation that blacks were planning an attempt to enter the University of Texas. In response, the legislature finally dealt with the issue by authorizing Prairie View State Normal and Industrial College to teach on demand any course offered at the University of Texas. As if attempting to make educational opportunities equal by merely decreeing that they were, the lawmakers also changed the name of the Negro institution to Prairie View University.[8] In reality nothing had changed in the eight years since the *Gaines* decision. When Sweatt applied to the University of Texas on February 26, 1946, a law school for blacks did not exist.

The NAACP launched the law school effort with unprecedented determination. Invigorated by a major court victory over the Democratic white primary and near its peak in membership and fund-raising potential, the organization carefully laid the groundwork in 1945 for the lawsuit. For almost a year before Sweatt appeared at the registrar's office, the Texas NAACP leaders collected finances, briefed the state laws, and studied the University's admission requirements. Locating a qualified plaintiff who would agree to attend the school afterward was the most difficult part of their preparations. In fact the Association almost gave up their search before the thirty-three-year-old Houston letter carrier, a graduate of Wiley College,

came forward and indicated his willingness to serve as the plaintiff.[9]

The NAACP attorneys had several reasons for selecting the target they did. Not only were they themselves more experienced in law school cases than in other desegregation suits, but they realized that the Supreme Court justices also knew more about legal education than other fields. Association lawyers believed that there would be less public opposition to desegregation of law schools. Since few women attended, the public's perceived threat of intermarriage would be minimized. General awareness that white and black lawyers competed against each other in court was also expected to mitigate opposition. Texas, where racial hostility was less intense than in the Deep South, was a logical site. The fact that a Negro law school did not even exist made the state a tempting target, and the University, with its secure financial base and its prestigious law school, would be a sharp contrast to any facilities for blacks the state might hastily improvise. Finally, the existence of a numerically and financially powerful NAACP organization in Texas was another consideration, for it would have to bear the cost of the litigation.[10]

While desegregating the University of Texas had loomed as a long-term goal of the Association leaders, many envisaged a more limited achievement. Although a stated objective of blacks in founding the Texas State Conference of NAACP Branches in 1937 was to open the University, few of them expected the lawsuit to sweep aside suddenly the barriers they had faced for a lifetime. If the Association's policy stood steadfastly against all forms of segregation, to many African Americans the creation of their own state university would be a successful, if temporary, resolution of the case. Even the legal strategy of invoking the "separate but equal" doctrine to force the state to provide equal facilities for blacks or admit them to white institutions encouraged the establishment of Jim Crow schools. As the *Sweatt* litigation proceeded, however, and the NAACP's strategy changed to a frontal assault on segregation per se, the ultimate objective of desegregating the University came into sharper focus.[11]

The University administration had no doubts that Sweatt's action was to be a constitutional test. Although the applicant denied membership in any "crusading Negro group," the NAACP had for months publicized its intention of filing such a lawsuit. Another indication was the fact that a delegation of NAACP leaders accompanied Sweatt and engaged University officials in a dialogue on the lack of black educational opportunities. By rejecting Sweatt solely on the basis of his race, the University made the lawsuit inevitable. Filed in the 126th District Court of Travis County, the petition asked Judge Roy C. Archer to order the University to admit Sweatt, whose exclusion had been a denial of his equal protection rights under the Fourteenth Amendment.[12]

The initial proceedings served only to delay Sweatt's efforts and allow time for the University to make some provision. As Board of Regents chairman Dudley K. Woodward Jr. wrote, "the Court gave the State every possible break under the facts." While granting that the plaintiff had a right to the same educational opportunities provided for whites, Judge Archer allowed the state six months to establish a curriculum. When the interval passed without the creation of a law school, he again denied Sweatt's petition, this time on the strength of an action by the Texas Agricultural and Mechanical College Board of Directors. The Board, which supervised Prairie View, had resolved to provide legal education on demand at that institution. Sweatt appealed Archer's ruling to the Court of Civil Appeals, which remanded the case to the district court for a full hearing on the merits in May 1947.[13]

Despite the appearance of inaction, Sweatt's registration attempt had mobilized powerful forces in the political establishment to press for a Negro university. Among them was Woodward, who wrote of his institution's "moral responsibility" to make some provision for blacks. Behind humanitarian instincts and the fear that blacks would be admitted to the University, Woodward had a deeper consideration. Guarding his institution's share of the Permanent University Fund was his foremost concern. The Board of Regents chairman and others took the lead in advancing the establishment of an African American university to make certain that it developed in a way that would not threaten the giant endowment. The same article of the 1875 state constitution that had established the University of Texas had also provided for a Negro branch when the legislature should deem "practicable." There was an additional stipulation that no taxes or appropriations from the general revenue could support the institution. Financing would have to come solely from the Available Fund, the income from the Permanent Fund. To Woodward the prospect

of a black university sharing the endowment would "entail consequences of the most destructive character." On the other hand, if the legislature would create another African American university by statute, the possibility that lawmakers would ever act on a constitutional branch would be indeed remote. "It is of great importance," Woodward wrote of the constitutional option, ". . . that this possibility be effectually destroyed."[14]

With encouragement from men such as Woodward, the legislature awakened into action. An appropriation of $2,750,000 and a transfer of the land and existing facilities of Houston College for Negroes created a new institution, Texas State University for Negroes, later to be known as Texas Southern University. Since the upcoming *Sweatt* hearing necessitated that an interim law school be in operation even sooner, the legislation also authorized a temporary facility in Austin. University officials leased the basement of a building from a petroleum firm and set up the law school of the Texas State University for Negroes. With an emergency appropriation of $100,000, they started assembling a law library. Rather than hire a separate faculty and administration, the dean of the University of Texas law school became the part-time dean of the basement school, the University registrar became the part-time registrar, and three faculty members received dual appointments: Leo W. Leary, Starling T. Morris, and Chalmers M. Hudspeth.[15]

The only ingredient that the University could not supply was students. When the basement school opened for registration in March 1947, no one enrolled. Although the deadline for registration was removed and a number of African Americans made inquiries, none matriculated. Heman Sweatt even received a personal announcement of the school's opening, but he showed no inclination to attend. An Austinite named Henry E. Doyle, after indicating that he would register, declined to do so. The NAACP dissuaded him and others from applying, so the institution had no students at all when the *Sweatt* hearing convened in May 1947.[16]

The five-day hearing was the highlight of the *Sweatt* case. An overflowing crowd of spectators gathered in Judge Archer's courtroom to witness a rare legal battle. Some University law professors reportedly even dismissed their classes so that students could observe the polished trial performance of Thurgood Marshall. Facing him and the other NAACP lawyers were Attorney General Price Daniel and his assistants, including Joe Greenhill.[17]

The state's counsel attempted to prove that although the basement school was not the monetary equal of the University of Texas Law School, it afforded the opportunity for an equal or "substantially equivalent" legal education. A succession of witnesses came forward to testify that the library provisions were sufficient, the lack of accreditation immaterial, and the school's part-time nature unimportant. They reasoned that classroom space and the library's size could be more limited and the number of faculty fewer without sacrificing equality, because fewer Negroes would attend the basement school than the number of whites who attended the University of Texas Law School. Nevertheless, the NAACP lawyers' cross examination of the witnesses forced several University officials to concede that some inequalities existed. James M. Nabrit's dogged interrogation of Dean Charles T. McCormick was particularly devastating. Besides quantitative factors such as the size of the library, there were obvious differences of a less tangible nature. It was impossible for the basement school to match the University of Texas in such areas as extracurricular activities, prestige, and the positions University alumni held in the legal community.[18]

The hearing marked a new strategy on the part of the NAACP, which now leveled a frontal attack on segregation per se. Departing from their customary insistence on strict equality of facilities under the mandate of *Plessy v. Ferguson*, Association lawyers now challenged the "separate but equal" doctrine itself. A law school that was separate, they argued, could never be equal. The statutes and provisions of the Texas Constitution calling for segregation were therefore unconstitutional. To prove that segregating students by race was unnecessary, unfair, and unconstitutional, the NAACP enlisted experts in the fields of anthropology, sociology, and legal education. The introduction of this scientific testimony marked an important innovation that would later become identified with *Brown v. Board of Education of Topeka*. Although Archer agreed to hear this evidence, he later ruled that most of it was inadmissible.[19]

If Judge Archer's ruling in favor of the state surprised no one, neither did the NAACP's appeal, which advanced the case on its way to the Supreme Court. More than three years elapsed before the lawsuit's final resolution. Meanwhile there were submissions of countless briefs and decisions by and appeals from intermediate courts. The NAACP concentrated on fund raising for the *Sweatt* case and planned other lawsuits against the University of Texas.[20] The state devoted its attention to the development of Texas State University for Negroes.

The basement law school became a going concern when three students registered in the fall of 1947. Henry E. Doyle incurred the scorn of the NAACP by enrolling as the first student and accepting a job as the school's janitor. Two other Austin blacks, Heuallan E. Lott and Mrs. Fornie Ussery Brown, registered soon afterward. With a student body of three, the professors took their teaching assignment seriously. Several of those involved have stated in retrospect their belief that the quality of instruction at the basement school exceeded in some respects that at the University of Texas. They based this view largely on the individual attention that the students received as a result of the high teacher-to-student ratio. When the school transferred to the Houston campus in August 1948, its quality, however, declined. Not only were the classes larger, but they were without the benefit of the University of Texas faculty.[21]

Had the NAACP leaders known the extent to which the dual law schools would tax the system of segregation, they might never have discouraged students from registering. For its one thousand students the University of Texas Law School had only nineteen full-time faculty, five of whom were detailed to the basement school. With the prospect of a second class entering the temporary facility for the spring semester, three more professors were assigned to the basement school, increasing its faculty to eight. Dean McCormick feared that a summer session would tie up practically the entire University faculty in order to teach six to ten students. The University of Texas Law School, he wrote Painter, was "faced with the prospect of successive increases of the burden which will be almost impossible to sustain."[22]

The burden described by McCormick was only a fraction of the strain that University segregation underwent in the next two years. It had been the Association's strategy all along to file a variety of suits relating to different fields of graduate and professional training. The unavailability of qualified plaintiffs and the NAACP's concentration on the *Sweatt* case had temporarily delayed additional actions. But beginning in late 1947, University officials encountered what

Early civil rights demonstration on the UT campus. *From the UT Texas Student Publications, Inc. Photographs Collection—Negroes at UT: Miscellaneous, Center for American History, the University of Texas at Austin. (DI 02401)*

must have seemed to them a procession of blacks challenging various barriers of segregation. The targets were graduate, medical, and dental schools, use of the library, and even correspondence courses. Having no doubts about the NAACP's objective, Painter wrote in January 1948, "It is fairly obvious that the Negroes are determined to make it as embarrassing as possible and as expensive as possible for us to maintain separate institutions for the two races. . . ." Nor did Painter fail to understand the consequences, for he concluded that, "in the end, the financial burden will be extremely heavy. . . ."[23]

The first of these challenges came in December 1947, when W. Astor Kirk applied to the graduate school in political science. A Tillotson College professor with bachelor and master's degrees from Howard University, Kirk had inquired at Texas State University for Negroes and learned that it had neither the faculty nor the library to sustain a doctoral program in his field. When officials suggested the out-of-state scholarship arrangement, he rejected that alternative with the explanation that since he planned to teach in Texas, he desired to complete his education there.[24]

Although the state later offered to provide a facility, it became apparent—in fact, Kirk stated—that he planned to test the validity of his exclusion from the University of Texas. The Board of Regents proposed establishing a graduate program for Negroes in the basement law school, a plan which the Texas State

University for Negroes Board endorsed in February 1948. Kirk, meanwhile, applied to the NAACP for assistance. While the organization had not initiated his registration attempt, it readily consented to take charge of his case. When the Association's attorneys filed the lawsuit that spring, A. Maceo Smith declared that, before the year's end, the NAACP expected to have many more such suits, "all hitting strategic blows at the system of Jim Crow."[25]

Almost two years later Kirk renewed his effort to enter the University. His case had not yet come to trial since attorneys for both sides agreed to postpone the litigation until the Supreme Court had decided *Sweatt v. Painter*. This time he actually registered under a contractual arrangement and attended one class during the spring semester, 1950, before withdrawing in protest. The contract between the University and Texas State University for Negroes stipulated that the former would offer graduate courses to blacks in classes "operated separately and apart from the campus." Although Kirk acquiesced in the concept of separate classes on the campus, he rejected the formula of having members of the government faculty teach him at the nearby YMCA. He then applied to the University as a regular student. His rejection sparked an indignant letter to registrar H. Y. McCown in which the applicant argued that the state law did not require a mode of separation "deliberately calculated to embarrass the person to whom it is proffered [sic]—a mode, mind you, that makes the University look ridiculous in the eyes of the rest of the nation and the world." Kirk also pointed out the inconsistencies in the University's interpretation. Since he had received the assurance of unrestricted access to the library, he would be admitted to that part of the campus in a nonsegregated arrangement. He noted also that officials applied the contract's imperative of physical separation differently at other branches of the University.[26]

In 1949 the NAACP found a new way to dramatize inequalities in higher education while increasing pressure on segregation. The Association that April orchestrated a mass registration attempt by thirty-five black college seniors. Organized by Bishop College students with the approval of the school's president, Joseph J. Rhoads, the protest was designed not only as a civil-rights demonstration at the University of Texas campus and the State Capitol, but also to present multiple applications for graduate and professional training, the denial of which could generate lawsuits similar to Sweatt's. The NAACP promoted the youths' activity by coordinating procedures, generating publicity, and offering to handle any subsequent lawsuits that would be appropriate. Although the group "was not directly under our control," wrote one branch official, "they accepted our leadership." Thurgood Marshall in New York even advised the effort. While enthusiastic, he weighed the possibility that picketing at the Capitol might prod the legislature into increasing the appropriation for Texas State University for Negroes, or, in his words, further "guilding [sic] of the ghetto." He therefore emphasized that the placards and press releases state explicitly that the group opposed segregated education and that their objective was to gain entrance to the University of Texas. Marshall also warned that the leaders exercise care to prevent communists from taking over the demonstration, as apparently had happened to a protest in Oklahoma.[27]

On April 27, thirty-three black students from five African American colleges arrived in a bus at the University campus. They were joined by NAACP officials Donald Jones, U. Simpson Tate, and James H. Morton, and two other students. Carrying placards with such inscriptions as "Civil Rights are Everybody's Rights," they marched to the registrar's office. Spokesman Astor Kirk politely informed the University officials that the students were there to apply to graduate, medical, and dental schools. Refusing to give them the appropriate forms, Assistant Registrar Max Fichtenbaum

told them to apply to Texas State University for Negroes. The students then departed quietly and walked across the campus toward the Capitol.[28]

Photographers' shutters clicked wildly at the rare spectacle of blacks marching two abreast on the Forty Acres, and the event received widespread radio and newspaper coverage. Nevertheless, it attracted only passing attention among University students. The *Daily Texan* noted that the placards "were nearly blanketed out by the spring political signs on the campus." Eleven sympathetic white students did, however, join the group on their march to the Capitol. Filing into the House and Senate galleries, the blacks continued their orderly demonstration while the legislators ignored them. A few of the group, including Donald Jones and James H. Morton, also met with Governor Beauford H. Jester to present a statement asking that blacks be allowed to attend the University's graduate and professional schools. Jester agreed only to give the petition to the proper authority. When he asked them what they would think of separate facilities, they responded that such a provision would not be equal to the University of Texas.[29]

The demonstration, which NAACP lawyer U. Simpson Tate characterized afterward as "the most impressive experience" in his civil-rights career, was a clear signal that the Sweatt case was only the first stage in the assault on segregated education. "A plan to hit the state's educational system in every place it is vulnerable. . . ." was the Houston *Post*'s analysis of the march. In fact, two of the thirty-five black students had already been designated as the NAACP's next potential plaintiffs. Although a reporter noticed that the two, escorted by Tate and Donald Jones, stood somewhat apart from the main group, he had no way of knowing that the NAACP had already prepared the groundwork for the lawsuits against the University's medical and dental schools.[30]

With the range of specializations, high salaries, expensive equipment, libraries, and hospital facilities, the cost of medical education exceeded all other forms of University training. When the state first contemplated establishing a Negro university in 1946, Painter received from the medical branch an estimated budget requirement of $192,000 for the first two years of operation. The creation of Texas State University for Negroes the following year led a number of blacks to inquire about attending medical school. At least two African American students applied to the University of Texas, while several others brought up the matter with Prairie View University's principal emeritus, Willette R. Banks. Banks then raised with Painter the possibility of sending the students to Meharry Medical College in Nashville. Heartily approving the proposal, Painter discussed it a length with Dr. M. Don Clawson, president of Meharry. The following spring, Painter also expressed support for a plan to join with other southern states in establishing a regional medical school for Negroes. Yet neither alternative was sufficient to meet the legal challenge that the NAACP posed. While the Meharry plan was adequate for those students that Banks described as "not inclined to press their claims to the point of embarrassing the state," the scheme would not withstand a constitutional test. Painter was aware that the *Gaines* decision had made out-of-state provisions unacceptable if similar opportunities were offered within the state to white students. For the same reason, the regional black universities were also vulnerable. Perhaps Painter was grasping at alternative solutions to compensate for the inaction of Texas State University for Negroes trustees. Disturbed at their failure to deal with the issue, he wrote early in 1948 that "if they do not make adequate provisions before September, we are going to have a hard time keeping Negroes out of our Medical and Dental Schools."[31]

The main reason that the state had not received a challenge was the NAACP's difficulty in finding a qualified student who was willing to file suit. Since the Galveston medical school accepted only the one hundred most qualified students, state officials had relied on self-exclusion by black youths emerging from inferior secondary and undergraduate educations. Perhaps the few who were qualified did not want to jeopardize their scholarships by attempting to enter the white facility. Yet the NAACP had tried to recruit a plaintiff as early as 1946. By 1949 the organization had intensified its efforts. Maceo Smith met with the dean of the Howard University medical school to find a student from Texas who would apply to the University's medical school in Galveston while continuing his course work at Howard. He subsequently outlined the procedure to a student in Washington, but that spring the Association located an ideal plaintiff in Austin. Herman Barnett, an honor graduate and student-council president at Samuel Huston College, had served as a pilot in the Army Air Corps during World War II. His scholastic attainments were exceptional,

and in a nationwide medical aptitude test he ranked in the highest third. As T. S. Painter observed, Barnett appeared to be "thoroughly qualified for the study of medicine."[32]

Barnett's application jolted the state into motion. In July the legislature belatedly appropriated $175,000 for a medical school in connection with Texas State University for Negroes. But if a basement law school could be set up in a matter of days, a medical school could not. Not only was the funding late—coming less than two months before the start of the fall semester—but the Houston officials simply lacked the considerable technical expertise necessary to establish a medical school. They therefore decided to turn the task over to the University of Texas under a contract. Since the latter, however, was unable to set up a curriculum for one student in such short time, officials decided to provide Barnett with training alongside white students at the Galveston facility. His enrollment would be officially at the Texas State University for Negroes, which would bear the cost of instruction, and his presence at Galveston would not reduce the number of white students accepted.[33]

Logistical difficulty, expense, and legislative delay had forced the state to scrap its policy of physical separation in Barnett's case. As Painter concluded: "Under the circumstances obtaining we really had no option. . . ."[34] The only remnant of segregation was the student's technical affiliation with the Texas State University for Negroes medical school, which did not exist. Since it could no longer segregate Barnett, the state simply segregated his registration card.

After his enrollment, the state made no serious attempt to establish a Negro medical school. This fact was perhaps due more to the enormous task of setting up a medical school than to monetary considerations. Barnett's acceptance among white medical students and the absence of widespread objections to the contract arrangement also eliminated the urgency of creating a separate school. Officials seemed content to await the outcome of the *Sweatt* case before investing in additional facilities.[35]

Mindful that the *Sweatt* case was a social struggle as well as a legal one, the NAACP strategists were always conscious of white public opinion. They particularly wanted the support of the University of Texas students, whom they regarded as the state's future lawyers, officials, and community leaders. There was also a more immediate reason. A show of student support would enable them to refute the attorney general's claim that, if Sweatt attended the University, whites would ostracize him and violence might even erupt.[36]

Heman Sweatt could not have picked a better time to apply to law school, for the climate was more favorable than at any previous time in the University's history. The campus changed in the postwar years. Enrollment soared from a prewar high of 11,000 to over 17,000 in the fall of 1946. But it was not the number of students that made the impact, as *Texan* editor Horace Busby observed; it was the kind of student: "older, more purposeful, considerably more wise." Returning veterans swelled the registration lines, comprising 63 percent of the student body. These older, more mature students had seen life in other regions of the country and of the world. While the diversity of their views spanned the political spectrum, they were as a group more broadminded than their prewar counterparts. Having fought in a world struggle to preserve democracy, they were now vocal in defending its ideals at home. Although the burning issue of Homer Rainey's dismissal, which had ignited the campus in 1944, was now in the past, there remained a smoldering resentment toward the regents and University administration.[37]

The prospect of an African American attending law school did not concern the students in general nearly as much as the acute housing shortage did. Most of them did not view the *Sweatt* case as a serious attempt to open the University to blacks. "The real issue," noted a *Texan* editorial, "is not whether Negroes shall attend the University—it is whether or not Negroes shall be give equal education [*sic*] opportunity in Texas." In October 1946, a student panel on the topic of interracial education viewed the subject as so remote that it focused instead on the need to improve African American education beginning with grade school.[38]

If liberal elements on the campus were largely sympathetic to black civil rights, they were only vaguely familiar with the issues. A number of such students became more aware when they fell under the influence of Melvin B. Tolson, a black poet and English professor who spoke on several occasions to the University community. During a talk in March 1946, he discussed the economics of discrimination and praised students who were circulating a petition that called for opening the law school to blacks. While lecturing

the following fall on the nature of law and authority, he described the NAACP's operation, confiding that "the Southern highways to Washington are chock full with small Negro leaders going to the Supreme Court to give their interpretation of every law and appeal their case." The *Texan* reported that Tolson held his audience's complete attention for two hours. "He just scintillated," one of his listeners remembered thirty years later.[39]

In the fall of 1946, a variety of organizations became involved in the *Sweatt* case. That November sixty University students, representing the Canterbury Club, Wesley Foundation, Lutheran Students Association, Baptist Student Union, American Veterans Committee, YMCA, and other groups held a rally in support of Sweatt's admission. They formed a campus committee, headed by John W. Stanford Jr., to distribute information about the case and to collect money for the lawsuit. When University administrators barred the fund-raising from campus, the committee members set up booths across the street and continued. Austin police warned the students that they were violating a city ordinance, but since no one filed a complaint, the officers did not interfere with the activity. A news story noted that, judging by their articles of military clothing, the students were predominantly veterans.[40]

The following month a number of University students and faculty participated in a large NAACP rally at Doris Miller Auditorium. James W. Smith, president of the Students' Association, announced his support for admitting blacks to the University. Smith's involvement had followed a visit to Sweatt's home in Houston to find out more about the African American who wanted to attend the law school. Prominent educator Dr. Frederick Eby condemned the "shameful" treatment of Negroes in the field of education. He reported that an informal poll of his students revealed abut 40 percent favored admitting Negroes while 30 percent were opposed and the same number undecided. The rally's main attraction was the noted writer and English professor J. Frank Dobie. A constant critic of the University administration who had drawn heavy fire from segregationists in 1945, Dobie delivered an impassioned plea for racial justice. Labeling the Jim Crow provision a farce, he advocated admitting Sweatt and other qualified blacks to the University at once.[41]

To NAACP officials the quintessence of support

from the University community was the formation of a University of Texas chapter of the NAACP. Suggested by the national youth secretary, the organization apparently evolved from the Sweatt Fund Drive. University students saw it as an opportunity to coordinate activities of the various organizations that were sympathetic to Sweatt's bid for legal education. They also believed that the publicity attending the group's formation would stimulate opposition to the proposal for a Negro university. To the NAACP's Austin branch and State Conference, a University chapter would be an important vehicle for advancing interracial work and establishing additional contacts with the white community while familiarizing students with the Association's programs and policies. The national office was especially enthusiastic about the University chapter. In addition to opportunities for interracial activity, the new group would serve as evidence of students' acceptance of Sweatt.[42]

While NAACP chapters existed on the campuses of major universities in the North and Midwest, the University of Texas branch was the only one on a segregated campus. In order to receive approval as an official University organization, the chapter's membership had to be composed exclusively of registered students and independent of outside direction. This requirement not only necessitated less supervision from the Austin branch, it also meant that the University unit was ironically a "white-only" NAACP chapter.[43] Yet its segregated status caused only a fraction of the difficulties that its internal strife and its relations with the Austin branch created.

Power struggles, purges, and propaganda disputes between communists and socialists discouraged many of Sweatt's original backers. Attacks on the leadership of the Austin branch and an intervention by the NAACP's national office on the side of the student chapter caused a serious disruption of Austin activities. In 1950, the national office finally revoked the charter of the University group, ending an embarrassing episode for the Association.[44]

If the ideological conflicts within the University NAACP did little to attract students to Sweatt's cause, other developments also siphoned off some campus support. Not only did the rise of anticommunism generally make students more tentative on social issues, but the fact that the state's political pendulum was swinging hard to the right had influence as well.

John Sanders Chase (right) in 1950. *From the UT Texas Student Publications, Inc. Photographs Collection—Negroes at UT: Miscellaneous, Center for American History, the University of Texas at Austin. (DI 02431)*

With the establishment of Texas State University for Negroes, some students considered the issue moot. Disillusioned by Sweatt's refusal to accept the newly created law school, they regarded the NAACP's attack on segregation per se as too much too soon.[45]

Nonetheless, a majority of University students through the end of the decade appear to have favored admitting blacks at the graduate level. Polls conducted in 1948 and 1950 indicated that approximately 56 percent approved. The canvasses also revealed that students made a distinction between graduate desegregation and admitting blacks as undergraduates. Only 37 percent endorsed the latter. A referendum that would have registered student views in March 1950, on several issues, including the admission of blacks, was blocked by the University Student Court.[46]

The Supreme Court announced its decision in *Sweatt v. Painter* on June 5, 1950. In a unanimous ruling the justices declared that the separate Negro facilities were not equal to the University of Texas and ordered the petitioner's admission to the latter. Looking beyond the physical differences, which included scope of the library, number of faculty, and availability of courses, the court considered such intangible qualities as the institution's prestige and the influence of its alumni. It also recognized that the value of associating with the state's future lawyers, judges, and officials at the University of Texas was an important element in preparing for the legal profession. By weighing such factors, the justices established a standard of equality so rigid and absolute that it would be virtually impossible to achieve in segregated schools.[47]

The University reacted quickly to the *Sweatt* decision. As soon as the announcement came, President Painter and other officials met with the attorney general to devise a policy that would meet the new legal requirements. Perhaps they even faced the task with a trace of relief. Until the creation of Texas State University for Negroes, the state had often invoked but never actually tried "separate but equal" facilities. In reality its policy had been "separate and nonexistent." The brief attempt at "separate but equal" professional schools had been an expensive, embarrassing, and bothersome experiment for dignified, intelligent men to have to implement. In addition to opening the University Law School, officials admitted blacks to other graduate and professional fields of study that were not offered at a state-supported Negro school. The first black graduate students, Horace L. Heath and John Sanders Chase, registered for the summer session. Throughout the early 1950s black enrollment ranged from sixty to sixty-five during the long term and increased to nearly one hundred during the summer session.[48]

Interpreting the *Sweatt* ruling as narrowly as possible, the University continued to exclude black undergraduates and graduate students whose fields of study were available at Prairie View and Texas Southern University. Once admitted, African American graduate students were allowed to take undergraduate classes when it was necessary for them to make up credit deficiencies or obtain prerequisite courses. The University admissions policy must have deeply puzzled a black high school graduate who applied for the fall semester of 1954. Marion George Ford Jr. was first rejected, then accepted after he stipulated that he wanted to enroll in chemical engineering. Less than two weeks after he received an acceptance letter from the University in which the registrar urged him to "get over your inferiority complex and the idea that you are being discriminated against," Ford was reject-

ed again, along with four other black undergraduates. Under pressure from University regents, officials now concluded that while Prairie View and Texas Southern University lacked an equivalent chemical engineering curriculum, Ford could obtain at least the first year's required courses at Prairie View before transferring to the University of Texas.[49]

Only after the Supreme Court's second *Brown* decision in 1955, which called for an end to educational discrimination "with all deliberate speed," did the University admit black undergraduates. The board then voted unanimously to desegregate, effective September 1956, with the adoption of an admissions standard based on merit. The NAACP decided not to challenge the year's delay, which the regents had justified by citing overcrowded conditions and a housing shortage. Yet segregated dormitories and more subtle forms of discrimination persisted even into the 1960s.[50]

What happened to those unwanted black students who had challenged the system in pursuit of an education? After the *Sweatt* decision, officials changed Herman Barnett's registration to the University of Texas medical school. Following graduation he became a prominent Houston surgeon and was president of that city's school board when he died in an airplane crash in May 1973. Astor Kirk, while earning his doctorate in the political science department at the University, held various academic and government positions. Thereafter he rose to the position of Mid-Atlantic regional director of the Office of Economic Opportunity. Exclusion from the seminar in business psychology and salesmanship evidently had no detrimental impact on George Allen, who prospered as a successful businessman, member of the Dallas city council, and local judge. At age thirty-seven, Heman Marion Sweatt entered the University of Texas law school, four and a half years after his original application. After two years of failing grades and disappointment, he dropped out. He later earned a master's degree in social work from Atlanta University and capped a career in community service as assistant director of the National Urban League's southern region.[51]

In an episode rich with ironies, a final irony is worth mentioning. Henry E. Doyle, who had incurred the NAACP's disfavor by attending the basement law school, became the first graduate of the law school at Texas State University for Negroes. The attorney general even cited him as the fine product of segregated education. Official pride in Doyle quickly evaporated, however, once he passed the bar examination and began filing civil-rights lawsuits against the state.[52]

NOTES

1. George L. Allen to M. L. G., Feb. 14, 1982, interview; Dallas *Express*, Oct. 15, 1938; Texas *Constitution* (1876), Art. VII, Sec. 7 (quotation). Article 2900 of Texas Civil Statutes required separate schools. See *1928 Complete Texas Statutes* . . . [*Vernon's Texas Statutes*] (Kansas City, Mo., 1928), 637.

2. Dallas *Express*, Oct. 15, 1938; Allen to M. L. G., Feb. 14, 1982, interview.

3. Dallas *Express*, Oct. 22, 29, 1938; Allen to M. L. G., Feb. 14, 1982, interview. For the scholarship provision, see House Bill 255 in Texas, Legislature, *Special Laws of the State of Texas Passed by the Regular Session of the Forty-sixth Legislature* . . . (n.p., n.d.), 359.

4. *Sweatt v. Painter*, 339 U.S. 629 (1950); James E. [*sic*] Nabrit Jr., "The Negro," [First Southwide Conference on Discrimination in Higher Education], *Discrimination in Higher Education* (New Orleans, [1951]), 25.

5. J. R. Parten to M. L. G., Apr. 13, 1982, interview; Orville Bullington to John A. Lomax, Jan. 7, 1944, "Homer Rainey Controversy" file, John A. Lomax Papers (Eugene C. Barker Texas History Center, University of Texas, Austin; cited hereafter as BTHC); release prepared by the Committee of Correspondence, Students Association, University of Texas, analyzing the charges made against President Homer P. Rainey, Charge No. 3, "Rainey Controversy" scrapbook, Homer P. Rainey Papers (BTHC); Texas, Legislature, Senate, Committee Investigating the University of Texas Controversy, *An Educational Crisis: A Summary of Testimony before a Senate Committee Investigating the University of Texas Controversy, November 15–28, 1944* (n.p., n.d.), 2–3; *Sunday American-Statesman* (Austin), Nov. 19, 1944; Seth Shepard McKay, *Texas and the Fair Deal, 1945–1952* (San Antonio, 1954), 120–130; Homer P. Rainey, *The Tower and the Dome: A Free University Versus Political Control* (Boulder, 1971).

6. *Defender* (Houston), Mar. 9, 1946; Dallas *Express*, Mar. 9, 1946; *Informer* (Houston), Jan. 17, 1942; A. P. Brogan to Theophilus S. Painter, May 3, 1946, General Files, "Negroes in Colleges, 1939–1954," University of Texas President's Office Records (BTHC; these records are cited hereafter as UTPOR).

7. Homer P. Rainey to Fred C. Smith, July 13, 1939, General Files, "Negroes in Colleges, 1939–1954," UTPOR; Missouri *ex rel.* Gaines v. Canada, 305 U.S. 337 (1938).

8. Dallas *Morning News*, Feb. 4, Mar. 20, Apr. 25, May 2, June 6, 1945. The text of Senate Bill 228 appears in Texas, Legislature, *General and Special Laws of the State of Texas Passed by the Regular Session of the Forty-ninth Legislature* . . . ([Austin, 1945]), 506.

9. Two other articles by the present author deal with the Texas NAACP during this period. Michael L. Gillette, "The Rise of the NAACP in Texas," *Southwestern Historical Quarterly*, 71 (Apr., 1978), 393–416, traces the growth of the organization and its defeat of the white primary in *Smith v. Allwright*, 321 U.S. 649 (1944). A discussion of the NAACP's preparations in the *Sweatt* case appears in Michael L. Gillette, "Heman Marion Sweatt: Civil Rights Plaintiff," Alwyn Barr and Robert A. Calvert (eds.), *Black Leaders: Texans for Their Times* (Austin, 1981), 157–188.

10. Charles H. Houston, memorandum for the use of Roscoe Dunjee in re Texas State Conference, May 7–8, 1937, Box G-200, NAACP Files (Library of Congress); Thurgood Marshall to Erwin N. Griswold, June 14, 1948, "University of Oklahoma, June to December, 1948," Legal Files, ibid; Marshall to M. L. G., Oct. 31, 1974, interview.

11. Resolutions—State Conference of Branches, Dallas, Texas, June 19, 1937; Minutes of the Texas State Conference of Branches, NAACP, June 18, 19, 1937, Box G-200, NAACP Files; A. Maceo Smith to Carter W. Wesley, Mar. 21, 1946, "Branch Files, Houston, 1944–1946," ibid.

12. Houston *Post*, Feb. 28, 1946; *Daily Texan* (Austin), Mar. 3, 1946 (quotation); Dallas *Express*, June 9, 30, Oct. 13, 1945; *Informer* (Houston), Jan. 22, Feb. 12, 1946; Brief for Petitioner at 2, *Sweatt v. Painter*, 339 U.S. 629. Details of the NAACP's role in Sweatt's registration attempt may be found in Gillette, "Heman Marion Sweatt," 158–168.

13. Dudley K. Woodward Jr. to Gibb Gilchrist, June 20, 1946, General Files, "Negroes in Colleges, 1939–1954," UTPOR; Dallas *Express*, Dec. 21, 1946; *Daily Texan* (Austin), Mar. 28, 1947.

14. Texas, *Constitution* (1876), Art. VII, Sec. 14 (second quotation), 15; Woodward to Gilchrist, June 8 (third, fourth, and fifth quotations), June 20 (first quotation), 1946, General Files, "Negroes in Colleges, 1939–1954," UTPOR. In December 1946, a biracial commission appointed by Governor Coke R. Stevenson recommended the creation of a statutory university, after University of Texas and Texas A&M officials reported that the endowment would not be sufficient to support a Negro university in addition to their own schools. Mark McGee to Coke R. Stevenson, Dec. 17, 1946; "Bi-Racial Commission Report," Dec. 6, 1946, ibid; Dallas *Morning News*, Feb. 25, 1947.

In late 1946, Dr. Everett H. Givens, a black Austin dentist, filed a lawsuit in an attempt to force the creation of a constitutional university. An election held in the late 1800s had determined that such a school should be located in Austin. Dallas *Morning News*, Feb. 12, May 8, 1947; *Informer* (Houston), Oct. 5, 1946; *Daily Texan* (Austin), Oct. 29, 1946.

Education officials concluded that expanding Prairie View to include graduate and professional programs was impractical, primarily because of its rural location, vocational emphasis, and already crowded conditions. Houston *Post*, Feb. 25, 1947.

15. For Senate Bill 140, see Texas, Legislature, *General and Special Laws of the State of Texas Passed by the Regular Session of the Fiftieth Legislature* . . . (n.p., n.d.), 36–41; Painter to Gilchrist, Oct. 9, 1946, General Files, "Negroes in Colleges, 1939–1954," UTPOR; Announcement of courses for the spring semester, 1947, of the School of Law of the Texas State University for Negroes, General Subject Files, "Texas State University for Negroes, 1946–1952," ibid. Walter Prescott Webb, H. Bailey

Carroll, and Eldon Stephen Branda (eds.), *The Handbook of Texas* (3 vols.; Austin, 1952, 1976), III, 993.

For the history of Houston College for Negroes, see *Informer* (Houston), Feb. 3, 1945; Ozie Harold Johnson, *Price of Freedom* (Houston, 1954), 16.

16. *Daily Texan* (Austin), Mar. 16, 1947; Henry E. Doyle to M. L. G., Jan. 29, 1982, interview. For Doyle's testimony (in the *Transcript of Record: Supreme Court of the United States, October Term, 1949, No. 44. Heman Marion Sweatt vs. Theophilus Shickel Painter, et al.*), see Record, vol. 1, at 299, *Sweatt v. Painter*, 339 U.S. 629 (1950); Dallas *Morning News*, Mar. 22, May 13, 1947.

17. Austin *American*, May 13–17, 1947; Chicago *Defender*, May 17, 1947; Pittsburgh *Courier*, May 17, 1947; Joe B. Frantz to M. L. G., May 3, 1982, interview.

18. Dallas *Morning News*, May 13, 1947 (quotation); Record, vol. 1, at 8–20, 86–111, 309–311, *Sweatt v. Painter*, 339 U.S. 629 (1950); Heman M. Sweatt to M. L. G., Feb. 10, 1973; C. B. Bunkley to M. L G., Mar. 23, 1973; Marshall to M. L G., Oct. 31, 1974, interviews.

19. Dallas *Morning News*, May 15, 1947; Record, vol. 1, at 228–286, 441, *Sweatt v. Painter* 339 U.S. 629 (1950). In *Plessy v. Ferguson*, 163 U.S. 537, a decision in 1896 involving separate railroad cars, the Supreme Court introduced the standard of "separate but equal." It was overturned in 1954 in the school desegregation case *Brown v. Board of Education of Topeka*, 347 U.S. 483.

The NAACP's direct assault on segregation drew criticism from a number of black Texans, including the influential publisher Carter W. Wesley. Although Wesley did not oppose this strategy in the *Sweatt* case, he favored simultaneous efforts to equalize existing facilities. Wesley to Marshall, Dec. 23, 1946, Oct. 8, 1947, NAACP Files.

20. In 1947 the NAACP established a five-state regional office in Dallas and divided Texas into districts to perfect a grassroots organization and strengthen control over local activities. In 1948 a massive fund-raising campaign was promoted through the sale of Freedom Bonds. Dallas *Express*, Feb. 28, May 22, Oct. 16, 1948; Report of Southwest Region NAACP, Oct. 2, 1947; Robert L. Carter to the legal staff, Nov. 14, 1949 (memorandum); Marshall to Amos T. Hall, Aug. 4, 1949; Report of Southwest Regional Conference, Mar. 25, 1950; Donald Jones to district officers, Jan. 19, 1948 (memorandum), NAACP Files; Donald Jones to Aaron Jefferson, Feb. 5, 1948, Juanita Craft Papers (BTHC).

21. *Daily Texan* (Austin), Sept, 23, 25, 26, 28, 1947; Doyle to M. L. G., Jan. 29, 1982, interview; Jerre Williams to M. L. G., June 4, 1982, interview.

22. Painter to Craig F. Cullinan, Oct. 20, 1947; Charles T. McCormick to Painter, Oct. 17, 1947 (quotation), Jan. 13, 1948, General Subject Files, "Texas State University for Negroes, 1946–1952," UTPOR. Since no new class actually enrolled at the basement law school for the spring semester, 1948, the three additional professors were taken off its faculty. McCormick to Painter, Feb. 11, 1948, ibid.

23. A. M. Smith to James H. Morton, July 10, 1947; A. M. Smith to Robert L. Carter, Aug. 9, 1946, NAACP Files; Painter to Woodward, Jan. 31, 1948, General Files, "Negroes in Colleges, 1939–1954," UTPOR.

24. *Daily Texan* (Austin), Dec. 5, 10, 1947, July 8, 1948.

25. *Daily Texan* (Austin), Jan. 15, Feb. 12, Apr. 15, 1948; W. Astor Kirk to M. L. G., Feb. 15 1982, interview; Austin *Statesman*, Jan. 26, 1948; Dallas *Express*, Apr. 3, 1948 (quotation).

26. William J. Durham to O. T Martin Jr., Dec. 17, 1949, enclosing motion for continuance, Kirk v. Painter, #80509, in the District Court of Travis County, Texas (microfilm, District Clerk's Office, Civil Division, Travis County Courthouse, Austin); copy of the agreement between T.S.U.N. and U.T., dated Sept. 1, 1949, signed by Cullinan and Woodward (first quotation); Kirk to H. Y McCown, Feb. 15, 1950, General Subject Files, "Texas State University for Negroes, 1946–1952," UTPOR. Kirk alluded to the medical school provision made for Herman Barnett, which did not involve physical separation. For a discussion of Barnett, see below.

27. U. S. Tate to Marshall, May 10, 1949 (first and second quotations); D. Jones to A. M. Smith et al., Apr. 20, 1949; A. M. Smith to Marshall, Apr. 5, 1949; Marshall to A. M. Smith, Apr. 18, 1940 (second quotation), NAACP Files.

28. Austin *American*, Apr. 28, 1949 (placard quotation); *Daily Texan* (Austin), Apr. 28, 1949; Tate to Marshall, Apr. 28, 1949, NAACP Files.

29. Austin *American*, Apr. 28, 1949; *Daily Texan* (Austin), Apr. 28, 1949; Tate to Marshall, Apr. 28, 1949, NAACP Files.

30. Tate to Marshall, Apr. 28, 1949, NAACP Files; Houston *Post*, Apr. 28, 1949. The black student who was to be the NAACP's plaintiff for a suit against the dental school was rejected on the grounds that he had not fulfilled the application requirements by the deadline. Association lawyers decided not to pursue this case but to concentrate on Herman Barnett and medical school. Tate to Marshall, May 10, 1949; Marshall to Tate, May 18, 1949, NAACP Files.

31. Chauncey D. Leake to Painter, Aug. 26, 1946; Painter to Ben Davis, Mar. 22, 1947, General Subject Files, "Texas State University for Negroes, 1946–1952," UTPOR; Painter to E. J. Matthews, Mar. 5, 1947; Willette R. Banks to Painter, May 31, 1947 (first quotation); Painter to Banks, June 2, 1947, June 26, 1948; Painter to Woodward, Jan. 31, 1948 (second quotation); Painter to J. W. Holly, Apr. 21, 1948; Painter to Charles L. Morgan, May 26, 1948, General Files, "Negroes in Colleges, 1939–1954," ibid.

32. *Negro Labor News* (Houston), Aug. 27, 1949; A. M. Smith to Carter, Oct. 18, 1946; A. M. Smith to J. Don Jackson, Jan. 14, 1949; Tate to Marshall, May 10, 1949, NAACP Files; Painter to Mrs. H. L. Madden, Sept. 1, 1949, General Files, "Negroes in Colleges, 1939–1954," UTPOR. In the fall of 1949 the number of medical students accepted was expanded to 162, not including Barnett. Painter to Goelzer, Sept. 1, 1949, UTPOR.

33. Painter to Madden, Sept. 1, 1949, General Files, "Negroes in Colleges, 1939–1954," UTPOR; Cullinan to Painter, July 13, 1949, General Subject Files, "Texas State University for Negroes, 1946–1952," ibid.

34. Painter to Dick Cason, Sept. 1, 1949, General Files, "Negroes in Colleges, 1939–1954," UTPOR.

35. Cullinan to Painter, July 20, 1949, General Subject Files, "Texas State University for Negroes, 1946–1952," UTPOR; Herman Barnett to Morton, Nov. 19, 1949, NAACP Files; Mack Hannah to M. L. G., Mar. 26, 1982, interview.

36. Robert L. Carter to Stuart Chamberlin, Sept. 29, 1947; A. M. Smith to Morton, Nov. 25, 1946; Marshall to Donald G. Murray, Apr. 9, 1947, NAACP Files.

37. William G. Noble to M. L. G., Jan. 23, 1982, interview; *Daily Texan* (Austin), Sept. 29, Oct. 4, Mar. 3, 1946 (quotation); James W. Smith to M. L. G., Apr. 12, 1982.

38. *Daily Texan* (Austin), Mar. 1 (quotations), Oct. 5, 1946.

39. Ibid., Mar. 12, Oct. 31, 1946 (first quotation); Ben N. Ramey to M. L. G., July 28, 1973.

40. "Texas vs. Heman Sweatt," *Newsweek*, Dec. 30, 1946, p. 74; *The Texas Spectator*, II (Dec. 20, 1946), 4; John W. Stanford Jr. to Painter, Dec. 13, 1946, General Files, "Negro Question: Sweatt Case, 1946–1950," UTPOR.

41. *The Texas Spectator*, II (Dec. 20, 1946), 4 (first quotation), 5; Austin *American*, Dec. 17, 1946; *Daily Texan* (Austin), Mar. 22, 1945; James W. Smith to M. L. G., Apr. 12, 1982.

42. Marshall to Wesley, Dec. 20, 1946; Lulu B. White to Marshall, Dec. 11, 1946; A. M. Smith to John J. Jones, Dec. 6, 1946, NAACP Files; Dallas *Morning News*, July 6, 1948; A. M. Smith to Gloster B Current, June 12, 1947; Morton to A. M. Smith, Feb. 8, 1947; Ruby Hurley to Morton, Mar. 13, 1947; press release, "NAACP Chapter Granted University Students," undated, in "U.T. Chapter NAACP File," James H. Morton Papers (copies in author's possession); *Daily Texan* (Austin), Mar. 25, Apr. 1, 1947.

43. Dallas *Morning News*, July 18, 1948; L. B. White to Current; May 15, 1947; Hurley to Morton, Mar. 13, 1947, Morton Papers.

44. Marion C. Ladwig to Hurley, Feb. 14, 1947; Morton et al. to Walter White, Apr. 1, 1947; Morton to A. M. Smith, Apr. 2, 1947; Ladwig to W. White, Apr. 4, 1947; A. M. Smith to W. White, Apr. 8, 1947; Ladwig to Current, Apr. 9, 1947; Current to Morton, May 1, 1947; Morton to A. M. Smith, May 7, 1947; L. B. White to Current, May 15, 1947; Oliver W Harrington to Current, May 19, 1947 (memorandum); A. M. Smith to Current, June 12, 1947; Marshall to W. White, July 11, 1947 (memorandum); Herb Gilmor to Morton, July 18, 1947; Roy Wilkins to Morton, Sept. 2, 1947, "U.T. Chapter NAACP File," Morton Papers; Stanford to M. L. G., Mar. 1, 1982, interview.

45. *Daily Texan* (Austin), Mar. 26, 1947; Noble to M. L. G., Jan. 23, 1982, interview; Gilmor to L. B White, May 15, 1947, "U.T. Chapter NAACP File," Morton Papers.

46. *Daily Texan* (Austin), Mar. 7, 1948, Mar. 2, 7, 14, Apr. 18 1950.

47. *Sweatt v. Painter*, 339 U.S. 629, 70 S. Ct. 848–851 (1950).

48. McCown to Logan Wilson, Aug. 30, 1954., General Files, "Negroes in Colleges, 1939–1954," UTPOR; *Daily Texan* (Austin), June 9, 1950; Austin *Statesman*, July 8, 1955; Dallas *Morning News*, Feb. 15, 1956.

49. McCown to Wilson, Aug. 30, 1954; Wilson to McCown, Aug. 31, 1954; McCown to Marion George Ford Jr., July 23, 1954 (quotation); Tom Sealy to Board of Regents, Sept. 2, 1954 (memorandum), General Files, "Negroes in Colleges, 1939–1954," UTPOR.

50. Dallas *Morning News*, July 13, 1955; Austin *Statesman*, July 8, 1955; *Daily Texan* (Austin), July 12, Dec. 6, 1955; Almetris Marsh Duren, *Overcoming: A History of Black Integration at the University of Texas at Austin* (Austin, 1979), 8, 14; *Brown v. Board of Education of Topeka*, 349 U.S. 294 (1955) (quotation).

51. D. Jones to Barnett, Oct. 17, 1950, NAACP Files; Houston *Post*, May 28, 1973; Kirk to M. L. G., Feb. 15, 1982, interview; Allen to M. L. G., Feb. 14, 1982, interview. For a biographical sketch of Heman Sweatt, see Gillette, "Heman Marion Sweatt," 157–188.

52. Doyle to M. L. G., Jan. 29, 1982, interview.

"Going Towards a Great Library at Texas" Harry Ransom's Acquisition of the T. E. Hanley Collection

RICHARD W. ORAM }

In late 1956, Dr. Harry H. Ransom, then vice president and provost of the University of Texas, proposed "that there be established somewhere in Texas—let's say in the capital city—a center of cultural compass, a research center to be the Bibliotheque Nationale of the only state that started out as an independent republic" (Ransom [1957], 3). Less than two years later, Ransom's bold conception was well on the way to becoming concrete reality. In 1957 he founded the Humanities Research Center (HRC) at the University and purchased the 40,000-volume library of New Orleans book collector Edward Alexander Parsons the next year. Ransom almost immediately topped this acquisition with an even more significant one: the T. Edward Hanley library of English and American literary manuscripts and books, one of the most significant block purchases in the recent history of American research libraries. With this masterstroke, Ransom succeeded in giving Texas, the owner of a modest rare books collection, immediate credibility in the library world, or "instant ivy," as some wits put it. Ransom exulted at the time of the Hanley purchase that "this action now puts the modern collections at Texas in the forefront of international libraries. We talk a good deal about 'first class.' In this regard, we have now achieved the title" (HHR to W. J. Burke, September 28, 1958). To Jake Schwartz, he wrote, "we are going towards a great Library at Texas" (Staley 18).

The Hanley purchase of 1958 (it was followed by a less spectacular sequel in 1964) was *the* defining moment in the early history of the Humanities Research Center. Without this massive acquisition (155,000 items from the 1958 purchase alone) and its distinguished array of manuscripts by the likes of George Bernard Shaw, D. H. Lawrence, and Dylan Thomas, the Univer-

---

As chief librarian of the Harry Ransom Humanities Research Center, Richard W. Oram oversees the curatorial and public services aspects of the Center. In 2004, he was named an associate director of the HRHRC. This essay appeared in a somewhat different form in the April 2000 issue of Antiquarian Books Monthly *(now* Rare Book Review*), under the title "Harry Ransom Brings the T. E. Hanley Collection to Texas."*

sity of Texas would have taken years to come up to full speed in twentieth-century literary collecting. As luck would have it, the availability of the Hanley Library coincided with the great oil boom of the 1950s, which allowed Texas to invest over a million dollars in a single collection. Furthermore, the Hanley purchase was, in Ransom's remarkably prescient words, "one of the really signal developments in the collection of modern literature" (HHR to James H. Drake, August 6, 1958). In effect, Ransom's acquisition legitimized institutional collecting of twentieth-century literary manuscripts, although there were precedents at other universities, most notably the University of Buffalo's Lockwood Library.

Thomas Edward ("Ed") Hanley (1893–1969) was a pioneer in the acquisition of manuscripts and correspondence by modern writers, though his name is unfamiliar to many, if not most, of today's librarians, booksellers, and collectors. He was also one of the most zealous collectors of his day, an extraordinarily acquisitive yet retiring man who collected on behalf of several institutional libraries as well as his own and put together a major collection of modern art during a half century of accumulation. Hanley's diffidence was equaled by the flamboyance of his wife, Tullah, a sensual former exotic dancer of Egyptian-Hungarian heritage who came to share Ed's love for books, manuscripts, and art and who played a key role in the eventual transfer of the entire Hanley Library to Austin. Ed Hanley was born in Bradford, Pennsylvania, where he spent most of his life. His family owned a brick-making company, oil and gas leases, and real estate. The family fortune allowed him to attend Harvard (class of 1915), where he majored in architecture and later fine arts. Hanley began collecting rare books while still at college and, after returning to Bradford to work in the family business, he began collecting modern literature and art. Hanley's art collecting merits separate treatment; suffice it to say that he put together a superb collection of Impressionist, Post-Impressionist, and other early modern paintings, the bulk of which is now at the DeYoung Museum in San Francisco.

While traveling through Arizona on vacation in the thirties, Hanley stopped at the library of the fledgling state university in Tucson and was appalled to find how poor its humanities holdings were (Sorensen 6). He offered to serve both as donor and book scout for the University of Arizona. Over the next thirty years Hanley spent countless hours on buying trips se-

lecting books, which he then personally packed and delivered to the post office. Hanley's generosity to Arizona, for which he was awarded an honorary doctorate, was matched by his cantankerousness: he held no truck with modern library science and waged running battles with administrators over cataloging and disposition of duplicates from the collection. Hanley also donated books to other institutions. Throughout his career as a book collector, he was keenly aware that the fruits of his collecting were destined for institutional collections and, despite his Harvard degree, tended to favor non-Ivy-League colleges and universities, perhaps because his roots were in a small, backwater Pennsylvania town.

In 1945, Ed Hanley and his brother visited a club in nearby Buffalo and took in the dance act of two shapely sisters, Tullah and Amy (or Ami) Innes. Tullah (1924–92) was a poor immigrant from Hungary with Egyptian blood and the avowed intention of landing an American millionaire. Upon meeting Ed Hanley, Tullah realized that her prize was in hand: "Yep, you've *sighted man, sank same*," she wrote in her memoirs (152). Tullah soon towed Hanley into port, and she and Amy moved into Ed's Victorian frame house, where its closets and the garage and outbuildings overflowed with thousands of art, rare book, and manuscript treasures. Tullah, who was always easily assimilated, became almost as obsessed with collecting as her husband. When Ed began building up a vast collection of Shaw letters in the late 1940s and early 1950s, Tullah brushed up her Shaw and used original correspondence of Janet Achurch, Charles Carrington, and Shaw in Hanley's library as the basis for a novel with the racy title of *The Strange Triangle of G.B.S* (1957). She was, as she writes in her autobiography, *Love of Art & Art of Love*, "a self-educated Cindertullah" who was earthy, generous, street-smart, and quite funny. She once quipped that "it's a lie that I make out with perfect strangers; nobody is perfect!" and that "home is wherever I hang my G-string" (135). Because of Tullah's candor we know somewhat more than we would care to about Ed's sexual problems, her extramarital escapades, her run-ins with the Bradford establishment, and her tips for good living (high-quality sex, yogurt, and health foods), but we also get an intimate psychological portrait of book collecting as seen from the inside.

Hanley spent much of his free time prowling bookstores and avoiding dealers: "I have myself always preferred playing the 'lone wolf,' making my own decisions and mistakes, and staying out of all book-collector clubs, etc. As a result, I am scarcely known anywhere and that is what I prefer" (to Jacob Schwartz, December 14, 1951). Harry Ransom echoed Hanley's self-characterization in his description of the Hanley modus operandi: "he has stayed completely independent of auction-room melodramatics, back-fence bibliographical gossip, and all the other avocations of the professors and professional bookmen" (Ransom, "Hanley Library," 35). Hanley was also unconventional in his preference for the manuscripts and correspondence of modern writers, believing that this material was underappreciated and undervalued on the market.

Hanley had a longstanding special relationship, going at least as far back as the early thirties, with the former dentist turned book "purveyor" Dr. Jacob Schwartz. Schwartz devoted himself to ferreting out important manuscripts of the moderns, and in many cases obtained his stock directly from the writers themselves, often for a relative pittance (no wonder that Samuel Beckett dubbed him "The Great Extractor"). Since Hanley preferred to leverage his purchases by buying on the installment plan and Schwartz was willing to extend credit, the relationship worked well. In the 1930s and 1940s, Hanley bought intermittently from the dealer, typically carrying balances of a few thousand dollars or less. In the early 1950s, however, Hanley began to accelerate his purchases of important manuscript material from Schwartz. Unquestionably the greatest of these items was the set of corrected final page proofs of James Joyce's *Ulysses*. Schwartz had bought these at auction on November 9, 1951, for $2,300 and sold them to Hanley a few days later for $4,300 (Watson 256).

About the same time, Hanley set about aggressively buying George Bernard Shaw letters from the same source. He had already staged a coup by purchasing the remaining stock of Shaw material from the estate of the bookseller Gabriel Wells. After acquiring a large group of Shaw letters from Schwartz in early 1953, Hanley now owned 1,400 letters, for which he reckoned he had paid roughly ten dollars each, and his balance on account rose alarmingly to $44,000. Jake Schwartz now faced the classic dealer's dilemma of wanting to encourage his client's Shaw habit while trying to get him to pay off a larger part of the ever-increasing balance; in 1953 he wrote to

Hanley that he could continue to get Shaw material economically because he went directly to the sources, principally Shaw's secretary Blanche Patch. However, Schwartz also complained about Hanley's indebtedness: "I WILL make your collection a world celebrity . . . but I am broke" (August 20, 1953). Ed Hanley was being pressured on the domestic front as well, by his wife. Even though Tullah had been kept in the dark about his large recent purchases, Ed wrote Schwartz that Tullah was already quite upset about the extent of his indebtedness and the insurance coverage problems that were beginning to develop.

These irritations notwithstanding, Hanley continued to pursue manuscripts not only by Shaw but also by other modern writers, such as Dylan Thomas, Samuel Beckett, and D. H. Lawrence. Lawrence's widow, Frieda Lawrence Ravagli, had been selling the late novelist's manuscripts to Hanley since the 1930s. In 1956, he wrote Schwartz, "In a letter to me a few years ago, [Frieda] stated that mine is the greatest D.H.L. collection in the world" (June 19, 1956). Though he complained constantly about paying Jake "too dam [sic] much," Hanley was also beginning to corner the market on manuscripts of Dylan Thomas, including a typescript of *Under Milkwood*, which were mostly acquired from his impecunious widow and friends. Another interest was Samuel Beckett, from whom Jake Schwartz had managed to coax manuscripts in exchange for paltry sums—in one case, for a tin of tea (Lake 2). In October 1956, Hanley paid Schwartz $5,000 for a substantial group of Beckett manuscripts.

Meanwhile, word was beginning to get out among scholars and bibliophiles about the spectacular manuscripts tucked away in Hanley's Bradford garage and outbuildings and which were now beginning to spill out of the closets of his office downtown. The University of Texas had just started a collection of D. H. Lawrence manuscripts and had been cultivating Frieda Lawrence Ravagli. Harry Ransom, then dean of the College of Arts and Sciences, and F. Warren Roberts, a young Lawrence scholar who later succeeded Ransom as director of the HRC, soon learned about Hanley's Lawrence holdings from her. In September 1954, Ransom made his first overture to Ed Hanley:

Dear Sir: By almost uncanny coincidence I have been brought [sic] acquainted with your great modern collections twice within the past few weeks. At a dinner given by the President of Baylor University last month

I gathered that the Baylor Browning Library was seeking your advice. Within the week, we have learned from Mrs. Frieda Lawrence Ravagli (whose remaining collection at Taos is now on option to the University of Texas) that with your permission we might inquire about your plans for your Lawrence Collection (September 10, 1954).

Ransom went on to describe how the Hanley materials might fit into a proposed "live center for research and writing." This center had been a preoccupation of Ransom's since the late 1940s, when he had served on a committee to chart a future course for Texas' special collections. Thus was born what Ransom called "the plan for the library." While Ransom was climbing the University's administrative ladder in the early 1950s, he was beginning to contact prominent dealers of twentieth-century books and manuscripts. The Ransom strategy was based on the acquisition of first editions and, even more importantly, manuscripts by modern writers. The field of modern manuscripts was a relatively open area in which Texas could compete successfully with older and wealthier universities, particularly if the legislature would see its way to allowing the expenditure of the postwar oil revenues piling up in the Permanent University Fund.

Shortly after writing Hanley, Ransom met briefly with him, presumably at Bradford in late 1954 or early 1955, and was "very excited" by the collection (F. Warren Roberts to TEH, April 13, 1955). There follows a substantial gap in the Hanley-Ransom correspondence. From a Schwartz letter to Hanley in June 1957 we know that the dealer was now showing signs of alarm about his client's balance of $99,022. Schwartz hinted at a convenient exit from the dilemma: "I also know privately that if you really wanted to raise money the University of Texas would buy your entire book and manuscript collection EN BLOC . . . I heard something about their desire from a highly confidential source here in London . . . it is their DREAM—Dr. Ransome [sic] was willing to pay Mrs. Lawrence a HUGH [sic] sum for that D. H. Lawrence collection (including the $75000) for the three versions of Chatterl[e]y" [June 25, 1957]). In his reply of June 30, Hanley revealed that the Lilly Library at Indiana and its librarian David A. Randall were also seriously interested in his library and pointedly added that he had not heard from Texas in some time.

Things developed rapidly in the summer of 1957. In addition to Schwartz's increasingly panicky demands for money, Hanley had to contend with his insurance agent, who paid another visit to the house in July and delivered an ultimatum that his company could no longer insure both the art and the library; clearly, part of the collection would have to go. In August and again in October, Randall inspected the books and manuscripts at Bradford, despite Hanley's continuing reservations about selling. The Lilly librarian returned home, having arrived at a cost figure of around a million dollars for the bulk of Hanley's library. Indiana University was, it turned out, unable to raise this sum. At an opportune moment in late 1957, Ransom sent a telegram to Hanley offering an honorary degree. This turned out to be decisive in sealing a deal with the collector. As Hanley wrote after the negotiation concluded, "Texas knew absolutely nothing that any part of my library was for sale [this was probably a bit naive on Hanley's part] and when I told Tullah about the Texas degree, we concluded right off to give Texas first chance if it wanted it, and Texas grabbed at the opportunity, and as for the price, never haggled whatsoever and considered the price absolutely fair and reasonable" (to JS, August 28, 1958). Ransom was justly celebrated for this sort of grand gesture that, sprung at just the right moment, could clinch big deals. In later years, friends and foes alike would refer to having been "Ransomized" into submission by this soft-spoken, ineffably charming man. His negotiating skill arose from his knowledge that such things hinged upon personal vanity—that is to say, psychological as well as economic issues. The prospect of an honorary degree for Ed and Phi Beta Kappa membership for Ed and Tullah (neither of which cost Texas a thing) was exactly the sort of academic recognition that the collector's ego craved.

Negotiations with Texas went on for months, but as a letter of May 18, 1958, from Hanley to Ransom makes clear, the outcome was no longer in doubt by then. The matter of whether the $1,080,000 would be paid in installments with interest or in a lump sum had to be decided. Ransom used Randall's million-dollar valuation and a comparable appraisal by the New York bookseller James H. Drake, acting as the University's agent during the final stages of the sale, to convince University and state officials to come up with the whole sum. This he did by July 1958, when the Texas regents approved the deal. There remained the problem of how HRC staff could inventory such a huge collection on-site, which was solved by having it packed by a crew of Bradford ex-convicts over ten days and then having the cataloging done back in Austin, where it arrived in September. Warren Roberts vividly remembered the unpacking: nobody "knew what he had or what was going to come out next. It was one of the most exciting things that ever happened" (Basbanes 318).

It is entertaining to compare Tullah Hanley's account of the 1958 sale in her autobiography, which varies from my reconstruction based on correspondence in the Ransom Center. She boils the whole episode down to a single dramatic visit by Ransom to Bradford, which supposedly took place sometime during the summer of 1958. In Tullah's version, Ransom's masterstroke was not offering Ed an honorary degree but rather his offer to *her* of an honorary fellowship in George Bernard Shaw studies, based on his admiration for her recently published novel about Shaw's love life. It was this gesture that supposedly set up Ransom's single trip to Bradford. Following dinner with Ransom, "whose wildest imagination could not grasp the variety and the extent of Ed's collection" (227), Ed was still wavering, but after some skillful pillow-talk that night and other psychological manipulation on Tullah's part, he decided that Texas should have the Hanley Library. We know from Hanley's correspondence that Tullah's condensed and highly dramatized account is fundamentally inaccurate, yet there is no reason to question her assertion that she helped push the deal through. She was highly motivated in seeing the negotiation with Texas consummated, since she and her sister had been promised a large chunk of the proceeds by Hanley. Also, she loved playing the role of "undercover conspirator" (227) on behalf of Texas, and it is entirely possible that without her assistance the Hanley Library might not have ended up in Austin.

It took a few months for Ed Hanley to heal after the loss of most of his literary treasures, but after paying off Jake Schwartz, he went right back to buying from his old friend. The 1958 agreement with Texas contained an option for the University to purchase additional manuscripts by Dylan Thomas, the Powys family, Samuel Beckett, and some literary portraits, all of which remained behind in Bradford. These were collections that Hanley continued to develop over the next few years, so that by 1960, Hanley's balance on account with Schwartz was over $150,000. Embarked

on one of the largest acquisitions sprees in library history, Harry Ransom had little time to attend to an increasingly forgetful Ed Hanley, an omission that did not dispose the collector to sell the rest of the collection to the Humanities Research Center. On the other hand, he was hopeful of seeing his entire collection united in Austin as a semi-independent T. E. Hanley Library, perhaps in a separate wing of a proposed new library building. As it happened, the Hanley books and manuscripts were absorbed into the general HRC book, manuscript, and art collections and the promised wing was never built. On October 5, 1964, Tullah wrote her friend "Dr. Harry":

A little inside info. For you prior to negotiations. Because I've never ceased to be your undercover agent on this side of the Culture-Curtain. Ed's friendship for you never lessened but he can't grasp why you stopped personal contact with him—and why do negotiations via lawyers? [She added that his library was worth $650,000,] but I say unto you, that verily, if you personally shall tell him, when you shall be convinced of the value, that could you give it for 600,000, he shall do so . . . These are the Intimate Knowledge.

With Tullah's assistance and relatively little ado, the sale of the second installment of the Hanley library, or "Hanley II" as it was known, was closed by late 1964, with Ransom paying $650,000. Tullah helped Texas once again by throwing in various items that Ed was unaware of, in an effort to clean out the entire Hanley stock of books and manuscripts. After Ed Hanley's death in 1969, a small group of literary art came to the Humanities Research Center as a bequest.

After viewing the materials in Hanley II, the rare book dealer Franklin Gilliam wrote Ransom that "There is here what can only be described as an embarrassment of riches. While there are many choice books present, the manuscript materials are the heart of this splendid collection" (November 13, 1964). This was, if anything, even more true of the earlier purchase. By late 1958, the Humanities Research Center at Texas now owned the largest collection by far of manuscripts by D. H. Lawrence and a Shaw collection nearly comparable to that of the British Library. One could single out smaller but important groups of letters and manuscripts by Robert and Elizabeth Barrett Browning (including her autograph of the "Battle of Marathon"), Lewis Carroll (his early illustrated work

"The Rectory Magazine"), John Galsworthy, Aldous Huxley (the corrected typescript of *Brave New World*), Ezra Pound, Algernon Swinburne, Walt Whitman (nearly 150 items), Virginia Woolf, and W. B. Yeats. The rare books include presentation copies from Carroll, Joseph Conrad (to Henry James), T. S. Eliot, Bret Harte, Somerset Maugham, Whitman (to his lover Peter Doyle), and Yeats (*Mosada*). Among other noteworthy individual items are a copy of Christina Rossetti's *Goblin Market* with original drawings by D. G. Rossetti, Ezra Pound's *A Lume Spento*, and Adam Smith's *Wealth of Nations* in the original boards. There was even a smattering of notable Americana and history of science. With the 1964 purchase from Hanley, Texas added superb groupings of manuscripts by Dylan Thomas and Beckett to the list.

From the perspective of over forty years later, we can say that the acquisition was a stupendous bargain. Or, as the bookseller Anthony Rota put it, "the gods were smiling on the University of Texas the day that it bought the Hanley collection" (42). The corrected proofs of Joyce's *Ulysses* alone are now likely worth more than the sales price for the entire library. Even today, when the collections of the Harry Ransom Humanities Research Center, as the HRC is now known, have grown to encompass over thirty million manuscripts and 800,000 rare books, the Hanley items make up a large part of the Center's crème de la crème. For example, in 1999, the Ransom Center mounted an Oscar Wilde exhibition. Many of the centerpieces of the show derived from the Hanley Library: one of the original drafts, in a notebook which Wilde purchased down the street from his lodgings in Paris, of *Salome*, and the corrected page proofs of *The Importance of Being Earnest*, not to mention several of Wilde's first editions inscribed to his mother and numerous letters (Hanley collected Oscar Wilde and James Joyce in part because of his pride in his Irish heritage.)

In his survey of the world's great libraries, Anthony Hobson writes that "a single coup raised [the HRC's] collection to the level of international importance; this was the purchase of the major part of the library formed over thirty years by T. E. Hanley of Pennsylvania" (309). Though all the principals are dead, the story of the acquisition of the Hanley Library by Harry Ransom can be reconstructed in considerable detail. It is very much the kind of larger-than-life story that Texans cherish. There is intrigue, drama, big oil money (on both sides of the deal, no less), and high stakes. There is the compulsive collector Ed Hanley, a bibliophile and art collector of gargantuan appetites, and Dr. Harry Ransom, "the Grand Acquisitor," driven to realize his vision of a Texan "national library." And, in a supporting role, there is the vivacious Tullah Hanley, "Dr. Harry's" undercover agent.

WORKS CITED

All letters cited in the text are from the Ransom Center's own archives or its collection of the correspondence between T. E. Hanley and Jacob Schwartz.

Basbanes, Nicholas A. *A Gentle Madness: Bibliophiles, Bibliomanes, and the Eternal Passion for Books.* New York: Henry Holt, 1995.

Hanley, Tullah. *Love of Art & Art of Love: Tullah Hanley's Autobiography.* Blue Earth, MN: Piper, 1975.

Hobson, Anthony. *Great Libraries.* New York: Putnam, 1970.

Lake, Carlton. "Ed the Collector, Jake the Dentist and Beckett: A Tale That Ends in Texas," *New York Times Book Review* 7 Sept. 1987: 2.

Ransom, Harry H. *The Collection of Knowledge in Texas.* El Paso: Carl Herzog, [1957].

———. "The Hanley Library." *Library Chronicle of the University of Texas* 6 (1959): 33–35.

Rota, Anthony. "The Collecting of Twentieth-Century Literary Manuscripts," *Rare Books and Manuscripts Librarianship* 1 (1986): 39–53.

Sorensen, Lee. *Determined Donor: T. Edward Hanley & His Gift of Books to the University of Arizona Library 1936–1964.* Tucson: Friends of the University of Arizona Library, 1989.

Staley, Thomas F. "Literary Canons and Library Collections: A Retrospective on Collecting Twentieth-Century Writers." *Rare Books and Manuscripts Librarianship* 5 (1990): 9–21.

Watson, Richard. "The Provenance of the Final Corrected Page Proofs of James Joyce's *Ulysses*." *Joyce Studies Annual* 2 (1991): 251–57.

The University Interscholastic League and the Integration of Texas High School Athletics

BOBBY HAWTHORNE

Every state has an organization to govern and protect high school athletics. Generally, they pass rules and dole out punishments designed to keep cheating to a discreet minimum. The largest and most powerful of these associations is Texas' University Interscholastic League, best known by its acronym—the UIL. It's revered by many, reviled by others who've called it heartless and dumb, arbitrary and capricious, to which the League, for most of its history, has simply replied, "Pfffft."

Not only does the UIL keep scholastic sports under its thumb, it sponsors huge marching band competitions, one-act play festivals, and academic tournaments involving contests in areas such as literary criticism and computer science. Its activities are part of the public schools' DNA. But the League didn't earn its reputation by sponsoring wind ensemble contests or debate tournaments. It earned it by ruthlessly enforcing the nation's harshest rules governing interscholastic sports. Only Texans fear that feeding an athlete a cheeseburger can get their hometown team booted from the high school state playoffs.

THE UT/UIL CONNECTION

Few people realize the League was hatched and raised by the University of Texas at Austin. If they're aware of the UIL at all, they figure it's part of either the Texas Education Agency, the NCAA, or the Department of Public Safety. They rarely connect it to UT-Austin, which has been fine for the most part with the big-wigs in the Tower because they don't want to have to apologize for an organization that has been rumored to disqualify football players for accepting Bibles. Whether this story is fact or fable is

Bobby Hawthorne was a journalist working for several Texas newspapers before he began his work with the University Interscholastic League in Austin. Hawthorne is recognized nationally and internationally as an authority on teaching high school journalism. He retired from his position as the UIL's director of academics in 2005.

irrelevant. School people and parents assume it's true and have developed an appreciable paranoia about all things related to the UIL.

Fortunately, no one blames UT for the League's quirks and flaws, and UT has benefited generously from its relationship with the UIL. Each year, hundreds of the state's brightest young high school students converge on the Forty Acres for the Academic State Meet and return a year or so later as undergraduates, assisted financially by UIL scholarships. Many high school athletes connect UT to championship basketball or track experiences held at the Erwin Center or Royal-Memorial Stadium. No department or division within the University reaches as many schools, their teachers, administrators, and students, and other institutions of higher learning as the UIL.

Despite the advantages of housing the state headquarters and hosting Texas championship events, UT rarely trumpets familial ties with the League other than at the occasional meeting or banquet. The fact is, UT spawned the UIL for the same reason it does about everything: to show up the Aggies and the Sooners.

This is complicated so pay attention. In 1905, UT hosted a track meet, attended by 11 high schools and prep academies. It wasn't a huge success. A heavy rain ruined the track at Clark Field, and the races were run up and down Speedway. According to Thomas H. Shelby, dean of the Division of Extension from 1921 to 1951, "The trip to Austin was expensive; no medals, banners or tangible proofs of prowess were given; and there was no real state championship involved."

The meet director, Homer F. Curtiss, director of the Men's Gymnasium and coach of the Longhorn track team, tried to compensate for the lack of glitz by offering to organize the schools into a league, which he called the "Texas Interscholastic Athletic Association." This didn't work either, at least not immediately.

Over the next six years, interest in track declined, then recovered, thanks mostly to huge invitational track meets up north and at Texas A&M and OU. Conspicuously missing, of course, was organization. No rules, eligibility standards, or procedures existed, and it wasn't uncommon for coaches, graduates, drifters—ringers of every stripe—to suit up and run and jump if that's what it took to win. "As track and field athletics began to be taken up more and more by the Texas high schools and academics, the school author-

ities felt the need of organization and supervision," Shelby wrote. "It became evident that these teachers felt the need for the development, under sane control, of school athletics."[1]

In 1910, the typical athletic coach was a self-appointed, untrained, poorly educated, crude, loud, profane, tobacco-chewing tyrant who conducted four-hour workouts in the blazing Texas sun and thumbed his nose at the school superintendent or anyone else who questioned his authority.

Okay. I know what you're thinking. But it was worse back then. For example, this 1923 letter to the UIL:

As a matter of fact, the . . . team was the dirtiest team that we have ever met. They kneed our men constantly. They knocked out of place the kidneys of one man, broke the collar bone of another, and shattered the ribs of a third. During the time between halves, substantial citizens heard their coach tell his men to do all they could to knock out our strong men in order that weak substitutes might be put in the line.

And this was more than a decade *after* the UIL had attempted to wrest control of athletics from the hometown fieldhouse cabal.

As the date for the first meet approached, Shelby said he worried that no one would show up. The Aggies ran their meet a week earlier and paid the athletes to attend, old habits being hard to break. UT couldn't match the offer, and "the better teams found A&M's offer the more attractive," Shelby said. "The only effective bid we could make was membership in a prospectively wider and more liberally self-governing organization." It would be called the Interscholastic Athletic Association.

About that same time, UT president S. E. Mezes commissioned registrar John A. Lomax to visit various Midwest universities and report on the activities of their extension departments. Upon his return, Lomax told Dr. Mezes that interschool associations for academic competitions—debating leagues in particular—appeared about as promising as anything. Lomax later became famous for collecting cowboy songs and frontier ballads, and for plucking blues legend Leadbelly out of a Louisiana prison and foisting him on New York socialites, but that's another story.

Mezes summoned Professor E. D. Shurter, then head of the UT Deptartment of Public Speaking, and suggested that he organize a debating league among Texas secondary schools. In 1910, Shurter took the idea to school administrators attending the Texas State Teachers Association meeting in Abilene; the group agreed to form the Debating League of Texas High Schools so long as UT would house and administer it. Shurter accepted, and UT hosted the first statewide contest on May 6, 1911. The next year, declamation was added, and the name was changed to the Debating and Declamation League of Texas.

In the spring of 1913, the debating league merged with the athletic association, forming the University Interscholastic League. Shurter was appointed its first director, thus ushering in the sometimes rocky, sometimes aloof marriage between UT and the UIL.

THE LEAGUE GROWS

Although a part of UT, the League doesn't beggar tax dollars from the legislature. Instead, it generates its own funds, mostly through membership fees and receipts from high school football playoff games. Controlling its own purse-strings has given the UIL an amazing degree of autonomy. Today, it answers to UT only when it comes to matters of policy and accounting. To its credit, UT rarely interferes with the League's decisions or rules. The following statement, issued on April 16, 1946 by D. K. Woodward, chairman of the UT Board of Regents, illustrates UT's mostly hands-off philosophy: "All rules and regulations are made by the public school people through democratic processes. The University provides a staff to enforce and administer these regulations. The Board of Regents, as such, has no authority to determine the eligibility and other rules relative to conducting contests."

There have been exceptions. In 1940, UT regent Lutcher Stark of Orange tried to bully UT president Homer Price Rainey into firing League director Roy Bedichek and athletic director Rodney Kidd for their support of an eligibility rule change which would have rendered Stark's twin sons ineligible. Rainey refused, further greasing the skids for his impending ride out of town, but that's another story too.

Though perhaps embarrassed or irritated by provincial League rules, the University has kept its distance beyond providing lawyers to defend the UIL in court and professors to create and direct its growing academic and fine arts programs. Now and then, the League's State Executive Committee—its Supreme Court—found it necessary to cattle-prod the UIL into the twentieth century. For example, in the 1980s, the executive committee ruled that girls could play on boys' teams if the school failed to provide a corresponding sport. School people weren't entirely prepared for this, girls playing on boys' teams. But they yielded, begrudgingly.

As Rhea Williams, the UIL director from 1964–79, noted, "The State Executive Committee has always been ahead of the schools in regard to philosophy and constitutionality," which is natural since the SEC consisted of UT faculty and staff members, whereas school administrators answered to locally elected school boards consisting of used car dealers and café owners with ninth-grade educations. Not that I see a big problem with this—my daddy had a ninth grade education, and he was a pretty smart fellow.

Today, the League is a shadow of its former self. Power is disbursed among a legislative council, the SEC and the state commissioner of education. Most of the League's archaic rules—such as the one that restricted basketball players from attending summer camps—have been abolished, generally by the UIL itself though rarely without some judge or legislator or big-eared billionaire twisting its arm.

In lawsuit after lawsuit during the 1970s and 1980s, the League's rules were challenged as arbitrary and capricious, which they were. When I joined the League in 1977, then UIL director Rhea Williams handed me a copy of the *Constitution and Contest Rules* and said, "Always keep this book between you and them." If he had ripped out pages and burned them in my hand, this moment of UIL *omerta* could not have been more serious.

This "us versus them" mentality produced and reinforced the League's big-net philosophy: toss out a huge net, pull in a lot of fish, and hope to catch the ones you plan to fry. But those days are over, even if UIL directors now occasionally lament the passing of an era when parents, school administrators and teachers displayed a Pharisaic deference to UIL rules. If a young man transferred into a new school, it was assumed he did so for athletic purposes, even if the kid was 5'2", weighed 115, and carried a flute and a slide rule.

Little wonder society revolted against the League in the 1980s. Parents sued and started winning, and today, the UIL recognizes the concept of due process, waives attendance rules for students in dire circumstances—like kids battling cancer—and seems genuinely more interested in service and policy than surveillance and policing. Sure, now and then a team gets kicked out of the football playoffs the day before the state championship, but they probably deserved it and more.

INTEGRATING THE UIL

Though it ditched its most restrictive rules, the UIL still has a hard time shirking its persona as the IRS of high school sports. Principals dread the possibility that by allowing their cheerleaders to leave a goodie bag in the quarterback's locker, they'll step within the UIL's cross-hairs. The amount of misinformation among teachers, coaches and school administrators regarding League rules is staggering. And so it is ironic that this organization, so renowned for its hidebound stubbornness, as resistant to change as an Afghan mullah, would play such an important role in desegregating Texas public schools. But it did.

From its birth in 1910 until 1965, UIL membership was open to white public schools in Texas, except those for "correctives or defectives." No evidence exists to suggest that the League's founders or early directors questioned the status quo of public education for blacks in the South. Even the inveterate liberal, Roy Bedichek, who served as UIL director from 1922 to 1948, never mentions blacks, Negroes, race, or segregation in *Educational Competition*, his history of the UIL.

Though perhaps best remembered for his Texas nature writing and his literary relationships with J. Frank Dobie and Walter Prescott Webb, Bedichek's day job was shaping the League into an extension of his philosophy of competition. He was an intellectual, but not an effete intellectual inasmuch as some of his personal habits would make a longshoreman blush. Still, he read Plato with his pre-dawn coffee and morning stroll through his garden. He knew by heart long passages of the *Iliad* and the *Odyssey* and had read deeply in Tolstoy and Dostoevsky, Greek tragedies, Shakespeare, Wordsworth, and Whitman. Though he believed that life was a matter of survival,

Roy Bedichek. *From the Prints and Photographs Collection—Roy Bedichek, Center for American History, the University of Texas at Austin. (DI 02423)*

he feared unfettered competition for the sake of local entertainment. He wrote:

> Just how to develop the fighting instinct without making gamecocks or bulldogs out of our children; just how to utilize rivalry in education without allowing the genie to run amuck; just how to graft upon this bitter stock cutting that shall bear the fruit of kindliness, goodwill and mutual aid and mutual respect; just how to turn the power behind an absolutely egotistic impulse to good uses in the life of the individual and to society—this is the problem that has exercised not only the minds of philosophers but of practical educators in all ages.[2]

It is strange that his sense of kindliness, goodwill and mutual aid did not extend, at least in any public statement or act, to African Americans, though he was clearly sympathetic to their plight. In a 1944 letter to Dobie, who had spent the year teaching in England at Cambridge University, Bedichek wrote, "You have been away for a year in an entirely new envi-

Rodney James Kidd. *Courtesy of the University Interscholastic League, University of Texas at Austin.*

ronment and I daresay you have become conscious of how we treat the Negro. Do you remember drinking fountains in every dirty east Texas courthouse labeled 'For Negroes' side by side with those labeled 'For Whites'? Nothing comparable to this exists outside of India."

But this sentiment didn't translate into anything tangible, and Bedichek played out his final years as UIL director, ensconced at Friday Mountain Ranch, writing *Adventures of a Texas Naturalist*, his history of the UIL, two other books, and box loads of letters to his friends in which he grumbled about the general state of everything, as old men are wont to do.

Grappling with the effects of desegregation would fall to Rodney Kidd, Bedichek's successor. The doctrine of "separate but equal" ended as a defensible legality in 1954 when the U.S. Supreme Court declared in the case of *Brown vs. Topeka Board of Education* that segregated public schools were unconstitutional. At the time, fewer than 20 percent of Texas school districts had even token desegregation, and the prospect of race-mixing was mostly unthinkable, particularly in East Texas, where whites agreed with kindred Southern bigots who blustered, "We are engaged in the greatest struggle and the greatest crusade in the history of mankind. If you're a white man, then it's time to stand up with us, or black your face and get on the other side."

No self-respecting Texas racist or political opportunist was going to miss the greatest crusade in the history of mankind, so the backlash began. Memberships boomed in White Citizens' Councils, exerting tremendous pressure on politicians to drag their feet

on desegregation. Like all Southern governors, Govenor Allan Shivers railed against the Supreme Court. "We are going to keep the system that we know is best," he said. "No law, no court, can wreck what God has made. Nobody can pass a law and change it." Snared in a bitter campaign for governor against liberal Ralph Yarborough, Shivers warned local school boards that their state financial aid might be jeopardized if they rushed into desegregation.

In May of 1954, Dr. J. W. Edgar, the state commissioner of education, told public schools that they should continue to segregate since the U.S. Supreme Court instructed public schools to admit black students to public schools on a racially, nondiscriminatory basis "with all deliberate speed," which was interpreted by many Southerners as "not in my lifetime."

But desegregation was inevitable. In July 1955, Kidd received a telephone call from Mortimer Brown, El Paso ISD superintendent, who said his schools were desegregating and wanted to know whether, in light of the Brown decision, "certain colored students" transferring to the white school would be eligible to compete in UIL activities. As it was, El Paso had only 735 black students, most of whom, Brown said, would continue to attend the Douglass School, which graduated between 12 to 17 seniors per year. The others would attend the "white" school closest to their home. "It was the first time our committee [the State Executive Committee] had before it the eligibility of Negro students representing white high schools," Kidd wrote.

The SEC's members at the time included James R. D. Eddy, the director of the UT Bureau of Extension; two government professors, Howard A. Calkins and Emmett S. Redford; B. C. Tharp, a botany professor; Thomas A. Rousse, a speech professor; I. I. Nelson, a professor in the Department of Curriculum and Instruction; Kidd; Williams; and Shelby, the former director of the extension bureau who had taught LBJ at Johnson City High. Eddy directed the war training program for the State of Texas during World War II. He was most likely Rainey's final hire as UT president. On the same day that Rainey hired Eddy, the UT regents fired Rainey.

From the League's inception in 1912 until 1956, the State Executive Committee had final authority in administering the affairs of the League. It passed rules and doled out punishment to those who broke them, reflecting Bedichek's high, almost unrealistic, ideals.

Texas historian Walter Prescott Webb served a five-year stint on the committee and said, "I was struck by the savage intensity with which he (Bedichek) enforced the rules in an effort to preserve some morality in school athletics." Added Shelby,

> In athletic activities, as such, he [Bedichek] had little or no interest, and he seldom attended games or other contests to enjoy the spectacle. In dealing with those who broke rules, whether contestants or school officials, Bedi never wavered in applying the rules of the League. He might be sympathetic with those who received penalties for rules infractions, but he was never soft.

Nor was Kidd. Though not the pure intellectual that Bedichek had been, Kidd provided the League what it needed most at the time: boundless enthusiasm, unwavering commitment to League principles, uncanny vision, common sense, and a stern Irish constitution. When a secretary once asked for a day off to observe the silver anniversary of her wedding day, Kidd is said to have replied, "My goodness, don't tell me we're going to have to go through this every 25 years." Slow spoken, honest, rigidly fair, he was a 12-sport letterman at Southwestern University. When he became UIL athletic director, one of his friends said he should be able to do a good job since Kidd himself had broken every UIL rule during his career as a coach at his alma mater.

Kidd called the SEC members together to discuss the El Paso situation, ironically on the same day the University Board of Regents gathered to decide whether Negro undergraduates would be admitted to UT and its branches. Other than a few thin minutes, records of the meeting are unavailable, and those who attended have long since died. Press accounts were based on a statement released by the UIL, which Kidd most likely wrote himself. We don't know how long the meeting lasted, who spoke, or what they said. But the power of their written statement suggests unanimity.

After a proper series of whereas this and whereas that, the SEC finally reached its therefore: "BE IT RESOLVED that the State Executive Committee of the Interscholastic League interpret the language 'public white school' as not excluding any public school in Texas which has previously limited its enrollment to white students but which has modified its rules so as to admit students of the Negro race."

There being no further business, the committee adjourned. Williams called Brown in El Paso, and Eddy, the SEC chairman, sent the statement to UT President Logan Wilson for his discussion with the Board of Regents. "We do not intend to disseminate this information until after you and the Board have had a chance to see it," Eddy wrote.

On July 8, Wilson responded:

> Since the Texas Interscholastic League is a relatively autonomous body, making its own policies, the Regents took the position that any action of your Executive Committee in this regard is its own affair. For the record, I wish to state that they saw no objection to the course of action set forth in your resolution concerning interpretation of the language, "white public school."

Brown applauded the SEC's quick decision. "In my opinion, the Executive Committee was wise in acting quickly on this matter before temperatures rose and discussions became more complicated," he told Williams.

South Texas and West Texas, where desegregation came easily, welcomed the ruling. The *San Antonio Express* called it "a most kindly human exemplary development which would go far in easing the desegregation transition." And though the League took pains to assure schools that the ruling would not permit black schools to enroll a couple of white students and then petition for UIL membership, complications arose soon enough, mostly in northeast Texas. A good share of the state, say everything east of Interstate 35 and north of I-10, more closely resembled the Deep South than the Old West. In the early 1950s, African Americans made up 13 percent of the state's population, but 90 percent of those citizens lived in 88 counties in east Central and northeast Texas, from a long line drawn roughly east of Paris and north of Houston.

On Feburary 22, 1956, at the direction of its board of trustees, Wharton forfeited a bi-district girls' basketball game against Beeville because, its superintendent C. Graves Sivells Jr. said, "of the fact that there is a colored girl on the Beeville team." The item took up three lines in the Feb. 22, 1956 minutes of the

Wharton ISD Board of Trustees meeting. Henry Stolle made the motion to forfeit. It was seconded by B. D. King and passed unanimously.

At the time, Wharton was undefeated and had defeated Angleton, the eventual state champion, 37–35. The Wharton head coach, Meta "Mickie" Holesovsky (pronounced hole-a-shos-kee), was in her fourth year as girls coach, physical education teacher, and cheerleader sponsor. "The girls were terribly upset," she said. "I was told [by Sivells] when I went in after I heard the rumors that I would not be rehired if I tried to get that game played. And I told him, 'Well, I wouldn't ask you to rehire me anyway.'"

Oddly, it wasn't the first time Wharton had cancelled a game to keep its white kids from playing against blacks. In the fall of 1955, Wharton was to play Port Lavaca in a non-district football game, but Sivells cancelled the game, most likely on Thomas Abell's orders, although neither took responsibility for the act. Boyd Tingle, the athletic director and head coach at the time, said Sivells told him one day, "You can't play that game. Get yourself another ball game."

Why, Tingle asked.

Because they had a couple of black players, Sivells replied. "They made it sound like I didn't want to play them," Tingle said. "That was as wrong as wrong can be. I would have played them. I didn't feel that way about black boys. I didn't have anything against them. Sivells told me it was canceled."

Tingle said he was besieged with telephone calls in the following weeks. "I didn't cancel the ballgame," he repeated. "But I got blamed for it. And all those sportswriters, from Galveston and Dallas and Fort Worth and, I don't know. I don't know how many times I talked to them when I came in in the evening. The phone would be ringing. God, that was a horrible year."

Tingle's wife, Pat, a fourth-grade teacher at the time, added, "People don't understand how ugly it was back then. They don't believe it. But I remember what they told me when it came up about playing Port Lavaca. Sivells said, 'We'll never play those black bastards.'"

On February 23, after the girls had played their final game, the Wharton school board, Sivells, and a few administrators convened in the gymnasium ticket office, a cold, cramped room barely large enough for 10 or 12 people, to explain themselves. Coach Hole-

sovsky stayed home. "I was told I could not come in," she said.

I had heard about [the board's intentions] from the West Columbia coach. She called me and said, "You're in for trouble," and I said, "What do you mean?" It didn't dawn on me that someone could be that narrow. So I went to Sivells and said, "I would like to know what's going on," and he said he didn't think that was any of my business.

One of the few players allowed to speak at the called meeting was Doris Housworth Teague, then a 16-year-old junior forward. "It was a dead-set thing," Teague said. "In a small town like this, a handful of people ran the school and said what was going to be done. I can remember Thomas Abell saying—and, as young as I was—he stood there and said, 'If we let you do this, we will have those niggers knocking down the doors to get into this school. And we're not going to have that.'

I was just so mad, and I said, 'Mr. Abell, do you think when you die, they're going to let you in because you're white?' He gave me that 'shut up kid' look. It was very traumatic in that room."

Though he wasn't president of the board, Abells controlled it. A lawyer from a ranching family, he married the daughter of a banker and looked like the small-town politico that he was: tall, lanky, with drooping ears, a fading hairline, and an adam's apple the size of a golf ball, he resembled Chet Atkins in a bow tie. "He was a very Southern gentleman," Holesovsky said. While he rarely raised his silky voice, "He ran that school," she added. "He didn't want any black kids, didn't want their children playing with black kids. Later on, I asked him, 'Do you think that skin is going to rub off?' I asked him that point blank later on. He never did answer me."

Sivells, on the other hand, was not an overt racist, but he wasn't going to stand up to the racists either. "He was weak. He was going to stay with the people who kept him going," Holesovsky said. "He didn't rock the boat."

In the weeks and months afterwards, various citizens—board members included—approached the coach to apologize. What with business and all, they explained, they couldn't afford to oppose Abell. "And I said, 'Don't tell it to me now. I don't want to hear it.'"

Holesovsky said. Forty-six years later, she's still bitter. "It was a lot of heart ache, and at the time, I didn't ever want to teach school again." She did, and coached as well—ending her career in 1988 after sixteen years at El Campo High. "Mickie always had good teams, but this was her cream that year," Teague added. "And it was going to mean a state championship. We never lost a ball game. Never lost a tournament. There was no one could touch us."

THE UIL RESPONDS

Informed of Wharton's decision to withdraw from the playoffs, Kidd informed Sivells in an April 13 letter that the State Executive Committee would convene "to determine whether the reason given by Wharton for not participating in the Girls bidistrict championship basketball game was valid."

Unless Wharton's explanation for dropping out of the playoffs was deemed reasonable, it would have violated Rule 27, which held that any school failing to participate or complete the official schedule of games, unless excused for valid reasons by the State Executive Committee (SEC), shall be guilty of a breach of contract and suspended for one year. Kidd invited Sivells and "any of the school officials you wish" to attend the meeting, which was scheduled for 2:15 p.m. on Tuesday, April 24. Kidd added, "Your coach asked me whether she would be permitted to attend and I told her this was a matter for her superintendent to determine. We would be happy to have her appear before the State Executive Committee and make any statement she may wish." Instead, Holesovsky was ordered neither to appear nor to make any statement to the UIL. Sivells and four members of the board would argue their case in Austin.

Married into an old, prominent family, for whom the school district's elementary school is today named, Sivells tried as best he could to explain Wharton's predicament. Since the school had complete segregation, he reasoned, the school board and administrators didn't consider it wise to play a game with a desegregated school because the colored folk in his community might not understand how a black child from Beeville or some other school was allowed to play in the white high school gymnasium against the white high school players—kids they'd known all their lives—but their children were not. They weren't

even allowed to attend games in the white gym. They darn sure weren't going to open the doors to outsiders.

Each member of the Wharton delegation agreed: the current school board would never allow the school to play any opponent that had a Negro on its team. Never. Ever. Besides, they argued, their colored people had no desire to attend the white high school because the facilities at their own school were roughly equal to those in the white school.

"That is a bald-face lie," said Tingle, who left Wharton at the end of the 1955–56 year to accept a coaching position at Brazosport High in Freeport. "I once went out [to the black school] with Sivells. He had some books that the white school had worn out. I don't know what kind of books they were, but they were in the back of his car. And he wanted me to go out there with him." The black school was a wood frame building, "dilapidated, needed paint," Tingle added. "Doors falling off. Windows broken. Doors hanging off hinges. The steps were wigglely-wigglely. And I was so shocked. Is this the black school?"

Because each member of the Wharton delegation was given an opportunity to say their piece, the meeting had stretched well into the evening, so the SEC decided to postpone action on the case until 4 p.m. Friday, April 27. That meeting opened on a sad note: longtime SEC member C. A. Wiley had died unexpectedly. Eddy appointed a committee to compose "a suitable resolution in memory of Dr. Wiley." Then, Kidd turned to the Wharton case. He reviewed the genesis of Rule 27, reminded members that it was crucial in order to insure an orderly playoff of the state basketball race, then opened the floor to discussion. According to the minutes of the meeting, "after considerable discussion and study, it was moved that Wharton be suspended in girls' basketball for one year, beginning with the school term, Sept. 1, 1956. Motion carried."

Once again, the League displayed a bare-knuckle commitment to its rules. *Rule 27 says you have to play out your schedule or give a good reason otherwise. The penalty for violation of Rule 27 is suspension. The rules don't say anything about refusing to play another team because one of their players is a Negro. Wharton violated the rule and is suspended for one year. Meeting adjourned.*

Back home, Sivells took a telephone call from Williams, informing him of the SEC's ruling and penalty.

Had it merely been a matter of not playing girls' basketball the next year, the board might have accepted the UIL decision as a mixed blessing. Girls' athletics in the 1950s were hardly worth a potentially exhaustive and expensive legal battle. But higher stakes were at risk, so on May 9, at the school board's next regular meeting, Sivells circulated the formal notice from the UIL—in the form of a telegram and two letters—regarding the suspension. Rather than accepting the decision, the board unanimously approved a motion authorizing Abell to appeal directly to the UT Board of Regents, to leap-frog the UIL. In a three-page letter dated June 15, Abell reiterated the school's position: "Wharton has not integrated the Negroes and Whites in its school system *and has no intention of doing so.*"

Rule 27, he argued, was formulated "at a time when segregated schools were required by law, hence it was not the intention that forfeiture of a game for racial reasons be a violation of the rule" and that avoidance of an integrated situation "was certainly valid." Furthermore, Abell held that the University of Texas was, albeit indirectly, "penalizing the preservation of segregation" and "forcing compulsory integration."

The ultra-conservative regents—*native fascists*, J. Frank Dobie called them—were long accustomed to, perhaps even took pride in being called reactionaries. But being called race-mixers, well, that stung, so the regents directed UT president Logan Wilson to investigate the matter. Wilson contacted Kidd, who in a June 28 letter rehashed the historical facts and precedents, especially those regarding UT's hands-off policy regarding UIL rules. To reinforce the point, Kidd warned Wilson,

It is my understanding that the members of the League are of opinion that their organization is single and complete in itself. This position has been adopted by the Board of Regents on several occasions. Although appeal has been made to it, the Board has consistently declined to accept jurisdiction. Should the Board of Regents undertake to review the action of the State Executive Committee, there will probably be one hundred or more cases presented to it each year.

Clearly peeved by the regents' intrusion, Kidd expressed his gratitude for the University's many generosities before reiterating the League's independence. In closing he added,

The League receives much aid from the University. Doubtless it would not function as efficiently without this aid from the University or some other source. The League is grateful for this help. At the same time, it is felt that the organization does much to further one of the chief purposes for which the people maintain the University and that the aid given by the University in furthering the purpose of the League does not in any way change the independence of the organization or subject the decisions of the State Executive Committee to review.

Though he signed the letter "Respectfully yours," Kidd was in essence telling the UT regents to bug off.

Instead, the regents dug in. Chairman Tom Sealy, a Midland oilman, warned Eddy in a July 31 letter that the League's actions were "not in conformity with either University policy or State policy or law. Clearly, the timing, and presently the decision, on integration is a matter of local determination by each independent school district."

Conceding that the regents had no direct jurisdiction over this matter, Sealy suggested the State Executive Committee reconsider its decision because "we are deeply concerned with its implications."

While it has been established that the Executive Committee is an official agency of the Interscholastic League and not subject to the direct control of the Board of Regents, it is our opinion that the decision in this case is not in conformity with either University policy or State policy or law. Clearly, the timing, and presently the decision, on integration is a matter of local determination by each independent school district. While it is our present feeling, subject to possible review at our September meeting, that we do not have any direct jurisdiction over this matter, it is our earnest hope that the Wharton case will be referred back to the Executive Committee for reconsideration with a view to arriving at a decision more in conformity with existing policy and law.

In addition, he suggested that the League's Legislative Advisory Committee initiate "a re-study of these rules with a view to writing regulation which will not unduly penalize local school districts acting within their legal rights on policy matters."

At its regular meeting, August 1, the SEC revisited its decision. Eddy opened the meeting by reading Sealy's letter, then Abell's letter to the Board of Regents, then Eddy's response to Wilson. At that point, the SEC began to crack. Rousse, who had missed both the April 24 and 27 meetings, objected to portions of Eddy's response to Abell's letter and asked to be allowed to file a minority report, which was granted. The nature of Rousse's objections are unknown insofar as the report is missing and the minutes of the meeting do not reflect his concerns.

After considerable discussion, the State Executive Committee voted to send the issue to the UIL Legislative Advisory Council, a group of school superintendents elected to recommend to the SEC legislation that it considered vital to the best interests of the League.

Two days later, the rift widened. Kidd drafted a letter to Sealy, to be signed by Eddy, reiterating the League's position. Kidd noted that the University had not objected to the League's 1955 interpretation of what constituted a "white public school." Nor had the University objected to the possibility that a Negro child might play in the State Basketball Tournament, might even use the Gregory Gym dressing rooms and other facilities.

"It is the practice of the State Executive Committee of the League to study every case from a neutral and unbiased point of view, and render decisions in accordance with the Constitution and Contest Rules, which the organization has adopted for its guidance," Kidd continued. "It will be noted that the Committee in the Wharton matter followed its regular judicial procedure, and assessed penalty prescribed as mandatory in the rules."

But Kidd understood the regents' not-so-veiled threat—*While it is our present feeling, subject to possible review at our September meeting, that we do not have any direct jurisdiction over this matter . . .*—and announced that "I am pleased" to call an emergency meeting of the Legislative Advisory Council early in September "for consideration and interpretation of rule 27 of the Girls' Basketball Plan."

Reduced to sarcasm, Kidd closed his draft, "Very respectfully yours," which Eddy removed in the final draft. But Eddy went farther in his revision. He added, "The State Executive Committee recognizes that the ruling of the U.S. Supreme Court on 'segregated schools' has created many new and unusual problems not covered by existing policies. In order to develop *proper policies* that are in conformity with University policies, we would appreciate receiving a statement of the Board's policies on this matter."

On August 27, Kidd and Norris A. Hiett, associate dean of the Bureau of Extension, met Wilson in his office—Eddy did not attend—and agreed to summon the Legislative Advisory Council to Austin on September 23 to "formulate a general policy on League competitions between integrated and non-integrated schools." Then the conversation turned philosophical. Though they had neither anticipated nor wanted this grudge match with the regents, they saw in it a chance to fundamentally change the League, an opportunity for the UIL to crawl from under UT's thumb. First, UIL rules should be made and amended by public school superintendents—not University professors and staff—who should be elected by the schools themselves and serve on a legislative council that had real power, not merely "advisory" status. And members of the council should elect their own chairman, who would preside at annual meetings instead of the dean of the UT Bureau of Extension.

For the next few weeks, the U.S. postal service was swamped by letters flying back and forth among Sealy, Kidd, Wilson, and Sivells.

On August 29, Sealy informed Eddy that he was authorized by the Board of Regents "to advise you that it is our unanimous opinion that the determination of integration problems posed to the Interscholastic League by local schools which are members thereof should be on a local basis, and no school should be penalized by any policy of the University or the Interscholastic League, either because it has desegregated at the local school level or because it still maintains a segregated system."

Meanwhile, several SEC members denied that neither Sealy nor any of the UT regents had any say in the matter whatsoever. That Eddy had altered Kidd's original draft to the regents, asking them to help develop "proper policies," infuriated Redford and Calkins, who charged that Eddy's letter made no distinction between University policies applicable to the University proper and policies set by the University which may "impinge upon the freedom of the League to determine its own policies outside the University proper through the machinery provided by its own Constitution and Contest Rules. The language used here is capable of being construed so as to constitute a general invitation to the Board of Regents to lay down policies which are to be followed by the State Executive Committee in *all* questions involving integration."

By now, the turmoil had taken its toll on Eddy, who'd decided the Division of Extension had little to gain and much to lose in this scrimmage between the UIL and the Board of Regents. On September 6, Wilson wrote Sealy a one-page letter, suggesting the changes he, Kidd, and Hiett had discussed. "In my judgment, such a reorganization would remove completely any basis for thinking that the University 'runs' the Interscholastic League," he wrote. "At the present time, as you well know, we cannot escape the onus which invariably attaches to us when the League gets into difficult situations."

Sealy agreed. "I hope the officials of the League will adopt your suggestion and accomplish this divorcement," he responded, adding that "I also devoutly hope and anticipate that the Council . . . will so amend its rules as to relieve Wharton from the penalty inflicted upon it. Please do whatever you can to see that this is accomplished."

A BITTER LOSS, A PROFOUND VICTORY

September 23 was unseasonably hot in Austin, 94 degrees at 4 p.m. Three days earlier, the mercury had topped out at 103 degrees, an all-time high for that date. It had been an eventful week all around. Middle East diplomats scrambled in a failed attempt to resolve the Suez Canal crisis. The presidential race between President Eisenhower and Adlai Stevenson headed into its final month. And across the South, civil rights advocates began the long struggle to dismantle the systems that required African Americans to inferior educations, solely on the basis of their color. And it would be a furious struggle. In Tyler, state district court judge Otis T. Dunagan ordered the NAACP to stop attempts to register black students in schools. Prodded on by state attorney general John Ben Shepperd, Dunagan ruled NAACP efforts to organize, solicit money and register voters tended "to incite racial prejudice, picketing, riots and other unlawful acts."

Shepperd claimed legal action was necessary because the NAACP and "its affiliated organizations have indulged in and are continuing to indulge in political activities contrary to the laws of Texas." He did not specify what the NAACP or its affiliates had done or were doing, but noted, "I know many Texans will be stunned by the import of our evidence," which he refused to divulge. It might be useful in any lawsuits "arising from this investigation," he added. Before the end of the week, Thurgood Marshall, legal counsel for the NAACP, said the most important battle on the integration front was being fought in Texas and vowed to use all of the NAACP resources to fight the restraining order.

On the Forty Acres, student registration swelled to almost 18,000, an all-time record. The class of 1956 included the first Negro undergraduates in UT history, nearly 100 of them. According to the *Austin American-Statesman*, "there were no incidents." Meanwhile, the Longhorn football team prepared for its September 22 season opener against Southern California, a game it would lose, 44–20. The Trojans were led by C. R. Roberts, a 206-pound fullback—"the giant Negro," *American-Statesman* sports editor Lou Maysel called him. Roberts rushed for 251 yards on twelve carries and scored four touchdowns, including scoring runs of 73, 50, and 74 yards. At the end of the 1–9 season, head coach Ed Price would be fired, and UT would lure a young coach from the University of Washington. His name was Darrell Royal.

Though it was the first state university in the South to admit black undergraduates, UT remained a segregated institution. The few black students on campus battled discrimination at every turn. Campus traditions, institutions, organizations, and events were all-white. The Longhorn football team would remain all-white for another decade. Black students were not even allowed ordinary visiting privileges in white dormitories, not that many were regularly invited to socialize with the era's flat-topped and ponytailed children of Texas privilege.

No newspaper covered the League's historic meeting of September 23, which isn't surprising. In the days prior to the state's Open Meetings Act, reporters were about as welcome at UIL meetings as bats at a baby shower. Twenty-one of the 23 members—all white, all men, representing schools from San Antonio's Alamo Heights to Pyote, Denton to Sinton, Odessa to Baytown—gathered at the Driskill Hotel. In Eddy's absence, Shelby presided. He rehashed the history of the League and various precedents and policies before ceding the floor to Kidd, who reviewed the Wharton case and called for the election of a chairman from the membership. Chester Strickland of Denton was nominated, elected and took the chair. After a lengthy discussion, the council unanimously approved a resolution that, in short, censured Wharton for forfeiting the game and protesting its punishment, and then commended the SEC for its fair and impartial hearing and for standing up to the regents "to the great benefit of the public schools of this State."

But after this empty act of defiance, the council amended Rule 27 of the Basketball Plan so that future schools unwilling to play teams with Negros would forfeit the game and rebate privileges, but would not be suspended. It closed by appointing a special committee from the council to meet on Oct. 10 with the SEC to outline "very clearly the duties and responsibilities of the Legislative Council and set forth definitely its source of authority." Though it took him another year to steer his plan through UT's bureaucratic maze, Kidd had turned a bitter loss to Abell, Sivells, Sealy and the regents into a profound and long-term victory for the member schools of the UIL.

Unfortunately, that didn't help Holesovsky and the girls at Wharton High. The council refused to overturn the suspension, and the Wharton school board filed no further protests or appeals. They got what they'd wanted all along: assurance that in the future, their white kids would not be forced to line up against blacks. Teague and the other juniors lost their senior years, at least in basketball. "We played volleyball, but not basketball," she said. And Holesovsky lost her job. "It was a sad situation there because she was an excellent coach," Teague added. "She knew how to teach, and to do her the way they did her, it was terrible. She couldn't get a job around here because they blackballed her good. She ended up in some little elementary school"—in Hungerford, a tiny community six miles north of Wharton. "Sivells didn't even bother to write me a decent letter," Holesovsky said. "He just put a note in my box, 'You won't be back next year.'"

TOWARD FULL INTEGRATION

"On the whole, I think we had extremely good fortune with the integration process," said Rhea Williams. "We had no riots. We weren't forced to move our games to the afternoons, like they had to do up and down the East Coast, although one or two schools did it—not because they had a problem but because they were trying to avoid a problem.

"The superintendents and the school people understood the problems," Williams added. "They were caught in the middle and then reacted according to where they were. But I think as a whole, we were very successful here."

Had it all been scripted, the black athletes, now free to showcase their talents, would have obliterated their white opponents. It didn't happen. Overall, blacks were slow to try out for white teams. Among the first to surface was Junior Coffey, who lead Dimmitt to the 1960 2A state basketball finals and went on to a successful football career with the Atlanta Falcons. Two years later, Fred Rocker of Austin High ran a 13.7 in the 120-yard high hurdles to tie a national record. One of his schoolmates was a Hall-of-Fame baseball player and coach Don Baylor.

The next fall, Johnny Roland ran 37 yards for one touchdown and caught a pair of 39-yard passes to push Corpus Christi Miller past Wichita Falls, 13–6, in the 4A championship. Roland went on to be an all-American halfback for the University of Missouri and all-pro with the St. Louis Cardinals.

In 1962, the electrifying Warren McVea scored three touchdowns on the ground and intercepted a pass and returned a kickoff 52 yards leading to two other scores in pacing San Antonio Brackenridge to the state 4A title. A year later, in a 55–48 bi-district loss to San Antonio Lee, McVea carried the ball 21 times for 215 yards and scored on runs of 54, 48, 45, 20, 14 and 4 yards. He also scored on a two-point conversion.

His efforts were matched by a bruising white halfback, Linus Baer, who scored five touchdowns, including a 95-yard touchdown that came with 18 seconds left to play. On the ensuing kickoff, Lee gang tackled McVea, and the game ended. Moments later, both teams knelt in the center of the field to pray. Sportswriters and fans in a position to know say it was the greatest Texas high school game ever played, probably the best ever played anywhere.

Changes were also starting at the college level. On the University of Texas campus earlier in 1962, the men's 440 relay team from Texas Southern, a historically black university, was warmly greeted by white fans at the Texas Relays, held in Memorial Stadium.

The 1962 Texas Relays were marked by the excellence of Texas Southern University's sprint relay team. *From the Russell Lee Photograph Collection, Center for American History, the University of Texas at Austin. (DI 02438)*

These few exceptions aside, the faces in the photos of state team champions through the mid-1960s remained as pink as a Mary Kay Cadillac because all-black schools weren't allowed to join the UIL. Instead, they participated in the Prairie View Interscholastic League. It wasn't until 1966 when the State Executive Committee, acting on a motion introduced by Calkins under the watchful eye of UT Chancellor Harry Ransom, voted unanimously to removed the word "white" from its membership requirement.

And then, schoolboy athletics in Texas changed forever. In the spring of 1968, Houston Wheatley edged Dallas Jefferson, 85–80, to win the first of its three consecutive 4A state basketball championships. Meanwhile, Fort Worth Kilpatrick set a national record (41.1) in the 440-yard relay, and the next fall, a mostly black Lubbock Estacado squad outscored its four opponents, 128–20, including 30–0 wins over Joe Wylie-led Henderson in the state semifinals and 14–0 over Refugio in the finals, to win the 3A state football crown.

1969 proved even more successful. In basketball, Fort Worth Kirkpatrick captured the 2A title, and Snook won the first of its string of Conference B championships. Two months later, the Pouncy twins, Joe and Gene, led Dallas Lincoln to the 4A state track title while setting a national record—40.7 seconds— in the 440-yard relay, a mark they would shatter the next year by half a second.

I remember those days quite well. I had two cousins fighting in Vietnam. My three brothers and I watched Detroit burn on the CBS evening news, trying to make sense of the war, the protests, the marches, the anger.

Into all of this came the word that my all-white East Texas junior high would be integrated the next year. I recall some redneck eighth grader saying that he didn't want to eat off the same fork "as some nigger." And I suppose, in my timid ignorance, I nodded in silent agreement. But then, the next year, the black kids arrived, and they were polite and probably scared half to death, and half a dozen of them played football. On the varsity, the starting fullback was a kid named Leroy something. Pine Tree High School had never seen a running back like him, and it's hard to dislike a bulldozer of a kid who just helped your kid or team score a touchdown, even if he is black. Whatever qualms I or my brothers or my friends had about going to school with Negro students floated away, like the blue and gold balloons released at the halftime of every home game. Sure, the hard-core racists survived, survive even now. I figure their parents had shoved nigger this and nigger down their throats for so long, they didn't, couldn't know any better. After Martin Luther King had been murdered, I recall a classmate prancing around, taunting black girls by singing, "He's gone. He's dead. They shot him in the head."

But, best I can remember, he sang alone. We didn't know Martin Luther King, really didn't understand what he meant to the black kids. We'd grown up, driving back and forth past a billboard on Highway 80 right outside the Longview city limits on the way to Gladewater, displaying an out-of-focus photo of a black man in a classroom, with a huge headline that read, "Martin Luther King at Communist School."

Not too much farther down the road, there was another billboard: "Vote Wallace. Equal Rights. Not Riots."

To me, Martin Luther King was just a name on a billboard. But to a lot of other whites, he represented everything they hated and feared, and they clinked their bottles of Schlitz or Old Milwaukee in jubilant toasts when they heard he'd been gunned down in Memphis.

I'm convinced that had it not been for football in particular, high school sports in general, folks attending the bonfires of autumn might have worn white robes rather than cheerleader outfits. Like most Texans, we loved football more than we feared sharing silverware with black kids.

And so integration came to Texas—a son of the Confederacy, still largely backwater, xenophobic, low-brow, racist—more smoothly than anyone could ever have hoped or feared or imagined.

NOTES

1. T. B. Shelby, "Development of Extension Education at the University of Texas, 1909–1952," University of Texas Extension, 1966.

2. Roy Bedicheck, "Interscholastic Non-athletic Contests," 1927 Master's thesis, University of Texas—Austin, 1927.

JOHN
SCHWARTZ
} # The View from the Tower

The day I finally got to look out from the observation deck of the University of Texas Tower, I wasn't prepared for the shocking beauty of the view from a perch known mainly for its association with mass murder. I looked a few blocks south to the pink granite dome of the State Capitol Building and the Colorado River, and down around me at the swarming university community. Seeing the University of Texas at Austin all at once, I truly felt connected to the place.

It was just as author Willie Morris had described in his memoir, *North Toward Home*:

> That first morning I took the elevator to the top, and looked out on those majestic purple hills to the west, changing to lighter shades of blue or a deeper purple as wisps of autumn clouds drifted around the sun; this, they would tell me, was the Great Balcones Divide, where the South ended and the West began.

As I stood there that day in 1981, thanks to a UT administrator willing to indulge my desire to enter the forbidden site, I wished that others could share the amazing experience. But they couldn't. UT had closed the Tower's observation deck in 1974 after too many tragedies there: seven suicide leaps and UT graduate student Charles Whitman's 1966 shooting spree, which left 13 dead and more than 30 wounded.

When the school announced in 1999 that it was going to reopen the Tower, I felt the thrill of the experience all over again. During my long-ago days as the editor of the UT newspaper, I had tried to persuade UT officials to throw open the Tower doors. The school has decided to charge admission to defray the costs of securing the deck, which is a pity. But I'm glad

---

John Schwartz was editor of The Daily Texan *in 1981–82, when he was enrolled in the UT Law School. He continued his career in journalism, working successively for* Newsweek, *the* Washington Post, *and the* New York Times. *He currently is a science reporter for the* Times, *where he has written extensively about NASA and New Orleans after Hurricane Katrina.*

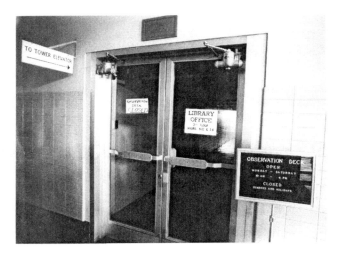

Doors leading to the Tower elevators. *From the Prints and Photographs Collection—UT Building: Main and Tower, Center for American History, the University of Texas at Austin. (DI 02425)*

that UT, instead of trying to ignore its tragedies, is finally confronting its past.

Even before I ascended to the observation deck, the Tower had always been a magical place for me. On my childhood trips to Austin, my folks would point out that the Tower clocks, when viewed from the building's corners, took on the appearance of owls' eyes. The eyes of Texas really were upon us.

I was just 9 when Whitman opened fire from the Tower. By chance, my family was visiting Austin that August day. We had even been shopping on Guadalupe Street—"The Drag," which ran along the western edge of the campus—where some of Whitman's victims were hit. Oblivious to the mayhem, we didn't find out what had happened until my Mother and I turned on the TV that evening.

Once I enrolled at the University in 1975, the Tower became a part of my daily life, the 307-foot structure visible from all angles as I crossed the broad lawns and malls on the way to class. My friends and I steeped ourselves in Whitman lore, trying to understand how a young man not much older than we were—a one-time Eagle Scout, a former Marine, a well-liked guy—could explode so catastrophically on the Tower's 27th floor. We wondered about the doctor at the counseling center who hadn't followed up after Whitman told him that he was "thinking about going up on the Tower with a deer rifle and start shooting people."

As an orientation adviser in the late seventies, I invited tour groups of new students to run their fingers in a groove in the sandstone between the balusters that separate the upper and lower terraces of the South Mall. It's a bullet groove, I'd explain to them, recounting how Whitman had spied Billy Paul Speed, a 22-year-old Austin police officer, crouching behind the limestone railing. Whitman fired a six-millimeter round through the narrow gap between two of the balusters, leaving Speed's wife a widow and his 16-month-old daughter fatherless.

A street vendor told Gary M. Lavergne, author of *A Sniper in the Tower: The Charles Whitman Murders,* that the Florida-born Whitman "was supposed to be an all-American boy. The sad thing is, maybe he really is." Songwriter and sly philosopher Kinky Friedman said it even better in "The Ballad of Charles Whitman":

Most folks couldn't figure just-a why he did it
And them that could would not admit it,
There's still a lot of Eagle Scouts around.

Whitman was only one part of my Tower fascination, though. I remember sitting in the morgue of the *Daily Texan,* reading clips about Tower suicides. One in particular, the 24-story leap of Alton Parker Thomason in 1945, stayed with me. Mr. Thomason was a 41-year-old English instructor from Nacogdoches and the son of a state senator.

While Whitman was a violent enigma, Thomason was a more purely tragic figure. He was deeply troubled by the key political event at the University at the time, the power struggle that led to the ouster of UT president Homer P. Rainey by a reactionary Board of Regents. He had recently written an essay for the *Antioch Review* that referred to the Rainey fight and compared it to the struggle against fascism worldwide. He opened the essay, engagingly, with the story of a Tennesseean, "a man named McNeil, I think it was," who in the 1830s "got into trouble, bad trouble."

McNeil's friends urged him to escape, so he went to Arkansas, and got into trouble there as well. And so he went to Texas, the place people seemed to end up when they had thoroughly messed up their lives. And when he got into trouble yet again, and friends urged him to flee, he wrote, "Where in the hell can I go—I'M IN TEXAS NOW!" Thomason then wrote, "I am in Texas now, writing in January of the year 1945;

nothing is very funny to me and my associates." A half a year later he opened the window of his office in the Tower and jumped.

It all added to the mystery of the place, and made it all the more rich. Yet during our time at Texas, we couldn't go all the way to the top: After Whitman's spree, the Tower was closed for a while, and then reopened. After a young man jumped in October of 1974, the University closed the observation deck again, seemingly for good. But students in Plan II, the venerable liberal arts honors program, could at least get access to the stacks of the main library and read in the dusty silence. My red-haired girlfriend, Jeanne, and I would ride up in the cramped elevator ("big enough for two people or three close friends," we joked) into the warrens of bookshelves. Jeanne and I would sit at the scarred wooden tables, where we could study and catch a slice of the view out of the narrow windows. But we couldn't take in the panorama that Willie beheld.

Our years passed at the University; we graduated and continued to hang around, stuck in Austin's strong gravitational pull. I went on to law school and fell in with the crowd at *UTmost* magazine and the *Daily Texan*, where people worked round the clock to put out the best college newspaper in the country. In a chain of events that still baffles me, I ended up getting the job of editor of the *Daily Texan*. The staff had walked out on the previous editor, a luckless guy who the summer after his election was caught plagiarizing an editorial from the *New York Times*. Things didn't really improve much for him after that, and tensions with the staff continued to mount through the fall, when he resigned. In a whirlwind of a week, I was appointed to the editor's post by the Texas Student Publications board to serve out the remainder of the 1981–82 school year.

In an instant, I had gone from being comfortably anonymous on the vast UT campus to being what passes for a celebrity, or even a student leader. Not that I had any time to do anything about my new status: Being editor was a grueling job which a former editor, Mark McKinnon, spoke of as getting the "keys to the gates of Hell." But I loved having a soapbox to stand on and deliver my poorly formed opinions. Some of the editorials, in retrospect, were shudderingly bad. But I was proud of a fair number of them—and the ones I was most proud of called for the Tower to be reopened.

The year after I left the editor's job, I was approached by a group I had never heard of, "The Eyes of Texas," a secretive honor society. I have little patience with secrets and initiations and the ersatz grandeur of newly minted rites. But the other members were all people I knew from campus activities, and they were good hearted; joining "The Eyes" seemed harmless enough. The group's stated purpose is "To promote student spirit, to preserve campus traditions, to promote the best interests of the University," and each new member has to "plan and execute a project fulfilling the purposes of the organization."

I instantly knew what I wanted to do: to carry on the work that I had started with my editorials about the Tower. I began to agitate for the Tower's reopening, lobbying. One afternoon, I visited the chairman of the UT Board of Regents in his large office downtown; he became wistful as he reminisced about taking his girlfriend to the 27th floor during his undergraduate days. I laid out the estimates I'd worked up of the costs of barriers to prevent suicides. He listened politely and sent me on my way.

I did wangle that lone visit to the observation deck, which I insisted that I needed in order to continue my quest. It was a beautiful Austin day. The guard who let me up to the top showed me where Whitman stood when a police officer killed him with a shotgun blast. Focusing on the view was a little tougher after that, but the breeze up there cleared my head, and I lived one of those long moments that Robert Earl Keen sings about, when you know that life is good.

Everything changes. Whitman's long act of violence, which seemed unthinkable in 1966, is now an extreme expression of adolescent rebellion by middle school students in Kentucky, Arkansas, and Colorado. Whitman also has become academic: Students who want to visit the Tower might prepare themselves for the experience by taking English 330E, "The UT Tower Shootings and Public Memory." The Tower and the Capitol Building no longer dominate Austin's skyline; downtown is full of ungainly giants that make the lovely town look pretty much like every other. The purple hills are scarred with malls and dotted with mansions.

But the lessons of Austin remain. I once interviewed film director Robert Benton about how going to the University of Texas prepared him for success in the world of film, and he said growing up in

The view from the Tower, looking east, 1967. *From the Prints and Photographs Collection—UT Building: Main and Tower, Center for American History, the University of Texas at Austin. (DI 02424)*

Texas makes you unafraid of "being a son of a bitch." At a place like Texas, he said, you learn that breaking rules, or at least ignoring them, gets you a lot farther than playing by the rules. And that helped me to realize that the thing I thought would be impossible—getting a real live job in journalism—wasn't impossible if I just ignored the impossibility of it all. Somehow, that worked. And my friends share a bond from those days that time does not break. Once in a while, my friend Steve Smith, a Texas Ex who moved to New York to find his fortune as a chef, will occasionally look me in the eye over dinner, and say, "Where in the hell can I go—I'M IN TEXAS NOW!"

The redheaded girl I kissed in the Tower's stacks now pops a Moxy Fruvous disc into our minivan's CD player as we drive our kids to school, piano lessons, and the mall. Our oldest will be ready for college in just three years. When we tour the UT campus, I'll probably show her the groove in the limestone where Billy Speed was killed; she'll probably roll her eyes and wonder why I'm pushing ancient history on her.

No matter. I'm glad that when we tour the campus I'll be able to take her to the top.

DOUGLAS
LAYCOCK
}

Desegregation, Affirmative Action, and the Ten-Percent Law

The University of Texas at Austin has been embroiled in problems of race and admissions for decades. Segregation and desegregation, the rise and fall and restoration of affirmative action, the ten-percent law and other efforts to maintain racial diversity without considering race, lengthy lawsuits and even longer proceedings before administrative agencies—these are all part of one continuous and tangled story. The University adopted affirmative action in admissions as a means to desegregation, partly because the faculty thought affirmative action to be sound policy and partly because federal courts and federal agencies demanded it. Some of those same federal courts and agencies later switched sides; the University found itself ordered to abandon what it had previously been ordered to commence. The very individual who had most vigorously demanded affirmative action as a bureaucrat became the one who most vigorously denounced it as a justice of the Supreme Court.

As the legal and political controversy dragged on and key actors switched sides, the demography of the state changed dramatically. Minorities formerly oppressed are now a majority of the Texas population; educating the future leaders of Texas necessarily means educating black and Hispanic Texans as well as Anglo Texans. The University is now firmly committed to racial diversity in its student body; the University is also committed to academic excellence. The University has experimented with many ways of pursuing these goals; by far the best way to achieve both goals simultaneously is affirmative action that admits students on the basis of academic excellence and race, selecting the very best students from every racial and ethnic group. It is no surprise that affirmative action is a means of achieving racial and

Douglas Laycock held the Alice McKean Young Regents Chair in Law at the University of Texas until 2006, when he joined the law faculty at the University of Michigan. He helped represent the University of Texas in the Hopwood litigation, and represented law school deans as a friend of the court when the Supreme Court decided the landmark University of Michigan affirmative action case. He is a fellow of the American Academy of Arts and Sciences and a member of the Council of the American Law Institute.

Picketers outside Kinsolving Dormitory. *From the UT Texas Student Publications, Inc. Photographs Collection—Negroes at UT: Miscellaneous, Center for American History, the University of Texas at Austin. (DI 02402)*

ethnic diversity; it may be a surprise that affirmative action is also a means of protecting academic excellence from pressure to reduce admission standards across the board. Surprise or not, affirmative action is both. How the university came to understand this is a long and winding tale.

FROM *SWEATT* TO *HOPWOOD*

It is one of history's ironies that *Sweatt v. Painter* in 1950, and *Hopwood v. Texas* in 1996, both involved race and admissions at the University of Texas Law School. In *Sweatt* the Law School considered the race of applicants to ensure that African-Americans were excluded; in *Hopwood* the Law School considered the race of applicants to ensure that all races were included. The Law School was sued both times.

Public colleges and universities in Texas abandoned formal exclusion of African-Americans after *Sweatt*, but segregated attendance patterns persisted. Segregation persisted partly from inertia and the preferences of white and minority students; partly because of institutional hostility from some of the formerly all-white institutions; and partly because the long history of discrimination in Texas, and especially of segregation in elementary and secondary education, meant that proportionately fewer minorities than whites achieved the highest levels of academic success. As political resistance to desegregation faded, admissions became more competitive. The baby boom and exploding rates of college attendance made college admissions much more competitive just as schools were willing to admit minority students. At the time of *Sweatt v. Painter*, admission to the Law School was open to any college graduate; today, the Law School receives about six thousand applications, nearly all of them from students with strong academic records, who compete for fewer than five hundred seats.

Minority enrollment in the Law School remained

Outside Memorial Stadium, 1967. *From the Prints and Photographs Collection—UT Demonstrations, Center for American History, the University of Texas at Austin. (DI 02426)*

small in the years after *Sweatt*, and it actually declined as admissions became more competitive. For a time in the late 1960s, the Law School participated in the CLEO program. CLEO (the Council on Legal Education Opportunity) provided summer training for minority applicants to law schools. But in 1971, the Law School withdrew from the program. The faculty found that CLEO "had shifted its focus from students who were just below the level where law schools would seriously consider them for admission to students who were significantly below that level." This distinction—between "just below" and "significantly below"—makes an enormous difference to the effectiveness and legitimacy of an affirmative action program. It is important both to the academic success of the minority students admitted and to the program's benefits for education and race relations that minority students be able to succeed when admitted. Minority applicants might be given a preference, but the preference cannot be too large.

The faculty was right to withdraw from CLEO, but the results for minority enrollment were disastrous. With a color-blind process and increased competition for seats, the Law School admitted no African-Americans in 1971. The faculty responded with a separate committee to give special consideration to minority applications.

The Law School's experience was typical of the University's experience overall. For southern schools with selective admissions standards, affirmative action that directly considered race was an essential step in efforts to meet their desegregation obligations. After the period of massive resistance, and after the period of passive resistance and deliberate foot-dragging, one of the greatest remaining obstacles at the historically white schools was selective admission standards. Across-the-board changes in admission standards threatened to destroy the mission of selective institutions. Affirmative action enabled selective institutions to maintain their admission standards, to admit greater numbers of minority students, and to select the best minority students as evaluated on the same criteria applied to all other applicants.

The University worked to increase minority enrollment in part because faculty and administrators came to believe that was the right thing to do, but also because the federal government demanded it. For a generation, the courts measured progress toward desegregation by "racial identifiability." Once a school district, or a university system, was found to be segregated, it incurred an "affirmative duty to take whatever steps might be necessary to convert to a unitary system in which racial discrimination would be eliminated root and branch." States and school districts were required to "convert promptly to a system without a 'white' school and a 'Negro' school, but just schools." Past deliberate segregation was generally undisputed, and it was generally impossible to prove that present racial identifiability was *not* caused by past deliberate segregation. So litigation and negotiation centered on the presence of racial identifiability and on the adequacy of the steps taken to eliminate it. States and school districts were obliged to "make every effort to achieve the greatest possible degree of actual desegregation." This obligation "necessarily" required efforts at "elimination of one-race schools" and "a presumption against schools that are substantially disproportionate in their racial composition."

In 1980, the federal Office for Civil Rights (OCR)

found that Texas had failed to eliminate vestiges of its former *de jure* [by law] racially dual system of public higher education, that Hispanics were significantly underrepresented, and that investigation of discrimination against Hispanics would continue.

The state submitted a proposed compliance plan, which OCR rejected as inadequate. The Assistant Secretary of Education who rejected this plan was the same Clarence Thomas who repeatedly and sarcastically described desegregated higher education as a mere "aesthetic" preference after he became a justice of the Supreme Court. The earlier Thomas first rejected the Texas plan because the numeric goals for black and Hispanic enrollment were insufficient. He rejected a revised plan because it set black and Hispanic enrollment goals on a statewide basis, instead of separately for each institution, and it did not project achievement dates for the stated goals. In 1983, a federal court in the District of Columbia ordered enforcement action against Texas unless the state submitted a fully complying plan within forty-five days.

At this point, OCR submitted thirty-seven suggested measures for increasing black and Hispanic enrollment. One of these "suggestions" was that schools reevaluate their admission criteria and "admit black and Hispanic students who demonstrate potential for success but who do not necessarily meet all the traditional admission requirements." Texas amended its plan to comply with the demands of OCR, and in June 1983 OCR accepted the plan, contingent on adequate funding and actual performance. As the 1988 expiration of this plan approached, OCR notified Texas that it was reviewing the state's compliance and that Texas should continue to operate under the plan pending further evaluation. The state's own officials determined that Texas had not yet achieved the plan's goals and adopted a second plan in hopes of avoiding a further federal mandate. In January 1994, on the eve of trial in *Hopwood v. Texas*, OCR notified Governor Ann Richards that it was still reviewing the state's compliance with its desegregation obligations.

During the Carter Administration, OCR embodied its negotiating position in regulations that have remained in effect, with only technical amendments, through the Reagan, George H. W. Bush, Clinton, and George W. Bush administrations. These regulations provide that "[i]n administering a program regarding which the recipient [of federal funds] has previously discriminated . . ., the recipient *must* take affirmative action to overcome the effects of prior discrimination." The regulations went on to specify that affirmative action included "*making selections* which will insure that groups previously subjected to discrimination are adequately served."

There was also a more detailed Notice, published in the *Federal Register* in 1978. This document contains many of the demands that OCR made in its negotiations with Texas. States were required to adopt "specific numeric goals" and "timetables for sequential implementation" to achieve equal matriculation rates for black and white high-school graduates and a 50% reduction in the black-white disparity in enrollment at historically white four-year and upper-division schools. These goals would require changed admission standards: Schools "may need to broaden definitions of potential; to discount the effects of early disadvantage on the development of academic competence; and to broaden the talents measured in admissions tests."

Developing a sound and workable affirmative action program took many years of trial and error. When I joined the UT Law School faculty in 1981, the Law School's program was too aggressive; some of the minority students admitted were still too weak. The effects of going too low in the pool were visible and disruptive in the classroom and in grading curves and a source of racial tension. The program was controversial among the faculty, and the faculty gradually changed the program. We invested more effort in recruiting the strongest minority students, and we deliberately reduced the racial gap in academic credentials. By the time we were sued in 1992, the visible gap in classroom performance had largely disappeared, and the program had become uncontroversial among the faculty—save for one outspoken dissenter.

The Law School was proud of its affirmative action program and believed that it was one of the most successful such programs in the country. Minority law students at Texas graduated at higher rates than at most other national law schools, and most of those graduates went on to successful careers. By the mid-nineties, the Law School had trained more African-American and Mexican-American lawyers than any other historically white law school, and it had trained a significant fraction of the national total of minority lawyers.

HOPWOOD V. TEXAS

In 1978, in *Regents of the University of California v. Bakke,* the Supreme Court set the legal framework for a generation of university admissions. The Court affirmed a court order that prohibited a fixed quota reserving 16% of seats in the medical school for minorities, but it reversed an order forbidding any consideration of race in admissions. Universities were free to consider race as one factor in an admissions process, and they were free to prefer minority applicants, but they were not free to reserve a fixed number of spaces.

The University of Texas operated under *Bakke* and its agreement with OCR. It considered race in admissions, and gave preference to minority applicants. Ten years later, as the country drifted to the right, we were sued over Law School admissions.

Cheryl Hopwood and the other plaintiffs applied for admission to the Law School in 1992. They had high grades and test scores, and they alleged that they would have been admitted but for the Law School's preference for minority applicants. The Law School said they had weak majors at weak undergraduate institutions and that, with or without affirmative action, they would not have been admitted.

The Law School conceded that it had preferred minority applicants, but it insisted that it had done so for compelling reasons—to achieve and maintain desegregation of legal education in Texas, to remedy past discrimination in public education, and to ensure diversity in its classrooms.

Plaintiffs emphasized that if some minority applicants were preferentially admitted on the basis of race, an equal number of white applicants were denied admission on the basis of race. That is a mathematical fact, which the Law School did not dispute. The Law School acknowledged that affirmative action has costs, but it insisted that those costs were justified by the compelling reasons for the program. And it argued that the costs were thinly spread over a substantial part of the applicant pool; a properly run affirmative action plan has only a minuscule effect on any particular white applicant's chances for admission.

Critics sometimes wonder how a small preference can make a large difference in minority enrollment. The key to the explanation is that at schools where minorities are seriously underrepresented, there are many more white applicants than minority applicants.

In the range of academic talent at the margin between admission and non-admission, the number of minority applicants is often substantial when compared to the number of minorities already admitted, but small when compared to the number of white and Asian applicants in the same range. If all admissions must be color blind, only a small fraction of the minority applicants in this range will be admitted. But if a school can directly consider race, it can admit most of the minority applicants in this range, thus significantly increasing minority representation in the student body, without significantly changing the range from which students are admitted.

As it happened, in 1992 the Law School had created a separate committee to review minority applications. This two-committee system became the subject of much criticism later, but neither side thought the dispute was about the administrative details of the program, and neither did the Court of Appeals. The Law School's Admissions Committee in 1992 thought that two committees would lead to a fairer and more accurate process. The two committees were part of the continuing effort to *minimize* the credential gap between affirmative action admits and other students. Consolidating consideration of minority files made it easier to identify the strongest minority applicants, and easier to enforce uniform limits on the magnitude of racial preferences.

For their part, the plaintiffs objected to any degree of racial preference, however it might be administered. The Court of Appeals in the first appeal adopted plaintiffs' position. The two-committee system was thus irrelevant to the sweeping decision in the Court of Appeals, and it was irrelevant to plaintiffs' decision to sue. But the two-committee system did have procedural consequences along the way.

The case was tried before Judge Sam Sparks, without a jury, in May 1994. Both sides offered evidence concerning the admissions process and how it worked, the reasons for affirmative action, and the effect of affirmative action on the four plaintiffs. Plaintiffs initially took the position that *Bakke* had been implicitly overruled and that any consideration of race was unconstitutional. When Judge Sparks made clear that he was not inclined to accept that argument, plaintiffs also argued that the two-committee system of 1992 was unconstitutional even under *Bakke.*

Judge Sparks held that the two-committee system had indeed been unconstitutional. But on the issue both sides cared about, he held it constitutionally permissible for the Law School to prefer minority applicants. And he held that plaintiffs had not shown they would have been admitted to the Law School under a one-committee system with racial preferences. He declared that the two-committee system had been unconstitutional, ordered that plaintiffs be permitted to reapply under the newly adopted one-committee system without paying a new application fee, and awarded each plaintiff one dollar in nominal damages. Plaintiffs appealed; the Law School did not. On the issues both sides cared about, the Law School had won a sweeping victory.

On appeal, plaintiffs successfully pursued their argument that any consideration of race would be unconstitutional. A panel of the Court of Appeals held that *Bakke* was no longer the law—and even more remarkably, that it had never been the law, because the opinions in the case had been so divided. The court held that the Law School could consider the race of applicants only if that were necessary to remedy discrimination *by the Law School*. Diversity of the student body was not a justification; indeed, the court said, pursuit of racial diversity is irrational, like pursuit of diverse blood types. And the Law School could not act to alleviate the effect on its applicant pool of past or even current discrimination in elementary, secondary, and undergraduate education. The effects of such discrimination were too difficult to measure, and the Law School was not responsible for those effects in any event. The Court of Appeals dismissed as irrelevant the state's continued obligation to fully desegregate its institutions of higher education, and it dismissed the desegregation plan negotiated with OCR as both irrelevant and unconstitutional. It was unlawful for the Law School to consider race, even as one factor among many. This time plaintiffs had won the sweeping victory.

There was more. The holding of the Court of Appeals fundamentally changed the question of whether plaintiffs would have been admitted under a constitutional system. The question in the trial court had been whether plaintiffs would have been admitted if racial preferences had been administered in a one-committee system; now the question would be whether plaintiffs would have been admitted if race had not been considered at all. And the court held that the burden of proof on that point would be on the Law School; if it were im-

possible to tell whether plaintiffs would been admitted under a color-blind system, Judge Sparks should award damages. The Court of Appeals reversed the judgment permitting the Law School to consider race, and sent the case back to Judge Sparks. The issues remaining for consideration were plaintiffs' claims for admission, for damages, for an injunction (a formal court order) directing future compliance, and for attorneys' fees.

The sweep of the opinion and the importance of the issue made the case seem an obvious candidate for Supreme Court review, and delay threatened serious declines in minority enrollment and even resegregation of the Law School. The Law School promptly filed a petition in the Supreme Court, omitting the other possible remedy of asking the Court of Appeals to rehear the case *en banc*—that is, before all fifteen judges. Meanwhile, one of the judges of the Court of Appeals requested an *en banc* vote without waiting to be asked, and by a vote of 8–7, the court decided not to hear the case *en banc*.

The Supreme Court also refused to hear the case, and two justices took the unusual step of publishing their reasons. Judicial opinions are implemented in a separate document, the judgment. The judgment from Judge Sparks addressed only the administrative details of the long-abandoned 1992 plan; the judgment of the Court of Appeals merely sent the case back to Judge Sparks for further proceedings. Despite the sweeping deterrent effect of the Court of Appeals' opinion, there was no judgment formally ordering the Law School not to consider race in admissions. Reminding the parties that the Supreme Court "reviews judgments, not opinions," the two justices viewed the Law School's petition as a challenge not to any judgment of a lower court, but only to the rationale of the Court of Appeals.

In 1997, *after* the Fifth Circuit had banned any consideration of race in university admissions, and after the Supreme Court had refused to review the case, OCR briefly threatened to cut off federal funding to Texas if the state abandoned affirmative action. In OCR's view, *Hopwood* applied only to facts "identical" to those found in the law school, and the state remained under "a clear legal obligation" to consider race in its efforts to completely desegregate its system. More reasonably, OCR wrote Governor Bush to request additional information needed to evaluate the state's compliance with its desegregation obligations.

As of this writing late in 2005, OCR has still not found that Texas has eliminated all vestiges of its prior dual system of higher education.

The *Hopwood* case was tried again in 1997. The first issue was whether plaintiffs would have been admitted under a color-blind admissions system. A long-time member of the Law School's Admissions Committee reconstructed the entire 1992 admissions process and identified numerous applicants who were denied admission despite having better qualifications than the four plaintiffs. The District Court concluded that plaintiffs probably would not have been admitted even under a color-blind admissions process; once again, he awarded $1 in nominal damages.

The two trials together reveal much about the actual workings of an admissions system. They show that grades and test scores are important but far from dispositive predictors, and that this is true with or without consideration of race. The plaintiffs were passed over in favor of minority applicants with lower grades and test scores, but they were also passed over in favor of a larger number of white applicants with lower grades and test scores. These latter decisions could not have been based on race; they were based on other predictors of academic success that have always affected admissions decisions—the quality of the applicant's undergraduate school, the rigor of courses taken, letters of recommendation, and the like.

Another issue in the second trial was to embody the opinion of the Court of Appeals in a formal judgment ordering the defendants to comply and specifying the terms with which they must comply. The trial judge entered an injunction, prohibiting defendants "from taking into consideration racial preferences in the selection of those individuals to be admitted as students at the University of Texas School of Law."

Both sides appealed. A second panel of the Court of Appeals affirmed the findings that plaintiffs would not have been admitted under a color-blind system, affirmed the judgment refusing to award more than nominal damages, and affirmed the award of attorneys' fees as against plaintiffs' demand for more and the Law School's argument that no fees should have been awarded at all.

Most importantly, the Law School appealed the injunction, thus raising the whole underlying controversy over the legality of affirmative action in some

form. The injunction implemented the opinion of the Court of Appeals on the first appeal, but unlike that opinion, it was a formal judgment subject to appellate review. The injunction had nothing to do with the administrative details of the 1992 affirmative action plan; it was a prospective ban on any consideration of race by any means. The injunction was thus in substance identical to the injunction that the Supreme Court reversed in *Bakke*. The Law School wanted the injunction reversed *on the merits*—on the ground that consideration of race in admissions is not unlawful.

The panel in the second appeal vacated the injunction on the procedural ground that the trial court had not entered formal findings of fact and conclusions of law supporting the injunction. The full court twice declined to hear the case *en banc*, once before argument to the panel and once after the panel's judgment. These judgments left the case in a difficult procedural posture, in which the 1996 opinion of the Court of Appeals operated like an injunction, controlling the behavior of the Law School and of higher education throughout the state and supporting a large award of attorneys' fees, but not set out in the usual form of an appealable final judgment. Once again, the Supreme Court declined to review the case.

On remand, plaintiffs said they no longer wanted an injunction, and Judge Sparks declined to enter one. But he rejected the Law School's argument that plaintiffs were entitled to no attorneys' fees because they had not personally benefited from the case and had never obtained a final judgment. Without a final judgment, there was no remaining possibility of appealing the merits, and both sides decided not to appeal their dispute over attorneys' fees. The case thus ground to a halt in a sort of limbo. A generous donor paid the attorneys' fees; that burden did not fall on the university or the taxpayers.

As an abstract resolution of a broad public policy dispute, the case had dramatic consequences. Plaintiffs and other ideological opponents of affirmative action never got a formal judgment, but they did get a sweeping opinion, complete with threats of actual and punitive damages against any law school official who ever again considered race in admissions. The Law School lost its best tool for achieving both academic excellence and racial and ethnic diversity.

ADMISSIONS UNDER *HOPWOOD*

In 1997, the first full year after *Hopwood*, minority admissions plummeted. The number of blacks in the University's freshman class dropped by about half, the number of Hispanics by about 15 percent. In the Law School, where the competition for seats is more fierce, the number of blacks dropped by 90 percent and the number of Hispanics by 60 percent.

The principal legislative response was the ten-percent law, guaranteeing admission to any public undergraduate program to any student who graduates in the top ten-percent of his or her high school class. California and Florida have adopted similar programs administratively. These plans differ in important ways; the Texas law is the most generous, because it guarantees admission to any public university the student chooses, including the flagships. What all percentage plans have in common is a promise of admission to the best students in each high school, as distinguished from the best students in the state.

The ten-percent law is much misunderstood by both its supporters and its opponents. By itself, it did very little to restore minority enrollment. But when combined with aggressive recruiting, financial aid, and retention programs, all targeting students from minority high schools, it helped ensure that some minority applicants are admitted and retained. It does not operate automatically; it depends on a strong commitment from the university to make it work. It achieves less diversity, at greater cost to academic admission standards, than a properly run affirmative action program. For the most part, it targets a different set of minority students than a traditional affirmative action program. The ten-percent law is great for students at the top of their class in low-achieving high schools; it does nothing for middle-class minority students in the second ten-percent of strong suburban high schools. The law also had unanticipated advantages: it is a powerful motivational and recruiting tool in low-achieving high schools.

The ten-percent law was enacted in 1997, and first affected admissions in 1998. Not much happened; minority enrollment rose only slightly, and remained well below the long-term average from 1982 to 1995. In the years that followed, with the help of substantial recruiting, financial aid, and retention efforts, black enrollment gradually recovered to the bottom of the 1982–1995 range. The experience with Hispanics is superficially better, but in some important ways worse. Hispanic enrollment did not drop so far, and it recovered somewhat more. In 2003 and 2004, Hispanic enrollment ticked up to new highs, slightly above what had been achieved in earlier years. The future, of course, is uncertain, but there is every reason to believe that percentage plans have achieved all their easy gains, and that further improvement will be much harder.

These simple comparisons of minority percentages in the freshman class conceal the extent to which Texas is falling further behind in the effort to educate its minority population. The principal reason for modest growth in Hispanic enrollment is surging growth in the Hispanic population. From 1990 to 2000, as the Hispanic fraction of the freshman class declined from 16.1% to 13.2%, the Hispanic fraction of the college-age population in the state increased from 30.9% to 40%. Hispanic representation in the freshman class as a percentage of Hispanic representation in the college-age population thus declined from 52% (16.1/30.9) to 33% (13.2/40). The record high Hispanic enrollment in 2003, at 16.3%, is only 41% of Hispanic representation in the college-age population in 2000, and undoubtedly a smaller percentage in 2003. Texas in the twenty-first century is doing considerably worse at enrolling Hispanics with the ten-percent law and aggressive targeted recruitment than it did in 1990 with affirmative action.

Blacks were doing worse even before *Hopwood*, and they have also lost ground since, but not as much. Principally because of the explosive growth in the Hispanic population, blacks as a percentage of the college-age population have declined slightly, from 13.3% in 1990 to 12.3% in 2000. In 1990, blacks were 5.0% of the freshman class, or 41% of their percentage in the college-age population; in 2000, they were 3.9% of the freshman class, or 32% of their percentage in the college-age population. The 4.1% black enrollment in 2003 was 33% of the black percentage of the college-age population in 2000.

I compare minorities in the freshman class to minorities in the college-age population as a crude measure of the degree of underrepresentation. I do not use high-school graduates, college applicants, or college applicants with controls for credentials, because no one seriously claims that the University now discriminates against minority applicants, and I am not testing that theory. Nor do I assume that the goal of affirmative action is racial balance, which in any event would not be remotely achievable in the foreseeable future. Rather, these comparisons follow the Supreme Court's recent decisions in the Michigan cases in assuming that gross underrepresentation is a legitimate measure of the need for affirmative action. Despite the University's best efforts with the ten-percent law, the largest minority groups in Texas are more grossly underrepresented at UT-Austin today than they were in the era of affirmative action.

To achieve some degree of diversity under the ten-percent law, the flagship schools in Texas developed recruiting, financial aid, and retention programs that deliberately target minority high schools. The University of Texas Longhorn Opportunity Scholars program selected these schools on the basis of low application rates and low parental income. These criteria are formally color-blind, but, in combination, they are a strong proxy for identifying minority high schools. These targeted programs have been essential to making the ten-percent law work. Of course there had been minority recruiting programs during the affirmative action years, but the ten-percent law required the addition of new and more elaborate efforts to produce a lower level of diversity.

In addition to not working very well, percentage plans have serious costs. Most obviously, they require serious departures from academic admission standards. Class rank is one important predictor of academic achievement, but only one. Pure percentage plans require universities to ignore everything else they know about an applicant. Test scores, high school curriculum, recommendations, writing samples, and other activities and accomplishments all become irrelevant. No affirmative action plan that considers race would ignore all these predictors, and no affirmative action plan that considers race would give anyone a guarantee of admission no matter how weak the rest of the file. But percentage plans make no difference if they provide no guarantee and if they admit only students whose class rank is consistent with other predictors of academic success. One of their principal functions is precisely to guarantee admission to applicants who would be rejected if the full file were considered.

The actual experience with percentage plans has been better than one might reasonably expect from these conceptual problems. Relatively few students with very low SAT scores have chosen to attend UT-Austin, and less than one percent of the entering class failed the Texas Academic Skills Program, an undemanding test of college preparation that focuses on minimal skills. The top-ten-percent students who have chosen to attend have done relatively well. If the admission guarantee is set at a level where most applicants benefiting from the guarantee would have gotten in anyway, and if there are retention services for those who would not have gotten in anyway, students admitted even under a pure percentage plan can perform reasonably well.

Holding other things equal, class rank is a powerful predictor of academic success. Admission officers defending their own performance under the ten-percent law have emphasized that top-ten-percent students have higher first-year college grades than bottom-ninety-percent students with SAT scores as much as two hundred points higher. This is merely another way of stating the unsurprising fact that class rank has predictive power after controlling for test scores. But it is equally true that test scores have predictive power after controlling for class rank. Among the top-ten-percent students, and also among the bottom-ninety-percent students, freshman grades rise uniformly and substantially with each hundred-point increment in test scores.

Any school attempting to admit the strongest possible class would consider both—class rank *and* test scores, or grades *and* test scores. There are many students in the second ten-percent and below with strong test scores and strong high school curricula who would reasonably be predicted to outperform students in the top ten-percent with low test scores and weaker high school curricula. The freshman class at Texas has not gotten weaker as compared to earlier years, but there can be little doubt that Texas admits a weaker class under the ten-percent law than it *could* admit *today* if it considered a full range of predictors. And because the weaker students guaranteed admission come from all races, not just underrepresented minorities, there is little doubt that Texas admits a weaker class than it *could* admit if it considered a full range of predictors and gave preferences to applicants from underrepresented minority groups.

As the ten-percent law has become better known, more and more high school graduates have claimed its guarantee. At Texas, the fraction of the class guaranteed admissions under the ten-percent law has risen every year, from around 40% in 1998 to about 75% in 2005. From the beginning, there were complaints from strong high schools that talented students in their second ten-percent were being squeezed out. These complaints were largely self-serving and baseless at first; there was little evidence of such an effect in the early years. But such an effect is inevitable as the fraction of the class committed to guaranteed admissions grows, and as the fraction available to discretionary admission decisions correspondingly shrinks.

Despite all these problems, percentage plans have had one unanticipated benefit that is very much worth saving. The school-specific guarantee of admission turns out to be an important aid to recruiting and motivating minority students. The guarantee enables officials of a flagship university to go to a minority high school, speak to an assembly, and promise seats in the freshman class. In a community that may mistrust the University and disbelieve promises of fair treatment or even of affirmative action, the guarantee enables University officials to say, in effect, "You don't have to trust us. You are not competing with rich kids from the suburbs. Your competition is in this room, and fifty of you are guaranteed admission. The seats are reserved, and we will provide financial aid." A closely related benefit, not confined to minority high schools, is evidence that students who have heard about the top-ten-percent law are much more likely to plan on going to college.

The key to these benefits is the school-specific guarantee. It is essential that the guarantee be offered to individual schools, and it is probably important that the guarantee be simple to explain. But it is not important that the guarantee be any particular percentage, or that it be based on class rank. What seems to be critical is that the competition is within each school, and that every school's student body understand that it will have winners who get admitted to the flagship campuses.

This essential guarantee can be separated from the percentage plan that first produced it, and this suggests possibilities for reform that would keep the benefit of the guarantee and reduce the costs of percentage plans. The simplest and most important change would be to put a cap on the guarantee, so that students guaranteed admission never take up more than half the freshman class at any campus. The top-ten-percent would be guaranteed admission to most state schools, and some smaller percentage would be guaranteed admission to the flagship. This would greatly reduce the squeeze on strong students in the bottom ninety percent, and that would greatly reduce the costs of the program. If full-file admission standards are allowed to operate for a substantial fraction of the class, there is less distortion of admission standards, less unfairness to strong students in the second ten-percent, and less incentive for high-school students to avoid tough courses and tough competition.

A more ambitious reform would be to offer the guarantee only to high schools with an historically low rate of applications to the flagship campuses. These schools would be selected on a color-blind basis, but they would disproportionately include minority high schools and rural and small-town high schools. This would offer the guarantee to the schools that need it most, and it would ensure that graduates of these schools would be admitted in reasonable numbers without having to compete against graduates of stronger high schools. But it would not distort academic standards or incentives at high schools that already have a strong history of college applications. Applicants from those high schools would be subjected to full-file review, and thus would have the full incentive to take challenging courses.

Percentage plans depend on the continued existence of predominantly minority high schools, and this means that percentage plans are useless for admission to graduate and professional schools. There are not nearly as many predominantly minority colleges as there are predominantly minority high schools. Moreover, graduate and professional schools admit applicants to each program, not to the university as a whole. The percentage of college students admitted to law school or any other particular program is tiny compared to the percentage of high school students admitted to college. No law school could workably guarantee admission to the top x-percent of college graduates, no matter the level of x. The Law School had to find other ways of coping with *Hopwood*.

The search for race-neutral means of increasing minority enrollment depends on identifying a proxy for race. Proxy admission criteria are race-neutral criteria that benefit minority applicants disproportionately. Such proxy selectors avoid the explicit consideration of race, but that is their only virtue. In every other way, they are far inferior to the direct consideration of race. They achieve far less diversity and do far more damage to admission standards. This is for quite general reasons inherent in the basic approach.

For most of these proxies, the correlation with race is weak. This means that most offers of admission based on a proxy selector do not go to applicants from disadvantaged minority groups. It is therefore ineffective to use these weak proxies at the margin of a school's other selection criteria. Rather, to achieve substantial diversity through proxies, the proxies must be used across the board. They must displace standard selection criteria rather than supplement them at the margin. This is why the ten-percent law is taking up nearly the whole freshman class. Graduation in the top ten-percent is a very weak proxy for race. It is a proxy because it guarantees admission to minority students from the top ten-percent of segregated high schools; it is a *weak* proxy because it also guarantees admission to the top ten-percent of integrated and predominantly white high schools.

By contrast, when the University directly considers race, it does so for only a few seats in the class, and the minority students admitted are the best minority applicants as measured by the same academic criteria used to admit all other students. The impact on the quality of the class is minimal. Proxy criteria are admission criteria picked for their correlation with race, not for their academic merit, and they must be applied to the whole class, not to a few seats. They inherently damage admission standards far more broadly than affirmative action does.

The Law School could not use a percentage plan, so what did it do instead? First, it intensively recruited potential minority students, using both Law School personnel and volunteers from the private sector. A private association raised substantial funds for privately administered minority scholarships. Before the difficulties in the airline industry after September 11, 2001, two alumni persuaded airlines to offer free trips to Austin for admitted minority applicants.

We also emphasized geographic diversity, taking advantage of the possibly unique circumstance of a vast region of the state with an overwhelmingly minority population. Along the Rio Grande from El Paso to Brownsville are cities and counties with huge Hispanic populations: 78% in El Paso County, 84% in Cameron, 88% in Hidalgo, 97.5% in Starr, and similar numbers in less populated counties. The Law School has funded and assisted pre-law programs at undergraduate schools in these counties, guaranteed offers of admission to graduates of these schools, and taken other steps to address the underrepresentation of these counties in the Law School. These efforts use geography as a proxy for ethnicity. This proxy obviously could not be used for the whole class; no one wanted to reject all applicants from counties not along the Rio Grande. But because this proxy was so strong, it could help increase Hispanic enrollment even when applied, like race-based affirmative action, to only a few seats.

Few other states, maybe none, could duplicate this program. Geography is not so strong a proxy for Hispanics in other states; it may not be a proxy for blacks in any state, unless the geographic areas are defined by neighborhoods or Zip Codes. Even for Texas Hispanics, the effect of heavy reliance on geography was limited. The combined effect of this very strong proxy, heavy recruiting, privately funded minority scholarships, and surging growth in the state's minority population could not restore Mexican-American enrollment to even the lowest level achieved in any year when ethnicity could be considered—at least not until 2003, when we got an additional boost from a nearly three-year halt in employment growth. In a tough job market, more students choose to continue their education, and this effect appeared to be bigger among minority applicants.

I have said that all the race-neutral means of achieving diversity pursue the goal of increasing minority enrollment indirectly, and thus less efficiently. They require greater departures from academic standards to produce less diversity. This is true even of the strongest proxies; the difference between strong and weak proxies is one of degree.

To make this abstract point concrete, consider the following stylized hypothetical. In the last stages of the admission process, suppose the director of admissions is comparing two candidates. One is a strong minority candidate from Dallas County, who after full deliberation, falls just short of being admissible on a color-blind basis. The other, from El Paso County, is considerably weaker but probably capable of succeeding at the Law School. The El Paso candidate is likely to be Mexican-American but may be white or black or Asian. That candidate's race is irrelevant to the illustration. In a color-blind system, the Law School would admit the weaker candidate from El Paso, without regard to race or ethnicity, and we would reject the stronger candidate from Dallas. We could not consider the Dallas candidate's race, and we could not do affirmative action for Dallas County, because the minority population there, while large, is not large enough to make Dallas County a strong proxy for race.

Repeat that example enough times and it is entirely possible to produce a bigger racial disparity in entering credentials with color-blind admissions than with affirmative action. That happened at the Law School; in the later color-blind years after *Hopwood*, the credential gap exceeded what it had been before *Hopwood*. This result was predicted by economists simulating color-blind admissions. This is the effect of proxies and their inefficiencies. Schools using proxies cannot admit the strongest minority applicants; they must admit the applicants who fit the proxy.

The University's efforts to restore minority enrollment under the constraints of *Hopwood* were desperate efforts. They were well-intentioned, and they did some good; they were far better than nothing. Some of those efforts should be continued in modified form. The true contribution of the ten-percent law is the guarantee of some admissions at each high school; that guarantee should be continued in ways that preserve most of the advantages and much less of the disadvantages of the existing ten-percent law. The pre-law programs at undergraduate institutions should also be continued. But none of these efforts, taken separately or together, show that race-neutral means can achieve racially diverse enrollment at reasonable cost to academic standards. And a majority of the Supreme Court appears to have understood this.

THE MICHIGAN CASES

In June 2003, the Supreme Court largely resolved the status of affirmative action in university admissions, in two cases from the University of Michigan: *Grutter v. Bollinger* and *Gratz v. Bollinger*.

Grutter adopted the diversity arguments that the University of Texas had made in *Hopwood*; it held that diversity in university classrooms is a compelling government interest. As compared to Justice Powell's opinion in *Bakke* a quarter-century before, the Supreme Court expanded the meaning of "diversity" to include educating a diverse leadership class for the next generation and keeping the pathway to leadership visibly open to talented students of all races. For many supporters of affirmative action, this is a far more powerful rationale than diversity in the classroom, even though both are important.

Grutter and *Gratz* also clarified and expanded the procedural limits on affirmative action. Consideration of race is narrowly tailored to the compelling interests it serves, and thus is constitutional, only under the following conditions: schools must seriously and in good faith consider race-neutral alternatives; they can consider the race of applicants only as part of an individualized and holistic review that considers a broad array of contributions to diversity, not just race; and they must periodically review their programs to determine whether they are still needed.

Reporting *Grutter* and *Gratz*, Austin newspapers proclaimed that "Hopwood Is Dead." That is true enough as far as it goes, and I found that it was the only way to explain the status of *Hopwood* to reporters. *Hopwood* is dead in the sense that any university with competent lawyers and good management systems can comply with *Grutter* and *Gratz* and restore affirmative action, unrestrained by anything in the *Hopwood* opinion.

The full relationship between the cases is more complex. *Grutter* squarely rejected *Hopwood*'s holding that diversity in higher education is not a compelling government interest. *Hopwood* also held that desegregating higher education does not justify considering race in admissions. *Hopwood* said, and earlier Supreme Court cases have held, that remedying the present effects of past discrimination is a compelling interest that can justify affirmative action. But *Hopwood* defined the relevant past discrimination and its effects so narrowly as to render this rule inapplicable to any university in the real world. *Grutter* did not consider either the desegregation holding or the past discrimination holding from *Hopwood*.

Legislation accompanying the ten-percent law requires the University to give a year's notice of any change in admission standards. So despite the Court's decision in *Grutter*, Texas had to remain color-blind in 2004. We used that year to carefully prepare for implementation of affirmative action in full compliance with *Grutter*. UT-Austin and the UT System conducted an elaborate evaluation of race-neutral alternatives, including the ten-percent law, documenting their failures, their costs, and their partial successes. We devised new admission procedures that satisfy the Supreme Court's broader conception of diversity, giving consideration to anything in an applicant's background that contributes to the diversity of the campus. Rural students, disabled students, low- and moderate-income students, students who have served in the military, students who have lived abroad—everything about a student is potentially relevant in a system of individualized and holistic review.

Implementation of this approach to admissions varies across the campus. Individualized admissions works best in the graduate and professional schools, but it is hard to generalize; UT-Austin has nearly a hundred graduate and professional programs selecting their own students, ranging from tiny specialized programs to the Law School with its 6,000 applicants. At the undergraduate level, admissions is dominated by the ten-percent law; the individualized admissions process applies only to the small number of seats remaining after all the top-ten-percent students are admitted. The first class admitted under the new system is just arriving as this is written; it is too early to say much about what has been accomplished.

THE REASONS FOR AFFIRMATIVE ACTION

The story of race and admissions is a long saga at Texas, from the days of deliberate segregation to the current restoration of affirmative action. One might reasonably ask why the university has invested so much effort. Why do we see affirmative action as essential to our mission?

"Diversity" is the Supreme Court's chosen ground for upholding race-based affirmative action in admissions to higher education. "Diversity" has multiple meanings, and the Court's opinion in *Grutter* substantially expanded those meanings and shifted their base. But however defined, diversity is not the only reason for affirmative action, and perhaps not the best label for what diversity has grown to include.

Affirmative action has been the most effective method, and generally the only effective method, of desegregating schools with highly selective admission standards. Perhaps least understood of all the reasons for affirmative action, directly considering race preserves selective admission standards and thus protects academic excellence. Affirmative action is needed to create a leadership class for a diverse American future, including the rapidly approaching time when Texas and other states will be led by their minority populations. Affirmative action is a partial remedy for the effects of past and present discrimination in public elementary and secondary education.

And no race-neutral means work nearly as well, either at increasing diversity or protecting academic standards. Affirmative action that directly considers race is the one effective method that has enabled highly selective schools to simultaneously maintain their selectivity while achieving some degree of diversity.

In his controlling opinion in *Bakke*, Justice Powell chose diversity as the ground for upholding race-based affirmative action in university admissions. For Justice Powell, diversity meant diversity of background and experience within the classroom, for the purpose of improving the educational experience in that classroom. This was explicitly a First Amendment interest in the "robust exchange of ideas."

For the majority in *Grutter*, diversity starts with Justice Powell's opinion and includes Justice Powell's meaning. But diversity in *Grutter* is a much broader concept, anchored more in racial justice and the values of the Equal Protection Clause than in the First Amendment. In the longer and more elaborated discussion in *Grutter*, diversity is about promoting racial tolerance and understanding; developing workers, citizens, and leaders for a racially diverse society; and preserving the legitimacy of American government. Diversity in Justice Powell's sense is a plausible reason for affirmative action in admissions; diversity in *Grutter*'s sense is a much better reason.

The Court in *Grutter* emphasized that American higher education prepares young people to function as workers and citizens in a highly diverse society. Racial stereotypes are an important barrier to knowledge and understanding, and communication across racial lines is essential to America's future. Diversity in the classroom "promotes cross-racial understanding, helps to break down racial stereotypes, and enables [students] to better understand persons of different races."

For the *Grutter* Court, the label "diversity" also includes the education of a diverse set of future leaders. A much-noted brief from military leaders argued that one of the lessons of Vietnam was that the military could not succeed with a white officer corps and heavily minority enlisted ranks. Squarely relying on that brief, the Court said that a successful military requires an officer corps that is "highly qualified *and* racially diverse."

The Court then expanded this point from the military and national security to the population generally. It noted "the overriding importance of preparing students for work and citizenship" and said that education has "a fundamental role in maintaining the fabric of society." "[E]ducation . . . is the very foundation of good citizenship. For this reason, the diffusion of knowledge and opportunity through public institutions of higher education must be accessible to all individuals regardless of race or ethnicity. . . . Effective participation by members of all racial and ethnic groups in the civic life of our Nation is essential if the dream of one Nation, indivisible, is to be realized."

Then the Court extended this reasoning to the nation's leadership class. "[U]niversities, and in particular, law schools [are] the training ground for a large number of our Nation's leaders. This is especially so of highly selective law schools." And so finally the Court came to the question of political legitimacy:

> In order to cultivate a set of leaders with legitimacy in the eyes of the citizenry, it is necessary that the path to leadership be visibly open to talented and qualified individuals of every race and ethnicity. All members of our heterogeneous society must have confidence in the openness and integrity of the educational institutions that provide this training.

These passages go vastly beyond Justice Powell's conception of diversity. They are not about more effective learning in the classroom. They are not about informal interactions on the campus, or even about breaking down racial stereotypes. These comments are about access; they are about bringing more minority young people into the most selective schools and into positions of leadership. They are about the legitimacy of selective institutions of higher education and the legitimacy of the nation's leadership. They are about the perceptions of the minority community, which "must have confidence" in the openness of the system. The label, "diversity," is the same, and retaining that label had rhetorical advantages for the Court, but the meaning has fundamentally changed.

The Court's emphasis on educating a diverse class of future leaders is especially important in Texas. Failure to educate a leadership class among disadvantaged minority populations would be a permanent threat to equality and social stability. At the time of the 2000 Census, 53 percent of the college-age population in Texas was African-American, Hispanic, or Native American. That percentage is steadily growing. Steve Murdock, the State Demographer of Texas, projects that in 2040 Texas will be 59 percent Hispanic, nine percent black, twenty-four percent white, and eight percent other races. The median age of the Hispanic population will still be nearly twelve years younger than the median age of the white population, which means that the Hispanic population will be reproducing more rapidly and dying more slowly. Even apart from immigration, the Hispanic increase as a percentage of the state's population will not yet have peaked.

A state with such large "minority" populations cannot be indifferent to the educational success of those populations. Most of our future workers and most of our future voters are members of minority groups that have been historically disadvantaged. Unless there are radical changes in ethnic voting patterns, most of our future government officials are black and Hispanic. In the second half of the twenty-first century, the University of Texas at Austin will almost certainly be a predominantly Hispanic institution. If it aspires to still be "a university of the first class," then it must aspire to raise Hispanic achievement levels sufficiently to maintain that status. To maintain highly selective admission standards without regard to racial and ethnic consequences is to put the state on track to a Third-World future, with a wealthier and more educated white minority trying to protect its privileges from a poorer and less-educated black and brown majority. Any attempt to reserve a grossly disproportionate share of elite positions for the white population is madness, whether done in the name of old-fashioned racism or of unbending commitment to color-blindness.

All of this is but to elaborate the Court's point in *Grutter*. The pathway to future leadership must be visibly open to talented citizens of all races and ethnicities. If we want our future leadership to be both highly qualified and ethnically diverse, then we must educate more minority students at the highest levels. Some states, and some opponents of affirmative action, may believe they can have a leadership class that is highly qualified and *not* diverse. But in Texas, and in other states with minority populations only slightly smaller, that choice is not available. Future leadership will inevitably be diverse; the ordinary workings of democracy will see to that. The question is whether we can fix our educational systems in time to ensure that those leaders are also highly trained and highly qualified.

Perhaps the least understood benefit of affirmative action that considers race is that it protects the University's commitment to academic excellence. Affirmative action is the one successful method that has enabled selective schools to significantly reduce their racial identifiability—their tendency to be all-white or nearly so—without significantly reducing their selectivity. Each school can apply the predictors of academic success that work best for it, and it can apply those selective admission standards across the board, to all applicants. Such schools can then consider race at the margin, giving special consideration to those minority applicants who have already demonstrated strong academic qualifications under the usual standards. This marginal consideration of race is essential to negate the segregative impact of highly selective admission standards.

This marginal consideration of race is equally essential to hold back the political assault on selective admission standards. It is always hard to maintain political support for admission standards that only a small fraction of the populace can meet. A school that admits only the top ten percent of high school seniors, or a professional school that selects from the top five-percent of college graduates, is of course saying that ninety or ninety-five percent of the population need not apply. This is a hard policy to sustain in a public institution subject to democratic control. Selective academic requirements inevitably exclude far more potential students than they admit. The benefit to those admitted is direct, obvious, and concentrated; those not admitted get only their less-obvious share of the benefits that accrue to the state from having a distinguished university.

It may be that selective admissions are politically sustainable principally because of limitations of institutional size. No matter the admission standards, not many more students could attend the flagship state university. If students were not selected on some basis of merit, they would have to be selected randomly, or on the older bases of wealth, social and political connections, and who their daddies were. Those alternatives are too unattractive to displace admissions based on merit.

But if meritocratic admissions have the effect of excluding racial minorities who have long suffered from discrimination, and if that exclusion is to a grossly disproportionate extent, the political calculus changes. It is very difficult for highly selective admissions to carry the political burden of justifying the appearance of racial exclusion. And if much of the public has come to view disproportionately white institutions as presumptively discriminatory, then the selective admission standards themselves appear to many people to be presumptively discriminatory. Affirmative action that reduces the exclusionary effects of these standards protects the admission standards themselves; ending affirmative action would have created inexorable pressure to distort and reduce those standards.

This fear is not just theoretical; it was demonstrated in a series of Texas statutes modifying admission standards in response to *Hopwood v. Texas*. The ten-percent law is not all that the legislature enacted. Graduate and professional schools are forbidden to use standardized test scores unless they compare those scores "with those of other applicants from similar socioeconomic backgrounds"; they are forbidden to rely on any test score, no matter how low, as a "sole" or "primary" criterion that ends consideration of an applicant. The legislature also provides a laundry list of factors that "may" be considered in graduate and professional school admissions, and a similar list that "shall" be considered for undergraduate applicants not in the top ten percent. Many of the items on these lists are socioeconomic factors with little or no capacity to predict academic achievement, but which the legislature hoped might have some correlation with race.

Similar changes occurred, less visibly, inside admission offices. Admissions officers gave less weight to grades and test scores and rigorous courses, more weight to soft variables with little power to predict academic achievement.

When affirmative action is done right, a school selects admission criteria, based on its own experience, academic judgment, and institutional needs, to produce the best student body for its programs. In a large undergraduate institution, these criteria might be a simple matrix of grades and test scores, although that must change after *Grutter* at any school that wishes to engage in affirmative action. In graduate and professional admissions, the criteria are nearly always more complex and more dependent on human judgment. But whatever those criteria are, they can be applied to applicants of all races, and the school can identify the very best applicants of each race, as judged by the same criteria.

Primary reliance on each school's preferred selection criteria, applied to applicants of all races, serves important interests. It preserves high academic standards, it preserves the distinctive missions of different schools, and it preserves incentives to hard work and academic achievement on the part of potential applicants. Explicit consideration of race, confined to a relatively narrow band as measured by established race-neutral selection criteria, preserves these criteria and the interests they serve. If explicit consideration of race were ended, all the interests in diversity and desegregation would remain, and at least in some states, the political pressure would become overwhelming to reduce or abolish selective admission standards across the board.

The connection between affirmative action and academic excellence came to the fore in the *Grutter* case. Justices Antonin Scalia and Clarence Thomas, dissenting, argued at length that the problem was selective admissions. Michigan had no compelling interest in running an excellent law school; Justice Thomas argued that forty-six states had been unable or unwilling to build an excellent law school, so excellent public law schools must not be very important. (Texas was one of the four excellent public law schools he acknowledged; he also emphasized that unlike Michigan, the University of Texas Law School offers its excellent legal education mostly to in-state students.) The dissenters argued that if Michigan would lower its admission standards across the board, the diversity problem would solve itself without any need to consider race. Justice Sandra Day O'Connor for the majority responded that Michigan did not have to choose between excellence and diversity. It could have highly selective admission standards, and it could negate the exclusionary effect of those standards with affirmative action.

CONCLUSION

Carefully limited consideration of race, in conjunction with the full range of academic predictors, serves important interests in experiential and racial diversity, in avoiding resegregation and the appearance of deliberate racial exclusion, in serving state populations and educating future leaders, in alleviating the consequences of discrimination in earlier stages of public education, and in preserving selective admission standards and academic excellence. No alternative means are available to serve this combination of interests. If the Supreme Court had prohibited consideration of race, that would have led first to substantial resegregation in American higher education, and then to substantial erosion of academic standards to avoid that resegregation. Different states might allocate the harm among these interests in different proportions, but both diversity and academic standards would be substantially reduced.

No race-neutral means can achieve both diversity and academic excellence. But experiments with percentage plans have revealed the motivational power of guaranteeing that some students from each high school can be admitted to the flagship campuses of the state university system. This is a discovery worth preserving, and it can be combined with a well-designed affirmative action program.

The University of Texas is committed to maintaining academic excellence and to serving all the populations of the state. These dual commitments inevitably require some consideration of race. To the extent the lawyers and politicians leave us alone, we will consider race in the fairest, most efficient, and least intrusive way possible. If those methods are taken away, we will address the problem in ways that are clumsier, less fair, less efficient, and more costly to academic excellence. But the inescapable bottom line is that we cannot refuse to educate the "minority" groups that are now a steadily growing majority of the Texas population.

NOTE ON SOURCES

Facts and quotations in this essay are generally from federal court opinions, federal regulations, state statutes, or similar sources. Readers interested in a more detailed account, with full citation of all sources, should consult Douglas Laycock, "The Broader Case for Affirmative Action: Desegregation, Academic Excellence, and Future Leadership," *Tulane Law Review* 78 (2004): 1767–1842, and Professor Laycock's introduction to Kumar Percy, comp., *Hopwood v. Texas Litigation Documents* (Buffalo, NY: Wm. S. Hein, 2002).

Reminiscences

MEADE F.
GRIFFIN

From Cottonwood
to the Capital
The University Years

I came to Austin to attend the University of Texas in September 1911 when I was seventeen years old. I spent six years in the University, taking my B.A. in 1915 and my law degree in 1917. After graduating, I immediately went into the army during World War I and became a candidate in the First Officers' Training Camp at Leon Springs, Texas.

I entered as a freshman in the Academic Department. In that class there were several people who became quite distinguished in the State of Texas: Beauford Jester, who became Governor of Texas; Charles I. Francis, who became a renowned lawyer and philanthropist; Robert G. Storey, who became an outstanding world authority on international law and was invited all over the world after World War II to help various countries set up democratic governments; Walter Linn, an insurance executive in Fort Worth; Bob Wagstaff, a prominent Abilene lawyer; and Rex G. Baker, a Houston lawyer and benefactor to the University. The University of Texas at that time had an enrollment of approximately 1,500 students and a faculty of about 150 to 200 teachers. Sidney Mezes was president, Dr. W. J. Battle was dean of the College of Arts (later to serve as president), T. U. Taylor was dean of the Engineering School, and Judge John C. Townes was dean of the Law Department (as it was then known).

Many of the faculty members of my time have become legendary to later generations of U.T. students. Leonidas W. Payne and Morgan Callaway were famous professors of English literature. Stark Young was just beginning to make his reputation teaching what we called general literature. E. L. Dodd and Milton B. Porter were in the Math Department; Dr. E. P. Schoch in the Chemistry Department; Dr. E. T. Miller was head of

Meade F. Griffin graduated from the University soon after returning from service in World War I. He practiced law in the Texas Panhandle and then served in World War II as a lieutenant colonel. After the war, he prosecuted war crimes in Wiesbaden, Germany. In 1949, Griffin was appointed to the Supreme Court of Texas, where he served until 1968. This essay was first published in Texas Our Texas: Remembrances of The University *(Eakin Press, 1984), edited by Griffin's grandson Bryan A. Garner.*

the Economics Department; Professor W. T. Mather, a strong prohibitionist who was president of the athletic council, taught physics; and John H. Keen was in the Philosophy Department. Charles W. Ramsdell was to have a long and notable career teaching American history, as would Milton R. Gutsch in Medieval history and L. M. Keasby in institutional history. In the Law Department, we had Senator Robert Emmett Cofer, Dr. George Charles Butte, Judge Ira Polk Hidebrand, Leon Green, Judge Lauch McLaurin, and Judge Beverly Dudley Tarleton. In retrospect, the caliber of the faculty of that time is astounding.

The Law Department's building was southeast of the hill where the Old Main Building was. What was then called the Main Library had just been completed; it was just west of the Old Main and south of the walk that goes from the Main Building out to Guadalupe Street. The gymnasium had originally been in the Old Main Building, but about two years before I came, a new wooden gymnasium had been built. The English professors' offices were located in the basement of the Old Main, where the gymnasium had previously been, and the corridor running through there became known as the English Channel. It was a very popular place because everybody had an awfully hard time with English.

In 1914, after I had been in the University for a year or two, the European War broke out. I had been doing some odd jobs: I delivered papers by bicycle for a while, ran a laundry route for a while, and then worked a great deal for John A. Lomax, who was secretary of the Ex-Students' Association. He worked to publish the *Alcalde*, which had been started about two or three years before and which published many fine articles and poems. For instance, Fritz Lanham, a distinguished alumnus of U.T. who later became a member of the United States Congress—and whose father, S. W T Lanham, was a governor of Texas—wrote a memorable long-winded poem for the magazine entitled "Putting Trolley on the Sack." At the turn of the century, Fritz had served as the first editor-in-chief of the *Daily Texan*.

I worked for John Lomax for about a year. Because I could run a typewriter, he hired me for twenty-five cents per hour to address labels, put on the wrappers, and roll each *Alcalde* up in paper to mail to every subscriber. I worked at various other odd jobs: mowing lawns, moving furniture, setting type for a newspaper, and waiting tables. When the European War broke out,

I had a sister in the College of Industrial Arts, and my father, though he had a good deal of land, grew only cotton when the price was cut down to three cents per pound, which came very near breaking him. He couldn't keep both of us in school, so I told him in the summer of 1914 that if he could give me enough money to get back down to Austin, I would get myself a job.

My father borrowed $75 from his brother and gave it to me. It was to pay my railroad fare and my expenses for the first month. I put the word out among everyone I knew that I had to have a job. (I was supposed to be one of three people in U.T. who knew everybody—every student and every faculty member—and could call anyone on campus by name. Dr. Daniel A. Penick, a professor of Greek and the tennis coach, approached me and said, "Meade, I understand you need to have a job to stay in school. I've got a little room up in my house that I always give to some boy student. I have a room and a bath—just make up the beds and look after the kids." I was also responsible for sweeping the sidewalk and the halls and furnishing wood when it got cold. Naturally, I was glad to take the job.

I accepted immediately, and ended up staying in Dr. Penick's lodging with Bob Knight Jr., Marion Knight, and Henry Knight, all sons of Robert E. Knight, a well-known lawyer in Dallas. We got along very well, and they didn't think any less of me because I was their "chambermaid." Meanwhile, I also worked as a student assistant to Dr. Lewis W. Haney, chairman of the Economics Department, and kept the books in the Hill & Hill Grocery Store.

At Christmastime, a friend of mine came up to me and said, "Meade, I'm sleeping down at Dr. Goodall Wooten's office for my room rent. He has a room upstairs with a bath, and by having students stay there, he gets residential tax rates." He told me that it had been Thomas Dudley Wooten's residence built when he first came to Austin back in 1876. My friend explained that he was leaving, and asked whether I would like to sleep there for my rent. Naturally, I accepted the offer. Dr. Goodall Wooten's office, which he shared with his brother, Dr. Joe Sil Wooten, was at 107 East Tenth, just a couple of blocks from the grocery store where I had worked.

I had breakfast every morning in a little Greek restaurant called the Crescent Confectionary at Tenth Street and Congress. It opened at six o'clock, so I would get up early, shave and bathe, and be there waiting for Pete, the proprietor, to open so that I could buy a meal ticket. After I had been eating there for two or three months, he found out that I was a student working my way through the University. Rather than charge me twelve cents for the regular breakfast (coffee, hot cereal, and hot bread), Old Pete would slip me a hot cake or an egg or a couple of strips of bacon. On a holiday or Sunday, he might slip me one egg and a strip of bacon in addition to the regular food.

I think I had more money than ever in my life, what with drawing $50 per month from my odd-jobs, sleeping for my rent, getting my breakfasts for twelve cents each morning, and eating at the University cafeteria where I boarded for about $12 per month. For supper, I would get a bowl of grits for five cents and a glass of milk for three cents; the boys there knew me well and they would fill up the bowl and glass good and full. Frequently, they would put a slice of butter on my grits. I was living like a lord.

I even had money to take my girl to the shows. In fact, I once took her on a special train over to A&M College to see U.T. and A&M play football, paid her way, and got mine paid as chief ticket-taker. I let her wait outside while I went in and did the checking before and after the game to see that we had all our money. In those days, we called working our way through school "grafting," and I am happy that I had that experience.

While at the University I quickly got interested in politics. There were two parties: the Barbarian Party—the "Barbs," as we called ourselves, those who belonged to the multitude of the great unwashed—and the Fraternity Party. The Barbs had won most of the offices for some time. The Barb Party did not consist of socialites: most of the boys were from the country and had no time to do much socializing. We spent most of the time working and going to school and just trying to get ourselves through the University.

The powers that were, the heads of the Barb party, took me in and I became a "ward heeler"—I would go around from boarding house to boarding house advocating our candidates for student government in the spring election of 1912. From that position I worked on up to the point where Sam Holliday, Walter Linn, and I were called Caesar, Cassius, and Pompey by much of the student body; it was said that we controlled politics at the University. That was pretty nearly true,

because we elected everybody except the editor of the *Daily Texan*. (We never could elect an editor to the *Texan!*) We controlled the Student Council, not only for the men but also for the women, we elected the president of the Women's Student Council, and we consulted with the president of the Students' Association to have our candidates appointed in various places. We had quite an organization.

My part of that organization was to help get the women's vote out and to control it. I had girlfriends who were representatives in each one of the boarding houses, and some of the sororities worked with us. In each of these sororities and boarding houses, our representatives would see that our ideas got over and that all those girls got out to vote—and voted on our side.

In the spring of 1916, I was the Barb Party candidate for president and was defeated by Raymond Myers, who was a classmate of mine and who also had been a freshman in 1911. We had taken our academic degrees together and were now working toward our law degrees. I knew I was going to lose because certain situations had arisen whereby it would have been practically impossible for me to be elected. I had been too active, and it was said by many in the Barb Party that its bosses—I was considered one, apparently—had controlled politics in the University for too long, and that they should be put down. Despite our differences in University days, Lynn Landrum, Hines Baker, Rex Baker, Clarence Lohmann, Myron G. Blalock, Earl Zellers, Tom Gambrell, and various other such fine people later became my very fast friends.

I had nevertheless been able to serve as representative from the senior class to the Student Council for the 1914–15 term. I served on the Student Council, and had started taking tickets at the football games and ultimately worked my way up, as I said, to chief ticket-taker. When we played football games out of town, Sam Holliday and I were sent around to check up on the opposing school to see if we had gotten all the money that was coming to us out of that particular football game. The University would give Sam and me enough money to pay for our railroad tickets and each of us would get a lower Pullman berth and three meals per day.

Ordinarily, we would go up to Dallas the day before the Texas-Oklahoma football game and then come back the night of the game. Sam and I would usually take an upper berth and sleep together, so that we could use the money we saved on the two lower berths to go and see the fair. You could get nearly anything to eat, such as hamburgers and hot dogs, for ten cents. Sam and I would take our money for meals and spend it on the things we wanted to see in the fair and eat hot dogs or ham sandwiches for the day and a half we were in Dallas for the big game.

Meanwhile, Sam had started ushering for all the cultural events in the auditorium, which was in the Old Main Building. Among the performers who came to U.T. during the teens were Alma Gluck, a soprano who was one of the first singers to make phonograph records; Fritz Kreisler, the great violinist; Ernestine Schumann-Heink, the Austrian-American contralto; and John McCormack, an operatic tenor from Ireland. When Sam worked his way up to be head usher, he got me a job as one of the regular ushers. Thus I got to see all the cultural events, and Sam got to see all the out-of-town football games.

Before I ever came to the University, my father and I sat down and figured out my courses so that I could finish my B.A. and LL.B. in six years. I made very poor grades my freshman year and did a little better my sophomore year. I took two years each of Chemistry and Calculus, for some reason, and moved up from C's to B's. I also took an advanced Latin course taught by Dr. Edwin W. Fay, a distinguished Latin teacher who was renowned as one of the ablest Classics professors in the United States. Under Dr. Fay, I made B's in Homer and Ovid, and then pulled up my grades somewhat because, of course, I planned to enter the Law Department. Dr. Fay was an outstanding teacher, but one of the hardest in the University.

In the winter semester, Dr. Daniel A. Penick and Miss Roberta F. Lavender, under whom I had taken "Latin Prose Composition" (and busted it), stopped me and said, "Meade, we don't understand your situation at all. You took 'Latin Prose Composition' under me and busted it, but now you're taking Latin under Dr. Fay, one of the best and hardest teachers in the United States, and you're making B's all the time. Can you explain this?" And I replied, "Well, no, I can't exactly explain it, except that that doggone 'Latin Prose Composition' never interested me. It was always hard. Maybe I imagined it was harder than it really is."

Actually, Dr. Fay had a way of capturing a student's interest. He always went over the lesson from the previous day during the first half of the class. For the next half-hour, he would cover brand-new material; I knew that he was going to ask questions on this new material the next time class met. He would go over the new material and translate it for us aloud. Because I am more auditory than visual, I still had the new material on my tongue's end and did very well in recitation. I did not do very well in writing, because I still had trouble getting my translations from English back into Latin.

One could take four courses that counted toward both the B.A. and the LL.B. They were English, Government, one-third of a course in Philosophy, and American History. I had planned to take those so that when I became a junior in the Academic Department, I could go down to the Law Department and take a course in "Wills and Estates." The summer before, I had taken "Criminal Law" and "Criminal Procedure" by correspondence. By my senior year, I had completed all but two of the required subjects for my B.A. degree. So I took three courses over at the Law Department, one of which counted both ways, for a total of five courses—three in Law and two in Academic—and I graduated.

My parents couldn't come down for my graduation in 1915, because Cottonwood was considered a long way from Austin. One had to take the train from Putnam to Fort Worth, change trains, and then come down to Austin. It was a day-and-a-half trip and cost real money—and money was scarce in those days. Thus my father, not wanting to spend any money when he could avoid it, decided that the family would wait to come down to my graduation from law school in 1917.

When I first enrolled in the Law Department, I made up my mind that I was going to make better grades, that I would make A's, and I set an A minus—that is, ninety to ninety-five—as my passing grade in law courses. I really wanted to level off and study law. As an undergraduate, I had had a lot of other things to do: go with girls, politick, and participate in student activities. But in the Law Department, I had to do my best to get A minuses at least. And I got along in law all right; I may have missed ninety a time or two, but not very often. Judge William Stewart Simkins (or Colonel Simkins, as we often called him, for he had been a colonel in the Confederate Army) taught a course in Equity. Many students were scared of him, but I always got on well with him and did well in his class.

He lectured, and what he said, as well as the way he said it, was quite memorable—so I had no difficulty remembering his lessons.

When the United States' involvement in World War I began—war was declared on April 7, 1917—the government decided to begin training officers. The United States military had fewer than 7,500 officers and 200,000 men total, and it needed approximately two or three million men and 200,000 to 300,000 officers. Having been accepted as a cadet at the First Officers' Training Camp for this part of the country, to be held at Leon Springs, Texas, I had about thirty days in the University before reporting for duty on May 8, 1917. During that thirty-day period the army sent a Captain Martle, together with some noncommissioned officers who were at the University of Texas, to give fundamental military training to students interested in having such instruction. During that one-month period, I had an opportunity to refresh my memory on many of the basic movements and on the training of the individual soldier from the time he came into the service until he became an adequate company member. Sam Holliday, Bert Walker, Dave McGee (who later became a district judge in Fort Worth), and I went to San Antonio on May 7 so that we could report to Leon Springs on May 8, 1917. Dave could not join the army, because he had only one arm, but he wanted to go as far with us as he could, and when we left in a jitney for Leon Springs the next morning, Dave just stood on the sidewalk, crying like a baby because he could not go with us. Those of us who graduated in 1917 and were going off to war had our degrees conferred at Leon Springs by President Robert E. Vinson in a special ceremony. That was the only time in the history of the University, I believe, that such an exception was made to hold part of the commencement exercises off campus. But then the circumstances were rather exceptional.

I am happy to have had the experience in college politics, to have developed the many lasting friendships, and to have worked my way through the University of Texas, because it equipped me well when I came out to fight the battle of life where I had to make my living, and also where I held public office much longer than I ever intended to. It was at U.T., where we really had "ward politics," that I learned how to organize politics and win an election. This experience stood me in good stead during the rest of the time I held public office.

WALTER PRESCOTT
WEBB

The Search for
William E. Hinds

For more than fifty years now—since May 1904—I have been searching for
a man I never saw. Though he died forty-five years ago, the search grows
more intensive as I approach inevitably the time when I can no longer
pursue it. The reason I continue this search is that I owe this man a great
debt. It would mean a lot to me if I could report to him how a long-shot
investment he made in Texas finally turned out.

Since I cannot report to William E. Hinds, I am doing the next best
thing by reporting to other people—in hopes that at least some of them
may be enriched by the spirit that animated this man. I think this would
please him. Once when I tried to express my appreciation, he wrote: "You
cannot do anything for me, but if I help you now, perhaps in time you can
help someone else." This is the nearest thing to applied Christianity that I
know.

He never told me much about himself and I did not inquire because a
boy on a small farm in West Texas does not ask personal questions of a
mysterious and wonderful benefactor in New York. He died before I had
anything to say to him, before there was any return on his investment, of
which I was the sole custodian. I knew what I owed him, but for a long
time I feared that I might default on the obligation. As the years went by,
I prospered in a moderate way and gradually rose in my profession of historian and writer. The greater my success, the greater became my sense of
obligation to him. I have to find some way to partially discharge it.

---

*During his long career as a historian at the University of Texas, Walter Prescott
Webb published more than twenty books. Best known are* The Great Plains
(1931) and The Great Frontier *(1952). During his distinguished career he served
as president of the American Historical Association and received many honorary degrees, including one from Oxford University. Professor Webb was killed
in an automobile accident near Austin in March of 1963. A statue of Webb and
his old friends J. Frank Dobie and Roy Bedichek stands outside Barton Springs
Pool in Austin's Zilker Park. This essay was previously published in the July
1961 issue of* Harper's Magazine.

Walter Prescott Webb, photographed by Russell Lee. *From the Russell Lee Photograph Collection, Center for American History, the University of Texas at Austin. (DI 02403)*

So this is a sort of public acknowledgment of the obligation. It is also an appeal for more information about William E. Hinds. Surely there are some still living in New York who knew him, and there may be others elsewhere who were warmed by his spirit. Before I set down the scant facts I have about him, I must first tell how his life touched my own.

My parents migrated from Mississippi to Texas about 1884, destitute products of the Civil War in search of a new opportunity. I was born in 1888, and four years later they moved to West Texas. There I received the childhood impressions that account for the realism in my first book, *The Great Plains*. My father was a country schoolteacher, self-educated, and he never had more than a second-grade certificate. He was one of the last fighting teachers, employed to "hold school" in the country schools where the big boys had run the teacher off the year before. It was a rough life in a rough country. My father was usually paid a premium of $10 a month to teach these outlaw

schools. He got $50 or $60 a month for a five-month term—an annual income of $250 or $300, supplemented by what he earned in the summer farming or working at anything that came up, at about seventy-five cents or a dollar a day.

I learned to read early, and by the time I was ten reading became a passion. Since my father was a teacher, we had books in the house, and both my parents were readers. At that time the most popular brand of coffee was put out by Arbuckle Brothers, and you could get ten pounds of it for a dollar. The beans came in one-pound paper bags, with Mr. Arbuckle's signature on the side; if you collected enough of his signatures, he would send you a premium. The first book I ever acquired for myself, *Jack the Giant Killer*, cost me ten signatures. It was the first piece of mail that Uncle Sam ever brought to me, and I can never forget the thrill of receiving it at the Lacasa post office, the thrill of reading it on Old Charlie as I rode him home. It was the beginning of a long series of thrills and shocks that have come to me via the post office.

Not only did I read everything in our house, but I scoured the country for three miles to come up with files of *The Youth's Companion*, *The Saturday Blade*, and *The Chicago Ledger*. From a peddler I acquired a big file of *Tip Top Weekly*, which dealt with the doings of Frank Merriwell, who seemed to be running things at Yale. As far as I can recall, this was the first time I ever heard of college. From Frank Merriwell I got the first faint desire to go to college myself but it never occurred to me that I would ever do it.

This reading opened up such a wonderful world that I developed an aversion to the one that lay around me. I wanted to get away from it into the world where the books were.

When I was either twelve or thirteen, my father homesteaded a quarter section of land—160 acres—in Stephens County. This was about the last of the vacant land, since the open range was fast going under fence. The best land had already been taken, and this place lay back in what was called the Cross Timbers—deep sand with a red clay bottom, covered with scrub oak and blackjack. My father built a plank house in an open glade, and we began opening up a farm, the hardest work a boy can do.

This land had once belonged to Phil S. Lehman of New York, but he had wisely gone off and forgotten all about it. When we had paid the back taxes and lived on it ten years, that made it ours according to Texas law. We didn't exactly steal it, but we were mighty glad when the ten years expired. During that time my mother was always apprehensive when a stranger poked his head out of the brush, and it was not until after the limitation had run that we widened the road. From the time I was thirteen until I was seventeen seems an eternity. When we plowed, we plowed in new, stumpy land, and when we were not plowing, we were making more stumps and more new ground. For at least two years I did not go to school at all because my father was away teaching in the winter, and I was the "man on the place" except on weekends.

Very early in my career, my father made a casual remark that had enormous influence on my life. He said that when I grew up he wanted me to be an editor. Now I didn't know what an editor was, but his remark excited my curiosity. I finally learned that an editor ran the local paper. One day when we were in Ranger, I made bold to go into the office of the Ranger *Record*, and there was the editor, whose name was Williams, pecking away on an Oliver typewriter. This was the first typewriter I had ever seen, and it fascinated me. I stood looking over Editor Williams' shoulder at this marvel until he suggested that I do something else. By this time I had spied a treasure of untold magnitude, a great pile of "exchanges" which Editor Williams had thrown into a corner of the office because no waste-paper basket was big enough to contain them. Most of the papers were in the original wrappers, and all but the latest ones were covered with dust. I got up my courage to ask if I might have some of them, and the editor said go ahead. I carried off as many as I thought it would be seemly to try to get away with.

Among them were several copies of *The Sunny South*, edited by Joel Chandler Harris and published in Atlanta, Georgia. The official records tell me that *The Sunny South*, a weekly, was "devoted to literature, romance, fact, and fiction." It was then publishing A. Conan Doyle, Uncle Remus, Gelett Burgess, Will Irwin, and many other good writers, with lavish illustrations. It was wonderful, but the tragedy was that I had only a few copies.

In reading it, however, I learned that for ten cents I could have *The Sunny South* every week for three

months. I did not have ten cents, and I knew of no way of getting such an amount of money. My father was working hard and I was almost afraid to approach him, though I know now that he probably would have given me the dime had I asked at a propitious time. That winter he was away, and my mother and I often sat up late reading. One night I told her what I wanted, and why. She did not say anything, but I can see her now as she got up from her chair and went diagonally across the room in the yellow light of a kerosene lamp, and extracted from some secret place a thin dime. It may have been the only coin in the house.

That dime is the most important piece of money I have ever owned, for my entire life pivots on its shiny surface. It brought *The Sunny South* for three months, and soon the whole family was in love with it. There was never any trouble about renewing the subscription.

The letter column in *The Sunny South* was presided over by Mrs. Mary E. Bryan. One day I sat down and wrote her a letter which had one quality dear to an editor—brevity—and perhaps another essential to the writer, a willingness to lay bare something deep in the human heart. I said I wanted to be a writer, to get an education. I mentioned that my father was a teacher, and that he had been crippled in an accident. I signed with my middle name, which I always liked because an uncle who had the name was something of a writer.

The letter was published in the issue of May 14, 1904.[1] My father had come home from school, and we were then plowing corn with Georgia stocks. (A Georgia stock is a kind of one-horse plow.) The corn was less than a foot high. It was late in the afternoon, the time when the sun hangs unmoving in the sky for an incredible length of time. We were very tired and were sitting on the beams of our Georgia stocks letting the horses blow, when my sister came from the mail box of the new rural route which ran about a mile from the house and handed me a letter.

Few such letters have ever been received by tired boys sitting on Georgia stocks in a stumpy field. The envelope was white as snow and of the finest paper; the ink was black as midnight; the handwriting bold and full of character, with fine dashes. The flap was closed by dark-red sealing wax stamped with the letter *H*. The address was:

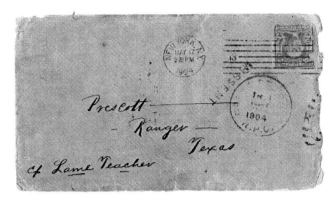

The envelope (above) and letter (below) from New York handed to young "Prescott" while he was helping his father plow a West Texas cornfield. *From the Walter Prescott Webb Papers, Center for American History, the University of Texas at Austin. (Box 2M250)*

Prescott
> *Ranger*
>> *Texas*

c/o Lame Teacher

The letter bore a New York postmark, May 17, 1904, but there was no return address. The envelope which lies before me now shows what care I used in opening this letter. It read:

"Prescott"
> Ranger
>> Texas

Dear Junior—I am a reader of the "Sunny South" and noticed your letter in the "Gossip Corner"—I trust you will not get discouraged in your aspirations for higher things, as you know there is no such word as *fail*, in the *lexicon* of *youth*; so keep your mind fixed on a lofty purpose and your hopes will be realized, I am sure, though it will take time and work.—I will be glad to send you some books or magazines, (if you will allow me to) if you will let me know what you like—Yrs truly

> Wm. E. Hinds
>> 489 Classon Ave

May 16/04
Brooklyn—New York

Now I realize how narrowly I missed this rendezvous with destiny. How did it come about that a letter addressed to "Prescott" reached me? *The Sunny South* came addressed to W. Prescott Webb, and it passed through the hands of Mr. John M. Griffin, the bewhiskered postmaster who was an ex-Confederate soldier. Since *The Sunny South* was pro-Confederate, Mr. Griffin got to reading my paper and fell in love with it. He and the rural mail carrier were probably the only people outside my family who knew that the name Prescott was really mine.

Even so, that letter nearly missed its mark. The envelope bears the post-office stamp "MISSENT," but I have no idea where it went before reaching me.

From that day on I never lacked for something to read—the best magazines in the land and occasional books. Every Christmas a letter would arrive from New York, and usually a tie of a quality not common in West Texas.

These books and magazines fired to white heat my desire for an education. Evidently my father, who was not a demonstrative man, was touched by my fervor. The stumpy farm had expanded and because of my father's love for the soil and his understanding of the principles of dry farming, it became productive. But there was still not enough of it, and we rented additional land from the neighbors. One day when we were clearing land my father asked me a question.

"Do you think," he asked, "that if you had one year in the Ranger school you could pass the examination for a teacher's certificate?"

To that question the only answer was yes.

"Well," he said, "if you will work hard, and if we make a good crop, we will move to Ranger for one year and you can go to school."

The year 1905 was one of the good years when the rains came. The fields produced bountifully, especially the new ground with the accumulated humus of a thousand years. The Ranger cotton gins ran day and night all fall. I know because I fed the suction pipe on Saturdays and after school. I had to make a sacrifice to go to school. Every boy in West Texas had a horse. Mine was a trim blue mare, close-built, easy to keep, fast, and lovely to look at. I sold her for $60 to get money for books; I got the tuition free by sweeping the school floors.

I pored over my books because I had a contract to deliver a second-grade certificate in the spring. My extensive reading gave me some advantage, but I had rough going with mathematics and grammar. I shall never forget J. E. Temple Peters, principal of the school and a near genius, who spent hours coaching a group of us to pass the examination at the county seat. When the time came, I had developed a severe case of tonsillitis, and my fever must have gone to 103 and over. Peters, who was one of the examiners, fed me aspirin while the fever fired my brain and seemed to sharpen all my faculties. I wrote on the eight required subjects for two days far into the night, but when I rose to turn in my papers I staggered in the aisle. There was never any thought of quitting. This was my only chance.

When school ended, I went back to the farm to await the decision of the examiners. Then one day there was an official envelope in the mail box. It was just a second-grade certificate which permitted me to teach in the rural schools, but to me it was a certificate of emancipation. I have acquired a good many parchments of finer quality in my career, but this one outranks them all.

My father not only moved the family back to the farm, but he quit teaching to devote all his time to it. I began where he left off, and through his influence had no trouble in getting an appointment. As a matter of fact, I taught three schools in that year, one for six weeks, one for four months, and one for two. My salary ranged from $42.50 to $45 a month, and I saved a bigger proportion of it than I have ever saved since. I had an affair of conscience because of the short hours. I had been accustomed to working from ten to fourteen hours a day, and there seemed to be something immoral about quitting at four o'clock.

With the money I saved I spent another year in school, and in the spring I passed the examination for a first-grade certificate. Suddenly I became a success. I was employed at $75 a month to teach the Merriman school which my father had taught two years at $60. (Underneath the stony Merriman school grounds and the nearby Baptist church yard lay a million or so barrels of oil, not to be found for ten years.) I was getting the maximum salary paid in the county schools. I was wearing good clothes and moving in the highest circles of local society, working five days a week and quitting when the sun was from two to three hours high.

Then in the winter of 1909 everything changed. One cold day, so windy that the pebbles from the playing field rattled like buckshot against the side of the school building, I walked down to the mail box and found a bulky letter from William E. Hinds. It was dated January 9, 1909. Here are the most important paragraphs:

My dear Friend.

. . . We have not had much winter as yet but the last few days have been cold and presume we shall have our usual amount before spring. My sister went to Washington, D.C., for the holidays and was at the White House New Year's. Secretary Cortelyou is our cousin, so she was invited to stay at the White House for luncheon. . . .

My friend, I wish you would *write me* what your

plans and wishes are for the *future*. We all have plans and hopes for the future and it is well we have, even if they are not always realized. Come, let us be *chums*, and write me *just what* is on your *mind*; perhaps I can help you and after all the best thing in life is to help some one, if we can. One would count it a great thing (to remember) if they had helped some one, that had afterwards become famous or great, say for instance Lincoln or Gladstone or any of the other great ones who were born a hundred years ago *this* year. And perhaps I can say, "Why I helped J. Prescott Webb when he was a young man."[2] And people may look at me, as a privileged character to have had the opportunity; so my boy tell me about *your* plans and *hopes* and then perhaps I may be able to help you carry them out.

Are there any books which you would like? *If so say so* and let me send them to you. If you don't "say so" I may send them anyway.

Your friend
Wm. E. Hinds

As an afterthought, he wrote on an extra sheet as follows:

I am interested in your teaching. How many scholars and are they mostly from the farm or town? Teaching is good training and I know it will benefit you.

Have you planned going to College in the fall, if you haven't planned it, is it something you would like to do, if so what College have you in mind? Now *answer all* these questions, *please.*

At the time the letter came I had not thought seriously of going to college. That was something for the sons of doctors and other prosperous people. Besides I was already a success, and rather enjoying the illusion. The letter faced me about, and made what I was doing insignificant—a means only.

I answered all his questions, telling him that I would like to go to the University of Texas. I had saved some money, for I had been at work three months, and I determined to save more. I reduced my social activity, and with some difficulty restrained myself from making a bid for a girl I had a very hard time forgetting. The road ahead was rough enough for one, and too rough for two.

Thus it came about that in September 1909, I boarded the train for Austin and the University of

William E. Hinds. *From the Walter Prescott Webb Papers, Center for American History, the University of Texas at Austin. (DI 02432)*

Texas with approximately $200. Our agreement was that I would spend my money, and when it played out, I would notify Mr. Hinds and he would send me a check each month. At the end of the second year, I owed him about $500, and he suggested that I should drop out and earn some money, saying that "I am not a rich man." I sent him a note for what I owed, but he would accept no interest. He never did.

In 1911–12, I taught the Bush Knob school in Throckmorton County, $90 a month. I reduced the note and told him I would like to return to the university. He approved, and I can sum it all up by saying that I never started a year at the university that he did not see me through. He never refused any requests I made of him, though I am glad to remember that I kept them to the minimum.

The nearest he ever came to a refusal was one summer when I made a good deal of money as a student salesman. I wrote Mr. Hinds that I would like to come to New York to see him, and that I had the money. He advised me to apply it on my college education. I did, but I have always regretted that I never saw him.

When I took the B.A. degree in 1915 I owed him something less than $500, which was our limit. And here I need to say something about my college career. I was twenty-one years old when I entered college, and I had no preparation for it. I had skipped too many grades and too many years of schooling. I did not have entrance credits, but because I was twenty-one the university admitted me on what is known as individual approval. My career as an undergraduate was completely lacking in distinction. I made fair grades in most subjects, but none to make Hinds proud. He never asked a question about grades. He never admonished me to do better.

But every month the check came. What he saw in me I have never been able to understand—but the fact that he saw something, that he seemed to believe in me, constituted a magnetic force that held me on the road. If I felt inclined to quit, or to go on a binge and spend money foolishly, as my friends often did, I could not do it for very long because there was a mysterious man in New York who trusted me.

Equipped with the B.A. degree, I got a job as principal of the Cuero High School at $133 a month. Then, in the fall of 1915 a letter came saying that William E. Hinds was dead.

The lawyers found my note in his papers, and they began to write me crisp and business-like letters. They had me make a new note to his sister, Ida K. Hinds, for $265. It was co-signed by my father and bore interest. Then came a letter from Miss Hinds, who had spent her life as a teacher in the New York schools. She said that she had taken over the note, and that I would not be bothered with the lawyers any more. In the fall of 1916, I married Jane Oliphant, and moved to the San Antonio Main Avenue High School as a teacher of history. Miss Ida Hinds came down to spend a part of the winter at the Gunter Hotel and she was often our guest.

She told me about all I know of her brother; that he had never married, that he had helped other boys,

and that he was an importer of European novelties. She implied that he was not intensively devoted to business, was rather casual about it. After his death I received an excellent photograph of Hinds, which is now before me. He had fine features, black hair, blue eyes, fair skin, a thin straight nose, and delicate ears. He wore a black mustache and had a full head of hair which appears to have been unruly.

Why didn't I get from Miss Hinds the information I now seek about her brother? There is no satisfactory answer to the question, as I look back now. From where I stood then, the answer seems reasonable to me. It never occurred to me that I would write this story. At that time there was no story because I had done nothing to justify one, and I was not yet a writer. Even had I thought of it, I would have considered that I had plenty of time, for youth is not conscious of the brevity of life. Moreover, I had just married, and at such a time each day seems sufficient unto itself.

Miss Hinds did not remain in San Antonio very long. It was probably in January of 1917 that she went to Los Angeles and took residence at 1316 South Vermont Avenue. Her first letter was dated February 18, 1917.

Then a letter arrived postmarked Burlington, Vermont, April 18, 1918. It marked the end of the trail. Inside was an undated memorandum from her to me, which read: "I enclosed your note in directed envelope so if anything happens to me, it will be sent to you. If you receive this, you will know that I have passed away and you are under no further obligation. Consider the matter closed as there is no one else that would be interested."

The note she enclosed was for $265 with 5 per cent interest. Endorsements on the back show that on April 17, 1917, I paid $100 principal and $16.56 interest, leaving a balance of $165 due in six months with interest "at 6% or 7%." The last endorsement is dated October 11, 1917, with a payment of $90 on the face of the note plus $5.68, leaving a balance of $75.

That $75 has never been paid to anyone connected with Hinds. It has, however, been paid over and over to those who needed it, and it will be paid again in the future as Hinds would have wanted it.

The act of this man is the unsolved mystery of my life. I have never been able to understand what motivated him. I find it easy enough to write a check for some student in temporary need, one that I can see and know, and I have written a good many such checks. But I still cannot understand how a man in New York City could reach far down in Texas, pluck a tired kid off a Georgia stock in a stumpy field, and stay with him without asking questions for eleven years, until death dissolved the relationship.

He did not live long enough to see any sign that the investment he made was not a bad one. In 1918 I became a member of the faculty of the University of Texas. My development there was slow—I have been late all my life—and it was not until 1931 that I published my first book, *The Great Plains*. Others followed in due course, but it was not until after 1950 that things began to happen which might have gratified William E. Hinds. When these marks of recognition came, my satisfaction was always tinged with regret that he could not know about them.

William E. Hinds was a great reader, and he probably was aware of Shelley's ironic lines:

The seed ye sow, another reaps;
The wealth ye find, another keeps;
The robes ye weave, another wears;
The arms ye forge, another bears.

I have reaped where he sowed, and I wear what he wove. Indeed, I keep a part of the wealth he found, but I have tried to keep a little of the spirit with which he used it. His spirit has hovered over me all my life. His name appears in the Preface or Dedication of my major books. I cannot now better describe what he did for me than I did in *The Texas Rangers*:

To the memory of
WILLIAM ELLERY HINDS
He fitted the arrow to the bow
set the mark and insisted
that the aim be true

His greatness of heart is known
best to me

This is the end of the story. I appeal to those who read it, for more information about William E. Hinds.

I would like to know when and where he was born, where he was educated, and what occupation he followed. If he helped other boys, as his sister stated, I would like to know who they are and what they did. His will might reveal something about his interests and activities.

I have consulted with private detective agencies about making a search, but found them just as vague about what they would do as they were specific about fees. I admit that this investigation should have been made long ago, but it was something easy to postpone. It might have been possible to make contact with the Cortelyou family, but I neglected to do it. While in New York once, I took a taxi to the place where William E. Hinds lived in Brooklyn, and I ran the index of the *New York Times* in search of his obituary, but could not find his name. In January 1961 I had a bout with the hospital and the surgeons, and came pretty close to losing. This was a warning that I could no longer delay; as soon as I was able, I went to work in earnest.

I now summarize the facts I have about him. His full name was William Ellery Hinds. For several years after 1904 he lived at 489 Classon Avenue, Brooklyn, New York. He later moved to another address, which I do not have. The only relatives he ever mentioned were his sister and some cousins, one of whom was George B. Cortelyou, Secretary of the Treasury under Theodore Roosevelt after 1907. I do not know the exact date of his death, but it must have been in the autumn of 1915 because my note made out to Ida K. Hinds bears the date of January 25, 1916.

The meager results of my search thus far suggest that if I remain silent, William E. Hinds may be forgotten. I want him to be remembered. Finally, it seems to me that what he did may encourage others to follow his example, and thus perpetuate his influence. He would want no better monument.

Anyone having information about William E. Hinds should address W. P. Webb, University Station, Austin, Texas.—THE EDITORS [*Harper's Magazine*, July 1961]

NOTES

1. *Editor's note*: Webb's letter reads as follows:

Will you welcome a stranger, "just a boy," into your circle? I am the only boy in the family and we live on a farm. This means a lot of all kinds of work to be done. But in the midst of it I keep my mind fixed on higher things. It is the height of my ambition to be educated and to become a writer—an author like our Mater and many others I read about.

But there is a host of difficulties in the way. Owing to a railroad accident my father is a permanent cripple. He is a teacher and his school is at a distance from home and he is away all winter, so that I am able to attend school only a little while every winter. The fates seem to be against me, but I shall keep trying. I am young—only 16—so there is time for me yet. I read and enjoyed the Knight's story, "Zeb's First Spree." I, too, once had a noble and intelligent dog. I would like to tell you a story about him if I am welcomed in the Household.

PRESCOTT.
Ranger, Tex.

The editor of *The Sunny South*'s Gossip Corner, where young Walter Prescott Webb's letter appeared, responded with the following advice:

Tell us the story, dear Prescott, and keep on aspiring and trying. One can become fairly educated without much school training. Some of the best writers never went to college, and cultivated themselves by reading with care, observing and thinking. Keep your eyes open to all that goes around you—the ways of men and the processes of nature. Read books of travel and study physical geography. A good physical geography is crammed full of information and food for thought.

M. . E. B

2. For years he did not get my first initial right, but addressed me as J. Prescott Webb.

WILLIE
MORRIS

From Mississippi
to Texas and Back

FROM "MISSISSIPPI," CHAPTER 10

One day that spring, two months before I was to graduate from high school, my father gave me some unexpected advice. He was reading the *Commercial Appeal* in our front room, and he turned to me and told me, quite simply, to get the hell out of Mississippi. I do not quite know why. Perhaps he knew something about doom, though his argument, he said, was based on a lack of *opportunity*. [. . .]

I saw no reason to leave. I was athlete, sports announcer, valedictorian, and, my greatest pride, editor of the *Flashlight*. I knew Mississippi and I loved what I saw. I had just been voted most likely to succeed. In Yazoo I knew every house and every tree in the white section of town. Each street and hill was like a map on my consciousness; I loved the contours of its land, and the slow changing of its seasons. I was full of the regional graces and was known as a perfect young gentleman. I was pleasant, enthusiastic, and happy. On any question pertaining to God or man I would have cast my morals on the results of a common plebiscite of the white voters of Yazoo County. [. . .]

My father took out one day for Austin, Texas, to see the campus of what we had sometimes heard was the best and certainly the biggest state university in the South. Four or five days later, my friend Bubba Barrier and I, quite by chance, ran into him in the lobby of the Edwards House in Jackson. He had just returned. "That's one hell of a place they got out there,"

Willie Morris is the Daily Texan *editor that everyone always remembers. His classic memoir* North Toward Home *(Houghton Mifflin Company, 1967) is an account of his growing up in Mississippi; his coming to Austin to attend the University and, later, work as editor of the* Texas Observer; *and his move to New York City, where he became the youngest editor-in-chief of* Harper's, *America's oldest magazine.* North Toward Home *is divided into three sections: Mississippi, Texas, and New York. This chapter is composed of excerpts from the book that deal specifically with Morris's experiences on the UT campus.*

he said. They had a main building thirty stories high, a baseball field dug right out of stone, artificial moonlight for street lamps, the biggest state capitol in the Republic, and the goddamndest student newspaper you ever saw. "I think you ought to go to school out there," he said. "Can't nuthin' in *this* state match it." [. . .]

FROM "TEXAS," CHAPTER I

I emerged from that bus frightened and tired, after having come 500 miles non-stop over the red hills of Louisiana and the pine forests of East Texas. The three men who met me—appalled, I was told later, by my green trousers and the National Honor Society medal on my gold-plated watch chain—were the kind that I briefly liked and admired, for their facility at small talk, their clothes, their manner, but whom I soon grew to deplore and finally to be bored by. They were the kind who made fraternities tick, the favorites of the Dean of Men at the time, respectable B or C-plus students, tolerable athletes, good with the Thetas or the Pi Phis; but one would find later, lurking there inside of them despite—or maybe because of—their good fun and jollity, the ideals of the insurance salesman and an aggressive distrust of anything approaching thought. One of them later told me, with the seriousness of an early disciple, that my table manners had become a source of acute embarrassment to all of them. That night they drove me around the campus, and they were impressed that I knew from my map-reading where the University library was, for two of them were not sure.

It was early fall, with that crispness in the air that awakened one's senses and seemed to make everything wondrously alive. My first days there I wandered about that enormous campus, mingling silently with its thousands of nameless students. I walked past the fraternity and sorority houses, which were like palaces to me with their broad porches and columns and patios, and down "The Drag" with its bookstores and restaurants, a perfectly contained little city of its own. On a slight rise dominating the place was a thirty-story skyscraper called the "Tower," topped

The UT campus in the 1950s. *From the Prints and Photographs Collection—UT Buildings: Main and Tower, Center for American History, the University of Texas at Austin. (DI 02407)*

with an edifice that was a mock Greek temple; the words carved on the white sandstone said, *"Ye Shall Know the Truth and the Truth Shall Make You Free,"* causing me to catch my breath in wonder and bafflement. That first morning I took the elevator to the top, and looked out on those majestic purple hills to the west, changing to lighter shades of blue or a deeper purple as wisps of autumn clouds drifted around the sun; this, they would tell me, was the Great Balcones Divide, where the South ended and the West began, with its stark, severe landscape so different from any I had known before. I saw the state capitol, only a few blocks to the south, set on its sloping green acres, its pink granite catching the morning light, and away to the east the baseball field dug into the native rock, and the football stadium, the largest and most awesome I had ever seen. Then down again to the campus, where all the furious construction and demolition was going on, and where the swarms of students back for another year greeted each other

23

Willie Morris, as he appeared in the "Outstanding Students" section of the 1956 yearbook. *From the* Cactus *yearbook (1956, p. 423), Center for American History, the University of Texas at Austin. (DI 02392)*

with such shouts and screams of delight, war-whoops, and hoohaws and wild embracing, and twangy "hello there's" with the "r's" exploited as nowhere else in the South, that I suddenly felt unbearably displaced and alone. Everything around me was brisk, burgeoning, *metropolitan*. It was bigger than Memphis when I was twelve. [. . .]

Old Brackenridge Hall, a yellow-brick affair with Spanish stucco roofs, stood right at the edge of the long intramural field, only a quarter of a mile from the capitol, and just across a narrow street from a line of dingy shops and greasy cafés. We called it "The Slum Area," not only for its general dinginess but for its violence, both organized and sporadic, which erupted inevitably on the weekend nights after the beer houses across the street closed down. Brackenridge Hall was

where life was, stripped of its pretenses, where one saw every day the lonely, the pathetic, the hopeless young men—often poor though sometimes not, often ignorant but not always, but never anything if not various. Here a fairly sensitive boy could not avoid a confrontation with his basic and bare-boned self, and see a big state university in its true dimensions. My first roommate, who flunked out soon enough with five F's and a D-plus, was an alcoholic from Dallas who saw giant roaches in the middle of the night, though the roaches may have been for my benefit. He would throw his sliderule against the wall, or piss in the trashcan from a range of six feet. As I sat in front of my typewriter composing my pieces for the *Daily Texan*, he and his friends played poker and drank rotgut bourbon on the other side of the table, interrupting themselves occasionally to make fun of my literary output which, when they read it, to their eternal honor, they did not appreciate.

I lived on the fourth floor, with a room overlooking the intramural field and the entire Slum Area, and down on the third floor lived the baseball players. I became a sort of poet laureate of that group, the resident egghead, it may have been, because I at least tried to study my books, and I actually did try to write for the student paper, which they called "The Daily Wipe."

Their floor was unquestionably the filthiest establishment I have ever seen, and from it emanated the most savage and grotesque, though until now unrecorded, happenings at the University of Texas in the 1950s. It was the decade of McCarthy, of Eisenhower and Dulles, the decade of students that David Riesman would characterize for posterity as outer-directed, the silent generation, I think it was called. These were promising labels, but they missed the closer truth, for real life at the University of Texas in the 1950s was like a circle with many rings—the smallest ring in the middle consisting of those students who were conscious of the labels and what they meant, the other inner circles progressively less aware. At the outside of that ring, the farthest out of all, was the third floor of Brackenridge Hall. They came from small ranch towns and middle-sized cities on the plains, and it was their decade right along with Ike's. Old newspapers covered the floors, and two of their number slept on cots in the hall so that one room could be a combination TV room, bar, and pornography library. Every so often they had rummage sales there, and for bargain prices tried to get rid of old water-wings, empty bottles, stale socks, and waterlogged baseballs. Dust and dirt covered the newspapers and the walls. Held most in contempt there were leaders of student government, fraternities, and deans, and they could smell out a stuffed shirt fifty yards away.

They wandered around at night in the pipes under the campus, breaking into office buildings through the sewage system in search of examination papers. Somewhere under there they found the mechanism which controlled the big clock on top of the Tower, and whenever the chimes struck eighteen, twenty, or twenty-four, I knew they were down there again. One afternoon I went up to the top of the Tower with one of them and his girl; when we were on the observation deck he suddenly climbed over the barrier, balanced himself on a rainpipe, looked toward the ground thirty stories below, and shouted: "*He-haw*: Sani Flush!" They would spend hours on cheat notes, for they felt that an elaborate and successful set of cheat notes was a work of art, and in itself a kind of intellectual achievement. These were cunningly indexed with rubber bands for manual maneuvering, so that for a quick look at the Causes of the American Revolution one had only to flick the rubber band to C—amid there, sure enough, were all seven causes, and in the right order. On a history identification test, one of them, his cheat notes not working, identified Daniel Webster as a colored Senator from Arkansas.

Once they caught several cadets from Texas A&M, the rival school out in the boondocks, marauding around the campus at night, and summoned aid from the whole dormitory; they shaved the Aggies' heads, painted them in orange and white enamel, paraded them at close drill around the intramural field, and in an unexpected burst of Christian charity sent them home in time for reveille. For fifty cents they would take anyone to see the cadavers in the Biology Building. They had a public address system which they would occasionally place in the window of the third floor and turn on at full blast. Once I was standing at rigid attention in the ranks of the ROTC on the intramural field while in total silence the troops were being reviewed by a general from San Antonio. Suddenly I heard a booming voice down the field, loud enough to be heard all the way to the capitol building: "Private Morris, Private Willie Morris, Company D, Squad

C, take charge of your troops and dismiss them!" At another ROTC drill I noticed them up in the window again, fiddling with the loudspeaker, and I feared the worst, but the voice merely said: "The War is over, boys! General Lee just gave his sword to ol' Grant! Go home to your families and your crops!"

They spied on parked cars behind the baseball field, sneaking right up to the windows and looking inside, then startling the passionate couples by setting off firecrackers under the cars and shouting and circling around like Apache Indians. Some two dozen of them, myself included, hiding in the grass under the bleachers at the baseball field late one night, watched while the starting pitcher for next day's game performed the act of love on a waitress on the pitcher's mound. The only times I saw them attentive, or ruminative, was during "Dragnet," or "The Ed Sullivan Show," or when they were listening to telephone conversations with an elaborate device that tapped the dormitory switchboard. All this was far more representative of the American state university generation in the 1950s than deans would likely have admitted. Nihilism was more articulate than silence, and more colorful than respectability. In the souls of all of us is anarchy, and it can erupt on a whim—especially in the young. That is why college administrators, like politicians, would have us believe they have had a glimpse of the higher truth. They need every defense they can get.

The student newspaper, *The Daily Texan*, turned out to be one of the two or three best college dailies in America, with an old and honorable tradition. It was housed in a brand-new building in the middle of the campus, and its physical set-up was impressive; there were individual offices for the important editors, a "city room" with a big copy desk and two wire-service tickers, and a chute to drop the copy down to a modern composing room below. I felt good just walking into those offices, for it was obvious they were designed for professionals.

In its finest moments, and they had been often, *The Daily Texan* had defended the spirit of a free university even when the University of Texas itself was unable or unwilling to do so, and in these periods it had reached an eloquence and displayed a courage that would have challenged the mature profession.

The tolerant seniors who ran it were bemused enough to give me a weekly column in my first semester, to report on the hundred or more college papers I was assigned to read every week. Here I began to read about strange ideas like integration, and issues of academic freedom, and observations that Dwight D. Eisenhower might be something of a bore. This was heady stuff indeed. On some nights I would stay up until three or four in the morning in my dormitory room, with the newspapers scattered on the tables and floors, trying to understand the incomprehensible goings-on in Berkeley or Ann Arbor or Colorado Springs or Chapel Hill. I gradually began to see the differences in all these papers; the ones from Harvard or Yale and a few big state universities were almost daringly outspoken, and kept talking about "conformity" and "self-satisfaction" in a way that both mystified and aroused me, but the great majority which poured in from all over America spoke a tongueless idiom, imploring students to turn over a new leaf at the start of each semester, give blood to a blood drive, collect wood for a bonfire, or use their leisure time more wisely. Something was out of order here, but I did not know quite what or why. I also wrote sports, covering the minor stories that would be given to me, and came under the blunt criticism of hard-headed types who may have been turning out the best sentences on the campus in those days. Once I wrote 2000 words on a baseball game; the six veteran sports writers, gleeful, pejorative, and smelling of Lone Star Beer, pointed out for me that the only thing I had neglected to provide was the score. . . .

Once I was invited to the apartment of a young graduate student and his wife. The walls of their apartment were lined with books, more books than I had ever seen before in a private dwelling—books everywhere and on everything. I was astonished; I tried to talk with those people, but I was unaccountably shy, and I kept looking at their books out of the corner of my eye, amid wondering if I should *say* something about them, or ask perhaps if they were for sale or if they formed some kind of special exhibit. It is a rare experience for certain young people to see great quantities of books in a private habitat for the first time, and to hear ideas talked about seriously in the off hours.

Good God, they were doing it for pleasure, or so it seemed. The wife, who was also a graduate student, asked me what I wanted to do with myself when I graduated from college. "I want to be a writer," I said, but not even thinking about it until the words were out; my reply surprised me most of all, but it was much more appropriate in those surroundings to have said that instead of "sports announcer," which probably constituted my first choice. "What do you want to write about?" she persisted. "Just . . . *things*," I said, turning red. That night, stirred by the conversation and by all the books I had seen, I went to the library, promising myself to read every important book that had ever been written. I was at a loss, because I did not have the faintest notion where to start. I picked out the most imposing volumes I could find—Lord Bryce on the American Commonwealth, which put me to sleep for ten nights in a row. But once this fire is lit, to consume and to know, it can burn on and on. I kept going back to the library, taking out tall stacks of books and reading them in a great undigested fury: Hemingway, Faulkner, Wolfe, Dreiser, anything in the American literature and American history shelves that looked promising. I started buying Modern Library books with the money I made writing for the newspaper, and I pledged to myself, as Marilyn Monroe had, that I would read them all, and in alphabetical order.

I believe now that the University of Texas was somehow beginning to give me an interest and a curiosity in something outside my own parochial ego. It was beginning to suggest the power not merely of language, but the whole unfamiliar world of experience and evocation which language served. That world was new, and the recognition of its existence was slow, uncertain, and immature. Books and literature, I was beginning to see, were not for getting a grade, not for the utilitarian purpose of being considered a nice and versatile boy, not just for casual pleasure, but subversive as Socrates and expressions of man's soul. It took me years to understand that words are often as important as experience, because words make experience last, but here, in the spring of my freshman year, there were men who were teaching me these things, perhaps with very little hope that anyone in their classrooms remotely cared, and I think perhaps I may have been listening. Freshman English was the first step; it was often the first and last time that many young people, headed in a state like Texas for insurance or business or the Junior League, might have had for a kind of small internal salvation.

For freshman English there was Frank Lyell, a fellow Mississippian, and it was his high values, giving my outrageous themes D's and C's when I had expected A's as something of a birthright, which first suggested that the editorial texture I had given the Yazoo High *Flashlight* would hardly serve in a world where English was master tongue. This was not merely a matter of syntax, discipline, and unheard-of-words. There came an awareness that loose, insensitive, and poorly formed language belie a loose, insensitive, and poorly formed mind. Lyell assigned a 2000-word autobiography, which I began with a description of the fading lonely sunlight outside Brackenridge Hall, went back through seventeen years of baseball, religion, and small-town hopes, and ended up in a volley of rhetoric in the same place six hours later. One sentence read: "My dog Skip and I wandered the woods and swamplands of our Mississippi home shooting rabbits and squirrels." To which the professor appended the comment: "Who was the better shot, you or the dog?" I was enraged. I can remember one morning the teacher reading a passage from a novel and asking "Isn't that marvelous?" The sorority girls sat there taking down everything he said, while in the back of the room I could see three or four ranch boys, who always sat there in a self-contained group, nudging each other and snickering over the teacher's unusual recommendations.

Yet there *was* loneliness in those fading Sunday afternoons, and madness in the meaningless activities that served to make one versatile and well rounded. The editors of the campus humor magazine, a cynical and knowing lot, must have recognized this. In May one of them told me to be sure and read the next issue; there was to be an article on me. It turned out to be a burlesque of a young campus character named Willie X, who had joined everything and wanted to know everything. Late one night he was walking down the University "Drag" reading a pamphlet, and as he crossed 24th Street something fortunate occurred for the University of Texas. He was run over by a two-ton truck. [. . .]

There was a core of serious, rather independent souls gathered around an institution called the "Christian Faith and Life Community," one of those robust experiments in community intellectual living that was in such stark contrast to the comfortable campus life of the 1950s. Despite the incomprehensible language they spoke, existential with a thin overlay of Calvin, which discouraged outsiders without training in structural linguistics or those who could not afford an interpreter, they kept their directions inside (sometimes, perhaps, *too* south-southwest of the inner light). The "Y" was a haven for other serious students, and as a forerunner to the flowering of the ecumenical movement encouraged controversial seminars and lectures on questions that usually mattered. These groups, and they were good people, were the repositories of whatever liberalism existed on a conscious level at the University of Texas at the time.

From all these things I had, by my junior year, become strangely removed, both intellectually and emotionally. I had ceased to be the torrid activist I had been before, and I was chiefly interested in the panorama. I knew so many different people—lonely twenty-year-old-failures who drank coffee and ate cheesecake at 1 A.M. in the Snak Shak, suave leaders of clubs amid committees, janitors, sorority girls, campus cops, lady booksalesmen, ranch boys from West Texas, grubby graduate students, and an occasional beauty queen—one in particular, though she was a Phi Beta Kappa. They are now lawyers, politicians, manufacturers of toilet seats and garbage-can lids, Junior Leaguers, schoolteachers, members of the John Birch Society, doubles in Hollywood westerns, and wives of New York editors. [. . .]

} {

I still lived in the same old dormitory, in a bigger and more officious room; I remember the place now on a late autumn afternoon of 1954. The sunlight streamed into the room from beyond the intramural field, and my roommate Collie, a genial West Texas ranch boy from Pecos, sat at the window chewing tobacco and watching the crowds drift by from the football game we had all been to in the afternoon. The football scores would start coming in on my old red portable radio that the radio station in Yazoo had given me—first from the little Eastern schools like Colby and Bowdoin and Amherst, or Niagara and Allegheny and Susquehanna, then the Ivy League scores which were just exercises, on to the big Midwestern or Southern ones that mattered, drifting slowly westward across the country like a great rolecall of America. Collie would sit there chewing and spitting into the trash can and complaining about his old hometown girlfriend, who had joined a fancy sorority called Zeta Tau Alpha and then promptly deserted him, and from downstairs we could hear the baseball players hooking up the dormitory firehose to wet down the Baylor band when they returned to their bus under the third-floor window. The lights on the beer joints of the Slum Area appeared, red-and-purple neons blinking on and off in the autumn dusk, and in the street near the gymnasium someone shouted, "Hook 'Em, Horns!" and the Texas band came by in their gaudy orange uniforms playing "Texas Fight." Then they halted and played "The Eyes," and from our window we could see all the Texas fans stop and come to attention and sing the words, for souls had been touched by the last-minute victory on that incomparable day. From the lower depths of the dormitory a voice could be heard shouting *"Chicken Farm!"* over and over again, the weekly call for the carload driving to the country whorehouse in La Grange. By this time the Greek temple on top of the Tower would be lit in orange, and the whole campus was sure to be a pendulum of activity—parties, dances, socials, beer-busts, barbecues, meetings of the old grads. Collie and I would go drink a beer in one of the Slum Area dives, already beginning to fill up with boys without dates or without cars to go anywhere; then I would leave him there, bitching about small-town women, and head straight for the sorority house where Celia lived. The Saturday night scene on the campus, as I walked across it to the "Drag," left nothing to the imagination—people in blue jeans and tuxedos, pedal-pushers and evening gowns, Stetson hats amid orange string ties, and tiny clusters of foreign students from Saudi Arabia or India with nowhere to go and no football game to talk about. . . .

Finally, in the spring of that year, having worked for *The Daily Texan* as sports editor, writer of my column called "The Round-up," and editorialist, and having viewed the campus for two and a half years as both a frenetic participant and a detached observer, I decided to file for the editorship. The race was an elective one, and I began campaigning from one end of the campus to the other. In the big student rally where all the candidates were questioned, someone asked me about integration. I replied:

> There's an inner turmoil in the United States; there's an inner turmoil in me. The Supreme Court decision was inevitable, but I don't think any universal rule can be applied to the entire nation when the time for integration comes. I don't think Ole Miss is ready for integration. I think the University of Texas is. [. . .]

FROM "TEXAS," CHAPTER 2

It was a viciously hot Texas afternoon in June when I moved my ten or fifteen favorite books, a toothbrush, an electric razor, an extra pair of shoes, and an emergency pint of Old Forester into the editor's office of the *Daily Texan*. Had I been able to predict the events of the next twelve months, I would have included the Book of Common Prayer.

We published the paper only twice a week in the summer, and the days drifted by in that heavy lethargy that anyone who has spent a summer in Texas would know so well. It was a time for lazy reading under the magnificent ancient trees of the campus, for swimming in the ice-cold waters of the natural springs at Barton's, for beer-drinking and political talk around the tables in the back of the old German beer hall. There was leisure enough to begin planning the editorial issues for the regular school year, when close to 20,000 students, a record number, would enroll, and to talk to anyone I wished to on the campus about the questions that would matter. [. . .]

FROM "TEXAS," CHAPTER 3

A great irony occasionally besets an American state university, for it allows and at its best encourages one to develop his critical capacities, his imagination, his values; at the same time, in its institutional aspects, a university under pressure can become increasingly wary of the very intent and direction of the ideals it has helped spawn. It is too easy, too much a righteous judgment, to call this attitude hypocrisy, for actually it is a kind of schizophrenia. This involves more than a gap between preaching and practicing; it involves the splitting of a university's soul. There can be something brutal about a university's teaching its young people to be alive, aware, critical, independent, and free, and then, when a threatening turn is taken, to reject by its actual behavior the substance of everything it claims for itself. Then ideals and critical capacities exist in a vacuum. They are sometimes ignored, and in extreme instances victimized. And the greater society suffers as well.

For a year I had been reading heavily in politics, history, and the journalism of the great editors. I took to my heart the memorable statement in Joseph Pulitzer's will, now reprinted every day on the editorial pages of the *St. Louis Post-Dispatch*, and which I subsequently tacked to the wall in my office next to my typewriter, as I have in every office where I have worked: "that it will always fight for progress and reform, never tolerate injustice or corruption, always fight demagogues of all parties, never belong to any party, always oppose privileged classes and public plunderers, never lack sympathy for the poor, always remain devoted to the public welfare, never be satisfied merely with printing news, always be drastically independent, never be afraid to attack wrong, whether by predatory plutocracy or predatory poverty."

I read the journalism of H. L. Mencken, Lincoln Steffens, William Allen White, S. S. McClure, Bernard DeVoto, Hodding Carter, Ralph McGill, and Brann the Iconoclast. I read the files of *The Daily Texan* itself, learning of different and more alive times—the great editorials of Horace Busby, who brought sanity and courage to the campus during the Rainey disaster of the 1940s, D. B. Hardeman, Ronnie Dugger, and others. The political climate of the state had become more pointed to me, and in long and sometimes agonizing talks with the brightest and most perceptive student leaders I had thought out the huge responsibility of the largest and most prominent student newspaper in the South in a period when the integration issue was coming alive; my experience with my hometown Citizens Council had helped me judge the extent of my own personal change, and showed the sad barbarism of intransigence. I was suffused with the ideals of freedom of expression and the open marketplace. I had the most emphatic belief that this freedom should be used to positive purposes, that freedom is as freedom does, that the pages of this newspaper should reflect the great diversity of the place I had come to know, that the University of Texas was too much a part of its state and of the rest of the world to avoid editorials on significant questions beyond the campus, and that the campus itself—as so many others then—was bogged down in dullness, complacency, and the corporate mentality. My deficits, as I fully realized later, were a self-righteousness, a lack of subtlety in polemic, and an especially underdeveloped awareness of the diplomatic approach.

President Kennedy, Theodore Sorensen later wrote, liked to improvise on the passage from Ecclesiastes: "A time to weep and a time to laugh, a time to mourn and a time to dance, a time to fish and a time to cut bait." I did not know as much about bait-cutting then as I would later. But I wanted the paper which would briefly be mine to be a living thing, distinctive and meaningful, in both its own tradition and the tradition of hard-hitting, outspoken American journalism. The University of Texas itself had taught me to place a high value on these qualities; the necessity of the free marketplace of ideas was apparently high on its list of formal priorities. It was in the books in its libraries, the valedictions of its deans, administrators, commencement speakers, even on the buildings and statues around its campus. You cannot make gestures of support for all these things and expect them to have no context. They either apply to a particular setting or they do not apply at all. They are either watered down to appease the distrusts of a power faction or they are not. But uphold these ideas long enough, frequently enough, and with such inspiration, and some young people are not only going to believe in them, they are going to believe in them with the fervor of the young, and even arrange their lives and their sense of honor by them.

So it was that I came out fighting hard, and the reactions were no sooner than immediate. I erred, first of all, into editorializing occasionally about state politics, particularly its twin deities, oil and gas. I suppose the authorities had not expected a gentle-natured Southern boy to overreach into areas ruled by hidden divinities; a student editor in Texas could blaspheme the Holy Spirit and the Apostle Paul, but irreverence stopped at the wellhead. We were going against a set of scandals and money frauds that had rocked Governor Shivers' administration. We were seeking intelligence and good will on integration and lauding most Texans for their tolerant attitude. Occasionally we chided John Foster Dulles' view of the rest of the world. Against the reactions from the school administration we categorically defended student press freedom and our right to comment as we wished on controversial state and national issues. We were committing the crime of being vigorous and outspoken, naïvely idealistic and exuberantly but not radically liberal in a state that at that time had little patience with either, on a campus where exuberance was reserved for the minor furies, and in a decade which encouraged little essential ebullience in the young.

There began a series of summonses to President Logan Wilson's office, much like a grade-school student who had been caught throwing spitballs in class being called to the principal; I was immediately reminded of my tribulations with my fourth-grade teacher, the evangelical Miss Abbott. Wilson's personal secretary would telephone and say, "Mr. Morris, the President would like to confer with you. Could we see you at three?" Ushered into the offices of the principal, who ruled over an academic domain stretching from El Paso to Galveston, I would wait in the outer chamber for an appropriate five minutes and admire there the lush carpet six inches deep; then the President was ready to see me. I would be offered menthol cigarettes and dealt with soothingly, charmingly, and with the condescension befitting the occasion. These biting editorials had to stop, though for a while the issue was not presented quite that frontally. There were meetings with the corps of deans, especially the one who had been a captain in the Navy and who believed that when an order is given, people should hop-to; anyone to the political left of Eisenhower, he once told me, was stupid if not downright treacherous. At first he was baffled, but this gave way to rage; there was no bemusement in these quarters. The slight liquid film that glazed his eyes as I came into his office suggested that he was keeping himself under control with some difficulty; his apparent preference was to assign me to the brig. A good part of the time I was scared, and Logan Wilson must have been equally miserable; he was beginning to get caught in a vicious crossfire. The political appointees who ran the University were beginning to use the old and tested dogmatisms. And in the end more people than President Wilson and I were to be involved.

Finally the regents erupted. At a meeting with several student leaders, including good friends of mine who were president and vice-president of the student body, they declared that the student paper should not discuss controversial state and national topics, and that college students were not interested in these things anyway. *The Daily Texan*, they said, had especially gone too far astray in commenting on a piece of natural gas legislature. There, now, was the rub! A little later they handed down a censorship edict. This was based, they said, not on principle but on legal considerations. They cited the rider on state appropriations bills, which stipulated that no state money "shall be used for influencing the outcome of any election or the passage or defeat of any legislative measure." Then they advanced one step further, a major step as it turned out, and announced that "editorial preoccupation with state and national political controversy" would be prohibited.

My friends and I on the *Texan* did some painful soul-searching after that announcement. Should we give in and avoid an agonizing fight? Was a fight worth it? The next morning, as I remember it, I drove out to Lyndon Johnson's lakes, to the one my beauty queen and I liked so much; I sat around under a scrub oak for a time reading some Thomas Jefferson. Then I came back to town and talked with Bergen, our managing editor, a shy, deceptive little man with an abundance of courage, and we decided in thirty minutes what Tom Jefferson likely would have recommended all along.

That began one of the greatest controversies in the history of American college journalism. Bergen and I stayed up all night in the editor's office, planning and writing editorials under the new censorship arrangement. We submitted critical editorials the next day, attacking the implications of the regents' order, along with a guest editorial from *The New York Times* on the natural gas legislation and several paragraphs from Thomas Jefferson on press freedom. All were rejected. The Jefferson quotes had been included in a personal column, and when he was censored there was thunder in the heavens, fire in the sky was reported over Monticello, and a thirty-minute moratorium on bourbon was declared in Charlottesville. But the student majority on the publications board outvoted the faculty representatives, and all the editorials were printed in toto in the next issue.

We kept right on going. We authorized a brilliant young law student, the "attorney general" for the student government, to examine the legal consequences of the Regent's order. He counseled with some of the state's most respected lawyers and legal scholars and refuted the applicability of the appropriations rider. The Regents' interpretation of this rider, he argued, had "terrifying implications" and could be used in the same way to stifle legitimate comment among students, faculty, and quasi-independent corporations housed on the campus like the alumni organization, the student government, and the law review.

In retrospect a number of things stand out clearly. One Regent saying, "The *Texan* has gone out of bounds in discussing issues pertaining to oil and gas because 66 percent of Texas tax money comes from oil and gas." And another adding, "We're just trying to hold Willie to a college yell." ("There are our young barbarians, all at play!") . . . A journalism professor coming up to me the day after the controversy began and whispering, "I just want to shake your hand. I'm proud to know you." . . . My parents phoning long-distance from Mississippi and asking, "Son, you in trouble? They won't kick you out of school so close to graduation, will they?" . . . At one of the interminable meetings of the publications board, one faculty representative saying to me, "You know what you are? You're a *propagandist*," a gripping judgment coming from an associate professor of advertising . . . And I recall one afternoon soon after the regents' action when I telephoned J. Frank Dobie, the indomitable and lovable old *pater familias* of Texas writers, who had lost his own teaching job at the University in the 1940s, and asked if he would consider writing to the letters column commenting on our troubles. "Hell," he said, "I been workin' on one all mornin'." The Board of Regents, Dobie's letter said, "are as much concerned with free intellectual enterprise as a razorback sow would be with Keats' 'Ode on a Grecian Urn'"—a well-known statement now despite the fact that this phrase, and many another colorful one, were deleted after I had gone home to sleep and the paper was going to press.

One day one of the few outspoken old souls on the faculty in that period, an English professor who had never ceased to fight the political appointees with scorn and satire even in the 1940s, stood up in a fac-

ulty meeting and asked what the student newspaper's troubles *meant* in terms of the entire university. "We should discuss this matter," he said, waving his walking cane at his colleagues, "and deplore a contemptuous, cynical attitude toward what the student body or what an elected student leader may say." He spoke of the "dignity of the student" as a "new citizen"; a university's funds, he said, "should not be meant to *stifle* discussion but to encourage it." There was no further discussion, however, from the faculty. I wrote a lead editorial on his speech and entitled it "Whispers in a Sleepy Lagoon." The night of its publication, as I sat at my desk eating a cold hamburger and drinking my fourth cup of black coffee, one of the administrative deans telephoned. "You published that editorial," he said, "but do you know that professor is runnin' around on his wife?" I had barely slept in a week, and at this point the fatigue had robbed me of any semblance of cynicism or humor. "Why you old bastard!" was all I could say, and hung up the telephone.

Looking back on it now, I had forgotten what a nasty time it was, how it sapped the patience of all of us on both sides, and the sad indignity with which many decent but weak men had to try to enforce official demands that I think they would have preferred in their hearts to ignore. One grew to be sympathetic, if not respectful, of some of these men, stripped as they were of power and sometimes, I believe, ashamed.

Finally, after more troubles, after we ran blank spaces and editorials entitled "Let's Water the Pansies," or "Don't Walk on the Grass" and held to our prerogatives to publish what we wished, there was a loosening up. There were no further official orders, and we remained free. But I was obsessed with the fear that in winning the battle we had lost the war, and that we had fought back wrongly and badly—and that the fight had not been worth it.

Yet I do not believe it was coincidence that in May of that year the Regents and the administration sought to impose in the general faculty a sweeping set of restrictions on the involvement of University of Texas faculty members in politics and political issues. One of the administration's spokesmen described these restrictions as the drawing of "a little circle" around political responsibilities. "That little circle," one young professor, the philosopher John Silber, said, "happens to comprise 90 percent of my political concerns." The issue was resoundingly defeated. For whom was the bell trying to toll? I believed then there was a connection there; the contempt for an independent student voice trying to engage itself in important issues in that age of McCarthy amid silence was reflected in an effort to do lasting damage to a state university's most basic civil liberties. Perhaps if the student newspaper had not chosen to meet the whole question head-on and in public, the controlling political faction would have thought anything easy and possible. Perhaps we won something more than a battle after all.

People would tell me long afterward that this sort of thing could never happen again in the later climate of the University of Texas, that everything became much better, that academic freedom, and freedom of expression, had been won, and were old issues now. I am convinced this is true. The 1960s were not the 1950s, and at our state universities these issues would become, not more straightforward, but more complex, involving considerations of the very quality of the mass society. In 1956 the issue was a direct one, and it became bigger than *The Daily Texan*, bigger than the Board of Regents, bigger than the University itself—and it could never be old-fashioned.

} {

I have often asked myself in the years that followed, would I do all this again? I would be less than honest if I answered that question simply.

At the time, as I understood later, the tone, style, and content of public discourse meant much more to me than the practical considerations of how one arranges complicated matters in feasible, flexible terms. There could have been more subtle and practical ways of dealing with the problem that confronted us. For this kind of personal diplomacy I was too immature and too impressionable.

Yet I was twenty years old; the real antagonists were in the seats of power. To my credit I knew who the enemy was. It would be an unwarranted personal renunciation for me to say retrospectively that the indignation I felt in 1956 was unjustified. It is legitimate to assume that editors of student papers at any university have a right to arouse the authorities, and within the laws of libel to bring them down on him. It is right

to be able to carry on an aggressive campaign against an ethic they consider sterile and contemptuous. The attempt to censor *The Daily Texan* in 1956 involved not a displacement of dissent, but the running roughshod over it by real power, and the more sophisticated kind of criticism that served as its forum—the kind of wealth which still encourages the idea in America that anything can be bought, including culture. A friend of mine in the state legislature would say to me a few years later, perhaps Texas can never become a truly civilized place until its great natural resources are gone.

For three years I had written my column, "The Round-Up," and in my "30" piece that spring, the last one I wrote, I said, with too many genuflections to Thomas Wolfe:

The University of Texas, I fear, has travelled all too swiftly toward beautiful buildings and sterling reputations. Its leaders, in submitting to those who relish the corporate purse, have too often, and even without reluctance, betrayed the corporation of ideas . . . It has existed at the whim of those forces which would readily crush its heart, its soul, and its mind.

The quick Texas rich, who apply the values of fast money to the values of higher education, have dealt foolishly and cruelly with the prerogatives of the spirit . . . As a result, our University condones the tyranny of the majority, and it encourages in its students sedate complacency to the national and regional arbiter.

It must lead, not follow . . . it must insist that society and the race can be made better. It must strive to show our people, our uneducated and our quick rich, that our civilization is doomed when the material can coerce the human spirit.

I believe that our University is lost, and that being lost has been silent and afraid, but that someday its destiny shall be fulfilled more courageously, more magnificently, and more humbly than we have ever imagined. It is in the bright promise of this vision that I close.

At graduation at the end of that year the air was heavy with the scents of the berry trees; most of the students were long since gone, and the campus was more lovely and still than I had ever seen it before.

The chimes on the Tower rang with stirring processionals to the Class of 1956, and proud country parents stood in diffident little groups watching their children march past. I received my diploma, and before a packed audience walked out the wrong door of the auditorium. At the reception afterward a journalism professor said, "I told my wife, there goes Morris, lost again," and the mother of one of my classmates walked up to me and said, "Why, you look too *innocent* to have caused all that newspaper trouble." The next day I left the campus, my '47 Plymouth loaded with books and the paraphernalia of four years, and drove all night one final time to the place I had come from.

RICHARD A. HOLLAND

Hairy Ranger, Wonder Wart-Hog, and the Sweet Young Thing Interviews with *Texas Ranger* Editors Frank Stack and Pat Brown

During the 1950s and 1960s a succession of talented individuals put their marks on Texas student publications that placed UT in the national forefront of college newspapers and magazines. To hit the high points, *Daily Texan* editors in the middle and late fifties included Ronnie Dugger, Horace Busby, and Willie Morris, all of whom went on to have legendary careers in politics and journalism; and a short-lived but influential sixties student literary magazine titled *Riata* was an incubator for high-caliber Texas writers such as Dave Oliphant and Dave Hickey. But it was another student publication, the sometimes scruffy and scurrilous *Texas Ranger*, that captured the hearts and minds of the students of the Silent Generation.

By the late forties the *Ranger* had been in existence for decades as a light humor magazine that featured topical jokes and the occasional cartoon that poked fun at various aspects of campus life. As a fixture of campus life, the *Ranger* was witty and topical but not much more than that. Then around 1950, the staff and the magazine began to change. American satire was beginning to change and the Korean War–era students were beginning to be influenced by the beginnings of Beat culture.

During the decade of the fifties, there were two notable groups of "Rangeroos": the 1949–1953 group that included Rowland Wilson, Harvey Schmidt, Liz Smith, and Robert Benton; and the 1956–1958 staff that was led by the young cartoonist Frank Stack. The earlier group individually became creative powerhouses after they left the University. Rowland Wilson, who edited the *Ranger* during the 1951 academic year, was a brilliant cartoonist who came up with the lasting image of the magazine: a fat, mustachioed, hat-and-boot–wearing outlaw named Hairy Ranger. In his postgraduate life Wilson became an influential cartoonist for magazines including the *New Yorker* and *Playboy* and had a very successful advertising career.

Among many other accomplishments, Harvey Schmidt co-wrote with Tom Jones the longest-running play in the history of the New York the-

Richard Holland was a devoted reader of The Texas Ranger *during his undergraduate days at the University.*

atre, *The Fantasticks* (1960–2002); Robert Benton became the influential art director for *Esquire* magazine and has had a distinguished film career, including co-writing the screenplay for *Bonnie and Clyde* in 1967 and directing over a dozen films including *Kramer vs. Kramer*, for which he won the 1980 Academy Award for best director; Liz Smith became one of America's leading syndicated columnists and was featured in a homecoming appearance at a Texas Book Festival.

Frank Stack enrolled at UT in September 1956 and immediately discovered the *Ranger*. By the February 1957 issue, the comical masthead identified him as "the power-mad freshman cartoon editor." Early in 2004 I conducted a series of e-mail interviews with Stack, who has had a distinguished career as a painter and professor of art at the University of Missouri, and who also is one of the country's best-known "underground" cartoonists and graphic novelists.

INTERVIEW WITH FRANK STACK

RICHARD HOLLAND: How was it you gravitated so quickly to the *Ranger* as a freshman?

FRANK STACK: I'd been seeing the *Ranger* since about 1952. My family visited Austin regularly, where my aunt Mozelle Morris was secretary to the director of libraries and my cousin Charles was a geology student. I loved Austin from the get-go, and I took *Rangers* back home to pore over and memorize. Of course I loved the work of Robert Benton, Rowland Wilson, John Frazier, and Harvey Schmidt, from '52 to about '54. Frazier was an art student, and a great cartoonist, whose gags were widely republished as examples of the best of college humor. He later went on to graduate school at Yale and a career as an art professor at one of the Ivy League women's colleges. The editors that immediately preceded my arrival in Austin were Jim Wright in '54 and James Hall in '55, both very funny writers, I thought. Some cartoonists I admired were Bill Klapp, Phil Bashara, Lee Ricks, and Bill West.

RH: Looking at a run of *Rangers* recently, I was struck by the similarities to the *Playboy* of the early days.

FS: I actually take exception to the idea that the *Ranger* was a rip of *Playboy*. The magazine scene then was very different than it was ten years later, and *very* different from what it is today. *Playboy* is one of the few magazines that hasn't changed significantly. We were

keenly aware of everything that was happening at the time, satirical art and writing across the board, and we were seeing such things in *Esquire, Punch, Life, Mad,* and especially the *New Yorker*—and also especially in the dozens of other college humor magazines, including *Yale Record, Harvard Lampoon, Ohio State Sundial, California Pelican, Arizona State Wildcat, Missouri Showme, Oklahoma State Cowboy.*

We stayed in close touch with the other humor mags and knew their history pretty well: distinguished alumni such as Robert Benchley and John Updike from the *Harvard Lampoon,* Mort Walker from *Missouri Showme,* Virgil Partch from *Arizona Wildcat.* William Faulkner and Chester Gould were college magazine staffers when they went to school.

Many of us later became pals of cartoonists and writers from other schools, such as Chuck Alverson from the *Pelican.* Some of us thought of *Playboy* as an overblown, rather immature but expensive and successful college humor magazine. Of course all of us aspired to work for something of the sort, and Bill Helmer (the editor who succeeded me in 1960) actually did, later, become a senior editor at *Playboy,* in charge of crime news.

RH: By your period of the magazine, it looks to me like the art dominated the copy—was that always true?

FS: It was by the time of Rowland Wilson, Harvey Schmidt, Robert Benton, and John Frazier (about 1950–55). The cartoons were always more important, I think, than the gray matter (and I don't mean brains). Or maybe they were just more important to me.

Creator of Hairy Ranger, Rowland Wilson went on to be a fabulously successful cartoonist and advertising man living for a time in London, whose cartoons have been appearing occasionally in magazines like *Playboy* and the *New Yorker* (if he's still alive—it's been 50 years!).

Benton, the only one of the group who I actually knew, went to New York to become art director of *Esquire* in its glory days, where he published illustrations by Robert Weaver and Tom Allen, as well as full-page watercolor cartoon ads (for New England Life Insurance) by Rowland Wilson. Later Benton wrote and directed movies, including *Places of the Heart, There was a Crooked Man,* and *Kramer vs. Kramer,* which won an academy award for best picture. He did an early screenplay for the first Superman (Christopher Reeve) film, but it wasn't used.

Schmidt was a very successful magazine illustrator for *Life, Esquire,* and others, but is perhaps best known as coauthor of the long-running off-Broadway musical *The Fantasticks*.

RH: So what was the *Ranger* like your freshman year?

FS: 1956–57 was a watershed year for the *Ranger*. The spring election '56 had resulted in Lee Ricks, a good cartoonist and illustrator, being elected editor, with Bill West and Jon Bracker as associate editor and managing editor, all talented and hard-working guys. But it turned out to be a disastrous first semester. The September issue had to be prepared during the summer, and Lee Ricks cracked under the pressure of having too much to do. It was his senior year, he'd just gotten married and had a new baby, *and* he was president of his fraternity. He resigned as *Ranger* editor before the October issue was ready to go. Bill West—wonderful funny cartoonist, chemistry major, pre-med—was promoted to editor and Jon Bracker to associate editor, and both of them were in a state of shock, with full responsibility for putting out the magazine suddenly thrust upon them. That was the state of affairs when I first walked in the door of the *Ranger* office as a freshman. I think I only saw Lee Ricks once. Bill West was rather desperate, but Jon Bracker held things together as the fortunes of the magazine sunk lower and lower. Poor sales led to poor advertising income and fewer pages. For at least one issue we were down to 24 pages, worst issue in memory by general agreement, and also the low point of circulation in many years, about 1,500.

Bill West didn't make his grades and flunked out at the end of the fall 1956 semester, so Jon Bracker (English major) took over as editor for the second semester, the third editor of 1956. It was the nadir of the magazine's career. To make matters worse, there was hardly any staff remaining. I think by November there were only five or six staffers, diehards only, including me, Jon Bracker, Harry Holland, Leonard Giesecke, and a couple of others. We did turn things around from that point forward, and by the end of the year we more than doubled circulation, got our page count back up to 32, then 40, pages and recruited an excellent and enthusiastic staff. So, naturally I developed an affectionate, and long-lasting respect for Jon Bracker in particular, but about equally for Harry Holland, Leonard Giesecke, Bill Klapp, Butch Barnes, and Robbie Powell (more than equal in her case—we were married in 1959, and stayed married until her death in 1998). To jump ahead a bit, by the end of 1958–59 school year, our official circulation was above 15,000, about ten times what it was at the end of 1956.

At the end of the 1956–57 school year Jon Bracker

graduated and started grad school, journalist Rudy Rochelle was appointed editor, and I, an art student, was associate editor. Bill Klapp, who had graduated earlier with an English degree, returned to Austin after a tour of duty as an army MP, to work toward an M.F.A. in art, and he enriched the *Ranger* art staff, along with Butch Barnes (art student), Harry Holland (flunked-out journalism major contributing remotely from the army), Rick, and me. Bill Helmer began to contribute articles, stories, and photographs, Lynn Ashby did regular humor pieces, and Murray Patton, already a professional commercial photographer, made our photo features, especially the cheesecake, look so good that *Playboy* contacted him about doing a photo shoot for them using one of our Girl of the Month models. She wouldn't pose nude, so that didn't happen. A couple of the Girl of the Month models that I (and Robbie) got to be long-term friends with were Nancy Schabbehar (who married cartoonist Butch Barnes) and Jackie Jenkins (later Alford). Rudy was a good editor, smart, clever and good to work with, and the *Ranger* thrived under his steady hand through the 1957–58 year. I was named editor for '58–'59.

RH: When I was a student I seemed to think there was an ongoing war between the Texas Student Publications Office and the *Ranger*.

FS: The Journalism School felt that it should have the *Ranger* under its control, and to a large extent it did, though there was never in my time a high percentage of journalists on the *Ranger* staff. They always had the power to close us down. TSP's manager, or whatever his title was, was Lloyd Edmonds, who controlled our production budget. There was a censorship board with at least one student member on it The main one I remember was a student council representative named Marjorie Menefee. The advertising people had little to do with the *Ranger*'s editorial staff. We all gave each other a hard time. Under my editorship I tried to work around the censors, and was annoyed by the censorship system (still am—forbidden words and subjects). My personal idea was, If they censor something we submit to them, I want *them*, not us, to be wrong. But there were some staffers, then and later, who relished the challenge of sneaking dirty stuff through.

We considered ourselves serious satirists with a sense of fun, not just naughty fellows. I argued that insults and zingers were not funny in themselves, unless there was an ironic or satirical point, and tried to apply that as editorial policy. "No insults unless they are true!" Jon

Bracker, Leonard Giesecke, and I aspired to the kind of authoritative satire of the *New Yorker* and *Punch*, rather than the sophomoric tone of *Playboy*. (I for one was absolutely appalled by the "Playboy Philosophy" and its guru Frank Sinatra). We were reading people like S. J. Perleman, James Thurber, Robert Benchley, Mark Twain, and some of our newer heroes were Jules Feiffer, Harvey Kurtzmann, Dwight MacDonald, J. D. Salinger, Walt Kelly, Ronald Searle, and even Charles Schulz.

RH: After your editorship, there was a period of a couple of years before the magazine reached its counter-culture peak, when it featured the art of Gilbert Shelton. I recall that Bill Helmer and Lynn Ashby ran the magazine in 1960–61.

FS: About the counter-culture question, I can only speak about the my own attitude and that of my close *Ranger* friends while I was involved with it, up to spring 1959. You couldn't say we were actually counter-culture. It was a few years too soon, and I think that the Helmer/Ashby years were, as you suggested, characterized by a different tone, more conservative in some sense, perhaps even less counter-culture, than my *Ranger* of 1958–59. But the Shelton, Crossley, Adkins time was the real thing. I think that Helmer, Bill Klapp, and I, and maybe even Lynn Ashby, considered ourselves as something of godfathers or elder statesmen of the Underground, with the youngsters like Shelton, Janis Joplin, Robert Crumb, and the other Stoned-Age real counter-culture folks benefiting from our more experienced tutelage. I think most of my generation of comic artists and satirists was friendly to the counter-culture and were proud of our role in helping form it.

RH: Did you know Gilbert Shelton when he was an undergraduate?

FS: Only for my last semester, when he brought a batch of cartoons to the office. And yes, he made a strong impression on everybody for both his comic talent *and* his extraordinary good looks. I loved his cartoons and immediately gave him a double-page feature in the middle of the magazine. We used everything he submitted. A year later I was in the goddam army. We got to know each other well in New York and have been close pals ever since. Gilbert entered grad school as a history major but then switched to art after doing a research paper on the Dada movement. He started from scratch as a freshman art major. According to him, Pat Brown stood head and shoulders above all the other art students and

he followed *her* to Cleveland. Others, including Pat herself, say that the two of them were the best artists in school at the time. Then Pat modestly asserts that there was little competition of the quality of Wilson, Frazier, Schmidt, Klapp, Barnes, etc. Of course, Tony Bell and Glenn Whitehead fell in there somewhere.

RH: How many of the other sixties folks did you know?

FS: Almost none except Gilbert. But I heard many stories about the group from Gilbert, who talked about them all the time. I knew Tony Bell a bit. Everybody knew what an extraordinary comic talent Lieuen Adkins was, and I did see a lot of his work. Pat I met only once, when Gilbert brought her along on a cross-country jaunt and crashed for a night in Columbia. Of course I liked her.

RH: Was their lifestyle really different from that of your late-fifties group on the magazine?

FS: Yes. The drug scene was only beginning by the time I left in spring 1959, and the music scene was pretty underground too. Most of the old crowd thought Gilbert was just way too wild— drug dealer, crazy motherfucker and all that. He didn't party with the old bunch much, except for Helmer, Ashby, Robbie, and me (and that was in NYC), and around us he was pretty conservative. But he was definitely the leader of the sixties group, and he and Helmer were the principal links between fifties and sixties folks.

RH: You also knew Shelton in New York? What was he like there?

FS: Gilbert was a masterful storyteller. In New York while I was in the army, stationed out on Governor's Island (pretty good place to be in the army if you have to be in the army), '61 and '62, Gilbert was in and out of the city, going back and forth between Austin, Cleveland, and New York. Helmer, with wife Pat and baby, was there editing men's magazines, Shelton worked on Stoopid Car Magazine (not the real title, but it might as well have been), and Ashby had a good job with the *New York Times* radio station, spending up all his money on telephone calls to Dorothy in Texas until they got married. Robbie and I got a housing allowance and lived uptown at 111 West 94th Street; Helmer was across the park on the East Side with a monumental collection of vintage comic books and a very pissed-off wife; Gilbert at first lived on the Lower East Side in [jazz bassist] Charlie Haden's apartment, on the walls of which he painted, at Charlie's request, horrific murals inspired by EC horror comics, then later moved to an apartment building in the Upper West Side 90s, where he learned to play 5-string banjo listening to Lester Flatt and Earl Scruggs records, and (to come to the point) hatched up the first batch of Wonder Warthog comics, with all the rest of us kibitzing and making suggestions, mostly and fortunately, of course, ignored by Gilbert. He originally roughed them out on yellow paper. I kept one of those sets of roughs, Masked Meanie maybe, among my papers for years. Maybe I could find it.

As Frank Stack suggests, the *Texas Ranger* of the early sixties became quite different. *Ranger* editor Bill Helmer was a graduate student in history who lived in a large house just east of the Capitol, in an area that is now state parking lots. His master's thesis was a history of the Thompson submachine gun, and it seemed a logical step for him to start a group that he called The John Dillinger Died For You Society. The occasional meetings of this group were a thin excuse for everyone who had a John Dillinger card to show up at the big house and drink quantities of beer.

If the art drove the pages of the *Ranger* in the fifties, it did so even more in the next decade. My second e-mail interview is with Pat Brown, the first female editor of the *Texas Ranger*. Like Frank Stack, she became involved in the magazine as soon as she got to campus.

INTERVIEW WITH PAT BROWN

RICHARD HOLLAND: You grew up in Austin?

PAT BROWN: I'm a second-generation Austinite. Like my father, I attended Austin High, graduating in 1962 with the plan to enter the University of Texas for a B.F.A. degree. (My father earned an M.A. in English Literature at UT in 1914.) I had benefited from the Saturday morning art program in the department during my high school years, and received a tuition scholarship from the program for my freshman year at the University. I had also received the Wellesley Award from a high-school division competition at the Laguna Gloria Art Museum—another tuition scholarship.

In the summer after I graduated from high school, my college-bound girlfriends and I dated "older men" who were already enrolled in UT, certain we would be increasing our level of sophistication with every encounter. The parties we were invited to were anything but sophisticated, however. We were unprepared to deal with the enormous quantities of beer being consumed, but the ensuing high jinx were too much fun to pass up. The boys who introduced us to the pranksters and partiers were soon sidelined, as we chatted up and flirted with the ones we were attracted to. By the time registration began in September, we were familiar faces at the gatherings where the Waller Creek Boys (Janis Joplin, Powell St. John, and Lanny Wiggins) played and sang for our entertainment (well, we *all* sang along).

Gilbert Shelton, *Ranger* editor for 1962–63, with his roommates, Joe Brown and Tony Bell, had a funky party pad on East 8th which was torn down at the end of the summer to make way for the new downtown post office. The Ghetto, however, was where most of the action was going on most of the time. Bill Killeen, a *Ranger* staffer from Lowell, Massachusetts, lived at the Ghetto, as did Janis and half a dozen others. There were probably more crashers than actual residents at any given time. Once the semester began, we all hung out at the *Ranger* office in the Journalism building or in the Chuck Wagon, then repaired to the Ghetto in the evenings. My girlfriend Marilyn Todd was attracted to Bill, so he and I were friendly as well. I confided to Bill that I was hoping to contribute cartoons to the *Ranger*, then showed my efforts to Gilbert, who was encouraging enough to publish one of my cartoons in the September issue. (Gilbert was in grad school at the time, hoping to defer his draft status, more than anything.) It wasn't until November—the UT vs. A&M game—that I became Gilbert's girlfriend, though. Bill wanted to take Marilyn to the game but needed a car. Gilbert had the car but no date. I was recruited, willingly went, and needless to say, we all had a real good time!

RH: So were you aware of the *Ranger* in high school?

PB: I don't recall that I ever saw a *Ranger* before the summer of '62. It immediately appealed to me, even though I felt that some of it was amateurish, which it was. Gilbert's writing matched his skill with cartooning. Lieuen Adkins stood out with hilarious little poems. Tony Bell could draw anything. Joe Brown and Bill Killeen both wrote cleverly, with doses of grand silliness. Lynn Ashby, Dave Crossley, and Bill Helmer were gone but contributed long distance occasionally. The cartoons and funny illustrations were better than any of the other college magazine comparables with the possible exception of the *Yale Record*, which had a pretty talented staff as well. I was as excited about being a "Rangeroo" as I was about being an art student! Although I had drawn and cartooned for the yearbook, the newspaper, football programs, and poetry journals in high school, I had never associated with any of the groups of students who were likewise involved. My friends and I hadn't been joiners. Now, here I was, eager to "belong" to this motley gang of hell-raising, fun-loving, talent-soaked misfits! Happily, acceptance wasn't a problem.

I met Gilbert for the first time at a swimming party out on Windy Point that June. I didn't visit with him at all . . . just got introduced. I didn't really get to know him until school started, although I saw him at parties throughout the summer. He was slight and pale with huge blue eyes, slightly curly hair, and a small mustache. It was the mustache that intrigued me. One afternoon, sitting around the *Ranger* office, I asked if I might sample a kiss to see how a mustachioed one differed from clean-lipped one. He complied. I liked it! Gilbert was somewhat shy and reticent, characteristics which disappeared after he consumed a number of beers. Once he was sufficiently lubricated, he assumed the position of pack leader, always ready with some clever and creative idea for a prank or a romp. He was obviously intellectual, but not arrogant or elitist. All the women, including Janis, were attracted to him, and his closest pals were devoted to him in the way that guys often are (nothing you can derive from their outward behavior). Coming into that fall semester not yet 18, I wasn't in his league at all.

Bill Helmer didn't return to Texas from NYC until the late spring of '63. Although I had heard of him from Gilbert's stories, I didn't meet him until then.

RH: Hadn't Gilbert and some of the others contributed to other college magazines at about the same time?

PB: Gilbert Shelton had decided to return to Texas after wintering in NYC with little success to show for his efforts at establishing a career in cartooning. His old UT buddies Dave Crossley and Kerry O'Quinn, who had been fired from the *Ranger* staff the previous year for slipping the now-famous expletive past the censors, were planning to publish an independent humor rag. *Bacchanal* was to be aimed at all the schools of the Southwest Conference, banking on a hot reception for its high-quality but irreverent brand of humor. For the premier issue in March, Shelton had ready an all-new comic which he'd conceived of while still in New York, enlisting the help

Texas Ranger cover, 1962. *From the University of Texas Archive, Center for American History, the University of Texas at Austin.*

of writer Bill Killeen on a script. Killeen and Shelton had met when Shelton visited him in his hometown of Lowell, Massachusetts. While attending Oklahoma State the previous year, Killeen had published *Charlatan*, an independent humor magazine of his own. Though his intention was to publish *Charlatan* again as a national magazine, introducing Gilbert Shelton's Wonder Wart-Hog in its debut edition, *Bacchanal* beat him to the punch. (Other contributors for the March 1962 inaugural issue of *Bacchanal* were J. Frank Dobie, Bill Helmer, Lynn Ashby, Jim Earle, John Weeks, and the staff, which also included managing editor Bob Lacy, associate editor Dave Helton, and assistant art director Tony Bell.)

When *Bacchanal* folded after only two issues, Shelton found himself without a venue for his new comic. It made good sense to apply for the editorship of the *Texas Ranger* for the '62–'63 school year, as his plan was to enter graduate school (history major) in an effort to avoid the draft. Duly appointed to the post, he gathered the talents of Tony Bell, Hal Normand, Lieuen Adkins, and others for his staff. Bill Killeen, too underfunded (penni-

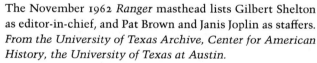

The November 1962 *Ranger* masthead lists Gilbert Shelton as editor-in-chief, and Pat Brown and Janis Joplin as staffers. *From the University of Texas Archive, Center for American History, the University of Texas at Austin.*

The first page of Gilbert Shelton's comic strip "Wonder Wart-Hog meets Super-Patriot," in the *Ranger*. *From the University of Texas Archive, Center for American History, the University of Texas at Austin.*

less) to publish his own magazine, drove down to Austin in his lumbering 1950 Cadillac hearse to join the Texas Rangeroos in producing a first-rate magazine. Needless to say, however, little thought was given to content, other than the Wart-Hog strip, for most of the summer. There was too much fun to be had.

RH: What was Janis Joplin like when she was at UT?

PB: Janis Joplin had hit Austin in the summer of 1962, entering the College of Fine Arts as a freshman that fall. Although she never contributed a thing to the *Ranger*, she was a vivid part of the scene, and an attraction at sales booths and all the parties. Inspired by Wonder Wart-Hog in modeling her persona, no doubt, every one else was inspired by her. Within a few months of arriving, she had sampled relationships with Powell St. John, Bill Killeen, Gilbert Shelton, and rather a lot of others. Many of the group were musicians, with Janis and Pepe Plowman being the featured singers. Impromptu performances were

always cropping up at parties and gatherings. Janis was also on hand for most of the summer's antic fun, such as the great three-hour water-balloon fight in Shelton's neighborhood, the bat-batting free-for-all at the Friendly Tavern, and a trip to the border town of Laredo, which confounded several barrooms full of Mexicans.

RH: Everyone was entranced by the adventures of Wonder Wart-Hog.

PB: Wonder Wart-Hog had been an instant success. The editors of *Mademoiselle* had spied the strip in *Bacchanal*, and featured the Hog in the August 1962 issue of their magazine. *HELP!*, Harvey Kurtzman's new venture, also published Wonder's first chapters. The September issue of the *Ranger* published chapter three, Wonder Wart-Hog meets Super-Hypnotist! The Hog of Steel was featured in each of the issues of the *Ranger* that year with the exception of the annual *Playboy* parody in March. It concluded with a chapter three which was different from the September chapter three! If Bill Helmer's tenure as editor had established the *Ranger* as a profit-making endeavor of quality campus humor, and Crossley's forays into censor-baiting made it controversial, the cartoons of Gilbert Shelton, not to mention those of Tony Bell, Jack Jackson, and Vin Sheihagen, elevated the *Ranger* to the position of top campus magazine in the country.

RH: Not everyone stayed in Austin.

PB: By January of 1963, Bill Killeen had returned to Massachusetts, absconding with a UT English professor's daughter, then heading to Florida to once again publish *Charlatan*. Janis had gone to San Francisco with Chet Helms, launching her career there. Joe Brown had returned from a stint in New York, where he had pursued acting for a time. After a year as a publisher in NYC, Bill Helmer also came back to Texas, intent on getting his master's degree in history. By now, I was Gilbert Shelton's steady girlfriend, and he used my illustrations and cartoons regularly in the *Ranger*. My title was "sweet young thing."

RH: It sounds as if there was a family-like atmosphere, punctuated by beer and perhaps other substances . . .

PB: The salary for *Ranger* editors in those years was a mere $100 a month. Somehow, Shelton managed to stretch that amount out to pay rent, eat sparingly, and always include cigarettes and the requisite alcoholic beverages. Many months, however, cash was in short supply by the last week. Poverty was one thing we all had in common. Most weekends were filled with amusements we invented, or just hanging around in the living room of Bill Helmer and his wife, Pat, who were somewhat housebound with two small children. Tony Bell, Lieuen Adkins, Joe Brown, Gilbert, and I spent almost every weekend with the Helmers. Bill Helmer, of course, was persuaded to contribute to the magazine as well as provide inspiration to his minions. Pat Helmer was persuaded to host family-style dinners of fried chicken and mashed potatoes, though Tony Bell often donned the apron and served up his personal recipe for jalapeño pinto beans and cornbread.

The *Ranger* parties themselves were the stuff of legends. The TSP board allowed the *Ranger* staff to use the profits from the on-campus sales booths for throwing a party each month. It was usually enough to buy at least a keg of cheap beer (Pearl!) and plastic cups. Someone had to volunteer their place (usually the Ghetto or Shelton's house), which would mean disastrous consequences for the abode. The parties usually started off quite genial and ended rowdy, with the arrival of the police or perhaps Inspector Harvey Gann in the small hours after midnight. There were always the fallen few who spent the night passed out in the wrong bed, on the floor, or under the shrubs. Bottles, cups, and cigarette butts littered every surface on the morning after. Hopefully, no doors were kicked in, windows broken, or furniture demolished, but often that was the case. Sunday morning hangovers were a given. Somehow, it all seemed like tremendous fun. (I, myself, never saw the end of the party, as I was required to be home by midnight, thanks to my cautious parents.) Still, I remember the music and singing, the inevitable flying pie, the camaraderie, the philosophical discussions, the drunken rants, the pranks and jokes. Rarely were there physical fights or even tussles among the Rangeroos.

At the end of the school year in spring of '63, appointments were made for the next year's editors. Lieuen Adkins had been forgiven for his part in the censorship debacle of spring '62, and was chosen to be editor while he was enrolled in graduate school. I was appointed associate editor thanks to some encouragement from my ex-editor boyfriend. I had a pretty good idea of what the job entailed, plus the knowledge that I had no qualifications for the job. Gilbert Shelton would be the de facto associate editor as well as the art editor, which was his new appointment. I was perfectly delighted to comply. Gilbert had done layout and design on the car magazines in New York, so the task suited him; besides, he had decided to switch from history to fine arts with the start of the '63–'64 school year. My artistic abilities had inspired him to learn more about technique, composition, and other rudiments of drawing and painting. He was always concerned with improving the quality of his work. The rest of us already drew well, but no one was able to embody a drawing with the inherent hilarity that Gilbert Shelton could achieve effortlessly.

RH: This sounds like an amazingly creative time.

PB: It must have been a mighty cosmic wind which gusted through Austin and the University of Texas during the spring of 1962. The elements were falling into place for one of those rare confluences of talent and originality from diverse sources which sometimes make their mark on history. This time, it was a group of historians, artists, writers, cartoonists, humorists, and musicians (plus one unique singer) who would be drawn together through the campus humor magazine.

BETTY SUE
FLOWERS

The Times
They Were A' Changin'

When I first came to the University in the fall of 1965, the campus seemed caught between the fifties and the future. The girls in Scottish Rite Dormitory had a weekday curfew well before midnight, and when we left to go on a date, we had to sign out at the door with "name of date" and "destination." To cross the formal living room in trousers required that you roll the trouser legs up above your knee, put on a raincoat, and persuade your roommate to follow you to the door so that she could take the raincoat back to your room. Our neighbors nearby, the Fijis, were rumored to have a powerful telescope trained on S.R.D.'s west wing, and there was a fearful story that some Fiji pledge had once been required to hide for twenty-four hours up in the attic where we stored our going-home luggage.

Except for the Fijis, we were basically secure. No man doubted that he would find a job, and no woman I knew talked about jobs at all. I was the only female in my Chemistry lab section and one of only two or three in my German class. During my four undergraduate years, I met only two female professors—but I didn't stop to recognize this fact or its significance at the time, even though I felt quite strongly the contrast between the lab with its rows of glass tubes and Bunsen burners and unnamed chemicals designed to foil the best attempts at identification, and the dormitory with its sit-down dinners, freshly cut flowers, and chocolate crumble balls for Sunday lunch.

During that first week in the dorm I heard a funny story about messages posted in the Texas Union saying, "Wife wanted immediately," with various incentives listed. One of the seniors told me that these weren't jokes, and that even some of the Fijis next door had hurriedly married before

---

Betty Sue Flowers has been director of the Lyndon Baines Johnson Presidential Library and Museum since 2002. Prior to that, she was director of UT's Plan II program and the Kelleher Professor of English. In addition to her work as a poet and editor, Dr. Flowers collaborated with Bill Moyers on four books and with Joseph Campbell on Joseph Campbell and the Power of Myth. *This essay was first published in* Texas Our Texas: Remembrances of The University *(Eakin Press, 1984), edited by Bryan A. Garner.*

the draft rules changed. In November of my freshman year I went to the Academic Center auditorium to hear the journalist Tom Wolfe give a witty lecture on "Why Baby Jane Holzer Is More Important than Vietnam." Two years later, no one would have laughed.

By 1967 the campus was swarming with back-to-back protests, some of them as small as five people with an audience of thirty on the West Mall, some of them with microphones and self-appointed student crowd-controllers with hundreds of students, non-students, and undercover investigators stretched from the Tower steps past the George Washington statue. The investigators were obvious—by 1967, many of them were known by name. The non-students weren't so obvious, because they dressed and talked just like the students and were just as afraid of being drafted to fight in what the West Mall speakers argued was an unjust war. Many of the non-students spent their time drinking ten-cent coffee in the Texas Union's Chuck Wagon, waiting for their draft notices and talking about times a couple of years earlier when Janis Joplin had hung around the Union singing. (Everyone had ignored her then.) Joplin and the Rolling Stones and the Beatles and Moby Grape and Jefferson Airplane and Simon and Garfunkle and Bob Dylan and Joan Baez were making music we all came to know. Every rally had some kind of song or chant—"All we are saying is 'Give peace a chance'" or "We shall overcome"—we'd taken the latter from the civil-rights movement, which we considered analogous to our own movement in its clear-cut presentation of right versus wrong. Unjust laws had recently been changed in our country, thanks to the civil-rights marchers. Those in the peace movement had no doubt that we could have the same effect on the Vietnam War.

And in this case, the movement was worldwide. We had a sense of solidarity with young people in France and Ohio and California—and many of the non-students who gathered in the Chuck Wagon were messengers from other colleges, traveling like circuit riders in their psychedelic-covered Volkswagen vans, talking about what was going on at Berkeley or at Columbia. A new day was dawning, we felt, and young people everywhere were to help the sun rise on a world of peace and harmony. There seemed to be nothing remarkable in the fact that our student government president was an Iranian, Rostam Kavoussi. Even the sessions of the Union's Model U.N. made front-page headlines in the *Daily Texan*, and feelings ran so high about the issues that when I was assigned to represent South Africa, a stranger yelled "Racist!" at me in the Co-Op.

The new world of peace and justice would look something like the Gentle Thursdays held on the grassy expanse of the West Mall. Beginning about ten o'clock on Thursday mornings, the "gentle people" began to gather, along with their children, dogs, and balloons. Some played guitars, and others played with the newly popular Frisbee. Over the entire group gathered on the grass hung wisps of the heavily pungent smoke that characterized almost all gatherings everywhere in the late 1960s. Visitors to campus would stare and say, "Look at the hippies," or sometimes, more ominously, "Look at those dirty hippies."

For the most part hippies weren't dirty; they were simply a contrast to the starched, ironed, sprayed, controlled look that had immediately preceded them. In 1965 men wore crewcuts or flat-tops and button-down shirts, and women ratted hair into enormous beehives or bouffants, spraying them to the consistency of steel wool. Every morning there was a line of girls outside the ironing room in S.R.D., and unless you indicated otherwise on the laundry list, blouses with Peter Pan collars would be starched. Three years later, even those of us who didn't consider ourselves hippies had let down our hair and parted it in the middle. The line outside the ironing room disappeared, except for those who regularly ironed their hair to achieve the straight flat look that was somehow felt to be more "honest" than teasing and ratting and curling and perming and spraying. Meanwhile, our boyfriends quit going to the barbershop, and many quit shaving.

The less time we spent fiddling with our hair, the more time our parents and other people over thirty seemed to spend commenting on it. The sense of community, even of family, among students was strong on campus in part because so many students had been told not to come home until they got a haircut. Others, cut off from family funding sources, moved into the large old houses around campus in groups of ten to fifteen both to save money and to try out new forms of communal living. This, too, people over thirty didn't seem to understand, imagining communes to be hotbeds of sexual license.

True, there seemed to be more flesh around in the late sixties than at any time previously. Earlier, every dress hem was a precise distance from the kneecap, varying from two inches below to perhaps a quarter inch above. By 1967, hemlines were thigh-high or down to the ground, and various undergarments began to be regarded as not really necessary. Students were arrested for swimming nude at what came to be known as "Hippie Hollow" on Lake Travis, and on campus a student play was banned because of a nude scene. The authors dropped out of school and took the play to Paris, where, we heard, it was a big success. In Texas, however, it was clear that "uptight" authorities would see as "decadent" what many students regarded as simply "honest." And when construction began on the West Mall, converting the grassy space of Gentle Thursday into a series of planter boxes and concrete sidewalks, many people saw it as another move to clean up the University by getting rid of the hippies.

From the student perspective, the major villain throughout the late sixties was the chairman of the Board of Regents, Frank Erwin. "I intend to build a university that the football team can be proud of," he was quoted as saying. It was Erwin who fired John Silber and broke up the College of Arts and Sciences. It was Erwin who ordered the trees along Waller Creek to be bulldozed and the protesting students in the trees to be pulled out. It was Erwin, we heard, who ordered walls to be built around campus to make it harder for non-students to enter, and Erwin who designed that circular flower box on the West Mall which, though it might have innocent-looking pansies in it, was rumored to contain a powerful fountain built to break up demonstrations by hosing out the peaceniks. It seemed that Erwin ran the University the way Johnson ran the United States, so it was easy for rally speakers to glide from Vietnam to the scandals at Waller Creek, arousing the same sense of outrage about both.

We were terribly self-righteous. We had no sense of the fragility of institutions, of the ease with which something precious and complex like a university can be damaged. We thought that those against us must be trying to protect themselves and their privileges and could not imagine that Chairman Frank might be working for the good of the University and yet still not think as we did. We saw policemen with gas masks on campus and knew that simply by attending a Vietnam rally we would end up being photographed and later identified for F.B.I. files. We knew that cer-

After the Chuck Wagon riot. *From the Prints and Photographs Collection—UT Demonstrations, Center for American History, the University of Texas at Austin. (DI 02404)*

tain service stations along the Drag and certain restaurants in town would not serve any male with long hair and that, even on campus, there were professors who would flunk a failing student, even though it meant that the student might be sent to Vietnam. We knew that all administrators were alike, and that when the University threw *The Rag* and its alternative news off campus, it was simply mirroring what the U.S. was doing: giving us only party-line versions of what was happening. Still, we knew what was happening in Vietnam because friends died there, and those who came back told stories so horrible about their experiences that most of us didn't want to hear them. Knowing so much, we couldn't imagine that there was so much we didn't know.

One day, sitting in the Chuck Wagon eating a hamburger, I looked up to see that outside, at both doors, crowds of policemen were gathering. An angry hum in the hall began to get louder and, remembering something about discretion being the better part of valor, I hurriedly picked up my books and headed for the nearest exit. The door was locked from the outside. Through the glass I could see a policeman shaking his head no. I pushed and banged on the door and yelled, "I'm going to be late to class!" He looked puzzled a moment, then unlocked the door, and I squeezed through sideways. The door shut after me, and the shouting began. Later I read about the "Chuck Wagon Riot" in the *Daily Texan*, the police having swooped in to rid the area of non-students. "Saying you were going to be late to class was a good excuse," someone told me later. "That's probably the only thing that got you out of there."

The truth was, though, that I didn't want to be late to class. There was a lot going on outside of class in the late sixties—but there was also a lot of excitement inside class. Students filled the Union Ballroom to hear Arrowsmith of the Classics Department read from his new Aristophanes translation. Shattuck of the French Department, speaking in his gentle, urbane way, opened up the worlds of Kafka and Stendhal to us, and Malof in English showed us the riches embedded in poetry. For American Government, Kraemer arranged war games and other simulation exercises. Menaker in Zoology challenged us with quizzes so difficult and witty that some of us spent precious minutes agonizing over the answer to a question that later turned out to be a ringer—it began, "Mitosis is bigger than your toes is." Meanwhile, across the campus, Raja Rao's Buddhism classes overflowed into the hall, and after every semester the new vision offered on the third floor of Waggener inspired students to travel to India and learn to meditate. And for those of us in Plan II, John Silber's philosophy class was at least as intense as the West Mall rallies.

No one missed Silber's class. Even the student who represented our nationally victorious College Bowl team was not allowed to miss a quiz in order to travel to the final competition. Anyone caught unprepared in Silber's class was simply thrown out on the spot. Once a young man excused himself for not having prepared on the grounds that he couldn't afford the textbook. Silber stopped the questioning, reached into his wallet, and threw some bills at the boy. The class was absolutely silent, waiting, until the boy reached down around him and gathered up the bills.

At Christmas break Silber required us all to go back to our hometowns and do a "slum project." We each chose a section of town, looked up the tax rolls to discover who owned the property, and then attempted to interview both the landlords and the tenants. "This is for your philosophy class?" my mother asked when I told her I needed the family car to drive over to the other side of the tracks. It didn't seem strange to me, though. Walking around the slums of my hometown on Christmas Eve seemed related to Kierkegaard and Kant in the same way that government and history and Milton's *Paradise Lost* and the study of circadian rhythms in Menaker's Zoology class and the protests against the Vietnam War all seemed related. My generation demanded relevance from our courses—but the demand was not that the professor make the subject matter relevant but that he acknowledge the relations which we felt already existed among subjects.

The sense that everything was connected to everything else also resulted in what was called "free-floating paranoia." Some students saw plots everywhere, and there was a general distrust of all institutions. Even those of us who weren't paranoid knew that students who went to the counseling center with a drug problem might find that their personal files had ended up in the district attorney's office. All around campus, unofficial helping services began to spring up—drug counseling or draft counseling or fund-raising centers for the Black Panther breakfast program or for bail money to help students arrested for one thing or another. We were remaking the world, and we thought anything was possible.

Even the curriculum seemed open for our reforming efforts. A sorority sister and I spent hours redesigning freshman English and then went to see Dean Silber about our plan. He referred us to the head of the National Translation Center, an English novelist named Keith Botsford, who had designed a new program with some similarities to ours. Botsford thought that freshmen should be exposed to the best minds on campus as early in their careers as possible, and so he brought in Don Weismann, the artist, and distinguished physicists and philosophers and scientists and said, "Explain what you're doing so that these kids can understand you and understand what's significant and interesting about your field."

The world seemed full of problems that could be solved if only the people over thirty could find enough goodwill to overcome tradition and self-interest. The issues were black and white, and the people you met were either young, long-haired, and against the Vietnam War, or older, short-haired, and against the Vietnam War protestors. Many days we could see this conflict dramatically re-enacted in the open-air debates between the bearded young philosophy professor, Larry Caroline, and Dean Silber. Those with free-floating paranoia were not surprised when Larry Caroline was fired.

But after Dean Silber was fired in 1970 and the College of Arts and Sciences was split, it became harder to tell who wore black hats and who wore white ones.

That spring more than 2,000 people marched to the Capitol to protest the Vietnam War, and many of the marchers were over thirty and had hair short enough to allow their ears to show. The peace rallies—half protest and half celebration—began to assume a harder edge now that four students had been killed in a demonstration at Kent State. On our own campus, we could still see the Tower sniper's bullet holes in the sidewalk, a reminder of the violence that, it now seemed, could erupt anywhere, anytime. And in California someone had been killed at a Rolling Stones concert, a death shocking to students, who had regarded rock concerts as the showcase for the peaceful communal activities of the future, after the world had learned to "Make Love, Not War."

The University of Texas in the sixties was not simply a campus experience, but an introduction to the larger world, to issues of war and peace and courage and betrayal and the need to question the values inherited from authority. At the University we met other members of our generation, a generation that still talks about itself as "children of the sixties." One of my colleagues in the law school, also a sixties child, told me, "I really do feel we are the goat being swallowed by the python of history."

Maybe we *were* an aberrant generation. I think so sometimes when I pass the sign on the Union patio announcing that at this one spot on campus, you don't have to get permission from the authorities if you want to hold a rally. Looking around at the Union barbeque tables and the sandwich carts and the donut-vending stands and the students sitting contentedly around the azaleas, I have difficulty imagining anyone gathering there in protest. The sign seems as anachronistic as those old iron rings for horses you sometimes see embedded in small-town sidewalks in West Texas. The last march I saw on Guadalupe consisted of a group of Iranians holding placards and walking down one side of the Drag and another group of Iranians holding placards and walking in the opposite direction down the other side of the Drag, while students waiting on the sidelines for the shuttle bus tried to figure out what the argument was all about.

One day in the spring of 1967, I took the little elevator up into the Tower stacks and found a place to study. I cleared the chicken bones left by the last occupant of the old wooden desk, opened the window and my poetry book, and then stared out beyond the red-tile roofs and the live-oak greenery to the blue Austin hills in the distance. At sunrise I had been setting up nets in a cow pasture north of town to catch birds for the laboratory at Balcones where I worked half-time. At noon I had been singing with a hundred others on the Main Mall: "All we are saying is 'Give peace a chance.'" At two, I had heard a brilliant lecture on T. S. Eliot. The week before had included a picnic at Campbell's Hole with the Junior Fellows, a group of two dozen liberal arts students who met for good meals and lively discussion at the Faculty Dining Room once a week. Even my Chemistry unknown had taken only one extra Saturday lab session to figure out. And the day before, lying under the sunshine at Barton Springs, I had, for an entire half-hour, thought I understood Kant's *Critique of Pure Reason*. On that sunny afternoon, high up in the Tower, I looked out at the blue hills, considered what a luxury it was to spend an afternoon reading Ezra Pound, and thought to myself that being at the University of Texas was wonderful.

It still is.

J. M.
COETZEE } # Remembering Texas

In September 1965 (this is an essay that can begin no other way) I sailed into New York harbor aboard an Italian ship, once a troopship, now crammed with young folk from foreign parts come to study in America. I came, immediately, from England; at the age of 25, I was heading for Austin, where the University of Texas was to support me to the tune of $2,100 a year for teaching freshman English while I studied in the graduate program.

In the colonies, where I came from ultimately, I had received a conventional undergraduate training in English studies. That is to say, I had learned to speak Chaucerian verse with good vowel definition and to read Elizabethan handwriting; I was acquainted with the Pearl Poet and Thomas More and John Evelyn and many other worthies; I could "do" literary criticism, though I had no clear idea what it was, how it differed from book reviewing or polite talk about books. All in all, this patchy imitation of Oxford "English" had proved a dull mistress from whom I had been thankful to turn to the embrace of mathematics; but now, after four years in the computer industry during which even my sleeping hours had been invaded by picayune problems in logic, I was ready to have another try.

In an Austin hotter and steamier than the Africa I remembered, I enrolled myself in courses in bibliography and Old English. From William B. Todd I learned the operation of the Hinman collator; for Rosamund Lehmann I wrote (a project of my own devising) a minutely detailed classification of rhetorical figures in the sermons of the 11th-century English cleric Bishop Wulfstaan. Mrs. Lehmann awarded me an A-, the minus, she said because studies like mine gave philology a bad name. She was right; I was not resentful, though unsure of where one went from there.

In the Manuscript Room of the library, I found the exercise books in which Samuel Beckett had written "Watt" on a farm in the south of France, hiding out from the Germans.

J. M. Coetzee (born 1940) is the author of ten novels. He was awarded the Nobel Prize for Literature in 2003. He lives in Adelaide, South Australia. This essay first appeared in his 1992 book Doubling the Point.

John Coetzee (third from left) on the 1968 UT cricket team. *From the* Cactus *yearbook (1968, p. 321), Center for American History, the University of Texas at Austin. (DI 02393)*

I spent weeks perusing them, pondering the sketches and numbers and doodles in the margins, disconcerted to find that the well-attested agony of composing a masterpiece had left no other traces than these flippancies. Was the pain perhaps all in the waiting, I asked myself, in the sitting and staring at the empty page?

One Charles Whitman, a student (a fellow student? were they all fellow students? all 23,000 of them?), took the elevator to the top of the clock tower and commenced shooting people on the quadrangle below. He killed a fair number, then someone killed him. I hid under my desk for the duration. In Cape Town a Greek assassinated Hendrik Frensch Verwoerd, architect of Grand Apartheid.

"If you dislike the war so much," said a friend, meaning the war in (on) Vietnam, "why don't you leave? There is nothing keeping you here." But he misread me. Complicity was not the problem—complicity was far too complex a notion for the time being—the problem was with knowing what was being done. It was not obvious where one went to escape knowledge.

The students I taught in my composition classes might as well have been Trobriand Islanders, so inaccessible to me were their culture, their recreations, their animating ideas. I moved in a single stratum of the university community, a stratum of graduate students living thrifty lives in rented apartments with baby toys scattered over the floors, laboring like tortoises to complete courses or prepare for orals or write dissertations. Their talk, when it was not of their teachers (their personalities, their deficiencies), was of getting out, getting a job in Huntsville or Texarkana, getting their hands on real money. With less tangible goals than these or perhaps with none at all, I toiled away at my Old English texts, my German grammar.

On Sundays I played cricket on one of the baseball fields with a group of Indians. We formed a team, traveled to College Station, played against a team from Texas A&M also made up of nostalgic castoffs from the colonies, lost. I remembered an Indian friend from the old days in England. He and I went for walks in the Surrey countryside, a countryside that, we agreed, meant nothing to either of us. "In America," he said (he had spent time in Columbus, Ohio), "you can stay up till 4 in the morning, and when you go out there will still be a hamburger stand open." I did not care about the hamburgers, but the picture he drew seemed a distinct improvement on the England I knew. Now I was in America, or at least in Texas; but the green hills, I was finding, were as alien as the Surrey downs. What I missed seemed to be a certain emptiness, empty earth and empty sky, to which South Africa had accustomed me. What I also missed was the sound of a language whose nuances I understood. Speech in Texas seemed to have no nuances; or if there were nuances, I was not hearing them.

I wrote a paper for Archibald Hill, the linguist, on the morphology of Nama, Malay, and Dutch, languages from unrelated stocks that had impacted on one another at the Cape of Good Hope. In the library I came upon books unopened since the 1920s; reports on the territory of South West Africa by its German explorers and administrators, accounts of punitive expeditions against the Nama and Herero, dissertations on the physical anthropology of the natives, monographs by the German ethnologist Carl Meinhof on the Khoisan (Hottentot and Bushman) languages. I read the makeshift grammars put together by missionaries, went further back in time to the earliest records of the Hottentots, word lists compiled by 17th-century seafarers, and then followed the fortunes of the Hottentots in a history written not by them but for them, from above, by travelers and missionaries, not excluding my remote ancestor Jacobus Coetzee, fl. 1760. Years later, in Buffalo, still pursuing this track, I was to venture my own contribution to the history of the Hottentots: a memoir, composed out of the air, of Jacobus Coetzee. The memoir went on growing till it had been absorbed into a first novel, "Dusklands."

A second track took me from Nama and Malay deeper into the syntax of exotic languages, on forays that ramified further and further as I found (I was rediscovering the wheel now) that the term "primitive" meant nothing, that every one of the 700 tongues of Borneo was as coherent and complex and intractable to analysis as English. I read Noam Chomsky and Jerrold Katz and the new universal grammarians and reached the point of asking myself: If a latter-day ark were ever commissioned to take the best that mankind had to offer and make a fresh start on the farther

planets, if it ever came down to that, might we not leave Shakespeare's plays and Beethoven's quartets behind to make room for the last aboriginal speaker of Dyirbal, even though that might be a fat old woman who scratched herself and smelled bad? It seemed an odd position for a student of English, the greatest imperial language of them all, to be falling into. It was a doubly odd position for someone with literary ambitions, albeit of the vaguest—ambitions to speak one day, somehow, in his own voice—to discover himself suspecting that languages spoke people or at the very least spoke through them.

I left Texas in 1968. It was never clear to me, from beginning to end, why the university—and the American taxpayer—had lavished so much money on me to follow idle whims. Sometimes I thought it an oversight, an insignificant oversight, allowed for in the system: that among the thousands of petroleum engineers and political scientists turned out every year, it did not matter if there were one or two of whatever I was. At other times the Fulbright exchange program seemed to me an extraordinary farsighted and generous scheme whose humane benefits would be felt by all parties far into the future. Where did the truth lie? Somewhere in the middle, perhaps.

Coming or going, I had no regrets. I departed, I thought, unmarked, unscathed, except by the times. No one had tried to teach me, for which I was grateful. What I had learned in the course of three years was not negligible, though picked up, for the most part, by accident. I had had the run of a great library, where I had stumbled on books whose existence I might otherwise never have guessed. Observing the linguist and scholar James Sledd at work at his desk at 5 o'clock on a Saturday afternoon, I had been reassured that the province of English studies was not, as the life style of my colonial teachers had always implied, reserved for dilettantes. I could have come away with less.

JULIUS
WHITTIER

The Last Bastion

My decision to attend the University of Texas is most appropriately captured by one of Coach Royal's famous homilies: "Luck is the meeting of opportunity and preparation." Well, maybe Coach Royal didn't invent it, but he was the first person I ever heard say it. The truth is that I was prepared to capitalize on the opportunity to become a part of one of the most significant institutions in the Southwest. I was prepared inasmuch as my experiences up to the spring of 1969 made the transition from a black eighteen-year-old San Antonio high school student athlete to a black University of Texas student athlete much easier. Ah, the wisdom and security of hindsight! I didn't know then that the adjustment would be modest and smooth. The more significant changes I went through as an undergraduate Longhorn had to do with growing up rather than with adjusting to the cultural, social, and psychological environment of the University.

I was raised in San Antonio, a very pastoral, slow-paced, and southern city. In atmosphere and culture, however, San Antonio is not a southern city; it is primarily a Mexican city. This has had a subtle yet pervasive impact on the development of my racial and cultural values. Although San Antonio had its distinctive southern racial heritage, both blacks and whites lived daily with the realities of a tri-ethnic milieu. Thus there was no simple "us" and "them" dichotomy so common to Southern American cities. This fact, coupled with the multiethnicity of my parents' background, made my adjustment to my experiences at the overwhelmingly white University of Texas much less of an ordeal than many expected.

Lest I be misunderstood, everything that I heard about UT was very important to me because it was all that I knew, and much of it in respect

Julius Whittier graduated from the University of Texas with a B.A. in Philosophy in 1974. After he received his M.P.A. degree from the LBJ School of Public Affairs, he worked for the mayor of Boston, and then returned to Austin, where he graduated from the University of Texas School of Law. Since then he has lived and worked in Dallas, where he has his own law practice. This essay was first published in Texas Our Texas: Remembrances of The University *(Eakin Press, 1984), edited by Bryan A. Garner.*

to race was bad. But I had the benefit of hearing good things—as well as predictions of a racial house of horrors. My high school football coaches, Clint Humphreys and Jim Stroud, saw to it during my senior year that I received no mail from colleges interested in my athletic skills. (By the way, the San Antonio Highlands High team won the 1968 District 31-AAAA football championship, and I was selected for the All-City first team.) I had from around mid-November 1968 until the signing date for Southwest Conference letters of intent to decide whether I would attend Texas, S.M.U., or North Texas State, the three schools I was then considering.

I visited all three schools. There was no comparison between the charge I got from my visit at Texas and my observations of the other schools. Here I was with an opportunity to compete for a spot on a nationally ranked football team. Here I could wander through a campus with 40,000 students to meet and get to know. Here was a school with an excellent collection of facilities for both my academic and athletic careers. Here was a school with a coach recognized all over the country as one of the most professional, and certainly one of the most genuine and successful. Realizing that this was a rare opportunity, I decided to shoot for Texas. I could play big-time football eighty miles from home, and my family could see me. There simply was no realistic alternative. Despite what some people had said about Texas, I had to try it. I had to accept the challenge of succeeding at Texas. The only real decision for me was whether I wanted to brave the possibility that everything I had heard from members of the black community was true just for a chance to play big-time football. I honestly did not give serious thought to going anywhere else.

Friends of my family in San Antonio and in Beaumont who were black schoolteachers and football coaches gave me, through my parents, the benefit of what they knew of Texas as a place for black student athletes. Based on what they knew and on what I've since heard, it is clear to me that the University had an overwhelmingly bad image in the black community. "You'll never get to play up there," these friends warned. "They say they will never play a nigger." Some people said that Coach Royal was quoted as having said this in some newspaper. One person told me she heard him say it. "You'll get flunked out as well as benched." Nobody knew anyone who had gone to Texas. "They ain't got no blacks on that campus."

At the time when I was trying to decide whether to attend Texas, there were probably just over one hundred black people spread over the vast Austin campus. People told me that I wouldn't know anyone and would be just another number. This is what I had heard from folks who genuinely had my best interests at heart.

Fortunately enough, my parents did not really appear to be turned off by the idea of my going to Texas just because it had a racist image and reputation. Their open-minded attitude left me to make my decision without fretting over whether they would be worried about me and my welfare. These were volatile times, and if my parents were worried for my safety they had good cause. These were the days when people took direct action to express themselves. We had heard of incidents on other campuses where black students were subjected to abuse simply for being on a lily-white campus. It was very critical to my final decision to chance it at Texas that I meet the right people from the Longhorn Athletic Department. It was important for me to hear how they described the program, what they felt was expected of the student athlete, what the school gave back to the athlete, what the school's athletic philosophy was, and how they assessed football skills and decided who would start. As luck would have it, I met the right people at the right time. Those people were Coach Mike Campbell, Leon O'Neal, and Head Coach Darrell Royal.

The first one I met was Coach Campbell. He was a relaxed man with a clear projection of quiet confidence. He came by my house on Dawson Street in San Antonio. We sat in my mother's living room and talked. My mother and I grilled him about what we had heard from others. We talked about racial prejudice at the University, in both the academic and the athletic programs. Why were there no blacks on the football team? What had been done to recruit black football players? In spite of these concerns, the central question for me was whether starting positions would be meted out according to ability. I was not looking for a promise that I would start, but for an opportunity to compete and a starting position if I earned it on skill alone. Coach Campbell assured me that my athletic career at Texas would be founded on this premise. My conversations with Coach Royal during this period made me even more confident that Texas was the place where I needed to be. And it was clear from both Coach Royal and Coach Campbell and from other people at the University that I was going to have to be aggressive and smart to get what I wanted from Texas.

What impressed me most was that Coach Campbell acted as if he had nothing to hide. He didn't try to run down the other schools that I considered attending. He didn't try to avoid my concerns by trying to impress me. Throughout the recruitment process no one tried to impress me, to put on a show for me, to make things look better than they were. I had fully expected that Coach Campbell and the other recruiters from Texas would not take my questions of race seriously. I had thought that they would scoff at me and my concerns. Coach Campbell told me and my family that UT could not recruit black athletes until 1963. He said that they had offered numerous black athletes scholarships, but that none had accepted until Leon O'Neal did in the spring of 1968. He said that, of those who declined scholarship offers to Texas, most eventually went to schools out of state or to all-black schools. I did not have any reason to doubt his forthright explanations for the lack of "color" in the Texas football program. Thus when he asked me whether I wanted to visit the school, I said yes.

I rode a Greyhound bus to Austin. It was in the middle of the winter, January 1969. Leon O'Neal met me at the station down at 4th Street and Congress Avenue. He took me over to the Villa Capri Motel on I-35 and Manor Road. (Remember, this was 1969, and there was no LBJ Library at that time; before the Library was built houses, boarding houses, and apartment complexes occupied that space.) Leon is one of the most disarming and friendly people anyone could know. He was the best possible guide to show me around the Texas Athletic Department and facilities. Meeting Leon had as much to do with my going to Texas as the fact that Texas was competitive nationally in football. Leon, who stood about six-foot-three and weighed about 230 pounds, was the first black student athlete to accept a football scholarship from Texas. He was from Killeen, where he had attended an integrated high school, and he believed that the only way for Texas football to change would be for blacks to come to Texas and change it.

This is exactly how I felt. I didn't think there was any leverage from the outside to force Texas to change to an integrated football program. Besides, the first step toward change would be for blacks to accept scholarships, show up, and seriously compete for starting positions. The experience of the first few

Julius Whittier. *From the Prints and Photographs Collection—Julius Whittier, Center for American History, the University of Texas at Austin. (DI 02405)*

blacks on football scholarships there would determine whether Texas had in fact progressed from the antebellum South into twentieth-century equal opportunity. My own experiences may be important to an assessment of that big step. However, the experiences of E. A. Curry, Leon O'Neal, Roosevelt Leaks, Lonnie Bennett, Fred Perry, Donald Ealey, Howard Show, and every other black who has been through the Texas football program, including Heisman Trophy winner Earl Campbell, are equally important.

The treatment a black football player received from the Texas athletic program had as much to do with individual character, personality, and athletic skills as with race. In my opinion the winning combination for matriculating at Texas includes a strong, well-developed character and personality and above-average skills at what one does best. In keeping with the frontier spirit of the state, the University holds no one's hand. If you are not an aggressive self-starter, you are not cut out for Texas. The additional problem to be overcome by the black student athlete was the fact that the institutional atmosphere of the University was more conducive to the success of his white counterpart. But this is exactly the same situation that minorities must face in other areas of life in America, so this was no real reason for me to decline the opportunity to attend Texas.

After checking me into the Villa Capri, Leon took me to the athletic business offices in good old Gregory Gym to sign papers for vouchers and recruiting allowances. Then he took me on a tour of the other offices in the Athletic Department, all located in Gregory Gym and its annex. We went by the athletic ticket office, which was located just inside the front doors of Gregory Gym where the caged windows still are. In looking back, it is hard for me to imagine that this cramped room was at the core of a multimillion-dollar college athletic program. But knowing Al Lundstedt, the Athletics business manager, I am sure he made it work as if it were all the space he needed. We then went by the sports information director's office, located upstairs just behind the bleachers at the front end of Gregory Gym. I believe that this space was later used to make student ID's. The sports information director at that time was Jones Ramsey. Leon even showed me the basketball team's locker room under the bleachers on the Jester Center side of Gregory Gym. At that time, we were still playing varsity basketball games in Gregory Gym. What a way to build school spirit: wherever you sat in Gregory Gym you could almost feel the knocks and bumps of the contact going on under the boards on each end of the court. You almost had the sense of actually playing each game with the team because you could work up a pretty good sweat, what with the excitement of such proximity to the action and to each call of the referee.

After leaving Gregory we walked through the annex, where the rest of the Athletic Department was. We started on the third floor, where the assistant football coaches had their offices. For a major college power these offices were rather spartan. On the B.E.B. end of the third floor was Lan Hewlett's office. Mr. Hewlett was the scholastic counselor for the athletes. He saw to it that we didn't get lost in the fall registration process and that we got registered properly for the classes we selected. This causes me to recall the unforgettable experience of going through registration and adds and drops in Gregory Gym. A good writer could make a lot of money writing about the sociology and atmosphere of those primitive days. Some people remember it as a nightmare. I had a grand time orienting myself, trying to negotiate Gregory Gym and the rest of the University's bureaucracy to get what everyone wanted: the perfect schedule of classes, with Fridays off and no class later than noon.

After we had looked around at all of the assistant coaches' offices, Leon took me to the office of offices. It was located on the second floor of the annex, which is on the same level as the main floor of Gregory Gym. It was Coach Royal's office. There was a rich, deep-pile carpet on the floor; it was a deep burnt orange and it was beautiful. The furniture's style and finish appeared to have been selected to enhance the beauty of this carpet. The walls were filled with numerous mementos of glorious times past, yet they were not cluttered. I remember seeing something on the desk, but I can't recall exactly what it was, except to note that it was part of the booty from the 1969 New Year's Cotton Bowl victory over Tennessee. My most distinct recollection of that visit to Coach Royal's office was that I knew then that you don't get trophies and awards such as I saw in that office without a strong competitive tradition—and, lily-white image or not, I wanted to become a part of that tradition. We had a strong competitive tradition at my junior high and high schools, and I wanted to continue to associate with the best athletes. After leaving Coach Royal's office we went to the Moore-Hill Dining Hall to eat lunch.

When I was being recruited, the athletes still ate in the old Moore-Hill dining room, tucked away behind everything. It was behind Moore-Hill, behind the R.O.T.C. building, behind Gregory Gym, and behind the Lila B. Etter Ex-Students' Center. It must also have been behind the times, because the following year, in 1970, we moved our dining facility to the new athletic dining hall in Jester Center. It's funny that our new dining hall was also behind a number of other buildings, namely, Brackenridge Men's Residence Hall, Roberts Men's Residence Hall, and Jester Center.

When Coach Campbell and all of the other coaches told me that the dining was family-style, I didn't have any idea what they were talking about. But the cozy and crowded atmosphere of the Moore-Hill dining hall was impressive, to say the least, and I found out what "family-style dining" meant. There I was, a rather small offensive lineman, aspiring to sit and break bread with the likes of All-America and All-Southwest Conference linemen Leo Brooks, Bill Atessis, Bob McKay and Bobby Wuensch. As it turned out, family-style dining meant that Dorothy Witt and her dining hall staff, which included the food preparers and the half-scholarship waiters, had the food piping hot in large serving bowls on the table when we came in to eat. Much as you would eat at home, you served yourself from these bowls. The rule set down by Coach Royal was: "Take all the food you want, but eat all you take." Beyond this, the style of eating in the athletic dining hall had no relation to family-style dining. Dining at the Texas training table is more accurately summed up by Charles Darwin's theory of natural selection: only the strongest survived. Simply getting to the table closest to the door of the kitchen took deft athletic skill and agility. Once at the table, your finer skills of manual dexterity and hand-eye coordination came into play. For the first five minutes at the table, there was more reaching and grabbing for those bowls of food than there was for the last plane out of Saigon in 1975.

It was a strange sensation being one of only five blacks in the room who were not working in the kitchen. But, apparently because Leon was well accepted, a number of guys came over to where I was sitting and asked my name, welcomed me, and said they hoped I liked Texas. I hadn't met Coach Royal yet, but he came in later, said hello, and reminded Leon to bring me by his office the next day.

The name "Royal" had a certain majesty to it that I am certain has left no small impression on many a Texas recruit. It certainly impressed me when I first heard it and found out exactly who he was. To be honest, I had no plans at all regarding college attendance after my senior year in high school, and had given it little or no thought. Thus, when Coach Humphreys told me with a big smile that Texas was interested in me, I didn't know how to react. Noting this, Coach Humphreys told me about the University of Texas and its head football coach, Darrell Royal. Royal had coached at Texas since 1957 and had been head coach the whole time. He had coached nine post-season bowl teams at Texas and had been named Coach of the Year several times. He had coached a National Championship Football Team and several Southwest Conference Championship Teams. Royal had one of the top winning percentages of all time among major college football coaches. With his record and his name, it was not surprising that he could field a team every year made up of the best athletes that the state, and the nation, could offer.

After lunch we went down to Memorial Stadium to look over the locker rooms and training facilities. At the time of my visit, the upper deck at the stadium was only in the planning stages. Waller Creek lay peacefully in the natural bed it had cut for itself, oblivious of the rapid changes the campus around it was going through. (Remember Waller Creek, and the important battle over it between the protectors of the Creek's ecosystem and Regent Frank Erwin, whose style was not appreciated, but who was backed by all the pro-Memorial Stadium expansion groups? The fuss was over whether Waller Creek should be moved twenty feet or so to the west in order to add the stadium's upper deck.) Before crossing Waller Creek, we walked past the prefabricated military barracks that constituted San Jacinto Men's Residence Hall to take a look at the huge, open, grass-covered field called Freshman Field (now, after complete renovation, renamed Clark Field), located between Prather Men's Residence Hall and San Jacinto Boulevard. Leon informed me that this was where the freshmen football team practiced. Back in 1969, before the Southwest Conference established a limit of thirty scholarships per school, all freshmen played on the freshman team. We had our own schedule, coaches, and workouts. I remember asking Leon whether he knew of any other black players being recruited by Texas because, as we walked through the Freshman Field, I contemplated what the rest of my teammates would be like. He mentioned several names, but the only one I remember now is John Harvey. I remember being impressed that Texas was trying to recruit him, for he was not only one of the best running backs in Texas, but also one of the best sprinters. It was encouraging to think that I might get to play football with athletes of his caliber. I'm certain this helped me decide before I left that weekend that I would accept a scholarship to Texas. We then walked across Waller Creek and San Jacinto Boulevard to Memorial Stadium.

We looked over the stadium—the field was still a grass oval with a cinder track around it—and then went up to the T-Room and the varsity weight room, both of which are located on the ramps between the ground-level and the second-level entrances to the bleachers on the west side of the stadium. Having trained in high school with cheap weights stacked in the corner of a small utility room, I relished thinking of what I could do with the equipment in the varsity weight room. It seemed as if there was an exercise machine for every muscle in your body, with plenty of space in between. The T-Room is a lounge that is opened for lettermen during home games and on other occasions. It contains numerous mementos of UT's lush athletic history, along with a list naming everyone who has lettered in a varsity sport at Texas. The pictures of recent Texas football teams contained no black players. Leon had been speaking constantly about how important it was for people like me who were offered scholarships to accept them in order to get blacks on the rosters of Texas football lettermen. He emphasized, as I have to numerous prospects since then, how much of an opportunity playing at Texas is. Yet this opportunity was being overlooked by black athletes.

It was being overlooked because of fear—fear based on Texas' lily-white image. What was clear to Leon, and later to me, was that this fear was not based on the concrete experiences of black scholarship football players. There was no one to whom these things had happened. We both thought that it was time for someone to go through the Texas scholarship football program and to meet this intimidation head on and either give it real life or destroy it. I knew when we left the T-Room that day that I would see to it that the University would no longer labor under the weight and embarrassment of a white-boys-only scholarship football program.

As I walked into the football locker rooms under the bleachers of Memorial Stadium, my first impression was of a hospital. The cleanliness of the place was striking. The locker rooms and taping room were the exclusive domain of a man I had heard about earlier that day, the head trainer. I'd heard that a player didn't merit being yelled at or chewed out until he successfully passed this man's uncompromising scrutiny. He conducted all condition training during pre-season and off-season, and after a player returned from an injury. This man was Frank Medina, and the locker rooms and taping rooms were reflections of his sense of order and purpose.

Frank Medina stood just a few inches over five feet tall. A full-blooded Indian, Frank is one of the legends of Texas' athletic history because of his untiring and relentless pursuit of excellence from the athletes in his charge. After Leon introduced us, Frank welcomed me and flashed that wide, toothy grin of his to relax me. Then he outlined the activities and functions of the taping room and of nearby training rooms. Frank was, it seemed to me, a huge asset to Texas football. It was obvious from his sharp, purposeful stride that Frank was always in charge. His deportment, his tone of voice, his self-confidence, his seemingly limitless experience made him highly respected—even revered—when it came to conditioning, injury prevention, and rehabilitation after injury. Frank had been the trainer for three United States Olympic Teams: 1960, 1964, and 1968. One could easily take an hour to look at all of the awards and certificates that testified to his peerless skill.

That evening Leon and I went out to dinner at a steak restaurant and talked about what dorm life was like and what it would be like having all white teammates. Leon was honest in what he had to say about these things. Dorm life, he said, would be comfortable but extremely easy to get enough of. He said that with all of these different guys from towns all over Texas, there would be something happening all the time, from quiet studying and television watching to . . . well, just about anything. Getting along with the white football players would not be much of a problem, Leon said, because most of them did not have a problem with having black teammates. Of course, there would be some guys who would, but there would be guys like that anywhere I might go. Leon pointed out that what commanded the most respect was showing everyone, coaches and players alike, that you "took care of business" on the football field. Leon said that most of the players who didn't have cars, like himself, had no problem borrowing a car from one of the other players who did. Little things like this, he said, helped him to learn that getting along with whites at Texas is much like getting along with anyone anywhere: you must treat persons as individuals because they are all different.

The following morning Leon picked me up from the Villa Capri and took me to Coach Royal. On the ride over to his office, I remember thinking that the meeting would be a turn-off if it took the form of a hard sell. I thought this despite Leon's having told me that Royal was "pretty cool, and easy to talk to." When we got up to his office, a few other players were standing with the recruits they had shown around, waiting to see Royal. As we stood outside it occurred to me that Royal must be pretty intense to bring in all these recruits and give each of them a one-on-one hard sell about signing with Texas. The recruits coming out of his office before me didn't appear to have been pressured or intimidated. Finally my turn came. I went in and was pleasantly surprised by Coach Royal's approach.

Coach Royal was very poised when he greeted Leon and me and invited us in to talk. I imagine that his tactic of bringing Leon in with me was designed to help me relax, and it worked. My first impression of Royal was that he wanted me to be comfortable with my choice of college and that, while he wanted me to attend Texas, he would not be offended if I chose to go elsewhere. By questions he asked, he made it clear that I should think about my choice of college as an important part of my future. Do you enjoy living in San Antonio and Texas? What kinds of things would you like to do if you do not make a career of football? What academic goals do you have? Instead of giving a hard sell, he really believed that this was a very important decision because it affected my future, and he wanted me to give it careful thought.

Before I could broach my concerns about race Coach Royal brought up the subject himself. He said that he was aware of my concerns and that he wanted me to feel free to talk about them. He would answer any questions I had. He seemed to believe that Leon and Coach Campbell had told me all about what I could expect at Texas. He said he would stand by everything they had said. His openness and his confidence in his staff and his program won me over as a friend and admirer from that day on. Leon and I had explored most of the things that concerned me, so our meeting was rather short. Coach Royal thanked me for coming up for the weekend and, as we walked to the door, he shook my hand and said he hoped that I liked the program and the facilities. I wonder whether he knew that he had just recruited the person who would eventually be the first black to play, start, and graduate from Texas.

On February 11, 1969, I signed the Southwest Conference letter of intent, declaring that I intended to accept the scholarship offer from Texas. On August 22, 1969, I arrived in Austin to begin pre-season football training and to begin my freshman year at the University. In the fall of 1971 I received my first varsity starting assignment on the Longhorn football team, as an offensive tackle. That season was ruined by a knee injury that caused me to miss the first five games of the season and to lose my starting position.

In the fall of my senior season in 1972 I received my second starting assignment, as a tight-end, and started for the entire season. During that season I caught *all* of the team's touchdown passes. The season ended with the 1973 Cotton Bowl game in which we defeated Alabama. And in May of 1974 I graduated from the University with a Bachelor of Arts degree in Philosophy.

BARBARA
JORDAN

Conviction Values
Two Speeches

CONVICTION VALUES

While thinking about and preparing what is to follow, I had a strong sense of the importance of tonight's event. I thought about the commencements in which I had participated as a candidate for graduation and tried to recall the addresses I had heard on those occasions. With great effort and total concentration, I could not recall the subject, subject-matter, or speaker at any of those events (and I am not ancient). (Though not particularly noted for my modesty, neither could I remember the subject matter of commencement speeches I have delivered in the past.) I therefore have no illusions about the impact of my presence nor of my words. But, listen anyway. Pretend that for the next fifteen minutes I'm the only game in town.

In spite of the odds against your remembering my words this evening in years—or days—hence, I did search for a topic that would be worthy of your time. In seeking such a topic, I spoke to students and faculty of this university and asked them what message they would like to convey, were they in my place. I was surprised at the common refrain: Values. Whether they be educational values or personal values, the concept was recurrent. I was surprised because I thought that a speech on values might be old hat; perhaps I assumed that by the time a student graduated from a university his or her values would be something that would need no attention. Perhaps I thought that many would feel that the subject of values

---

Barbara Jordan was Texas's first African American state senator in the twentieth century and the first African American woman from a southern state to be elected to Congress. After a long and distinguished public career, she is perhaps best remembered for her role in the House Judiciary Committee's Watergate inquiry. She left Congress to teach at the Lyndon B. Johnson School of Public Affairs on the University of Texas campus. She died in 1996. The first of these two speeches is the commencement address she delivered at the University's graduation ceremonies in May 1986; the second contains her testimony at a February 1987 panel discussion on university funding.

Barbara Jordan at the 1986 UT commencement exercises. *Courtesy of the Office of Public Affairs, the University of Texas at Austin.*

is one that should stay out of the educational arena. And maybe that is why I have chosen to speak about values: because the subject has been taken for granted and thus perhaps ignored; yet we apparently need to be reminded of what lies behind the facts and figures and lessons that we know as education.

I call what follows CONVICTION VALUES. By that I mean that one should have some principles, standards, or qualities which are firmly fixed, unwavering and immutable; that there are some traits of character which are or should be non-negotiable; that we should have a set of beliefs which is endemic to our concept of self.

Having said that, you might infer that conviction values are inherently good. Not always, not always.

If convictions cause one to be rigid, inflexible, and unwilling to compromise when compromise is necessary, such convictions do not serve a good end. If such values are antithetical to basic human rights and to maximizing hope, they are to be rejected. (The President of South Africa has convictions which apparently cause him to believe that it is right for a white minority to suppress and subjugate a black majority—a view which should be rejected.)

The values which I have in mind are those which should be universally agreed upon because they foster a sense of community: they are healing and civilizing.

They promote the general welfare and the common good. Those values include education, kindness, justice and responsibility . . . ordinary, pedestrian words which should require no particular or extraordinary commitment on our part. So why talk about convictions vis-a-vis those words? Why not just go with the flow and passively let things happen as they happen? Interventionism can be troublesome, frustrating, and time-consuming. Interventionism can require thought and action.

There is a poignant passage in Mark Twain's *The Adventures of Huckleberry Finn* which speaks to this point. At a time early in the story Huck has decided it was wrong for him to help Jim, Miss Watson's slave, escape. Huck determined that he would paddle ashore at first light and tell of Jim's whereabouts. However, enroute to the shore he encountered two white men on a skiff who were looking for runaway slaves. They saw that the raft had a man on it and asked Huck whether that man was black or white. After some hesitation Huck said, "He's white." Huck then reflects:

They went off and I got aboard the raft feeling bad and low, because I knowed very well I had done wrong, and I see it wasn't no use for me to try to learn to do right; a body that don't get started right when he's little ain't got no show—when the pinch comes there ain't nothing to back him up and keep him to his work, and so he gets beat. Then I thought a minute and says to myself, hold on; s'pose you'd 'a' done right and give Jim up, would you felt better than what you do now? No, says I, I'd feel bad—I'd feel just the same way I do now. Well, then, says I, what's the use you learning to do right when it's troublesome to do right and ain't no trouble to do wrong, and the wages is just the same? I was stuck. I couldn't answer that. So I reckoned I wouldn't bother no more about it, but after this always do whichever comes handiest at the time.

"Whichever comes handiest at the time" flies in the face of convictions. The alternative is not easy but must be pursued.

Education is a value at once general and specific. It was made a general principle of government in the Declaration of Independence of the Republic of Texas in 1836. The Texas Declaration of Independence states:

It [the government of Mexico] has failed to establish any public system of education, although possessed of almost boundless resources ... and although it is an axiom in political science that unless a people are educated and enlightened it is idle to expect the continuance of civil liberty or the capacity for self government.

From this statement of principle the people of Texas and their governors moved with alacrity to establish a system of public education. This university was subsequently established. In celebrating the centennial of the University of Texas, "first class" became "world class." Scholars and academic chairs proliferated. And then came 1986, the sesquicentennial of the state. That noble principle so well stated in 1836 came face to face with collapsing oil prices and revenue shortfalls. If our own rhetoric is a statement of conviction, then our course of action is clear. We change our revenue base to reflect present exigencies and reaffirm our faith in education as a value which will not be sacrificed ... a value of the state, of the people collectively.

State office holders will accuse me of proposing a most difficult political task. And they would be right. I urge them to put their revenue-raising ideas in the marketplace and see what happens. William Schneider reviewing David Stockman's book, *The Triumph of Politics: Why the Reagan Revolution Failed*, said, "There are two basic styles of political thinking. Pragmatists believe that whatever works is right. Ideologues believe that if something is wrong it can't possibly work even if it works." It is important that education be salient in this state, even if we have to try something which is considered to be politically wrong.

A conviction value which attaches to the person, the individual, rather than the state is kindness ... to be contrasted with cruelty or meanness. It is mean and cruel for anyone to be hungry and homeless in our midst. It does not require a course in ethics or moral analysis to know that wrong can result from action or inaction. It is not enough that we acknowledge the existence of the plight of the destitute. We must act.

Tomorrow it is anticipated that thousands of people will join hands across America to call attention to world hunger and raise funds for its amelioration. Such action may or may not have lasting impact.

What is required is a massive assault on those policies in whatever forum allows such conditions to exist. We know instinctively as well as intellectually what it means to be kind, yet at times we experience a gap between what we know and what we do.

Robert Coles wrote a column in the *New York Times* two weeks ago about a senior about to graduate who wrote the following:

> ... But it really does bother me sometimes when I stop and realize that I've learned how to think, to talk a good line, but a lot of the time I don't live up to what I know and say. There's a gap there between the "me" that's my grades and my "record" and the "me" who is living my life from one day to the next.

May we all live our lives in such a way that kindness is an enduring and actualized trait from one day to the next.

The value of justice ranks very high in the hierarchy of conviction values. Justice is fairness. A roll call of philosophers and political theorists from Aristotle to John Rawls would reveal unanimity in the rank and definition of justice. That all, each and every one of us, should be treated fairly and treat others likewise should brook no opposition.

Responsibility is a value which is both overriding and undergirding. Rights and duties run in both directions, notwithstanding the nature of the relationship: teacher-student, government-citizen, parent-child. Each relationship is rife with reciprocal rights and duties, and failure to honor them is destructive of the relationship. These mutual rights and duties are concurrent, not sequential. Our lives proceed apace without self-created disruption, if justice and fairness have been assured.

This listing of what I have termed "conviction values" is not exhaustive. I leave its completion with you as you get on with your life.

The ancient Hebrews wrote: "What doth the Lord require of thee? To do justly, love mercy, and walk humbly with thy God." In the vernacular, we could say, "What does civilization require of you? To love learning, be kind, do justly, and act responsibly." A task that is not easy, is never-ending and one which is in marked contrast with "always do whichever comes handiest at the time."

I conclude with a true story. A woman preparing for a large party had pressed her yard-man into household service. As they attacked the many tasks, she expressed second thoughts about the social event because of all the effort entailed. His response was weak in grammar, but the message was powerful: "Ain't nothin' worth nothin', that ain't no trouble."

SPECIAL BRIEFING TO THE
70TH LEGISLATURE AND
HIGHER EDUCATION FUNDING,
FEBRUARY 11, 1987

[Auditorium, LBJ Library. Briefing moderated by Jess Hay, Chairman, UT Board of Regents]
Thank you very much, Jess. I am delighted to be the wrapup for this session of gloom and somewhat doom that you have had here today, but you are going to leave here today, and your job will be to turn the Legislature around if it needs to be turned around, and you're going to have to communicate with them and make them understand what the message is that you have heard here.

Well, I want you to tell those Legislators—and the Governor and Lieutenant Governor and the Speaker if you get a chance to talk to them—that what you have discovered as you thought through what you have been told this afternoon is that the University of Texas is a citadel of strength in this state, that it stands tall, that it glitters, that it has a faculty—a research and teaching faculty—that is engaged in communicating with students and that they are in the business of creating life in a future generation, intellectual life in a future generation.

Ashbel Smith was the first—he was called President of the Board of Regents for the University of Texas, and he said, "I am delighted to be this first president of the board of directors of the University of Texas, and it's going to be a great school. The first order of business will be a first-rate faculty." He knew then in the 1880s, early, that a first-rate faculty was a good thing.

The Legislators of Texas have sense enough to know that 103 years later. Don't you know that those people who sit in the Capitol and vote on legislation have sense enough to know that education is the fu-

ture of this state, that this is not a partisan issue. We don't care whether the Democrats or the Republicans are in office.

On most issues I'm an intense partisan, but when it comes to excellence, there is no partisanship there. You can be liberal, conservative, Democrat or Republican, and you will know what excellence means. And you can tell those legislators, all of them, that the University of Texas is about excellence. It is about quality of intellect. It is about depth of understanding. It is about people learning to get along with each other and enjoying each other and discussing with each other issues that matter in a rational way. There is no reason for this school to collapse intellectually because of some fiscal strains.

Do you know the big well, Santa Rita? It blew in in 1923. Now that did not mark the beginning of excellence at the University of Texas. The school had been in business for over 40 years when the well blew in.

So because oil prices have collapsed, does that mean then that the quality of the education of this institution must too collapse? No. Our inside strength has never been tied to the price of oil. We have never relied on the price of oil to determine whether we are ahead of the game or behind the game. The price of oil does not determine whether we are mediocre or whether we are high and first-rate.

This is a strong and good and great institution. It has meant a lot to this state. I was born in this state, and I remember all of my life hearing about the University of Texas. For a long time I couldn't come here, and you know why. But I can now. I cannot only come here, I can teach here, and the school has opened up the minds of the citizens of this state so that even that kind of interaction is acceptable.

So you tell the people on the hill that you got a message here today that some people are making rustlings and starting rumors about the land that the University of Texas is in trouble and it might collapse; that it's not a good place to come and a good place to teach and a good place to work. You go over there and tell them that those rumors are false. Disabuse them. Tell them they lie and that we are going to, in the spirit of Texas and in the spirit of humanity, retain the greatness of this institution. That's your message.

Professor Jordan delivering her commencement address in front of the Tower. *Courtesy of the Office of Public Affairs, the University of Texas at Austin.*

Acknowledgments

The idea to put together a book of essays about the University of Texas resulted from a meeting called by Larry Faulkner in 1998, the first year of his tenure as president of the University. The topic of President Faulkner's meeting, as I recall, was how to make the University more user-friendly, and during the meeting one repeated observation was that many people, ranging from alumni to incoming freshmen, did not fully appreciate the rich history of the Forty Acres. After the meeting, Susan Clagett and Don Carleton and I chatted about the idea of a book on the University. Susan was then working out of the President's Office on special projects, and Don, in his position as director of the Center for American History, oversees an important book series published by the University of Texas Press.

I had just retired from being special collections librarian at Southwest Texas State University and was doing some editing and writing. I have three degrees from the University of Texas and had been a library bibliographer on its campus for sixteen years; my wife was teaching at the Law School and my two children had recently graduated from UT, one in Plan II, the other in Radio-TV-Film. From our upstairs bedroom window we have a view of the Tower through the trees, and we're pleased when it lights up orange—in other words, I passed the UT patriot test. After a brief conversation, I told Susan and Don that I could put together a book.

So here the book is, a number of years later, and it demands some explanation. First, the title: not an easy thing, naming this book, if one doesn't choose to feature the word "orange." In one of our early meetings, Susan Clagett loaned me a book from President Faulkner's office library titled, simply, *The Harvard Book*—a compilation of pieces written by Harvard faculty and graduates that encompasses 400 years of prose about the country's oldest college. Our university has had only 125 years, but much of what we have experienced on campus is a reflection of our state's tumultuous social history—and aspiring to be a "University of the First Class" automatically aligns us with Harvard. So I engaged in a little borrowing and put forward "The Texas Book" as a title.

Once you begin looking around, you find quite an extensive body of literature about the University, but not always just the thing one would want for balance and topicality. Fairly quickly I embraced the idea of putting together a book of essays, some comprehensive, some specific, some quite well-known pieces or excerpts from longer works already published, and the rest specifically written for this book at my request. I was looking for stories that had meaning, balance, and, when possible, literary flair.

My first thanks go to all of the living contributors to the book, quite an extraordinary group. They include librarians; professors of English, creative writing, and law; prize-winning journalists, novelists, poets, and playwrights; a science reporter for the *New York Times*; the executive director of Humanities Texas; and the director of the Lyndon B. Johnson Library and Museum. What they all have in common is a genuine attachment to the University of Texas. The no-longer-living contributors include Joe B. Frantz, Meade F. Griffin, Barbara Jordan, Willie Morris, Chad Oliver, and Walter Prescott Webb. I want to thank the institutions and individuals who granted us permission to present their words.

Susan Clagett and Don Carleton are the progenitors of this book. Susan has helped transform the University into a welcoming place for new students and an institution that honors its graduates. Don presides over the Center for American History, a unique entity on the Texas campus. Walking into the reading room of the Center is a geniune egalitarian experience—there, in the same room, one finds the finest scholars of American history working on their next books, seated next to Texans poring over old county maps that may settle an oil and gas dispute, next to undergraduate students learning about the music of the 1960s by examining posters from Austin's legendary Armadillo World Headquarters. For anyone working on the history of the American South or the history of twentieth-century journalism, the Center is indispensable. In any aspect of Texas studies, the researcher goes there first, and as the repository of the University Archives the Center provided the archival and photographic resources for most of this book. In addition to Don at the Center, I would like to thank Ralph Elder and John Wheat, those two founts of Texas knowledge who roam the halls of Sid Richardson

Hall. My friend Kate Adams, a recently retired associate director of the Center, always supported the work on this book. When it came to photographic images at the Center, Linda Peterson, Steven Williams, and Zachary Vowell did exemplary work.

In the collection of other images on the UT campus, Nancy Sparrow at the Alexander Architectural Archive at UT was crucial in the process of selecting architectural illustrations; Rich Oram and John Thomas helped with images housed at the Harry Ransom Center; and Nursing School dean Dolores Sands and her assistant, Jane Keller, unearthed a long-lost painting of Frances Hudspeth. Marsha Miller in the Office of Public Affairs and Marla Akin at the Michener Center for Writers were instrumental in finding images in their two offices.

Several of my friends, including Tom Zigal, Jim Magnuson, Jack Cargill, and Dennis Domer, demonstrated enthusiasm for this complicated project from the beginning. Austin historian and cartoonist Jack Jackson got me in touch with Pat Brown, who got me in touch with Frank Stack. In my delicate inquiries into the legacy of Frank Erwin, Austin lobbyist Nick Kralj generously talked with me about his old friend; Sheree Scarborough helped me reach Jeff Sandefer, who shared with me a portion of his huge Frank Erwin archive; J. C. Martin educated me about Erwin's colleagues on the Board of Regents; and Brenda Bell talked with me about her last telephone conversation with Erwin, shortly before he died.

The late Marquita W. Anderson, who was coordinator of special collections in the Robert J. Terry Library at Texas Southern University, provided important access to Barbara Jordan's unpublished papers.

At the University of Texas Press, Bill Bishel and Dave Hamrick have been patient and supportive of this extended project.

Finally I want to thank my wife, Cynthia Bryant, for listening to these stories over and over—she has the most astute editorial ear I know. Above and beyond has been the collaboration of David Dettmer at the Center for American History. Without David's hard work, good sense, and friendship, this book would not be in our hands. Thank you David.